Oxford Socio-Legal Studies

Economic Consequences of Divorce

Oxford Socio-Legal Studies is a series of books published for the Centre for Socio-Legal Studies, Wolfson College, Oxford. The series is concerned generally with the relationship between law and society, and is designed to reflect the increasing interest of lawyers, social scientists and historians in this field.

Already Published by Oxford University Press

Genevra Richardson, with Anthony Ogus and Paul Burrows
POLICING POLLUTION: A Study of Regulation and Enforcement

P.W.J. Bartrip and S.B. Burman
THE WOUNDED SOLDIERS OF INDUSTRY Industrial Compensation Policy 1833–1897

Donald Harris *et al*
COMPENSATION AND SUPPORT FOR ILLLNESS AND INJURY

Keith Hawkins
ENVIRONMENT AND ENFORCEMENT Regulation and the Social Definition of Pollution

Robert Baldwin
REGULATING THE AIRLINES Administrative Justice and Agency Discretion

John Eekelaar and Mavis Maclean
MAINTENANCE AFTER DIVORCE

Paul Rock
A VIEW FROM THE SHADOWS: The Ministry of the Solicitor-General of Canada and the Justice for Victims of Crime Initiative

Bridget Hutter
THE REASONABLE ARM OF THE LAW?: The Law Enforcement Procedures of Environmental Health Officers

Hazel Genn
HARD BARGAINING: Out of Court Settlement in Personal Injury Actions

David Downers
CONTRASTS IN TOLERANCE: Penal Policy in the Netherlands and England and Wales

Robert Dingwall and John Eekelaar
DIVORCE MEDIATORS AND THE LEGAL PROCESS

Christopher J. Whelan
SMALL CLAIMS COURTS: A Comparative Study

Paul Rock
HELPING VICTIMS OF CRIME: The Home Office and the Rise of Victim Support in England and Wales

John Eekelaar
REGULATING DIVORCE

Sally Wheeler
RESERVATION OF TITLE CLAUSES: Impact and Implications

ECONOMIC CONSEQUENCES OF DIVORCE

The International Perspective

edited by
LENORE J. WEITZMAN
and MAVIS MACLEAN

CLARENDON PRESS · OXFORD
1992

Oxford University Press, Walton Street, Oxford OX2 6DP

Oxford New York Toronto
Delhi Bombay Calcutta Madras Karachi
Petaling Jaya Singapore Hong Kong Tokyo
Nairobi Dar es Salaam Cape Town
Melbourne Auckland

and associated companies in
Berlin Ibadan

Oxford is a trade mark of Oxford University Press

Published in the United States
by Oxford University Press, New York

British Library Cataloguing in Publication Data
data available

Library of Congress Cataloging in Publication Data
Economic consequences of divorce : the international perspective /
edited by Lenore J. Weitzman and Mavis Maclean.
(Oxford socio-legal studies)
Includes index.
1. Divorce—Law and legislation—Economic aspects. I. Weitzman, Lenore J. II. Mavis, Maclean. III. Series.
K695.E26 1992 336.01'66—dc20 [342.6166] 91–14739
ISBN 0–19–825421–0

Typset by Pentacor PLC, High Wycombe, Bucks
Printed in Great Britain by Bookcraft Ltd
Midsomer Norton, Avon

For
William J. Goode

Preface

MANY of the contributors to this volume have been collaborating for over a decade, and have shared and cross-fertilized each other's research and policy perspectives, beginning in 1978 in Sweden, at the meeting Anders Agell chaired for the International Society on Family Law. Professor Agell's international horizon and Professor William J. Goode's keynote address on cross-cultural patterns in divorce inspired a small group of sociologists and lawyers to meet and to discover that they were exploring similar issues in their respective countries. They began to reformulate their questions comparatively and to challenge each other's 'simplistic solutions'. The cross-fertilization broadened their horizons about what was possible.

For example, during a sabbatical year at the Centre for Socio-Legal Studies in Oxford, Lenore Weitzman learnt about the 'children-first' principle in English divorce law and adapted it in her recommendation for the treatment of the family home in California. At the same time, Mavis Maclean and John Eekelaar of Oxford were designing their study of divorce in England, and they benefited from Weitzman's research in the 1970s in California. Similarly, the Australian Institute for Family Studies built on Weitzman's research and Irwin Garfinkel's suggestions for collecting child support. Sandra Burman (South Africa), Satoshi Minamikata (Japan), and Richard Ingleby (Australia) were also part of the nucleus of Oxford-inspired researchers who went on to study divorce in their respective countries.

In the spring of 1989 a group of scholars, sociologists, lawyers, economists, and anthropologists met at the Rockefeller Conference Centre in Bellagio, Italy, to discuss the economic consequences of divorce from an international perspective. The editors would like to express their appreciation of this opportunity to the Rockefeller Foundation and staff.

Drawing on the participants' own hard data as a basis for comparison, we asked each of them to consider what might reduce the hardships generated by the current system of divorce. Do the answers lie in specific features of the law (such as no-fault divorce laws or provisions for sharing pensions), or the social structure of the society (such as participation and distribution of women in the labour force) or the system of social welfare benefits? What factors are correlated with different patterns of results?

Our hope is that the comparative perspective in this volume will lead to a greater understanding of the types of societal arrangements that are most likely to minimize the adverse consequences of divorce. This analysis should also facilitate the formulation of better policy recommendations in individual countries.

The contributors to this volume are committed to conceptualizing divorce as a societal problem and to asking how each of their societies is allocating the responsibilities for the costs. While most societies have assumed that post-divorce support could be managed within the family, the results of our individual and comparative research suggest the impossibiity of that vision in the modern world. Our collective research suggests that no society can continue to see divorce as a private matter between individual husbands and wives, or between individual parents and children. Instead, we must ask about its impact on the larger society and on the public purse. Indeed, we must ask about the costs of divorce for the society as a whole—and how those tremendous costs can be borne without destroying the fabric of either the family or the society.

In a volume including contributions from all over the world, inevitably the same terms are used in slightly different ways and different terms are used for what may appear to be the same concept. Where a clear unambiguous term can be found, this has been used throughout. But where contributors have carefully chosen a term to indicate gender neutrality, or gender awareness by, for example, using, 'lone-parent family' or 'mother-headed family', these distinctions have been maintained.

This volume was prepared for publication during a period of exciting political change. Chapters 7 and 12 describe the position in the FRG in 1989, and are now of broader application as the law of the former FRG forms the basis for the law of all Germany. The editors' comments were written immediately after unification and therefore refer to Germany.

The editors would like to express their gratitude to Tracy Higgins, Lynne Farnum, Lisa Schoor and Madhavi Sunder of Harvard University, and to Jeannette Price of Oxford University, for editorial assistance.

Mavis Maclean
Lenore J. Weitzman

December 1990
Wolfson College, Oxford
Harvard University, Cambridge, Mass.

Contents

List of Contributors

ANDERS AGELL has been a Professor of Law in the University of Uppsala since 1962, and Dean in 1979–85. He is the author of many articles and books on family law. His most recent publications include *The Law of Marriage and Cohabitation according to the Legislation of 1987* (3rd edn., 1988; 4th edn., 1989) and *Maintenance for Children and Wives* (1988).

KAY BADER is currently a Research Associate in the Faculty of Law, University of Bristol, and has undertaken several research studies in the field of family law.

BENOÎT BASTARD is a senior researcher at the Centre National de la Recherche Scientifique and member of the Centre du Sociologie des Organisations in Paris. He has studied the functioning of courts, decision-making on the financial consequences of divorce, and family breakdown. Recent publications include *Practiques judicaires du divorce* (1988) with J. F. Perrin and L. Cardia Voneche.

SANDRA BURMAN is a Research Fellow at Queen Elizabeth House, University of Oxford, and at the University of Cape Town. Her publications have included books on the imposition of law, both in Lesotho and, more widely, on women and work, and on tort liability in both domestic and industrial settings. Over the past decade she has focused on the effects of urbanization and apartheid legislation on legal and family structures in South Africa.

LAURA CARDIA VONECHE is a sociologist working at the Institute for Social and Preventative Medicine at the University of Geneva. She works in the field of family and health, concentrating on family formation and family functioning, and particularly divorce and its consequences.

JEAN COLLINS is a social anthropologist currently Research Associate in the Faculty of Law, University of Bristol.

STEPHEN CRETNEY is Professor of Law at the University of Bristol and author of *Principles in Family Law* (5th edn., 1990) with J. Masson, and many other books.

GWYNN DAVIS is Senior Research Fellow in the Faculty of Law, University of Bristol. He has conducted several studies of negotiation upon divorce, and is the author of *Partisans and Mediators* (1988), and co-author with M. Murch of *Grounds for Divorce* (1988).

JOHN EEKELAAR is a Fellow of Pembroke College and the Centre for Socio-Legal Studies, and a Reader in Law at Oxford University, with particular interests in family law and social policy. Recent publications include *Divorce Mediation and the Legal Process* (1988) with R. Dingwall and *Maintenance after Divorce* (1986) with M. Maclean.

KATHLEEN FUNDER is a psychologist working at the Australian Institute for Family Studies, with a particular interest in parenting after divorce. Recent publications include 'Women, Work and Post-Divorce Economic Self-Sufficiency', in J. Eekelaar and M. T. Meulders Klein (eds.), *Family, State, and Economic Security* (1988).

MALGORZATA FUSZARA is a Senior Legal Researcher at the Department of Applied Social Science at the University of Warsaw. Recent publications include 'The Abortion Debate', in M. Maclean and D. Groves (eds.) *Women's Issues in Social Policy* (1991).

IRWIN GARFINKEL is a Professor of Social Work at Columbia University. His primary research interests are poverty and social welfare programmes. He has published numerous articles and five books. He is co-author with S. McLanahan of *Single Mothers and their Children: A New American Dilemma* (1986). His most recent work focuses on child support. He is completing a book on *Child Support, Poverty, and Welfare.*

WILLIAM J. GOODE is a member of the Sociology Department at Harvard University. He is a former President of the American Sociological Association and the author of 17 books including *World Revolution in Family Patterns* (1963) and *The Celebration of Heroes* (1978). He is currently writing a monograph on world changes in divorce patterns during the period 1950–90.

MARGARET HARRISON is a Legal Fellow of the Australian Institute of Family Studies, working on the economic consequences of marriage breakdown, and evaluation of the Australian Child Support Scheme. She is co-author, with G. Snider and R. Merlo, of *Who Pays for the Children?* (1990).

RICHARD INGLEBY is a Senior Lecturer in the Faculty of Law,

University of Melbourne, currently working in family law and dispute resolution. Recent publications include 'Rhetoric and Reality: Regulation of Out-of-Court Activity in Matrimonial Proceedings', *Oxford Journal of Legal Studies* (1988).

JACEK KURCZEWSKI is Professor of Sociology of Custom and Law at the Institute of Applied Social Sciences (WPRiDS), University of Warsaw, and author of many books and articles, including *Family, Gender and Body in Law and Society Today* (1990).

MAVIS MACLEAN is a Socio-Legal Fellow of Wolfson College, Oxford, working on families and the law at the Centre for Socio-Legal Studies. Recent publications include *Surviving Divorce* (1991).

KAREL MADDENS was formerly a researcher at UFSIA, University of Antwerp, studying the new Belgian Child Support Scheme.

SARA MCLANAHAN is Professor of Sociology and Public Affairs at Princeton University. Her primary interests are the family and family policy, poverty and inequality, and gender stratification. She is currently involved in several research projects dealing with the effects of marital disruption on children's economic and social well-being. She is also working on an evaluation design for the child support provisions of the Family Support Act (1988). She has published numerous articles in books and scholarly journals and is co-author with I. Garfinkel of *Single Mothers and their Children: A New American Dilemma* (1986).

SATOSHI MINAMIKATA is Associate Professor of Law at Ibaraki University with research interests in conciliation. Recent publications include Kaji Chotei: Mediation in the Japanese Family Court, in R. Dingwall and J. Eekelaar (eds.), *Divorce Mediation and the Legal Process* (1988).

PETAR ŠARČEVIĆ is Rector of the University of Rijeka, Visiting Professor in Law at the University of Florida, Director of Scientific Work of the International Association of Legal Science (Paris), and editor of *International Contracts and Conflicts of Law* (1990).

ANNEMETTE SØRENSEN is Associate Professor of Sociology at Harvard University. Current research interests include gender differences in the economic consequences of divorce, consequences of women's economic dependency, and comparative studies of women's economic position in advanced industrial societies.

Publications include 'Married Women's Economic Dependency, 1940–1980' (1987); 'Sex Differences in Poverty, 1960–1980' (1989); 'Divorce and its Consequences: the Distribution of Risk between Women and Men' (1990); 'Gender and the Life Course' (1990; published in German translation).

JEAN VAN HOUTTE is Professor of Sociology and the Sociology of Law at the University of Antwerp (UFSIA-UIA) and Director of the Centre for the Sociology of Law (UFSIA), President of the Research Committee on Sociology of Law of the International Sociological Association, and now Rector (President) of the University of Saint Ignatius, Antwerp. He has conducted research and published widely in the fields of the administration of justice, family law, and epistemological problems in the sociology of law.

WOLFGANG VOEGELI is Professor of Civil Law at the Hochschule für Wirtschaft und Politik, Hamburg, and involved in socio-legal research in family law. Recent publications include 'Multiple Disadvantages of One Parent Families', in J. Eekelaar and M. T. Meulders Klein (eds.), The *Family, State and Individual Economic Security* (1988), and *Das Finamt als Unterhaltesbehörde, Zur Reform des Kindesunterhalts in Australien, in Rabels Zeitschrift für ausländisches und internationales Privatrecht* (1990).

LENORE J. WEITZMAN is an Associate Professor of Sociology at Harvard University. She is the author of *The Divorce Revolution: The Unexpected Social and Economic Consequences for Women and Children in America* (1986) and *The Marriage Contract: Spouses, Lovers and the Law* (1981). She is currently writing a book on how married couples handle money and property, which will be published as *The Transformation of Property in Marriage: Ideology, Gender and the Law*.

BARBARA WILLENBACHER is Lecturer in Sociology of Law at the Faculty of Law, University of Hanover. Current research interests include the economic consequences of divorce and sex discrimination in the labour market. Main publications include 'The Multiple Disadvantages of One Parent Families', in J. Eekelaar and M. T. Meulders Klein (eds.) *Family, State and Economic Security* (1988).

The following were also participants at the Bellagio Meeting and contributed throughout individual sessions and particularly to the concluding chapter.

MARZIO BARBAGLI, Professor of Sociology at the University of Bologna.

HEATHER JOSHI, Research Economist at Birkbeck College, University of London.

ANDRAS KLINGER, Researcher at the Hungarian Academy of Science, Budapest.

JEANETTE PRICE, Administrator at the Centre for Socio-Legal Studies, Oxford.

Part One
Overview

1. Introduction to the Issues

Mavis Maclean and Lenore J. Weitzman

In the past decade there has been a remarkable cross-national convergence in the experience, research, and reaction to 'The Divorce Revolution'. As each country experienced spiralling divorce rates and adopted more liberal legal rules for divorce, it began to be concerned about the social and economic consequences of these changes. The contributors to this volume were among the pioneers in their respective countries, undertaking empirical research to find out how the new laws were working in practice and analysing the societal effects of the rapid changes. Surprisingly, there was a striking uniformity in the results of these studies. Throughout the world the new system of divorce was causing economic hardship for women and children and men (see Weitzman 1985; Eekelaar and Maclean 1986; McDonald 1986, Bastard, Cardia Voneche and Perrin 1987). This research, which is incorporated in this volume, attracted considerable attention, and policy-makers turned to the researchers for consultation. Thus the contributors to this volume have not only conducted research; they have also grappled with the policy implications of their results. Some have been actively involved in the policy-making process itself, because they shared a commitment to public policy that is informed by empirical research.

This volume begins with a broad overview of divorce patterns historically and cross-culturally. In Chapter 2 William J. Goode analyses the rising and high divorce rates in most of the Western world, and compares the high divorce societies of today with those of the past (in Japan, China, Malaysia, and most of the Arab world). He concludes that what distinguishes the present pattern, and what makes a high divorce rate problematic today, is not the high divorce rate itself, but rather the fact that women and children have become the 'casualties' of the present system:

> The high divorce societies of the past institutionalized remarriage after divorce and therefore most women (and most men) remained in families. In contrast, the high divorce societies of today have not

solved the problems of reintegrating women and children into the family—and/or into the mainstream of the society. Rather, as many of the chapters in this volume attest, they are often left in severely diminished economic circumstances and an increasingly larger percentage of children are raised in mother-headed households.

Goode concludes by noting that 'this is the challenge that confronts the high divorce rate societies of today'.

Part Two focuses on the legal rules and procedures for divorce. In Chapter 3 Anders Agell provides an overview of current legal thinking. He compares the consequences of the common-law and the civil-law approaches to the economic aspects of divorce, and points to the importance of the structure of the legal process as well as of the formal legal rules. As the chair of the subgroup of lawyers and law professors at the Bellagio meeting, he summarizes their views on the following issues: on what grounds should a divorce be granted; whether fault should be considered; whether or not grounds must be established in addition to the request by one party, perhaps with a waiting period; what rules govern arrangements for children; and the definition and distribution of property and periodic payments for ex-spouses and children.

Many of the themes of Agell's chapter are echoed in the more detailed chapters on specific countries that follow. Here we note only one: in comparing the clear guidelines and rules that are typical of marital-property systems with the common-law rules that leave basic uncertainty, he observes that this uncertainty may give rise to unnecessary bargaining and litigation which raise the social and economic costs of the divorce.

Richard Ingleby traces the striking developments in Australian law in the past few years and notes the significant impact of empirical data on the policy-making process. He points in Chapter 4 to the data on non-payment of child support and to the uniformity in the calculations of support and property awards as providing the major justification for the abolition of the discretionary framework of the old law.

In Part Three we begin our analysis of the key economic issues in divorce with a focus on marital property. In Chapter 5 Lenore J. Weitzman reviews both the empirical data on property division in the United States and the major legal developments in reconceptualizing the nature of marital property. Research in the United States reveals that most divorcing couples do not have very much property to divide. While the trend is to divide that property equally, in practice this has often meant the forced sale of the family home because it is the 'only' asset. This not only causes disruption in the lives of minor children (and older home-makers); it is significantly linked to the economic hardships that women and children experience after divorce.

Weitzman argues that property is not really being divided equally because the courts (and the traditional law) ignore the most significant assets acquired during marriage, what she calls career assets, including the earning capacities, and the benefits and entitlements of employment (such as pensions and medical insurance). These assets are not only as valuable or more valuable than traditional property; they are, for many families, the major fruits of the marriage. If they are not divided at divorce one spouse, typically the husband, leaves the marriage with a windfall. In the past five years, however, courts in the United States have begun to recognize these career assets and to divide them at divorce. Weitzman reviews the trends in the legal recognition of pensions, professional degrees, and medical insurance as marital property, and shows how the courts are dealing with the complexities of valuation and division.

There is a striking contrast between the basic theories that govern the division of the new property in the United States and in Australia. In the United States, as Weitzman reports, the theory is one of an economic partnership in which marital partners 'share the fruits of the marital partnership'. In Australia, in contrast, as Kathleen Funder describes it in Chapter 6, the theory focuses on 'sharing the debts'. Funder, who is a psychologist at the Australian Institute of Family Studies, outlines the disadvantages that accrue to women who are mothers and home-makers and calls on the legal system to divide these 'costs of marriage' between the husband and the wife at divorce. Funder points to the income disparity between men and women and notes that one component is due to the gender gap in earnings in Australia. Putting that aside, the second component is related to the 'differing effects of marriage, child-bearing and child-rearing upon the income earning capacity of men and women'. It is this disadvantage which is shared at divorce.

The pioneering FRG system for dividing pensions at divorce, which is described by Wolfgang Voegeli and Barbara Willenbacher in Chapter 7, is one of the most sophisticated and comprehensive attempts to implement the marital partnership theory by dividing the new property at divorce. As they note,

> the forms of new property which . . . have been accumulated during marriage [include] assets in social security insurance systems or private superannuation plans, in short, all work-related benefits. . . . The rationale for the pension-splitting scheme is that . . . marriage is a unity in which the couple share equally.

Continuing income support for women and children is discussed in Chapter 8. The guaranteed maintenance system recently established in Belgium is reviewed by Professor van Houtte and Karel Maddens in Chapter 9. The Wisconsin approach whereby the absent parent is required to share his income on a percentage basis with his children is reviewed by its architect, Irwin Garfinkel, in Chapter 10, and the scheme developed from this approach now in effect in Australia, with collection through the tax system, is reported by Margaret Harrison in Chapter 11. The system in the FRG is reviewed by Barbara Willenbacher and Wolfgang Voegeli in Chapter 12. Mavis Maclean and John Eekelaar address the issue of the difference between child support, spousal support, and family support in Chapter 13. Lenore Weitzman reviews the resurgence of interest in alimony in the United States in Chapter 14, and the debate surrounding the economic position of men and women after divorce is clarified by Annemette Sørenson in Chapter 15.

Part Five is concerned with society's response. Sara McLanahan in Chapter 16 reviews the ongoing disadvantages experienced by children who go through parental divorce in the United States. In Chapter 17 Gwynn Davis, Stephen Cretney, and their colleagues describe the complex interplay between public and private support for women and children after divorce in the British context.

In Chapter 18 we present basic information about divorce trends, rules, and consequences in the countries represented at the conference. The following chapters present case studies of particular aspects of divorce management in six countries. The conflict of laws in the federal state of Yugoslavia and in other federal jurisdictions is analysed by Petar Šarčević (Chapter 19). Sandra Burman describes the problems of attempting to import policies from other societies into the complex situation in South Africa in Chapter 20. Satoshi Minamikata outlines the difficulties of the newly emerged group of single fathers in Japan in Chapter 21. Malgorzata Fuszara and Jacek Kurczewski examine attitudes to financial support after divorce in Poland, during a period of national economic crisis, in Chapter 22. Lenore Weitzman analyses gender differences in custody bargaining in the United States in Chapter 23.

In the final chapter in Part Six Benoît Bastard and Laura Cardia Voneche describe various strategies for post-divorce survival adopted by women in France. The degree of stress or satisfaction was found not to be related directly to income level but rather to the development of a coherent, economic strategy for the family.

> One group of women were seeking to develop their capacities to the full, using divorce as an opportunity for self-development and economic interdependence. These women had often been held back from following a career within the marriage, had sought the divorce, did not wish to be economically dependent on ex-partner or public support and were seeking, though with difficulty, satisfying work. A second group were dissatisfied with their position and saw themselves as victims of divorce, and sought to claim all they could from their ex-partner or from the state. For a third group, living on the margin of society in poverty, income surprisingly was not the chief concern. For these women the survival of their family was the chief preoccupation. Success was represented by keeping their children with them, rather than losing them to state care. They worked to present themselves as good and caring mothers.

In the concluding chapter, Chapter 25, the editors aim to present the collective views of the participants at the Bellagio meeting, bringing together the world of research and the world of policy formulation and implementation. In some areas, particularly concerning legal rules, we present clear conclusions concerning the desirability of increased predictability and the reduction of discretion. We are also clear about the desirability of coming to terms with the new definitions of property, but recognize two distinct approaches—the American forward-looking view, which seeks a share for both partners in future benefits, and the Australian view of divorce, as the ending of a partnership, requiring the settlement of debts and compensation for loss.

Concerning income support, we describe the development of new administrative bases for defining and collecting child support, but recognize the renewed interest in spousal support. A key question is emerging concerning the boundaries of child, spouse, and family support.

But, as well as presenting data and searching for solutions to current policy problems, we have one further objective. We hope to challenge and extend the nature of the policy debate concerning the economic consequences of divorce. We subscribe to the view that question-setting is as important as problem-solving. Therefore, we see one contribution of this collaborative work as asking a different and broader set of questions about divorce and, in the process, reconceptualizing the policy agenda. Instead of the traditional focus on divorce as a matter of allocating cost between the individual parties (and their children), we ask about the costs of divorce for the society as a whole.

We raise three questions concerning the economic implications of divorce. First, what are the costs attached to a divorce? Secondly, who bears these costs? And, thirdly, do we wish these costs to lie where they currently fall, on the individual parties, on the public purse, and on the following generation? Or do we wish to intervene through legal regulation of individual decision-making on property division, and through public acceptance of shared responsibilities for child-rearing?

We propose a shift of focus from the marital dispute—concerned with the property and income arrangements between individual spouses—to a broader approach concerned with the outcome of divorce for the parties, their children, and society as a whole.

We now have a paradoxical situation: with increased earning capacity and higher participation in paid work, women are less willing to enter an unwanted marriage, less willing to stay in an unsatisfactory marriage, and have less incentive to remarry. On the other hand, the burden of child-rearing after divorce falls mainly on their shoulders, and, with lower wages for women, combined with the opportunity costs of child-rearing, we have a growing population of economically vulnerable female-headed households.

Underlying our discussion of the outcome of divorce there inevitably lies a variety of conceptions of the legal marriage which is ending. Are we thinking about divorce as the ending of an emotional relationship between two independent adults? If so, the appropriate procedures would be divorce on request, little waiting, no attribution of fault, equal sharing of property, and no continuing financial relationship between the partners. If, on the other hand, we see the family as a social institution centred around the married pair, and providing care to the older generation, investing in the nurture and socialization of their children, then we are likely to be more cautious about easing divorce procedures, more concerned to provide for regulation of income transfers to children, and more willing to make provision for the human capital invested in the family to be taken into account in any definition and division of the property of the marriage. We also present contributions from Catholic countries where marriage is viewed as a sacrament and divorce is held to be either totally unacceptable or reluctantly accepted for a small minority.

In this volume divorce is seen as the end of something more complex than a property-holding company. We retain money as our central focus, partly because the financial aspect of divorce is important *per se*, and also because of what it tells us about relationships between the individual, the family, and the state. Financial needs and means act as indicators for the underlying issues of dependency and power, individualism, and collectivity in the family: what may be described as the social contract within the family. We offer some answers—and hopefully some new questions—which may help the development of a new agenda.

References

Bastard, B., Cardia Voneche, L., and Perrin, J. F. (1987), *Practiques judiciaires du divorce* (Lausanne).

EEKELAAR, J., and MACLEAN, M. (1986), *Maintenance after Divorce* (Oxford).

McDONALD, P. (ed.) (1986), *Settling Up: Property and Income Distribution on Divorce in Australia* (Sydney).

WEITZMAN, L. J. (1985), *The Divorce Revolution: The Unexpected Social and Economic Consequences for Women and Children in America* (New York).

2. World Changes in Divorce Patterns

William J. Goode

This chapter examines a set of social processes that are important both theoretically and politically. They occur at an intersection of institutional forces which affect one another, though each has far-reaching independent effects as well. That concrete institutional intersection is the family system and its divorce processes, and the independent sets of forces are legal, sociological, and economic.

The legal forces determine whether and how divorce can be obtained at any given time, which resources can be considered property and income, who owns them, and the conditions under which they can be transfered. The sociological factors determine over the longer run what is the law, what are the roles of family members, who can or does use the law most effectively, the consequences of divorce, and who can or does enter the economic roles of production and allocation before and after divorce. The economic variables affect what is the law and to some extent the sociological forces, and set the structure of opportunity for husbands, wives, and children.

Within the Western world, the social conditions of our time have created the highest divorce rates in its history, and the interaction of these three sets of forces have faced the polities of the West with a wide range of economic and political issues because of those rates.

These issues will be noted in several contexts, but, briefly, very high divorce rates in nations where they were traditionally low, or a breakdown in the traditional divorce system where once they were high, will place a much larger segment of the population in difficult social and economic circumstances for which the existing institutions are not adequately prepared. When the numbers are large, a social issue arises which would have been viewed in the past as no more than the sum of individual misfortunes. However, when millions are affected, it is less acceptable politically, especially in the welfare state, to assert that these are merely diverse cases of personal fate or incompetence. Rather, it becomes more reasonable to say that the larger social system itself generates the problem.

Because the actions of human beings maintain that system, we can—and many people do—assert that, through social action, programmes, and collective effort, we can try to change the system. However, at the same time, because people in different positions in the social structure have very different stakes in the system as it is, they will see the problem differently, and therefore many will oppose, while others will support, a particular solution. Changing any system of such complexity is always difficult, and with near certainty, we can predict that the changes will be *multifarious*, while many of them will *not* be in the preferred direction.

I do not intend to suggest policies here. My goal is rather to analyse sociologically a few of the major changes in divorce patterns in several regions of the world. I shall first consider the rising social importance of divorce in research on family change, and thereafter outline what are in my opinion, the most important trends in the Western countries; I shall not consider them in depth: other studies in this volume will do that. Because divorce patterns are different when divorce first becomes possible after generations of being forbidden, a section will be devoted to that topic. In a succeeding section I shall consider changes in a type of system that (to my knowledge) has not been given explicit theoretical attention before, the traditional high-divorce society, or what I call here the 'stable high-divorce rate' society. In the last sections some data are also presented on China and the Arab world.

Both time and the lack of adequate data prevent consideration here of Latin America, sub-Saharan Africa, India, and the Eastern European countries, but in a larger forthcoming study they will be given more attention. Thus, although the perspective in this chapter will be global, because the larger work of which this is a part is global, in this smaller compass much will be omitted.

The Increase in Research on Divorce

In what was the first field survey of post-divorce adjustment in the United States, and possibly anywhere, I argued that marital happiness is not theoretically interesting, but that divorce is. (Goode 1956: 5–9). Divorce is a point of strain in a small social system—the individual family—and it takes on added importance in a kinship system that has valued marital stability highly. It is a point of conflict, and it both reflects and adds to conflicts in the larger social structure. It is an integral part of the marriage system, since it is one kind of mechanism for dealing with the pressures and problems inevitably arising within a family. In a basic sense, marriage 'causes' divorce.

Over the past fifteen years there has been a rapid increase in divorce research in Europe. This has occurred, however, not so much because European family theorists have come to recognize it as theoretically interesting, but because many have become *alarmed* at the higher rates. They have come to wonder whether the changes taking place mean that the family itself is being transformed—or even undermined. (Certainly, that very hypothesis suggests implicitly that divorce rates might also be theoretically significant.) Over many decades analysts could point to the United States as a special case of high divorce rates, in its dubious position as simultaneously the vanguard of the future and an example of capitalistic hedonism and possibly even decadence. Consequently, their intellectual interest in divorce was only modest.

Much of the current interest comes from moral and ideological concerns. (Are women neglecting their family duties? Is a breakdown in morals imminent? Are children being neglected? Should decent citizens have to pay for the welfare support of people who violate traditional family norms?) Most who are interested in the topic also wish to take various policy positions. However, precisely because policies are likely to be somewhat wiser if they are based on the facts, at least one of our tasks in this volume must be to find out and to understand what is really happening, so that future policies may be wiser.

Yet if divorce patterns are of some theoretical importance, that potential has not been much exploited, except on a *micro* scale. That is, most divorce research of both the past and the present has been concerned with why a particular set of couples got divorces. Or, instead, why a nation has experienced a slight rise or fall in the divorce rates. We have not often attempted macro studies, in which we try to ascertain why various cultures or nations have high or low divorce rates, or why divorce rates fall and rise similarly in sets of nations.

I think this theoretical failure has occurred for several reasons. The first is perhaps theological and moral. That is, in a culture which took marital stability as the ideal and the norm, divorce was seen as a personal failure, or a slight breakdown in the value system, and understanding that 'fact' surely did not require much deep sociological analysis, but rather no more than journalistic common sense or moralistic eloquence.

Another possible reason is that divorce was viewed as, at best, only a small, dependent variable, of too little importance to be examined seriously. After all, the Marxist canon asserts, the great variables of social change have to do with power and economic systems.

Indeed, it is only now and then—for example, when we consider some great social movement such as the French Revolution—that a few people assert the independent importance of values, norms, and ideologies. However, in social science generally, there is now a significant development of a renewed interest in that possibility.

Perhaps there has been an even more important reason for this neglect: generally Western theorists feel, without examining the question closely, that they already have a kind of 'theory' for the breakdown of marital stability in a social system. It is the notion that modern society is a transition *Gemeinschaft* to *Gesellschaft*. Since divorce is part of that transition, the theory would apply there. That is, for several hundred years society has gradually moved away from tight community controls, specific definitions of appropriate kinship behaviour, reliance on tradition, family surveillance of private behaviour, etc., and towards an opposite set of traits.

The acute reader will recognize, of course, that this is not a genuine *theory* but no more than a way of naming certain processes, with labels containing a rich imagery. That set of notions may well be adequate in speaking of the decline from virtue that is shown in modern Western societies. By contrast, however, it does not at all apply to traditional high-divorce societies of the past, which were all *Gemeinschaft* in character.

In addition, although Plato stated one form of this idea some two thousand years ago, and numerous commentators have noted the downfall of various high cultures, neither this nor any other grand theory tries to explain how or why systems of stable virtue get started in the first place.

In an important sense, Toennies's much more recent version—after all, a mere century ago—is simply an early version of what may be called 'convergence theory', that is, the hypothesis that the social patterns of each nation will become very similar, specifically like those of the industrial West. The most fruitful statement in my view is based on 'industrialization theory'. The various grand theories that might be applied are not analysed here, for this has been done elsewhere (Goode, forthcoming (*a*)), and they are in any event only minimally relevant in this context. However, I do want to make three important points.

First, my version of industrialization theory tries to *specify* the key variables that actually shape family transformation: (1) an increasing percentage of the population depends on *jobs*, not land or other resources in the control of elders; (2) efficiency requires that jobs and promotions be given out for competence, by people who basically have little stake in the family behaviour of the worker; and (3) wages and rewards are given to the *individual*, who can spend them as he or she chooses (Goode 1982: chs. 10, 11). Consequently, family controls are weakened. On the other hand, in countries that acquire high technology but keep those variables under family control—as may well have happened in Arab countries—we cannot expect the same kinds of changes that the West has undergone; industrialization in this precise sense has not occurred.

Secondly, under this view, the curves of divorce rates or any other family variable might go up *or* down under industrialization, depending on whether they were high or low to begin with. And, thirdly, this theory does not tell us much about the *future*. That is, after a nation is substantially industrialized, such a theory has little predictive power in sketching the future of family patterns.

That gap is relevant to our discussions here, for policies are designed to solve problems that now exist, and will probably exist in the future. We are very likely proceeding on the assumption that Western divorce rates will probably continue to rise. Is there a good basis for that expectation?

If we must predict future divorce in the West, we are forced to follow one of two time-worn clichés: (1) any existing trend will continue tomorrow as it has up to now; or (2) since these are organic curves, then like almost all curves based on biological or social factors, they will eventually slow down and flatten out.

It is easy to list the many variables that will cause divorce rates to continue upwards. Western culture can be said almost to *overdetermine* that movement: hedonism, individualism, competitiveness, sexually titillating mass media and philosophies, and so on. However, it is more difficult to state specifically what will be the factors which will surely and inevitably cause the rates to flatten out, other than the banal, ironic possibility that perhaps eventually everyone will be divorced, and there will be no one left married to run that risk.

However, since such guesses lie in the realm of imagination rather than the factual, and we are here to analyse the facts—and of course the forces that drive those facts—let us turn to them now.

Western Divorce Patterns

Instead of offering many details of changing divorce processes in the Western countries, I shall simply list a number of the *main* changes that have been taking place over the past generation.

The first of course is the very large upward movement of the divorce curves, especially from the 1960s onwards. Although some analysts write as though there was little change before this rise, the fact is that in all of these countries—including the nations in the Pacific that are culturally Western—rates had been moving upwards steadily since 1900 (Goode 1963 82 ff.) As usual, the United States is the most extreme in this regard, where the divorce rate has risen in every decade since the Civil War, over a century ago. In any event, among currently marrying cohorts it can be suggested that only about 40–50 per cent (from about 35 per cent in Sweden to about 55 per cent in Great Britain) will still be married after they have reached the age of fifty years (Sardon 1986: 479–81).

These rates exhibit several regularities over time. They rise with prosperity—that is, divorce is a consumer good, which people purchase when they can afford it. In a depression, the rates fall.

However, it is possible that this long-term (negative) relationship between economic depression and divorce rates is changing. South (1985: 31–9) suggests that in the prosperity of the post-war period the *relative* cost of divorce has declined. Thus, if we look at the shorter rises and falls of economic well-being over the past several decades, within this general context of a relatively lower cost of divorce, divorce rates will be higher during periods of unemployment and also during periods of rising unemployment, for both situations put additional stress on the family.

These rising rates have not affected the *duration* of marriage as much as one might expect (especially in the Netherlands, Austria, Great Britain, and Germany). In some there is even a slight increase (Sardon 1986: 475–7), because of the great

TABLE 2.1. *Western Europe and the Industrialized world, divorce rate for married females, 1950–198-*

Country	1950	1960	1970	1980	198-
Austria	6.7	5.0	6.1	6.8	
	(1951)	(1961)		(1977)	
Belgium	2.4	2.0	2.6	4.9	
Denmark	7.0	6.1	8.1	11.1	12.8
				(1978)	(1986)
England and	2.6	2.1	5.9	11.6	12.9
Wales	(1951)	(1961)	(1971)	(1978)	(1986)
Finland	4.6	4.0	6.0	9.8	
France	5.7	2.6	2.9		8.5
	(1946)				(1986)
Germany, Federal	7.7	3.7	5.1	4.9	8.8
Republic of		(1961)		(1977)	(1987)
Netherlands	3.0	2.2	3.3	6.5	8.7
Norway	3.2	2.8	3.7	6.6	(1986)
				(1978)	
Switzerland	4.2	3.9	4.4		

Source: U.N. Demographic Yearbooks and national statistics

effect of long duration on the numerical average. The reason is that the rate of marital dissolution among older marriages has also increased. However, among the younger marriage cohorts the duration has decreased.

Divorce rates drop during a long war, but rise sharply at its end. They drop or stabilize, or rise, when laws are passed that make divorce more costly (as in the FRG in 1976–7) or less difficult. However, as is well known, these laws have typically done no more than reflect the underlying changes in social attitudes and behaviour, so that the long-term upward movement, called the *secular trend*, is not affected much by such temporary legal shifts. On the other hand, some of these legal changes (e.g. the *spread* of no-fault divorce laws) do alter the bargaining position of husbands and wives and that can affect the divorce patterns, if not the gross divorce rates themselves (see Weitzman 1985).

Coupled with this major increase has been a general liberalization of divorce laws during this period, but it is worth noting that some countries had made that step *before* the sharp upwards movement of the divorce rate, while others took that step while it was occurring. A recent, detailed analysis sugests that it would be very difficult to prove that much of the increase has been caused by the liberalization of the law itself (Commaille and Festy 1981).

In addition, some countries which formerly did not permit divorce now do so (e.g. Italy, Spain, Portugal, and Argentina). Later on, I shall take some special note of the patterns in those countries.

Some Broad Regularities in Trends

A high-divorce system is a high-remarriage system, for societies do not let their women go unused (although Brahmins did and do) (Goode 1956: 216, 204 ff.). That generalization still holds true, but it is also clear that during the present period the rate of remarriage has dropped, and we suppose it will continue to decrease for some years. Specifically, until recently in most European countries, about 60 per cent of divorced husbands and wives remarried—more men than women of course—and a still higher percentage of the young divorcees eventually remarried (Roussel 1981: 778 ff.).

However, those figures have dropped steadily since the mid-1960s.

Several consequences and causes are intertwined in this change. One consequence is the continuing increase in woman-headed households. Most divorced mothers have custody of the children, either by judicial decree or in fact, and that creates a growing number of such households which face economic hardship and thus become a burden for the welfare systems of the various countries (and thereby creating a social issue). That is so because, whatever the divorce settlement, the divorced woman is not likely to be able to maintain the level of living she shared during the marriage.

In addition, since life expectancy has increased for the female more than for the male, while divorced men have more chance of remarrying a younger woman than divorced women have of remarrying a younger man, the divorced woman (especially the older one) is less likely to be able to find a mate in the available pool of divorced men not yet remarried, for it is a smaller pool.

One of the proximate causes of the decrease in remarriage is the spread of unmarried cohabitation as a kind of substitute for marriage (see Roussel 1981: 765–90). Cohabitation occurs mostly among the unmarried young, and is perhaps now coming to be socially viewed as a new, 'expected' phase of the whole courtship system. However, a large number of divorcees also enter such union, instead of (or before) remarrying. Thus, they do form adult households, often with one or more children, on a temporary or long-term basis. This process, then, partly substitutes for the drop in the remarriage rate, while also introducing some statistical (and social) ambiguity in the apparent rates. (For a sophisticated analysis of the statistics of cohabitation in the United States, see Bumpass and Sweet 1988.) In addition, of course, a large block of older people form such unions and do not marry because of insurance and pension problems.

For many divorcees the lesser rewards of such unions are partly balanced by their lesser costs and commitments. These balances are complex, and space forbids their discussion here. In any event, they are less stable than marriages, for the social commitments of the 'spouses' to each other are much weaker.

Some part of the decrease may occur because a larger number of women who can now manage to support themselves through jobs, even though their salaries are lower than those of men, feel a bit more reluctant than in the past to re-enter a relationship in which the traditional division of labour gives such great advantages to the husband. At a minimum, they are more cautious about entering a new marriage, since it is so difficult to find a husband who is willing to share the domestic burdens on a more or less equal basis.

In the United States the rate of remarriage has been dropping much more among blacks than among whites (Bumpass, Sweet, and Castro 1988); (Castro and Bumpass 1989). This change is in harmony with another finding from the United States, which has not been tested in Europe, that the higher the salary and education of the divorced wife, the lower the rate of remarriage. This finding supports the view that more women feel there is no great advantage in quickly entering a new marriage since that requires a heavier workload for her since new husbands are not generally willing to share domestic tasks. It also applies to black women, who are even more likely than whites to earn more than their husbands.

The next, and related, important change is the large-scale entrance of women, especially mothers, into the workforce, and the higher rate of divorce among working women. This is, of course, a reciprocal relationship, in which both variables are independently causal. That is, more women who get divorced have to work, even if they did not before; and more who work or who want to work will experience a higher divorce rate (see also Green and Questor 1982; Roussel 1988).

Neither of these two relationships between women in the workforce and the divorce rate is a change; what is new is the *scale* of women's entrance into the labour market, and especially the entrance of mothers with young children.

Some decades ago I noted that the difference between the husband's earnings and the wife's real or potential earnings is usually greater towards the upper social strata (Goode 1956: 63.). This is part of the complex of forces that generates a higher divorce rate towards the *lower* social strata (the wife has much less to lose towards the lower economic strata). That work and an earlier paper (1949) may have been the first studies to draw *theoretical* attention to this regularity, although since that time many researchers seem to have 'discovered' this robust fact for themselves.

Towards the lower social strata, and especially among blacks, women were more likely to be in the workforce even decades ago, and the divorce rate was higher as well. Moreover, in study after study, and with data from many countries outside the West, the rate of marital dissolution has proved to be lower among men in higher level occupations or some other index of class such as income (excluding the agricultural population).

In addition, and especially important in the present discussion, I have shown that this relationship is *reversed* for women who work: that is, the higher their incomes, the higher their divorce rate. The sophisticated reader will instantly see that several social factors may oppose one another here, and create some complexities in the resulting tables, and thus the robust negative correlation between male class position and divorce rate may also be changing, but the matter cannot be pursued here.

In simple terms, and stating the matter negatively, the more likely it is that the wife can support herself, even if the husband withdraws his support, the less likely it is that she will be willing to tolerate an unsatisfactory domestic life. With the spread of feminist notions of equality and fair treatment, and the opening of careers to women, more women than before have been able to express that dissatisfaction through divorce.

Of course, men, and especially social philosophers and public advisors, have charged women with abandoning their responsibilities, but only a few have been able to accept the view that it is the equal moral responsibility of husbands to take on the burden of domestic duties, from children to cooking, if both are working. This is almost as correct in Sweden, widely seen as especially 'egalitarian' (see, in this connection, the work of Elena Haavio-Mannila), as it is in Russia.

Investments in the Collectivity of the Family

A further consequence must be noted here, which Weitzman, Roussel, Lesthaege, and I have analysed, each in a very different way. Weitzman (1985) has pointed out that the social patterns of divorce help to define the meaning of marriage. Roussel (1988) has argued that the steep rise in divorce rates is not a temporary change, but a fundamental redefinition of marriage. Lesthaege (1983) has suggested that the basic Western values concerning the family have altered.

At the same time, I have presented data to suggest that people in the West are less and less willing to make serious investments in the collectivity of the family (Goode 1984).

One element in these new patterns is what some have viewed as the 'continual availability' of everyone, married or single, as a possible mate. Roussel suggests that people see the union as essentially 'precarious', that is, however *seemingly* stable it may be. All of us understand from observing the high chance of divorce—for the United States, Castro and Gumpass (1989) calculate on the basis of the present rates that about two-thirds of all new marriages in the United States will end in divorce or separation—that the union may not last.

In more econometric language, since we know that family life will pay off on our investments only over the long term, but increasingly may not last long enough to yield those pay-offs—social, emotional, even economic—it may seem wiser not to commit a heavy investment in a family. We may decide instead to invest more, say, in our careers, and view our family as an organization we shall leave if it does not seem to be going well. That feeling of precariousness *is*, in my view, a change in our time—though it has certainly been common in other cultures at different times in the past.

Custody and Support

The area of custody and post-divorce support exhibits another set of changes, although we do not have adequate data to be certain they are all changes. Some relationships are visibly being altered, while others may have existed in the past in a similar form but simply in smaller numbers.

Although there has been much discussion of no-fault divorce, strictly speaking that term should be limited to a divorce process in which the question of 'whose fault?' is not *permitted* to enter, and *neither* party can refuse a divorce if the other wants it. That is, it is not simply a divorce in which no fault is actually charged by a spouse who feels wronged (e.g. a divorce based on a long separation, where fault becomes irrelevant). What has come to be called 'mutual consent' has become more common, however that 'consent' may have been accomplished.

Whatever the legal grounds, in any event, custody has come to be generally given to the mother—certainly a change from the distant past, and an array of state payments or support has become part of the typical welfare system in the developed nations. About these changes, of course, much public concern has been expressed. This is especially intense in the United States, which has never felt comfortable with the state welfare system, in part because of its uneasy attitudes towards black poverty.

It seems safe to assert, though no full-scale European data on this point are available, that ex-husbands do not generally pay for the full support of mother and children (but see Kahn and Kamerman 1988). This has always been the case. More important, the apparent public acceptance of mutual consent conceals a significant bargaining process between husband and wife before the divorce, in which the greater resources of the husband—personal, economic, and social—enable him to press for advantages which an objective arbitration process might not view as egalitarian.

Instead, the couple typically presents to the court a settled agreement, which the court accepts without much question, and makes it official. In various European countries, possibly all of them (as in Japan), the court is supposed to examine the agreement, but its work-load is so great that mostly it cannot do that task adequately and thus the husband benefits from the hidden negotiations and that seemingly 'fair' consensus (Statistische Umschau: Bevoelkering 1982 for Germany). Again, this has probably been the case in the past as well. The difference now is that there are far more such cases.

It was noted earlier that wives have the burden, or pleasure, of custody in most divorces—this change has doubtless occurred at different historical dates in different countries—and I also note that husbands do not typically pay support that is adequate for the mother-child household. In addition, it is increasingly common in the United States, and also in

Europe, that men sometimes use the threat of a custody (or other) claim as a way of down-scaling the wife's demands for a better settlement (see Weitzman 1985: 309, and in Chapter 22 of this book). As part of this dynamic, although it is very complex, fathers typically do not maintain intimate and frequent relationships with their children after divorce if they do not get custody. (In the United States most children do not continue to see their fathers (Furstenberg *et al* 1983.)

In the next section I report on remarriage in the United States, which perhaps some of my European colleagues can test in other Western countries.

Divorce and Remarriage in the United States

In the United States some two-thirds of the marriage cohorts of the early 1990s can be expected to separate or divorce before death, and of these some three-quarters will also remarry. That is a lower likelihood of remarriage than two decades previously. The most important variables in remarriage are age and race. Ninety per cent of those who are under age 25 at the time of separation will remarry, but only one-third of those who separate or divorce over the age of 40. Less than half of black women will remarry, and that figure has dropped more than among whites, and most sharply among blacks under age 25 (Bumpass, Sweet, and Castro 1988). It is not surprising to find that men with higher incomes marry earliest.

Of course, age affects divorce to begin with: 35 per cent of US women in the early 1980s were married as teenagers, while one-half of recent marital disruptions (including separations) occurred to couples who had married as teenagers. But over 60 per cent of remarried women had married for the first time as teenagers(Castro and Bumpass 1989: esp. pp. 42, 44, 46 ff.). The differences are large, because the divorce rate in the United States, as in Europe, is higher among the young than among other age groups. After divorce, however, these divorcees are still in the younger age groups, where the remarriage rate is also highest.

US women with more education (one or more years of college) are somewhat less likely to remarry, but the rate is mostly a function of age, while their remarriage rate has not been declining as much as that of other women. Those who have had a longer marriage are also less likely to remarry, and take longer to remarry, but again most of this difference is a function of their higher age at the time of separation or divorce.

If people do remarry, of course they risk divorce again. People who remarry experience a higher rate of divorce than people who marry for the first time.

This is a finding that was noted in my early monograph on divorce (Goode 1956: ch. 22). More specifically, if those who remarry are asked about their second marriages within some early period, they say that they are happier than in their first marriages, but the research data are robust: their marital stability is nevertheless lower than that of first marriages. Part of this is doubtless a function of age at first marriage, and thus of *class*: some research suggests that much of the higher rate of divorce among the young is really a function of class. People who marry earlier are more likely to come from a lower economic stratum, where divorce is more common. When they remarry they again experience a higher rate of divorce than those who marry for the first time.

We would also suppose that those who have had the experience of divorce may come to think of it as less extraordinary, perhaps simply an adjustment that many people have to accept, as the final outcome of a difficult domestic existence. And, as more and more come to have that experience, perhaps divorces will come to be more similar to the entire population, in all important social traits.

Divorce in Countries that Formerly Prohibited It

The Catholic Church has successfully opposed divorce in many countries in the past, or pressed for a new prohibition after a period of liberalization. In the last decade, divorce has finally become possible in three Western countries: Italy, Spain, and Portugal. Culturally European, of course, Brazil can be added to that list, since divorce was made possible there in 1977, and in Argentina in 1986 (as the result of a Supreme Court decision and a 1987 law).

In all but Argentina the new laws were accompanied by much polemic, amid fears that a flood of divorce would lead to a breakdown of the family. Women, especially older ones, expressed opposition because they believed that husbands would hasten to throw off their family responsibilities. Partly as a result of widespread opposition, the resulting laws were severely restrictive—in Italy, for example, a minimum of five years' separation was made a prerequisite for divorce, and in some types of cases the period was seven years.

When such laws are introduced so late in the socio-economic development of a country, for some years afterwards the demography of divorce is very different from that of similar countries. The reason is that over the long years when divorce was not possible many of the same forces that lead to family dissolution in other Western countries continued to have their effect just the same. In short, husbands and wives fight and separate even though a legal divorce is not possible; men philander, and set up public or private relations with another woman; and so on—all without entering the status of 'divorced'. For example, in Italy in the 1950s it was estimated that perhaps 40,000 couples were breaking up each year in this manner (Goode 1963: 84). In 1984 almost 400,000 couples were living apart (Golini 1987: 703).

Those who were financially able to do so could go to another country, obtain citizenship, get a divorce, and then return to Italy (Sgritta and Tufari 1977: 258). Others could obtain, with some difficuty and at much cost, a church annulment. Many legal separations, both church and civil, were obtained, but of course neither party was free to remarry. And, of those who separated, legally or informally, only men could establish a new union without much social censure.

Thus, the number of 'candidates' for the new divorce procedure would not represent the normal distribution of divorce-prone people in a given country. It is skewed by the accumulation over time of many people who in other countries would already have obtained divorces, at a much earlier age. Thus, there would also be a skew towards more divorces at older ages, and those with more or older or adult children. At the same time, obviously, an unknown number of older people would have simply given up. Their passions and hatreds would have cooled over time, and they would have made some adjustments to the diminished domestic life that a prohibition on divorce enforces.

In addition, in Italy those who could take advantage of the new law, with all its complexity, were those who had been separated for some years (and thus were older), since the new laws required a lengthy period of separation. They were also beter educated, and somewhat better off financially. Because much of the rural population has a lower propensity to divorce, the new divorcees were mostly urban.

When the Italian divorce law was put into effect at the end of 1970 (in 1975 the grounds of guilt were abolished), divorces rose from 17,000 the first year (1971) to over 32,000 in the second, while legal requests in the first year numbered over 55,000 (Istituto Centrale di Statistica, 1982: 17). After that, the number of divorces dropped by 1975 to a steady 11,000 per year for a few years, leading some analysts to suggest that previous fears about a divorce flood were groundless.

However, that optimism was premature. In the period 1978–82 separations rose 30 per cent to almost 38,000, and in 1980–2 divorces rose 23 per cent, to over 14,000. By 1986 there were over 16,000 divorces (Golini 1987: 704). Not a flood, to be sure, but a continued increase.

Since a divorce first requires a separation, petitions for separations continue to rise. Of course, this legal requirement adds time to the 'official' marriage and thus to any calculation of the duration of marriage. The older age skew of the new divorcees also increases the average age of the divorced spouses, the time between separation and divorce, the duration of marriage, the number of children involved as well as their age, and of course the total number of divorces granted. Thus, *all* such figures are biased by the long history of *non*-divorce. We can suppose that in the future all these figures will become more 'normal', that is, closer to those of other European countries.

After the initial period in which divorce first became legally possible, the supposed 'grounds' (fault, etc.) usually became the simple assertion that a separation already existed, based on 'agreement' (thus, over 60 per cent were 'consensual'), and now guilt is no longer required. As might be expected, those who married in the church are less likely to get divorced, but modern Italians are less likely than in the past to marry by a religious rite, and in fact the differences between the two divorce rates (i.e. of the religious and the secular groups) actually increase. That is, the truly 'faithful' become more different from the rest of population, though almost all are nominally Catholic. In the contemporary cohorts, the statistical bias caused by age is also diminishing (Golini 1987: 10).

From the beginning, almost two-thirds of the requests for divorce were filed by men. We interpret this to mean that more men than women had entered upon new relationships, or simply wanted to be free, and they were economically able to support themselves. Because of women's more precarious economic position—more difficult in Italy than in other Western countries—more wives were reluctant to be divorced.

In general, sex differences in who files for divorce cannot be interpreted as an index of who is less satisfied with the marriage. *Who actually files* is shaped by the existing social customs, the technical legal grounds, and the dynamics of negotiations between spouses (see Goode 1956: 114–15). Thus, a rising percentage of women filing divorce petitions in a given country does not tell us unambiguously that more women would now like to divorce.

In Spain divorce became possible only in 1981, and thus the available data are much less rich and complete. From 1900 until 1940 the Spanish censuses did not even list the category of 'separated' (Instituto Nacional de Estadística, 1974: 54). There, too, there was no intitial flood of divorces—in the first year, barely over 5,000 cases. One hypothesis is that the Spanish are still less prone to go to court to settle personal problems than people in other nations at this level of socio-economic development (Presidencia del Tribunal Supremo, Secretaría Técnica 1981).

The skew in age at divorce (over 40 per cent of the men were over 40 years of age) in Spain in the initial years led the Technical Secretariat to suggest that domestic conflict increases after 18–20 years of marriage, a most unlikely hypothesis. Older people were simply better able to take advantage of the new law late in their marriage (e.g. they were more likely to have been separated already).

That the new generation will be different can be inferred from youth surveys done in Spain in recent years; (Alberdi 1986: 93–112; Borrajo 1987: 113–37; Conde 1983: 52–3). Younger people do not take for granted the indissolubility of marriage, and almost half assert that the public ceremony of marriage is only a formality.

Divorce was made less costly in Spain than in Italy, but still bound to the requirement of a legal separation, in this case two years. Couples must then take the *separate and distinct* step of filing a divorce petition. Thus, a substantial age skew remains. The total number of such cases in the early 1980s was about 40,000 a year. This rate is roughly that of other European countries, as it falls at the middle of the distribution in Europe.

Consensual suits have increased (in 1984 they formed about one-half of the total). However, that shift conceals an important counter-process. Women are agreeing to the separation, because they are under some pressure in the private negotiating stage; but they can accept disadvantageous terms at this stage, and plan to come back to the court for a change in settlement. Then the negotiations will be more public. In Madrid the court records for this period average a hundred pages per case (Alberdi 93–7; Borrajo, 114). In 1983 there were 39,000 separation and divorce suits, but the family courts faced almost 108,000 family cases, as couples sought to move from a supposedly consensual agreement to a settlement more under the scrutiny of the judge.

Declining Divorce Rates

As I noted earlier, social analysts have used some version either of industrialization theory or of the older notions of *Gemeinsschaft* and *Gesellschaft* to explain the breakdown of family patterns generally and the rise of divorce rates. The received wisdom in social science has been that life in rural areas or villages is more stable, and people invest more in the collectivity of the family. Wives and husbands share common values as well as customs and thus they conflict with one another less frequently and less intensely. Both need each other economically and so would see no reason to dissolve their relationship. 'Loss of love' would not even be taken seriously as a cause for divorce (if permitted at all), since they had not married for love to begin with. Elders and kin also press them to stay together.

In fact, hundreds of studies (in the West) support the general notion that divorce rates are higher in urban or industrial areas, that divorce rates begin to rise first in such areas, that traditional family norms and values begin to weaken there first, and so on. Certainly, some literary figures and anthropologists have dissented here and there, supporting Mark Twain's striking assertion that God made the country, man made the town, and the Devil made the little country town. They have not, however, convinced the majority.

Those general statements do not constitute a theory. Rather they are a complex, rich set of descriptive ideas. They do not, for example, explain the build-up of the traditional family system, in which consensus, fidelity to the norms, marital stability, and so on are supposedly common. They do partially explain the 'fall away from virtue', but then most of us feel little difficulty in understanding that fall anyway; just as we feel sympathetic with the angels who are banished from Heaven in Milton's *Paradise Lost*. Entirely apart from our personal experiences, we have been taught by our religious instructors that the two very first human beings on earth led the way, long before we ourselves were born, to follow them in that path.

A quarter-century ago I drew attention to the empirical fact that in some countries we could point to declining divorce rates, and to formerly high rates in some rural areas. Whether specific rates rose or fell under the impact of industrialization would depend on how high they were under traditional system. For example, Japan and the Arab countries traditionally generated high divorce rates (Goode 1963: 25, 155–62, 358 ff.; Murdock 1950: 195–201).

I also predicted that, although these societies might experience declining divorce rates, the rates would eventually climb again. They would at first fall, because the modern forces would begin to undermine the traditional ones that generated high rates in the past. It is not possible to analyse here all the cases that fall under this category, which includes at least Indonesia, Taiwan, Malaysia, and Japan, but probably not the Arab countries (which may not fit my dynamic definition of industrialization anyway). These cases can also be contrasted with modern China, which I correctly predicted would experience a declining rate but not because of anything like industrialization.

Traditional High-Divorce-Rate Societies

This section will focus on some of the general patterns of stable high-divorce societies. Some individual cases will be noted, however, at least in passing. The first general pattern of importance is this: *before* they were affected by the ideas, the culture, or the immediate direct pressures of industrialization or the West, and very likely over long time periods, perhaps hundreds of years, the rates of marital stability in any traditional society (including Western ones) showed *no trends at all*. The rates went up and down only modestly, in a form Pitrim Sorokin called 'trendless fluctuation'.

Secondly, in times of great change, such as revolutions and civil wars, epidemics, famines, or conquests, rates of marital dissolution almost certainly went up, as they did in periods of prosperity.

Thirdly, each such traditional family system generated a given level of marital dissolution, or divorce if it was permitted. This general rate was very different from that of other traditional societies of the same epoch (e.g. the high rate in Mahgreb—in what is now Morocco, in contrast to the low rate in the region that is now Afghanistan).

Fourthly, some of these systems *typically* created high rates of dissolution or divorce, while others did not. But the differences bear little relationship to such modern concepts as industrialization, 'modernization', world systems, and the like.

Thus, almost certainly, the indigenous Japanese system in the Tokugawa period (and extending into the Meiji for some decades) exhibited high rates of marital dissolution, especially in the *rural* areas. And so did many of the societies that form the great Muslim Crescent from North Africa to Indonesia. By contrast, the Chinese and Indian systems did not and Western nations (under the Catholic Church) did not either until modern times.

Finally, though we can take notice of these stable differences, we have no over-arching theory to explain why each of them occurred. In each case we can give only *ad hoc* accounts of the factors that seem to generate each set of rates. Attempts by economists have also been empty so far, because their assumptions about how marriage and divorce systems operate pay so little respect to reality (e.g. the work of Gary Becker).

Of course, for some cases we feel our explanations are sound enough. For example, matrilineal family systems are not simply 'mirror images' of patrilineal systems and they usually have shown high rates of divorce (the Crow among the Plains Indians, the Nayar in India, several of the societies across the belt of Africa, etc.). Women and their brothers remained firmly linked even after marriage, since they belonged to the same lineage, and they shared material and emotional stakes in lineage matters. The husband was not a member of his wife's lineage, but his children were, and their mother's brother had jural authority over them. If there was a divorce, the husband moved out and the children and mother possessed whatever lineage property there was. Many of these systems were also horticultural and thus women were very important in the productive process itself.

The implicit reasoning here seems to be that, when women are in a stronger position (as in a matrilineal system), they are less tolerant of smaller inadequacies or slights from their husbands. The social structure *creates* that stronger position. We apply the same principle when we assert that, because many wives in Western countries now earn good salaries, they feel free to be more independent and thus will not adjust to traditional male demands.

Unfortunately, that reasoning would not apply to most traditional Muslim and especially Arab societies. There the social analyst is tempted to 'explain' high Muslim divorce rates and the ease with which *husbands* could divorce their wives by the fact that the husbands were in a stronger position. Thus, we say the divorce rate is high in the one case because women's position is *strong*; in the second, because women's position is *weak* . Obviously an explanation that must be changed for each set of cases is not very powerful. I shall not develop a better one, but we can understand these systems better by making a few additional general statements about those high-divorce-rate systems.

First, one basic emphasis to be kept in mind is that a traditional high-divorce family system is not like that of a modern Western family system with similarly high rates. In crucial structural ways, they are very different.

Of course, these societies share with all others the general trait of male dominance, but this is always limited to some degree. If men were only husbands, they might use their power to shape a family system in which men could marry and discard wives at their whim. But since men are also the fathers, brothers, uncles, and cousins of women, it is in their interest to protect their female kin from other men. All family systems are in part the outcomes of these and other parallel tensions.

Another broad similarity is that societies try to make

certain that women should be *used*, for they are a valuable resource. Thus, the high-divorce society has typically been a high-remarriage society as well. But even where the divorce rate was low, as in Ch'ing China, widows and divorced women 'disappeared demographically' into the married status (that is, over successive population studies, women who were widows or divorcees did not remain so). It is only in modern Western and some Eastern (and Arab) countries that we find a large and growing number of divorced mothers who become single heads of family units at low wages or on social welfare, and who remain unmarried for long periods or indefinitely.

By contrast, since divorces typically occurred *early* in a traditional high-divorce society and almost everyone remarried, the percentage of the female population in the status '*now* divorced' did not increase over time.

In addition, divorce patterns in stable high-divorce societies were *institutionalized*. Whether and what part of the bride price was to be returned or finally paid, who got the children at which ages, who was responsible for arranging the remarriage—all such matters were determined by common acceptance and rule.

It hardly needs to be said that we cannot assume that domestic life was happier in a low-divorce society or more troubled by conflict in a high-divorce society. Conflict is *endemic, pervasive, ubiquitous*; how the social institutions deal with it determines the divorce or dissolution rate.

In the high-divorce society, later marriages were more likely to be stable than first marriages (unlike the Western pattern). Those who had been married once were given more freedom of choice. Divorcees were a bit older and more experienced. The divorced population was not 'deviant'.

Finally we can now predict (other things being equal) that the historical forces that once generated these high divorce rates would weaken as these societies move into the modern world. Thus, for a while those rates would *drop*. However, later, the modern forces that generate high divorce rates would eventually assert their power, and the rates would rise again, though not necessarily to their traditional levels.

Malaysia

Let us first consider the case of Malysia. Western family theorists have not spent much time in developing hypotheses about why the divorce rate of Malaysia has fallen rapidly since the 1940s since few have ever heard of the fact to begin with. We are not even surprised about the trend, since we have not thought about the matter at all.

The striking datum is that the divorce rates in some of the substates of Malaysia have been higher than any found anywhere else in the world. In some years the number of divorces in certain substates has been as high as 70 per cent of the number of marriages. On the other hand, by 1975 the trend lines of Western divorce rates (rising) and Malysian divorce rates (falling) were coming close together or even crossing. Whether, as we predict, Malaysian divorce rates will eventually rise again can not be ascertained as yet.

In traditional Muslim system, marriages were strictly arranged by parents and women married young (median age in 1947, 16.6 years). The population was rural and agricultural, mostly illiterate, and polygamy (one husband with two or more wives) was fairly common. With the exception of polygamy, these arrangements were typical for much of the world's population until the Second World War. Other factors combined to generate a high instability, especially in first marriages. I shall outline these briefly.

First, marriage was 'normatively unstable'. That is, people took it for granted that unions would be brittle. Parents did not concern themselves as much as they did in China with a very careful selection of the prospective spouse, since they did not expect the marriage to last anyway. There was little or no social disapproval of divorce.

Remarriage was easy, and not much under the control of parents. Economic obstacles to remarriage were minimal. The divorcee was not required to have a dowry. She was likely to be economically productive, especially in a wet-rice region or in the local markets. If the divorcee had any property, she kept it after the divorce. If they stayed together long enough to acquire property, it was divided equally.

After a marriage a wife was likely to enjoy a social and economic position nearly equal to that of her husband. She handled the money, and her economic contribution was important. Customary village life made husband and wife more equal than Muslim tenets would generally approve.

An additional factor contributed to marital instability: the

Malay's strong wish to avoid personal conflict. Personal dignity, sensitivity to affront, and the inability to confront and resolve disputes were intense and widespread. Kin and other villagers were likely to become involved in marital conflict. Marital conflict, however, was not experienced as a mere problem between a husband and a wife. It was a source of *spiritual* unease and discomfort for kin as well as the entire village.

Thus, when spouses considered divorce as a solution to the problem, their kin would usually prefer that step rather than endure and be infected by a continuing spiritual disharmony. Similarly, the wife who wanted a divorce against her husband's wishes could engage in a public conflict with him or even insult him, knowing that the ensuing humilitation and indignation would very likely persuade him to repudiate her, as a way of restoring personal and social tranquility.

All of these social patterns were most extreme in regions that were least educated, most traditional, most rural, least developed economically, and with the highest rates of polygyny. The indigenous social and family patterns, in short, generated high divorce rates.

That system was much undermined since the 1940s. By the mid-1970s the median age at marriage for women had risen to

TABLE 2.2. *Malaysia, divorce rate, 1948–1975*

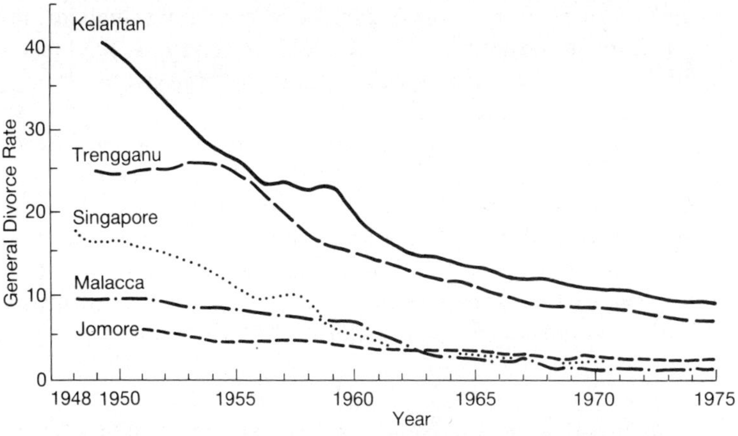

Source: Gavin W. Jones, "Marriage and Divorce in Peninsular Malaysia: Three Decades of Change" Population and Development Review (June 1981), p. 266.

about that of the United States, over 21 years. Almost all girls are now being educated and an increasing pecentage of them are going on to higher levels of schooling. The birth-rate has fallen. Job opportunities have opened up, because the government has insisted on jobs for Malays and encouraged economic expansion. By 1980 one third of all females aged 10 and over were in the labour force, about the same fraction of the currently married, and over half of the divorced. Women have moved into many sectors in the urban areas, such as teaching, electronics, factories, etc.

Young people have achieved more freedom of mate choice, and of course the age gap between husband and wife has narrowed considerably. Nuclear families have become more common, as more people have moved to the cities. Thus, couples are less likely to feel the pressures of relatives who, in the past, would have pressed them to restore harmony by divorcing. By marrying at older ages both the spouses are more likely to have accumulated property already and both would have a larger collective stake in marital stability.

Perhaps of equal importance is another change of attitude, very likely partly the result of the spread of the 'meaning of modern marriage' in the international culture of our era. Even in the past, the better educated, and the lower and higher governmental officials and professionals had come to feel that divorce was uncouth, 'country', backward, not 'modern' at all. Women's organizations have begun to campaign against these practices and to press for more restrictive legislation. Thus almost certainly an ideological change has been occurring, towards the attitude that divorce is no longer appropriate or even proper.

Obviously we can give no exact measure of the forces moving in these various directions, though we do predict that over the long term the divorce rates will begin to rise somewhat, though not to the high levels of the past.

A similar pattern of declining divorce rates is evident in Indonesia, which is geographically close and culturally similar to Malaysia (See Table 2.3).

Japan

In pre-industrial rural Japan, as in Malaysia, high divorce rates seemed to form part of an unplanned dynamic of

TABLE 2.3. *Indonesia, divorce rate, 1950–1986*

Year	Ratio
1950	45.9
1955	53.1
1960	47.8
1970	33.4
1975	25.3
1980	16.4
1984	15.2
1986	10.3

'marital sifting' or extended mate selection, through which more compatible marriages were eventually achieved through successive marital unions. However, the Japanese leaders *deliberately* planned to alter this pattern in the Meiji Restoration of 1868.

The Meiji Restoration aimed at nothing short of a revolution, not a socialist but a conservative one. It sought to keep intact Japan's ancient ways, but also to become the first non-Western nation to industrialize successfully. Its astonishing achievements extended to the family as well.

The new leaders sought through propaganda, formal education, and new legal codes to impose the family patterns of the *samurai* on all the Japanese and to reject the rural patterns as uneducated and primitive. As a result, Japan was the first high-divorce nation to decrease its divorce rate substantially. Industrialization certainly contributed something to the decades-long drop in the divorce rate, but the foundations of the shift were deliberate political decisions and legal acts, based on the ideology of the Meiji reformers.

Under earlier rural patterns, Japanese young men and women, unlike the Chinese, not only knew one another before marriage; they had some clandestine, but widely understood, access to one another. But they married only with the permission of their parents (as in eighteenth-century Sweden). Marriage in very early adolescence was neither an ideal nor a common practice. Young women married at an average of 19 years and were expected to shoulder the heavy adult burdens of rural tasks. Grooms were about 22 years of age and thus adult, but it was the parents of the young man who would decide that it was time for him to marry, and with whom.

Local custom ruled marriage practices, no state licence was required, and the marriage was not even typically recorded in the family records until weeks or even months after the ceremony. Consequently it will never be possible to obtain a correct divorce rate for the period before the Restoration, or for several decades afterwards. Innumerable breakups occurred without any mention of them in the family records. Although in the 1880s there were more than 300 divorces per 1,000 marriages—a ratio higher than the United States ever experienced until about the 1960s—almost certainly the true figures were higher. The higher rates were to be found in rural areas in the past, but now the divorce rates are higher in urban areas.

The young bride was sent back by her in-laws in perhaps most cases, for it was they who had to be pleased, not the young groom. The young woman was not in the situation of a Chinese bride, separated from village and kin, with no resources of her own. Peasant Japanese wives had not yet become so subservient as Chinese brides, or as much as Western travellers observed Japanese urban women to be. As a productive worker, the Japanese bride was valuable and knew that others before her had divorced and still found adequate husbands. The remarriage rate was high, almost total, and thus, at any given time until the death of a spouse, almost every adult was in the married state, whatever his or her previous marital adventures. In effect, the traditional rural Japanese bride who was confronted by rejecting in-laws always knew there was an alternative.

As noted above, the Japanese leaders set in motion a conscious ideological and legal programme towards changing the family system, more in harmony with *samurai* domestic ideals and practices, and, of course, closer to that of the Chinese ideal. The young woman was absorbed into the household of the adult groom's father, and expected to remain subordinate to her mother-in-law, and to devote herself to domestic duties. Many women worked in factories and came to be educated, but elders kept strict control over where they worked as well as their earnings.

Elders and leaders were quite conscious of the threat of

industrialization. The changes were guided by political beliefs that put a high value on service to the state. The aim was to intensify the family hierarchy and male power, and to strengthen family controls over individuals through dominion over access to land in the countryside and access to jobs and training in the cities. Women who worked in the new factories did not control their own wages or dispose of them, and did not work there after marriage.

Greater power was legally given to the head of the family line and a member of the family could not choose his or her residence, or marry without the permission of the head.

The 1898 code required state registration for marriages and thereafter divorces were not recorded unless the marriages had been previously recorded. This had the immediate effect of reducing the official rate of divorce. But in general the public stance of leaders was that the unofficial shuffling of mates was crude and countrified. These efforts at harnessing the strength of the family for state purposes, i.e. industrial and national power, were strengthened in the 1930s by an intensive campaign of nationalist propaganda. It was not until 1947 that a new civil code was passed. It was more in harmony with the industrialization that had been going on for more than half a century.

As I noted long ago, the Japanese rate of marital dissolution was *downwards* during industrialization, as its social processes eroded the traditional factors that had once made marriages fragile; but full-scale industrialization generates quite other, new forces, that have made marraiges unstable in almost all Western nations. These social forces eventually lead other people, particularly employers, to be less concerned with one's family role fulfilment; mass media urge self-seeking, material advancement, concern for self more than for the family collectivity, for lesser authority for elders, etc. All of these social forces will ultimately cause a rise in the divorce rate.

Beginning in the 1960s (see Tables 2.4 and 2.5) the divorce rate in Japan did start to rise again. It continues to rise, though it is unlikely that the rate will match those in Western countries over the next generation.

Thus, it was not until the 1960s that many of the results of the previous decades of change became apparent: the declining power of elders, high levels of education for both men and

TABLE 2.4. *Japan, divorce rate, 1947–1986*

Year	Crude rate	Rate (per 100 couples)
1947	1.02	
1950	1.01	0.54
1955	0.84	0.45
1960	0.74	0.37
1963	0.73	0.35
1965	0.79	0.36
1970	0.93	0.39
1975	1.07	0.43
1980	1.22	0.49
1986	1.37	

Source: Japan Statistical Yearbook 1988.

women, a growing approval of free choice in marriage, an increasing percentage of women working after marriage, low fertility, and so on, and—more recently—even a modest feminist movement. Thus elders cannot control as they once could the inevitable conflicts between husbands and wives, and husbands have lost some of their command over their wives.

The Japanese divorce rate reached its lowest figure in 1963 and has been gradually rising since then. It should, however, be kept in mind that, by Western standards, that rate remains low. Many other changes are taking place in the divorce process itself for example, the trend towards mother-custody, an increase in the percentage of ex-husbands who pay for their children's support, and an increase in the number of Japanese women who take the initiative in a divorce—but time does not permit us to discuss them here.

China

The political and social complexities of changes in the divorce patterns of China cannot as yet be fully unravelled; here I wish only to note a few basic facts.

After the early 1950s, when the divorce rate rose sharply in China, divorce disappeared from the public records. Clearly the regime was dismayed at the surge of divorce in the 1950s, for the leaders felt that, after some of the injustices from the

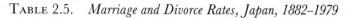

TABLE 2.5. *Marriage and Divorce Rates, Japan, 1882–1979*

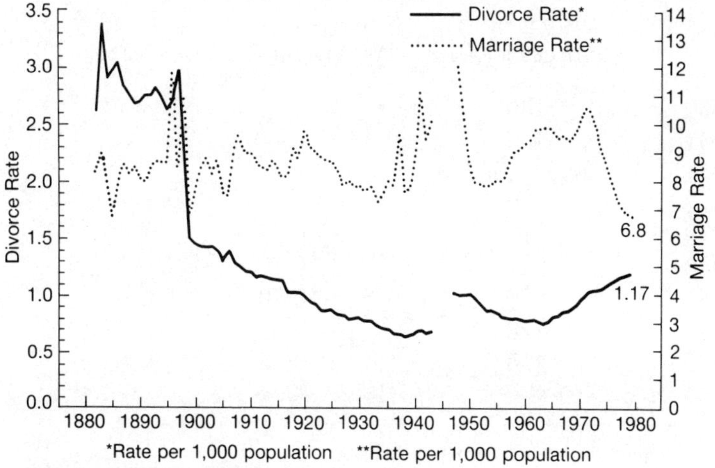

* Rate per 1,000 population
** Rate per 1,000 population

Sources: 1882–1899 *Nihon Teikoku Tōkei Nenkan*, Bureau of the Census, Prime Minister's Office, Tokyo, 1915.
1900–1978 *Vital Statistics: 1978, Vol.1*, Health & Welfare Statistics Dept., Minister Secretariat, Minister of Health & Welfare , Tokyo, 1980.
1979 Estimations, Health & Welfare Statistics Association, Tokyo, 1980.

past had been redressed, citizens ought to be happy or at least content in marriage. The Chinese had, in any event, always disapproved of divorce.

Divorce rose again after 1978, with the more liberal policies that began then, and has continued to rise. However, divorce continues to be a sensitive political topic, as is clear from reading recent Chinese newspapers and social science reports.

As I predicted many years ago (Goode 1963: 317–8), the divorce rate did go down, but for administrative reasons. Divorce creates many bureaucratic problems in a state-controlled society. For purposes of control, Chinese workers under the communist system were organized into factory units, which allocated (and still allocate) housing, which is scarce. A divorced person could not, as in the West, simply rent an apartment when a divorce occured. Even in the cities, family matters were never private, and under the communist regime there were several layers of social controls to prevent

TABLE 2.6. *China, divorce rate, 1950–1985*

Year	Number of divorces (000)	Rate (per 1,000 population)
1950	186	–
1951	409	–
1953	over 1,000	–
1978	170	–
1979	319	0.66
1980	341	0.70
1981	389	0.78
1982	428	0.85
1983	418	0.82
1985	–	0.9

Source: Unpublished data from official sources.

or reduce any public outbreak of marital disharmony. The easy divorce procedure of the 1950 law was not changed, but it became extremely difficult to get a divorce, especially for a woman. The courts were reluctant to concede 'irreconcilability', and sent couples back to local cadres and organizations (Parish and Whyte 1978: 194), who tried to convince them to try to work things out and stay together to 'preserve [their] marriage even if both partners desired a divorce'. Much bitterness was expressed in the freer 1980s about this earlier, long period when unwilling couples were forced to stay together.

Thus we observe the irony, in which powerful 'others'—in this case, local groups or committees organized by the state—required a reluctant couple to stay together, just as in Ch'ing China the family elders rigidly controlled both the mate choice and the later marital behaviour of their adult children.

Modern China offers another twist to the old theme of family controls. While remarriage was always frowned on, today new social science reports tell us that in the modern age it is often the *young adults* who put barriers in the way of their *parents'* remarriage. Apart from their moral disapproval, they have a material stake: their elders are a resource, their services are needed (for child care, etc.), and they sometimes own a bit of property or goods. In one study it was asserted that on marriage applications almost all of the people intending to remarry wrote that they had already obtained the agreement of their children (Chu 1984*a*).

The Arab World

The changes occuring in Arab divorce patterns are too complex to describe fully, but a few important conclusions can be presented here.

In 1963 I predicted that divorce rates in the Arab world would decline with industrialization, as in other traditional high-divorce-rate societies, and only later rise again (Goode 1963: 158). That expectation *cannot* be affirmed, in contrast to my predictions about China and Japan.

There are several reasons for this conclusion. First, in spite of the high technological developments in oil-rich Arab countries, the resources and opportunities remain overwhelmingly in the hands of family heads, and obedience to family rules continues to outweigh other factors of such importance in industrialized polities. In that precise sense, then, it can be argued that the Arab countries have 'industrialized' very little as yet.

Secondly, and more importantly, after much study of the data, as well as correspondence with Arab experts, I have found so many problems in the data themselves that it is not possible to have confidence in any reported trends. In addition, the reported rates of divorce are mostly based on the whole population, which, when compared with Western nations, is a disproportionately younger population (due to a continuing high birth-rate and lower infant mortality). Since there is a substantial rise in the female age at marriage, and thus a much lower percentage of the younger population at risk of divorce, any real changes are somewhat hidden or muted.

Thirdly, it is possible that the political, economic, and social turmoil in these countries has had so many contrary effects on the actual divorce patterns, that we should not really expect any consistent time trends from one nation to another.

In any event, the simple fact is that no such consistency can be discerned in the trends. Some have indeed declined, but others have moved up or down without basically changing, and others have risen (see Tables).

TABLE 2.7. *Arab countries, divorce rate, 1930–1985*

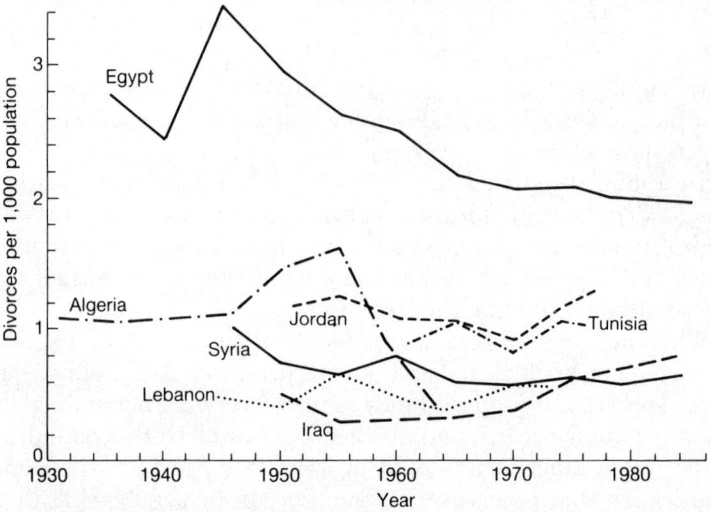

Numerous changes in marriage and divorce law have occurred, within a context of fierce debate and even violence, so that the rights of women in divorce have improved somewhat but moves in both directions have apparently occurred.

Perhaps the most important alteration is that divorce has increasingly come to be defined, recorded, and even scrutinized by officials, and by the civilian courts. In Morocco, divorce is still a matter for the religious courts, but generally these matters that were once clearly in the hands of family elders and the religious authorites must conform with bureaucratic rules. For example, it is generally recognized that women must give their consent to their own marriage. And in most countries they may even specify that they have the right to ask for a divorce if their husband insists on taking a second wife. On the other hand, if a woman wishes to initiate a divorce, she may have to pay back whatever bride price was originally given.

One fundamental change seems to be occurring in divorce patterns, which has resulted in what some have called the feminization of households. Under the traditional system a woman remained under the protection and control of a male:

first her father, then her husband. If she was divorced, she returned to her father's household to be remarried again. If her life was long, she might have ended her days in the house of one of her sons.

However, temporary or long-term migration is widespread. Many husbands may take a second wife anywhere, and divorce their first wives only much later (or not at all). Thus, many wives do not remarry, or remarry late, and those left behind may be forced to enter the labour force. It can certainly be claimed that conditions are somewhat better for them than in the past in one regard: more can survive in this manner than a half-century ago. It is also possible that the elder household male is no longer able to assure the remarriage of his divorced daughter. One result of these processes is that far more women than men are in the status of 'divorced and not remarried', and the number of women-headed households is increasing.

It also seems likely that real custody is increasingly becoming the continued responsibility of the mother. Under the traditional system, custody belonged to the father, and legally still does in most countries, except for the earliest years of the child. However, that system rested on a more permanent residence pattern, and the existence of a patriarchal household in which there would be some members (the man's mother, a sister, an aunt) who could assume that custody; and in the rural villages of the past, of course, the man was not typically going to the city to work in an office during regular hours. Thus, he would be there to assume some responsibility. Now, more fathers are 'absent', or work elsewhere at low wages, and cannot or at least do not reassume custody when the children reach the appropriate ages. Some legal codes have made some recognition of the new patterns, by raising the ages during which the mother has legal custody, or recognizing (in Egypt) some rights of custody among the mother's kin.

Thus, with respect to both remarriage and custody, the traditional system is weakening. State welfare support does continue to expand, although it may not be large enough to meet the apparent needs. But that very expansion reflects the decline in the power of the patriarch. As Mernissi (1978) has suggested, the state begins to replace the chief elder.

Final Comment

Most large-scale societies the world has known have been patriarchal and exhibited low divorce rates, except possibly in periods of great decline. Commentators, both then and later, have responded with alarm to increased divorce rates, seeing in them at least an index of coming societal failure. Thus far, it is not certain they were wholly incorrect. Such periods *are* likely to be epochs of important changes in the legal, social, and economic forces that have hitherto persuaded people to fulfil their social obligations.

Even if we do not deplore those changes, they do suggest the theoretical significance of the processes under way. Modern Western analysts have begun to examine with greater empirical care the details of the alterations and the dynamics that generate higher divorce rates in Western nations (including those in the Pacific).

This chapter has tried to enlarge the scope of this expanding enterprise by moving to a more global plane. Taking a world perspective, some of the complexities of the changes now occuring have been noted in different parts of the world—the West, including countries where divorce has only recently been permitted, nations where my theory of industrial ization would predict a fall in divorce rates (Japan, Taiwan, Malaysia, Indonesia) before (perhaps) rising again, China, and the Arab world (see Tables). A label has been suggested for this phenomenon, which has generally been ignored in the world literature on divorce: the 'stable, high divorce-rate system'.

Are there similarities between these stable high-divorce-rate societies of the past and the modern high-divorce-rate societies that are evolving in the United States and Western Europe today? Some have been noted in this Chapter, but the differences between the two are perhaps more striking. While the high-divorce societies of the past institutionalized remarriage after divorce (and thereby kept most women and most men in families), the high-divorce societies of today, in contrast, have not solved the problems of reintegrating women (and children) into the family—and/or into the mainstream of the society. Rather, as many of the chapters in this volume attest, they are often left in severely diminished economic circumstances, and an increasingly larger percentage of children are raised in mother-headed households. This is the challenge that confronts high-divorce-rate societies today.

This chapter has tried to place these issues in a larger perspective, so that we can more easily understand, or at least consider more carefully, the complexity of the factors that create high and low divorce rates, and some of the corresponding social consequences. We have also noted that many of the *consequences* of divorce change in magnitude and process as the rates move up or down; some of these may be viewed as primarily familial, but the polity is also affected by changes in such family behaviour and attitudes. To the extent that we set ourselves to grapple seriously with these multifarious issues of fact, social theory, and political action, we shall be better able to assess what should, or even what *could* be done about them.

References

ALBERDI, I. (1986) 'Divorcio y sociedad en la España actual', *Revista sistema*, 93–112.

BARBAGLI, M. (1990), *Provando e riprovando* (Bologna).

BARCLAY, G.W. (1954), *Colonial Development and Population in Taiwan* (Princeton, NJ).

BORRAJO, S. I. (1987), 'Estudio sociológico sobre la ruptura matrimonial en Madrid capital (1981–1984)', *Revista española de investigaciones sociológicas*, 37: 113–37.

BUMPASS, L., and SWEET, J. A. (1988), 'Preliminary Evidence on Cohabitation', *National Survey of Families and Households' Working Paper No.2* (Madison, Win.).

BUMPASS, L., SWEET, J., and CASTRO, T. (1988), 'Changing Patterns of Remarriage' (Madison, Wis.).

CASTRO, T., and BUMPASS, L. (1989), 'Recent Trends in Marital Disruption', *Demography*, 25, 37–51.

CHU, D. S. K. (1984*a*), 'An Investigation of the Remarriage Situation in HongKou District, Shanghai', in S. S. K. Chu,, (ed.), *Sociology and Society in Contemporary China, 1979–1981* (New York).

—— (ed.), (1984*b*), *Sociology and Society in Contemporary China, 1979–1981* (New York).

COMMAILLE, J. and FESTY, P. et al. (1981), *Le Divorce en Europe Occidentale: La loi et le nombre* (Paris), I.N.E.D.

CONDE, R. (1983), 'Tendencias de cambio en la estructura familiar', *Revista española de investigaciones sociales*, 12: 52–3.

FURSTENBERG, F. F., NORD, C. W., PETERSON, J. L., and ZILL, N.

(1983), 'The Life Course of Children of Divorce: Marital Disruption and Parental Contact', *American Sociological Review*, 48: 656–68.

Golini, A. (1987), 'Famille et ménage dans l'Italie récente', *Population*, 42: 699–714.

Goode, W. J. (1956), *After Divorce* (later: *Women in Divorce*) (New York).

—— (1963), *World Revolution and Family Patterns* (New York).

—— (1982), *The Family* (2nd edn. Englewood Cliffs).

—— (1984), 'Individual Investments in Family Relationships over the Coming Decades', *Tocqueville Review*, 6: 51–83. (Given at a meeting of the Tocqueville Society, Arc-et-Senans, 1983.)

—— (forthcoming (*a*)), 'Grand Theories of Family Change', Society for the Scientific Study of Population, Nov. (Tokyo).

—— (forthcoming (*b*)), *World Changes in Divorce Patterns*.

Greene, W. H., and Questor, A. O. (1982), 'Divorce Risk and Wives' Labor Supply Behaviour', *Social Science Quarterly*, 63: 16–27.

Instituto Centrale de Statistica (1982), *Dati statici su dieci anni di divorzio in italia, anni 1971–1980*, suppl. *Bollentino mensile d.d.i. Statistica, 23:17.*

Instituto Nacional de Estadística (1974), *Panorama social* (Madrid).

Japan Statistical Yearbook (1988) (Toyko).

Jones, G. W. (1980), 'Trends in Marriage and Divorce in Peninsular Malaysia', *Population Studies*, 34/2: 279–92.

—— (1981), 'Malay Marriage and Divorce in Peninsular Malaysia: Three Decades of Change', *Population and Development Review*, 7/2: 255–78.

Kahn, A. J., and Kamerman, S. B. (1988), *Child Support: From Debt Collection to Social Policy* (Newbury Park, Calif.).

Lesthaeghe, R. (1983), 'A Century of Demographic and Cultural Change in Western Europe: An Exploration of Underlying Dimensions', *Population and Development Review*, 9: 411–35.

Mernissi, F. (1978), 'The Patriarch in the Moroccan Family: Myth or Reality', in Alman, *Women's Status and Fertility in the Muslim World* (New York), 312–2.

Murdock, G. P. (1950), 'Family Stability in Non-European Cultures', *Annals*, 272: 195–201.

Parish, W. L., and Whyte, M. K. (1978), *Village and Family in Contemporary China* (Chicago).

Raybeck, D. (1974), 'Social Stress and Social Structure in Lelantan Village Life', in W. R. Roff (ed.), *Kelantan: Religion, Society and Politics in a Malay State* (New York).

—— (1976), 'Kelantanese Divorce: The Price of Kindred and Village Harmony', mimeo (Kirkland College).

ROUSSEL, L. (1981), 'Le Remariage des divorcés', *Population*, 765–90.

—— (1988), 'Die soziologische Bedeutung der demographischen Erscheutterung in den Industriellaendern der letzten Zwangig Jahre', in K. Luscher, F. Schultheis, and M. Wherspaun (eds.), *Die 'postmoderne' Familie* (Konstanz), 39–54.

SARDON, J.-P. (1986), 'Évolution de la nuptialité et de la divortialité en europe depuis la fin des anneés 1960', *Population*, 41 3: 479–81.

SGRITTA, G. B., and TUFARI, P. (1977), 'Italy', in R. Chester (ed.), *Divorce in Europe* (Leiden), 253–81.

SOUTH, S. J. (1985), 'Economic Conditions and the Divorce Rate: A Time Series Analysis of the Post-War U.S.', *J. Marr and the Family* 47: 31–41.

STATISTISCHE UMSCHAU: BEVOELKERUNG (1982), *Wirtschaft und Statistik*, 12/11: 6, 12, 55–6.

STRANGE, H. (1981), *Rural Malay Women in Tradition and Transition* (New York).

Tai Wan Statistical Abstracts (1956–86).

T'ai-Wan Sheng t'ung Chi Yao (1951).

TSUBOUCHI, Y. (1975), 'Marriage and Divorce among Malay Peasants in Kelantan', *Journal of Southeast Asian Studies*, 6: 135–50.

WEITZMAN, L. J. (1985), *The Divorce Revolution: The Unexpected Social and Economic Consequences for Women and Children in America* (New York).

Part Two
Legal Rules

3. Grounds and Procedures Reviewed

Anders Agell

In its legal context, the concept of 'divorce' functions as a link between the grounds for divorce and the effects of the divorce decree. The main effect of a legal divorce is the dissolution of the marriage and the termination of marital rights and duties, which are dependent on the ongoing marriage. Divorce also gives rise to legal effects concerning the future custody of the children, the right to stay in the joint dwelling, questions of maintenance after divorce, and the distribution of property. These effects have often been called 'ancillary matters', since they have to be solved in connection with the granting of a divorce.

It is a well-known observation that the ancillary matters are often more important than the granting of the divorce itself. The legal system cannot prevent spouses from drifting apart and separating, but it must at least try to offer tools for solving the problems that arise when the spouses have ceased to live together.

The existence of chidren in a marriage means that the relation between a child and both parents will, and normally shall, continue in the future. An ongoing relation between the child and both parents will, however, normally also presuppose contacts between the ex-spouses themselves. In the interest of the child, as well as of the personal well-being of the ex-spouses, it is therefore of profound importance that the divorce procedure does not promote conflicts and bitterness, but that it instead supports, if possible, good future relationships among all the parties.

In the past the emphasis in most countries was placed on the grounds for divorce and on the importance of preserving the existing family. Today, when there is a high divorce rate in most countries, we have learnt that the conditions for divorce offer very limited possibilities for preserving a marriage (Rheinstein 1972). If one spouse really wants a divorce, he or she will obtain it in one way or the other. But if we assume that family well-being and stability are valuable, and that marriage can promote instead of diminishing the well-being of the family members, we want to know how different legal rules, connected or unconnected with the divorce as such, can promote family stability. A further question is whether a balance can be found in the divorce procedure between the aim of promoting family stability and the aim of promoting a good future relationship between the spouses in the case where a divorce cannot be avoided.

This chapter contains few references to solutions in particular countries. Where examples are given, they tend to come from the civil-law countries in Western Europe and from the common-law countries. The approach is unavoidably influenced by the development of Swedish law, although not always in agreement with the changes which have taken place there. For the reader who wishes to improve his or her comparative knowledge there are valuable surveys written by others, not to mention the contributions to the meeting in Bellagio which have formed the basis for this book (Eekelaar 1984; Eekelaar and Katz 1984; Glendon 1989; Law Commission 1988; Meulders Klein 1989).

The blend of social, sociological, and legal perspectives present at the meeting provided inspiration for the participants, myself included. At the end of the meeting the participating university teachers of law formed a small working group, which tried to adopt a joint position on the issues of legal policy discussed below. This chapter will refer to some opinions expressed by or within the group, although most of what is said below represents only my own points of view.[1]

Grounds for Divorce and Family Stability

The Catholic attitude, that a marriage cannot be dissolved, and the Lutheran tradition, that only adultery and desertion were grounds for divorce, have been modified step by step in most countries. The first step or stage seems to consist of the acceptance of breakdown of the marriage as a ground for divorce, alongside different forms of 'fault' by one spouse (in

[1] The members of the group were Marzio Barbagli (Bologna), Richard Ingleby (Melbourne), Satoshi Minamikata (Tokyo), Petar Šarčević (Rijeka), Wolfgang Voegeli (Hamburg), and myself.

the Scandinavian countries since around 1920; in France since 1975). A second stage is to accept breakdown of the marriage as the only ground for divorce, although some countries have retained the importance of fault within the breakdown framework (as in England since 1969). A third stage is to make less stringent requirements for proving that the marriage has really broken down permanently (as in Italy, when the period of separation in 1987 was decreased from five to three years). A fourth stage in the liberalization process is to accept unilateral divorce in the sense that an application by one spouse is considered to be sufficient proof of the breakdown (as in California since 1970). A fifth stage is to accept unilateral divorce in the still more liberal sense that the desire of one spouse to terminate the marriage shall be respected as such, which makes reference to breakdown of the marriage superfluous (as in Sweden since 1974).

There are good causes to be sceptical concerning fault as a ground for divorce. One can ask, although the question is seldom put, why fault in itself should be a ground for divorce, if there is a chance of saving the marriage and thereby keeping both parents with their children. In a deeper sense it is also difficult to take a position as to whether one spouse alone must be considered as the party of fault. Another disadvantage is that fault as a ground for divorce can give rise to particularly unfriendly divorce proceedings which damage the future relationship between the ex-spouses to the disadvantage of the children and the spouses themselves. These points of view are well known and often referred to, as is the observation that, when fault is an alternative ground for divorce, besides breakdown of the marriage, it leads to abuse of the rules, since spouses arrange 'fault' in order to obtain a quick divorce. This leads to an unpleasant bargaining situation and diminishes general respect for the law. In countries where 'fault grounds' exist side by side with 'breakdown grounds', the former tend to represent an unrealistically large proportion of all divorces.

Breakdown of the marriage as a ground for divorce, however, also has its weaknesses. Very often a period of separation is requested as proof of the permanent breakdown of the marriage. It is also common to claim a longer period if only one spouse wants the divorce than when both spouses apply for divorce, or one spouse applies alone and the respondent consents to divorce. In my view it is rather artificial and probably without practical significance to let the length of a period of separation vary according to whether both spouses or only one spouse want to obtain the divorce. It seems unlikely that an especially long period can save any marriages. Experiences of breakdown as a ground for divorce seem, in the long run, to lead to the conclusion that no one other than the spouse who applies for divorce can really evaluate whether the marriage has permanently broken down. If the spouses obtain divorce after living apart for a very long period in order to show permanent breakdown of the marriage, this shows only that the legislature has tried in vain to save a dead marriage. In the meantime unnecessary suffering has been created for one or both of the spouses.

It seems that most industrialized countries which are somewhere in the middle of the above-mentioned 'ladder' will continue changing their legislation until they reach stage 4 or stage 5. A further reason for such a development can be based on the tendencies in many countries for men and women to cohabit without marrying. It may become necessary to adjust the rules on marriage and divorce in order to avoid a situation where a growing number of people decide not to marry at all.

A reconsideration period functions in another way from separation as a condition for divorce. Separation is in many countries claimed as evidence of permanent breakdown of the marriage, but only if it occurs before the application for divorce. A reconsideration period is based on the idea that the applicant for divorce should have an opportunity to reconsider the application which has been made earlier. If the purpose is also to prepare for the situation after divorce, one might speak of a period of transition. It seems, however, somewhat doubtful whether such an aim does not conflict with the function of the period to prevent, if possible, overhasty divorces (see below).

The participants in 'the lawyers' group' at the Bellagio meeting were unanimously of the opinion that the law should contain only one single ground for divorce, and that the desire of a spouse to terminate the marriage should be respected. There was also unanimous agreement on the desirability of having some period of reconsideration, the length of which can be discussed, between an application for divorce and the issuance of a divorce decree. It was also emphasized that it should not be necessary to claim that the spouses live apart during the transitional period.

Agreement on these basic points none the less leaves open the question as to whether, as a matter of principle, the sole ground for divorce should be the breakdown of the marriage or the pure desire by a spouse to terminate the marriage. In other words, the question is whether the law shall take the step from stage 4 to stage 5 in the 'ladder'. From a practical point of view, the difference may be of minor importance. The acceptance of the idea that only a spouse can judge whether the marriage has broken down means that it can normally be taken for granted that an application for divorce implies the breakdown of the marriage.

The chosen starting-point, however, causes at least one practical difference. If the legislation is based on the view that the wish of a spouse shall be respected as such (stage 5), there is hardly any basis for a reconsideration period if both spouses want the divorce and there are no children whose interests must be taken into account. If, however, an application for divorce is seen as sufficient evidence of permanent breakdown of the marriage (stage 4), the state as a matter of principle has retained control over the conditions for divorce. This makes it possible to require a reconsideration period, even when both spouses want to get divorced and there are no children.

One argument which might be used for keeping the latter approach—that divorce should be based not only on the wishes of one spouse but also on an irrebuttable presumption that an application for divorce means that the marriage has broken down permanently—can be found in the discussion paper issued by the English Law Commission in 1988. The Law Commission appeared to consider not only that public opinion would not accept the radical solution represented by stage 5 but also that the Commission itself had a role in influencing public opinion in the future and *should not support the attitude that divorce is a very easy way to leave a marriage.* Although social conditions in general probably influence the divorce rate much more than the divorce rules as such, it is likely that these play at least some part in forming the general attitudes of citizens. It may also be added that it would have been astonishing if the English Law Commission, which has engaged in a profound rethinking of legislation only twenty years old, should have gone directly from stage 3 to stage 5.

The general assumption, based on comparative experiences, that the grounds for divorce are not efficient tools for diminishing the divorce rate does not imply that family stability does not have a value for family members and indirectly for society as a whole. On the contrary, stable and happy families are of the utmost importance for the next generation. The question is whether such stability can be promoted by legal means.

It is, however, worth emphasizing that measures other than the rules on divorce offer much better possibilities for strengthening marriages. A wide range of problems occur in societies where an increasing proportion of both spouses with children work outside the home. The possibilities of alleviating these problems include alternating the number of working hours for both parents, improving the availability of day care for children, supporting changes in traditional gender roles, and a variety of different economic measures (e.g. rules on taxes and social welfare) in order to help families with children. It must, however, be admitted that some of these issues are probably controversial in a large number of countries.

A further important measure is the availability of family counselling in order to help spouses to sort out as early as possible problems of a serious nature. Views were also expressed within the informal 'lawyers' group' in Bellagio about the desirability of teaching about marriage, family, and parenthood as part of the compulsory school-curriculum.

Custody, Maintenance, and Property

The custody issue is the most important of the 'ancillary matters', as it is vital that children are given the best possible chance to develop balanced personalities and become responsible adults. In recent years joint legal custody of children by divorced parents has been promoted in many countries as a means of strengthening good relations between the child and both parents. This development is probably most workable in a society like Sweden, where men are encouraged to play an important role in parenting during marriage, and where the traditional division of labour between men and women is being challenged and in the process of changing. In Sweden joint custody can meet the psychological needs of a parent who does not live permanently with the child, and help him or her retain a good relationship with the child. It can also increase that parent's feeling of responsibility. If it works, joint custody promotes good relationships between the parents as well. In Sweden since 1983 divorced parents retain join custody automatically, if neither raises the custody issue in connection with the divorce, and if the court does not have special reasons to take up the custody issue for supervision.

If, however, there is continuing conflict between the parents, a joint-custody arrangement may put the child in the middle of the conflict, and that is clearly not good for the child. In these situations it may be better for one parent to have sole legal custody. In addition, if parents are willing to co-operate, a good relationship between the child and both parents can also be obtained when one parent has the sole legal custody. Thus the formal legal arrangements depend here, as in many other areas, on the social supports for those arrangements.

Irrespective of how legal custody is arranged, it is a tragedy for all persons involved if a court has to resolve the matter through litigation. A legal struggle between the parents can easily result in destructive consequences. This factor has certainly played a role in the efforts in many jurisdictions to organize family counselling or co-operative talks between the parents in order to help the parents understand their internal problems and reach the best possible solution for the child, which does not necessarily mean joint custody.

When the importance of understanding between the parents is emphasized in connection with the custody issue, it should, however, be added that this state of things does not imply that the parents should be allowed to conclude a contract that is formally binding for the future. The custody issue is a personal, not an economic matter, the primary aim of which is the well-being of the child. Thus it should not be the object of formally binding agreements. This means that a parent should have the freedom to withdraw his or her consent to an agreement until the agreement has been confirmed by the court. Even after the decree has been issued by the court, the possibility for reviewing the custody decision should be kept open, if conditions have changed.

The extent of a parent's obligation to pay maintenance allowances to a child with whom he is not living has to be fixed in connection with the divorce. Answers must also be given to the question of how the property of the spouses shall be divided, and whether support to an ex-spouse (usually the wife) shall be paid. As shown below, the basic solutions adopted within a country to each of these questions tend to have a decisive influence on the technical possibilities of reaching an agreement between the spouses.

In the common-law tradition there is a tendency to mix all the economic questions together in one pot. Since there is no marital property which is to be divided in a set way, the field is left open for a comparatively free redistribution of the property in accordance with what is considered reasonable with respect to the economic roles played by each spouse during the marriage, and both the spouses' and the children's economic needs for the future. A marital-property system, on the other hand, is normally based on clear guidelines which govern the division of different belongings in accordance with when they were acquired by a spouse, and with respect to later events during the marriage. Such a perspective does not basically take the future needs of a spouse into account, although this can be done in special situations and in accordance with special rules.

It has often been stated that a separate-property system offers low foreseeability but fair solutions in individual cases, while a marital-property system offers foreseeability but does not offer the same possibilities for achieving justice for the individual case. It is not, however, necessary to consider foreseeability and justice as alternatives. Both perspectives have to be taken into account and the objective of the law should be to find a proper balance. It can also be added that low foreseeability means bad justice in the sense that there is a considerable risk that equal cases will be decided unequally. In my opinion, a separate-property system, leaving the basic decisions on redistribution to a court, does not offer a reasonable possibility to foresee the outcome in an individual case. The starting-point, therefore, should be some sort of marital-property system. This requires comprehensive legislation regulating the distribution of property at divorce and not simply giving guidelines as a basis for discretionary decision-making by judges in individual cases. All participants in the lawyers' group in Bellagio agreed on the necessity of legislation on the basic principles for distribution of property and the impossibility of achieving satisfactory results if too much freedom is given to the courts in this respect.

There is obviously a risk that an observer from another country does not fully understand what is going on within a different legal system. My impression is, however, that experiences from common-law countries demonstrate the disadvantages of separate-property systems with low foreseeability. The difficulties are increased by the vague borderline between matters concerning property and matters concerning support. Such a situation has the further disadvantage of making it difficult for the spouses to conclude an agreement on economic matters, since the legal framework is comparatively uncertain. This means, in other words, that the legal uncertainty may give rise to unnecessary 'bargaining' and to unnecessary litigation. A conflict also costs money which could be used in a better way.

In such a bargaining situation the custody issue can also be used as a playing-card. In my opinion too much bargaining at divorce is a bad thing, especially if it includes the custody of the children. (See, for example, Weitzman, Ch. 23 below.)

In the United States the difficulties of foreseeing the financial outcome at divorce in states applying a separate-property system have increased the tendency to conclude antenuptial contracts between the spouses. Not even such contracts, however, can offer a good solution, since it is often impossible to establish in advance what will be reasonable at a divorce many years later.

My conclusion is that it is probably better to have separate legal provisions governing the different ancillary matters at divorce rather than flinging together in one pot the questions of maintenance to children, division of property, and support to an ex-spouse. At the same time it is of course obvious that the division of property can influence an ex-spouse's need for support. The policy should be to create clear rules, the outcome of which can be foreseen, which contain clauses to enable the court to avoid results which are unjust in exceptional, individual cases. As a matter of principle there is no need to deny spouses the freedom to conclude agreements on the economic issues at divorce.

Procedural Aspects of Divorce and Ancillary Matters

The rules on conditions for divorce and on ancillary matters must serve as starting-points for consideration of the rules on procedure. The procedure concerning the grounds for divorce can be simple if the application by a spouse is always respected or considered as sufficient evidence for the permanent breakdown of the marriage (see above).

One reason, however, for requiring an oral and not only a written procedure might be the wish to check if the spouse(s) genuinely support the application for divorce. If the possibility of unilateral divorce is combined with a period of reconsideration or transition, a further aim may be to offer the spouses family counselling. This may be offered by or within the court, but it requires considerable psychological expertise and social experience and so in my view should not be left to a judge. Experiences from countries in the Western world at any rate indicate that family counselling does not work well if forced upon the spouses. It should be offered as a service but not as a compulsory arrangement.

The procedural matters become much more complex when the ancillary questions are also taken into account. It has been pointed out above that the spouses cannot, as a matter of principle, conclude agreements which are formally binding on custody of a child. This fact does not, however, prevent an agreement between the spouses being respected by a court as consistent with the best interest of the child. The starting-point differs from that concerning purely economic matters. As a matter of principle, the spouses should have the freedom at divorce to conclude binding agreements, although a reservation might be made with respect to maintenance allowances to the children (see above). It should, perhaps, also be added here that the spouses cannot be entitled to conclude economic agreements which are binding for the state in so far as the agreement affects the right of an ex-spouse or a child to different social benefits.

Even if an agreement on an economic issue is valid as a

matter of principle, the question remains whether a court should be given the competence and the duty to check the contents of the agreement. In many countries divorce based on the application by one spouse alone or both spouses together presupposes that the ancillary matters have been solved and, in some cases, also accepted by the court. Such an approach seems to be based on a desire to protect the children and the weaker spouse, usually the wife. According to this approach, the children and the wife are given protection through the continuation of the marriage until the ancillary matters have been solved.

This approach may sound clear and reasonable. Nevertheless some question marks can be added. As a matter of principle there is special cause for hesitation if an application for divorce by one spouse alone is treated as ground for divorce, but the divorce decree can not be issued until a period of reconsideration has elapsed following the application. The primary aim of such a period should be based on the hope that the applicant will not insist on divorce when the period has expired. It is difficult to combine with this the additional purpose of using the time to settle the ancillary issues.

Since the spouses can live apart quite irrespective of the point of time when the decree on divorce is issued, it is also doubtful whether postponing the decree is an efficient method of protecting the children and the weaker party until the ancillary matters have been resolved. In any case, there will be a need for the court to issue interim orders, regulating the issues on custody, on the right to stay in the family home, and on maintenance, until final solutions are achieved. The interim orders can fulfil the same function as the regulation of the ancillary matters before the issuance of the divorce decree.

None the less, there are counter-arguments. If the main ancillary matters must be solved before the divorce decree is issued, this might make the husband more inclined to make economic concessions to the advantage of the wife and the children. This, however, is not certain either. Very often it is the wife who wants the divorce more than the husband. It is possible that she may be encouraged to give up her interests too easily if the divorce cannot be obtained until the ancillary matters are solved. It is in fact also possible that spouses with a bad relationship may reach agreement more easily when they live apart.

Once again counter-arguments can be raised. It could be said that the court should check every agreement between the spouses in order to protect the weaker spouse and the children, and that this could also be done after the divorce. Even this, however, has its price. If the court is supposed to check all agreements, the risk of conflicts between the spouses may be increased, which would be a considerable disadvantage. A compulsory court procedure also costs money.

What has been said indicates that the questions of whether the ancillary matters should be solved before the divorce decree is issued, and of whether the court should exercise some degree of compulsory supervision of spousal agreements, are very complicated matters. It seems probable that the willingness in many countries to supervise the agreements of the spouses before the divorce decree is issued survives from the time when the grounds for divorce were strict and not based on a liberal application of the principles of permanent breakdown of the marriage.

Organization of the procedure is complicated as so many considerations of a varying character have to be taken into account. In the interest of promoting family stability it is desirable that the parties should be offered family counselling as a service in connection with the divorce procedure. When, as in many cases, the divorce is unavoidable, the service should instead be offered in order to resolve the custody issue by agreement, and to create as good an atmosphere as possible for the relationship between a child and both its parents. In addition to this, the economic issues also have to be resolved, if possible by private ordering. Finally, a court has to adjudicate the remaining, contentious questions which cannot be solved by the parties.

In most countries divorce cases are handled by the ordinary civil courts. Such a system presupposes that some social authorities are also playing a role in offering family counselling or attempting to solve custody matters. There are, however, also countries (Australia, New Zealand, Japan) with special family courts which contain not only lawyers but also officials with special competence in psychology or social-welfare matters. The proceedings may be oral or, in uncontested cases, purely written. Considerable interest in later years has also been devoted to the alternative of administrative divorce procedure in Denmark and Norway, which means that an administrative body can handle both the divorce case and the ancillary matters, especially when a case is not contentious. The administrative bodies, which acquire great practical experience, help the parties to reach an agreement. The ordinary courts basically handle contentious divorce cases (Schmidt 1984). An even more complicated system exists in Japan, where different types of cases are treated differently (Shimazu 1984).

National traditions normally play a decisive role in the legal development within a country. The social situation of families also differs considerably between industrialized countries, not to mention the developing countries. It is obviously not possible to recommend legal solutions of universal validity. As this chapter has attempted to show, however, the problems of legal policy in this area are universal.

References

EEKELAAR, J. (1984), *Family Law and Social Policy* (London).

—— and KATZ, S. (ed.)s (1984), *The Resolution of Family Conflict: Comparative Legal Perspectives* (Toronto).

GLENDON, M. A. (1989), *The Transformation of Family Law* (Chicago).

LAW COMMISSION (1988), *Grounds for Divorce Law Commission No. 170 (HMSO, London).*

MEULDERS KLEIN, M. T. (1989) 'La Problématique du divorce dans les legislations d'Europe Occidentale', in M. T. Meulders Klein (ed.) *Revue internationale de droit comparé* (Brussels), 7–58.

RHEINTSTEIN, M. (1972), *Marriage Stability, Divorce and the Law* (Chicago).

SCHMIDT, S. (1984), 'The Scandinavian Law of Procedure in Matrimonial Courts', in J. Eekelaar and S. Katz (eds.), *The Resolution of Family Conflict: Comparative Legal Perspectives* (Toronto), 77–99.

SHIMAZU, I. (1984), 'Procedural Aspects of Marriage Dissolution in Japan', in J. Eekelaar and S. Katz (eds.), *The Resolution of Family Conflict: Comparative Legal Perspectives* (Toronto), 116–23.

4. Recent Australian Developments: Discretion Discredited

Richard Ingleby

THIS chapter considers two features of the law's involvement in the economic consequences of divorce in Australia. The first feature is that of 'dispute resolution'. The breakdown of the marriage relationship means that the parties must decide how they are to distribute their present and future resources and liabilities. The Australian Family Law Act 1975 (Cth) provides a set of rules for the courts to apply to disputes which are brought to them. This Act empowers the courts to make orders for financial provision and sets out a list of factors to be taken into account in the exercise of that discretion. The second feature of the law's involvement considered here, though not as directly as the first, lies in the rules which govern entitlements to benefits from the welfare state. Although welfare-law rules cover a broader category of people than divorcing parties, the role of the welfare state in financing post-divorce support means that it cannot be ignored in any discussion of financial provision on divorce.

The first section of the chapter describes the changes which have taken, and are taking, place to the laws relating to financial provision on divorce. These are manifested in the recommendations of the Australian Law Reform Commission's Report No. 39, *Matrimonial Property* (the Hambly Report), the Child Support Act 1988 (Cth), and the Child Support (Assessment) Bill (1989), developments which represent a major move away from the scheme set out in Part VIII of the Family Law Act 1975 (Cth).

The second section offers some explanations for these developments. The variables which seem to be of particular importance to Australia are outlined: first, the relationship between the various aspects of the state and the consequences of divorce; secondly, the extent to which legislative measures have the support of specific government departments and agencies; thirdly, the use of empirical data in the policy formation process; and, finally, the particular functions performed by trial courts. This list is not intended to be exhaustive and the factors are not divided by clear conceptual distinctions. The third section, considers what the implications of these developments might be for the economic impact of divorce. Both the second and third sections are obviously more speculative than the first. Their purpose is not to provide definitive answers, but to offer some tentative hypotheses so that others may consider the relative importance of the variables as regards their own jurisdictions.

Legal Charge: The Decline and Fall of Discretion

Matrimonial Property

The Family Law Act 1975 (see, generally, Wade 1988 and the authorities there cited), Part VIII, which is entitled 'Maintenance and Property', empowers the court to make orders for both spousal and child maintenance, and for the alteration of property interests between parties to the marriage. The court is provided with a list of factors to take into account in deciding whether, and if so how, to exercise its jurisdiction. The lists of factors will not be recounted here, both because of their length and, because of their irrelevance. The statute provides a long list of factors for the court to take into account, but no real guidance as to how to do this. In *Mallet* ((1984) FLC 91–507) the Family Court's attempts to establish precedents as to the interpretation of section 79(4) were struck down by the High Court. More recently, however, the High Court has suggested that guidelines, a concept borrowed from administrative law, may be permissible (*Norbis* (1986) FLC 91–712; Ingleby 1989).

Why did the legislature provide such a broad discretion for trial judges in matrimonial property law? The judiciary itself has offered two possible explanations. In *Norbis* (at 75, 166), Mason and Deane JJ stated that judicial discretion, 'maximises the possibility of doing justice in every case'. In *Mallet* (at 79, 110) Gibbs CJ said that

> The *Family Law Act* was passed at a time when great changes had occurred, and were continuing to occur, in the attitudes of many

members of society to marriage and divorce, but when it was (as it is now) difficult, if not impossible, to say that any one set of values or ideas is commonly accepted, or approved by a majority of the members of society . . . it is not surprising that, given this diversity of opinions, the Parliament did not require the power conferred by sec. 79 to be exercised in accordance with fixed rules.

More cynical explanations might be offered. The first is that discretion serves the legislature's interests by permitting it not to offend any particular interest group. The absence of consensus as to the 'economic consequences of divorce' is a superficially attractive argument but in reality a spectacular non-sequitur. There is an absence of societal consensus regarding road traffic law, and levels of both taxation and social security entitlement, but in these cases the figures are specified by Parliament. The absence of societal consensus is not of itself enough to justify the presence of judicial discretion. But it may explain the reluctance to specify clear legislative standards on any particular matter. Every matrimonial breakdown demands a consideration of the economic consequences of that particular marriage. Systems which provide for redistribution of matrimonial property on divorce have to assess the value of the contribution of those whose input to the relationship has been in unwaged services. Such a broad area of discretion devolves this decision from Parliament to trial judges. As Rein (1976: 22) argues, 'one of the consequences of passing ambiguous . . . legislation is to shift the area of decision to a lower level'. In fact, the devolution extends further than trial judges. As only about 5 per cent of cases are resolved in court (Australian Law Reform Commission 1987, para. 823), most decision are made by the divorcing parties and their legal representatives. Galanter (1974: 147–8) has written that,

by ambiguity and normative overload (the) system effects a massive covert delegation from the most authoritative rule-makers to field-level officials (and their constituencies) responsive to other norms and priorities than are contained in the 'higher law'.

Another possible explanation for discretionary schemes is that they serve the interest of the legal profession. The reality of the effect of the discretion in relation to matrimonial property is well summarized by Wade's (1988: 51–2) observations:

In theory at least, case law was reduced to a wilderness of single instances. . . . Nevertheless, in practice, registrars, lawyers, street law, and folk law contined to use the discredited 'precedent' as a basis for negotiating settlements.

The rhetoric of a mysterious discretionary process, beyond the comprehension of the lay client, combines with the reality of reasonable certainty. This provides lawyers with the predictability necessary for them to negotiate within recognized boundaries, and a justification for their professional standing.

In June 1983 public concern about the operation of the Family Law Act led the Attorney-General to give the Law Reform Commission a reference on the law of matrimonial property. A Discussion Paper was released in June 1985 and the Report was published in August 1987. The recommendations of the Report, which have not yet been implemented, were that the discretionary scheme in section 79 of the Act be replaced with statutory presumptions. The Report concluded (at para. 313) that there were 'compelling arguments for preferring legislatively prescribed guidelines to the process of developing guidelines through judicial decisions'. It recommended (para. 364) a presumption of equal sharing of matrimonial property on divorce, to be departed from 'to take account of certain special circumstances'. These include 'a substantially greater contribution to the marriage by one party than by the other'. But the report proposes (para. 375) that, after the decision has been taken whether or not to depart from the starting-point, the court should make an adjustment,

if it is satisfied that there is a disparity between the standards of living reasonably attainable by the parties, and that this disparity is wholly or partly attributable to a party's responsibility for the future care of the children of the marriage or to a party's income-earning capacity having been affected by marriage.

The presumption of equal sharing is of interest because it seems to indicate a common-law country adopting civil-law-type schemes. This common-law/civil-law dichotomy arises in other chapters in this volume, in particular Chapters 3, 5, and 18. It is relevant to the ease with which legal systems consider prospective superannuation (i.e. pension) entitlements to be property and it also seems to influence whether child support is considered to be primarily a responsibility of the parents, or of the state.

It is questionable whether this scheme would be more successful in protecting child-carers than the present law, nor is there any guarantee that the outcomes of individual cases would be altered by reformulating the trial process. In any event, the presumption may be little more than a legislative ratification of what is already happening. We should also note the limited nature of the 'property' to which the presumption of equal sharing is to apply (see Chapter 5). But it cannot be doubted that the recommendations represent a disavowal of the scheme set up in the 1975 Act.

The Calculation of Child-Support Payments

The second aspect of the rejection of the discretionary framework is the calculation of child-support payments. Here there are two related problems with the statutory framework. First, as regards its judicial interpretation, there was uncertainty as to the priorities between the various factors. In the leading case of *Mee and Ferguson* ((1986) FLC 91–716) the full court of the Family Court commented on the statute (at 75, 196), noting that 'The sections do not all sit comfortably with each other and there are inconsistencies in the expressions which they use.'

Furthermore, although the scheme in the Family Law Act may have envisaged payments being made in accordance with parental capacity, McDonald's and Weston's research (1986: 26) indicated that the effect of the provisions was a 'going rate' of about $20 per week per child. One explanation for this rate is that it falls just below the level at whch supporting parents' allowances (i.e. welfare benefits for low-income parents) would be curtailed (Mcdonald and Weston 1986: 43). In fact, the empirical research (McDonald 1986: 266) found little relationship between parental capacity to pay and the amounts which were actually paid. The figure of $20 fell well below the actual costs of child-care (Lovering 1984). It would, therefore, be fair to see the poverty of the children of divorced parties as being caused by the difference between the cost of child-care and the 'going rate' for child support.

In *Mee and Ferguson* the full Court (at 75, 196) stressed the priority which should be given to child support.

The question of child maintenance should be approached by considering the following issues:

(a) the financial needs of the particular child;

(b) the extent to which the child has financial resources to meet those needs;

(c) a comparison of what can be described for the moment as the respective financial circumstances of the parties to meet the needs of the child.

The Court criticized the tendency 'for this to be done in reverse order', and stressed that the financial needs of the child were a matter on which evidence should be called. They specifically referred to the Australian Institute of Family Studies publication *The Cost of Children in Australia* (Lovering 1984), saying that 'It demonstrates what most custodians know, namely the very high cost of maintaining a child in our society, and that the courts may be lagging behind reality.' This decision, in March 1986, emerged contemporaneously with the debate in and around the Department of Social Security about the relationship between levels and enforcement of maintenance and child poverty following divorce.

The immediate legislative response to *Mee and Ferguson*, assented to in December 1987, was a new Division 6 of Part VII of the Family Law Act, entitled 'Maintenance of Children'. Section 66A(1) stated that 'The principal object of this division is to ensure that children receive a proper level of financial support from their parents.' This object was pursued by stressing, in section 66B(1), that the duty of parents to support children was a 'primary duty'. Section 66B(2) provided that, without limiting the generality of section 66B(1), the duty was 'not of lower priority' than the parent's duty to maintain anyone else, and has priority over all the parent's commitments other than those, 'necessary to enable the parent to support: (i) himself or herself; and (ii) any other child or another person that the parent has a duty to maintain'.

Importantly for the interests of the welfare state, the section also provides that the parental duty is not affected by '(i) the duty of any other person to maintain the child; or (ii) any entitlement of the child or another person to an income tested pension, allowance or benefit'. This amendment prevents the court from refusing to make, or to approve, an order on the basis that the recipient of the ordered payment is also in receipt of welfare benefits.

These new provisions are an attempt to structure judicial discretion so that more priority is attached to the needs of children. Their impact can already be seen in recent decisions. For example, in *Ryan* it was held that payments should be made to the children rather than to build up the capital of the non-custodial parent.

Division 6 is probably best seen as a holding operation until the Child Support (Assessment) Bill, which took effect in October 1989. This Bill instituted the use of a formula to determine levels of child support. The concept was introduced in October 1986 by the Minister for Social Security (Howe 1986: 11–12), who identified the twin issues of inadequate amounts and enforcement of child support. He concluded in favour of a formula for the calculation of support levels (Howe 1986: 15).

In May 1987 the Child Support Consultative Committee was appointed to advise the government on the content of the formula. After exemptions for the non-custodial parent's living expenses, child support will be calculated as a percentage of income for those whose incomes are less than 2.5 times the national average wage. The figures chosen range from 18 per cent to 35 per cent depending on the number of children.

The use of the formula should have a much more dramatic impact on the economic consequences of divorce than the amendments to the Family Law Act which were made in 1987. The 'going rate' will be abolished. For families on low incomes there will be little difference, but such children would not even have received the $20 rate. In middle- and high-income families the rate will lead to an increase in payments from non-custodial parents to custodial parents, an increase rendered more significant by the greater likelihood of its being collected, given the developments to be discussed in the next section of this chapter (see also Chapter 11).

The Taxation Office and the Enforcement of Child Support

The third retreat from the discretionary scheme in the Family Law Act relates to the enforcement rather than the calculation of child support. The Child Support Act 1988 (Cth), which came into force in June 1988, removed the responsibility for the enforcement of child support from divorcing parties and transferred it to the Taxation Office.

There are two categories of registrable maintenance liabilities, those subject to mandatory registration (s. 23) and those for which registration is optional. Liabilities for which registration is mandatory are those where the payee is in receipt of social security (Kilger 1988). This suggests that the impetus behind the legislation is the desire to support the Department of Social Security as well as the children of divorcing parties.

The effect of registration is that the liabilities cease to be enforceable as between payer and payee and become debts to the government. The payee loses the right to claim through the court, and the payer loses the right to force the payee to pursue his or her claims through the court (s. 30). The liabilities are enforced by the Registrar, giving notice to the payer's employee (s. 45), the employer making the appropriate deductions from the employee's wages (s. 46), and the employer transferring those monies deducted to the Registrar (s. 47). The Registrar transfers these sums into the Child Support Trust Account (ss. 73–5), from which payments are made to payees. The Act has its own provisions for enforcement, which include the use of both fines and imprisonment as penalties.

Explanations: The Involvement of the Post-Liberal State

Why have these developments taken place within such a short period of time? A key feature is the involvement of the various aspects of the state in the economic consequences of divorce. It is impossible for the legislature to ignore the social consequences when so much of society is organized around the family unit, and the state is involved in so much of society (Unger 1976: 193). A characteristic of what Unger has referred to as the 'post-liberal' society typified by Australia is the involvement of the state, and in particular the Department of Social Security, in the consequences of matrimonial breakdown. In addition to providing rules for the resolution of disputes which are brought to the courts, the state provides mechanisms for supervising those agreements which divorcing parties make themselves.

The combination of the state's interest in the family, and the increased divorce rate since the Family Law Act, may well have forced the legislature to make the decisions which (arguably) were evaded by the discretion legislation and the consequent devolution of decision-making authority to lawyers and first instance judges (Ingleby 1988b; Rein 1976: 22) Divorce can no longer be regarded as exceptional or an accident.

Perhaps it is useful to make a comparison with the motor car. One hundred years ago these were the preserve of the rich. Now the level of car-ownership and the level of injuries arising from accidents have created the issue of loss allocation. In Victoria, for example, there is compulsory third-party insurance for personal injury, but not, though this is, at the time of writing, a source of debate, for property damage. The state might have done nothing, leaving all individuals to insure themselves against the consequences of injury from motor vehicles. But one of the reasons for the emergence of the loss-allocation issue is the prevalence of the phenomenon which causes the damage.

This suggests that the rhetoric about the welfare of the child may well be nothing more than a useful cloak to hide another benefit of the reforms to child support, the savings in public expenditure. This point is supported by the fact that section 23 of the Child Support Act makes it clear that the system of enforcement is directed at recipients of social security. Legislative reform concurrent with the Child Support Act made it a condition of receipt of the relevant benefits that the recipient take whatever steps were reasonable to obtain a court order.

The Welfare State and the Child-Support Secretariat

Australia's welfare state appears more generous than the UK system, perhaps as a result of the combination of relative wealth, and, for want of a better term, more strongly entrenched communitarian ideals. Perhaps linked to this is a political climate where there are fewer institutionalized interests than in other, longer-established, countries. Is it coincidental that the sorts of developments noted in the first section of the paper have taken place in a small (in terms of population), new, or more accurately newly Westernized (when compared to the rest of the developed world) country, which possesses both material wealth and communitarian ideals? Although this hypothesis is hardly susceptible to proof, comparisons might be drawn with the Scandinavian countries and with New Zealand.

The relationship between child poverty and divorce was made more important by the oft-cited 1987 election speech of the Prime Minister, who declared that no child need live in poverty by 1990. Although this pledge was optimistic, it is important to note the specific existence of the Child Support Secretariat in the Department of Social Security. Its part in the promotion of the child support legislation cannot be underestimated (Child Support Consultative Group 1988: 10). There are many instances of issues not becoming Papers, of Papers not becoming Bills, and of Bills not becoming Acts. This discussion is probably best left to the political scientist, but it is important to note that having a government lobby group has made a critical difference. Since the 'child-support' problem existed for some years before legislative initiatives were considered, the variable which seems to have precipitated the legislative measures is the political will and power in cabinet, particularly within the Department of Social Security.

Empirical Studies and the Policy Process

A striking factor in the developments of the last eighteen months is the use of empirical data in the policy process. In Australia there appears to have been extensive invocation of empirical data, compared to the extent to which they appear to have been used in the English reforms of the law governing financial provision on divorce (Ingleby 1986), though the English Law Commission does now seem to be making more use of empirical studies. The Hambly Report states (para. 10) that 'it was essential to the Commission's research program to conduct surveys to obtain, for the first time, reliable evidence about the operation of the present law.' The Report (para. 10) pays tribute to the studies conducted by the Institute of Family Studies. The Institute was itself established by the Family Law Act. It was part of the 1975 reforms that there be a body to 'promote, by the conduct, encouragement and co-ordination of research and other appropriate means, the identification of, and development of understanding of, the factors affecting marital and family stability in Australia' (s. 114B(2)).

These empirical studies have *inter alia* revealed the distinction between law and lore in the operation of the law governing financial provision on divorce. Particularly striking empirical findings are the non-payment of child support (Howe 1986: 11), and the apparent non-application of the statutory discretionary schemes for the calculation of support and property entitlements (McDonald 1986: 192). A less striking, but equally important finding was the conclusion that most matrimonial-property cases involved similar consideration (McDonald 1986: 319). If a large majority of cases are not unique or exceptional, this removes one of the justifications for the discretionary framework noted above.

A Reappraisal of the Functions of Courts

The archetypical image of the role of the common-law court is to resolve disputes between individuals which are not covered by the existing body of norms. As Cotterrell (1984; 220) states, 'the idea that the central function of courts is to process disputes is almost universal'. These 'hard cases' demand the resolution of conflicts between competing norms and principles, and thereby define the body of precedent which is to govern future fact situations. But this picture is not necessarily an accurate reflection of the functions performed by the Family Court.

First, in many cases the Family Court does not act to resolve disputes between divorcing parties. There are cases where a state agency is a party or where the action is taken at the insistence of a state agency. Here, the case is not really a dispute between the husband and the wife, but one between the state on the one hand and the husband or the wife on the other. There are examples in both the United Kingdom and Australia where public authorities, such as the Department of Social Security, the Taxation Office, or housing authorities, bring the case to invoke the third-party state-agency interests. Although these cases constitute 'disputes', they are not necessarily disputes which relate to the divorcing parties alone. (Ingleby 1988*b*).

Furthermore, many cases are brought before the court for ratification rather than dispute resolution. For example, under section 48 of the Family Law Act a dissolution cannot be granted unless the court is satisfied that there has been the necessary period of separation. Under section 55A a decree nisi cannot be made absolute unless the court has declared itself satisfied as to the arrangements which have been made for the children.

With courts engaged in more routine administration (see Friedman and Percival 1976: 301) administrative efficiency rather than judicial rigour becomes perceived as the dominant virtue of first-instance court (Cotterrell 1984: 226). As Lempert (1978: 990) noted, courts resolve disputes other than by adjudicating in contested cases. Disputes can be resolved by parties being aware of the norms which would be applied were the dispute to be litigated. The developments discussed in the first section of this chapter would seem to indicate that this function is best performed by more certain norms, with the legislature playing a more prominent role relative to the judiciary.

Finally, even the dispute cases which do reach the courts do not characteristically demand the creation of new principles or the reapplication of old ones. Cases which end in court are usually those where one of the parties refuses to accept the state's norms, cases which are marked by emotional rather than legal complexity. (Australian Law Reform Commission 1987, paras. 109, 138; Wade 1988:67).

As Cotterrell (1984: 223) states, 'the court's judgement is perhaps best seen then, not primarily as the resolution of a conflict but as an assertion of a normative order'.

The phrase 'licence not to pay' seems a convenient shorthand for the situation of child maintenance before the Child Support Act. The onus on individual payees to pursue enforcement of rights through the courts created a situation where payments were more or less at the payer's discretion. If the welfare of post-divorce children is a matter which the state regards as an issue of public policy, it makes sense for the state to enforce the obligations through its own agencies, rather than through the initiative of individuals, and to prescribe the norms more directly, through the creation of formulas, thus removing the possibility for the mystification of the law under the guise of discretion.

Implications

What might be the implications for the economic consequences of divorce for the sorts of developments set out above? As has been stressed throughout this chapter, we need to consider the impact of these reforms on the processes which take place outside the court-room.

A statutory presumption in favour of equal sharing of matrimonial property will not have made much difference to those cases which were in any event negotiated on the basis of 50 : 50 division. But it will have an impact in those case where the sole owner attempted to deny that the other party had any interest whatsoever in the property. The costs of processing such disputes might be lower if solicitors' advice to clients was more certain. Further, in those case where there are substantial business assets, the presumption could well produce a result where the home is transferred outright in return for extinguishing the claims regarding the business, by giving the weaker party more bargaining endowments. In other words, the removal of the discretionary framework, whose uncertainty cannot be borne equally by the parties (Ingleby 1989), would tilt the balance less in favour of the stronger economic partner.

The use of a formula for the calculation of child support would certainly prevent the 'going rate' of $20 per week. The use of the Taxation Office should not only enforce the obligation more effectively, but should also be important for ideological reasons. Equating child support with taxation responsibilities is a strong statement as to the social importance of such payments. The law would not function so much to resolve disputes, as to create, or reinforce, a climate where child-support obligations were the norm. Legislation on the basis of a problem of child poverty legitimizes the child-poverty lobby in a similar manner to which clean-break legislation might be thought to legitimize the myth of the alimony drone.

We should also consider the limitations of the measure outlined above. First, regarding their effectiveness, we should not presume that econimically stronger parties would be unable to evade the full impact of such rules in the same way that such people might be able to evade the full impact of taxation law. Regarding the scope of the measures, it might be argued that, if child support is a state responsibility, the state should ensure that such payments are made to custodial parents before assessing the non-custodial parent's contribution. As the Child Support Consultative Group (1988: 7) acknowledges, 'complete reform will not be achieved until a guaranteed minimum maintenance payment is established'. The system is still one where the custodial parent has to take action to obtain child support, and will indeed be subject to penalties if he or she does not. Perhaps the new scheme is part of a move towards a Guaranteed Maintenance Allowance.

It may be that the effect of these measures will be to reduce the gap between law and lore by providing more stringent mechanisms to enforce post-divorce obligations. The economic consequences could be that the effect of the 1988/9 developments will be to make the operation of the law what was, or might have been, intended by the 1975 Act. Whether the limitations of these changes are perceived as limitations depends on what the aims of such rules are deemed to be. If the problem is deemed to be 'child poverty', this might be alleviated to some extent, but if the problem is deemed to be 'inequality', it is difficult to see that the rules represent much more than a tinkering with the edges, as what is deemed to be 'property' does not comprehend all the sources of inequality, in particular, the unequal impact of child-care responsibilities on earning capacities. Changing the variables in the process by which disputes are resolved is limited by the inequalities which are influenced by that process. (These issues are discussed by Kathleen Funder in Chapter 6.)

The implications for the legal profession may be more important. The impact of these measures is to turn divorce into a more administrative process. Although it could well be argued that the present system is essentially administrative, given the going rates and presumptions in professional folklore, the effect of these reforms is to make the system officially administrative. Could it be that the removal of the mystique of discretion is a threat to the legal monopoly on the processes of resolving disputes? If formulas are to be used, why should accountants not be employed, or why should professionals be used at all? These questions are not unique to divorce law. Similar issues arise, for example, in conveyancing, where the removal of the monopoly has had an impact on the legal profession, though not as great as some might have forecast.

To conclude, the impact of the changes discussed here will be important as regards the day-to-day application of the law, but the laws which are being applied need to extend their scope more widely if they are to have a more significant impact on the economic consequences of divorce.

References

Australian Law Reform Commission (1987), *Matrimonial Property* Report No. 39 (The Hambly Report) (Canberra).

Cain, M. (1983), 'Where are the Disputes? A Study of First Instance Civil Courts in the UK', in M. Cain and G. Kulcsar (eds.), *Disputes and the Law* (Budapest).

Child Support Consultative Group (1988), *Child Support: Formula for Australia* (The Fogarty Report) (Canberra).

Cotterrell, R. (1984), *The Sociology of Law: An Introduction* (London).

Fowler, S. (1988), 'Current Maintenance Issues', *Bicentenary Family Law Conference* (Melbourne).

Friedman, L. M., and Percival, R. V. (1976), 'A Tale of Two Courts: Litigation in Alameda and San Benito Counties', *Law and Society Review*, 10: 267–301.

Galanter, M. (1974), 'Why the "Haves" Come Out Ahead: Speculations on the Limits of Legal Change', *Law and Society Review*, 9: 95–160.

Howe, B. (1986), *Child Support: A Discussion Paper on Child Maintenance* (Canberra).

Ingleby, R. (1986), 'The Clean Break: Allusions to Illusions and the Welfare of the Child', *Journal of Social Welfare Law*, 257–66.

—— (1988*a*), 'The Right to Protection from Poverty of Children of Divorced Couples', *Australian Child and Family Welfare*, 12: 11–17.

—— (1988*b*), 'Law Commission Working Paper No 96: Towards a Judicial Definition of Reasonableness?', *Family Law*, 18: 45–6.

—— (1988*c*), 'The Solicitor as Intermediary' in R. Dingwall and J. Eekelaar (eds.), *Divorce Mediation and the Legal Process* (Oxford).

—— (forthcoming) 'Australian Matrimonial Property Law: The Rise and Fall of Discretion', in Bradbrook, Ellinghaus and Duggan (eds.), *The Emergence of Australian Law* (Melbourne).

Kliger, B. (1988), 'The Child Support Scheme: Who is Reaping the Benefits?', *Legal Services Bulletin*, 13: 16.

Lempert, R. O. (1978), 'More Tales of Two Courts: Exploring Changes in the "Dispute Settlement Function" of Trial Courts', Law and Society Review, 13: 91–138.

Lovering, K. (1984), *Cost of Childrem in Australia* (Australian Institute of Family Studies, Working Paper No. 8; Melbourne).

Mcdonald, P. *(ed.)*, (1986), *Settling Up: Property and Income Distribution on Divorce in Australia* (Sydney).
—— and Weston, R. (1986), *The Data Base for Child Support Reform* (Melbourne).
Rein, M. (1976), *Social Science and Public Policy* (Harmondsworth).
Unger, R. M. (1976), *Law in Modern Society: Toward a Criticism of Social Theory* (New York).
Wade, J. H. (1988), 'Matrimonial Property Reform in Australia: An Overview', *Family Law Quarterly, 22: 41–69.*

Part Three

Property: Definition and Allocation

5. Marital Property: Its Transformation and Division in the United States

Lenore J. Weitzman

THE word 'property' evokes an image of substantial assets. When thinking of dividing property, most people assume that there will be enough to provide a cushion to weather the likely hardships of divorce. However, research in the United States indicates that most divorcing couples have very little property; most have cars and furniture and television sets, but only half own or are purchasing a home at the time of the divorce, and even fewer own a business or pension (Weitzman 1985).

Even more surprising is the low monetary value of the property they do own. In California over 60 per cent of the divorcing couples have less than $20,000 net worth (Weitzman 1985). This means that, if their property is divided equally, each spouse will receive less than $10,000 worth of assets. That is hardly a security blanket; it is rarely enough for the down payment on a home.

These data are open to two interpretations. One is that most divorcing couples simply do not have much property to divide upon divorce. The alternative is that most divorcing couples have invested in something else—something the courts do not yet label as property—and that their real wealth lies in this other type of investment.

In fact, *most couples do have another form of wealth: they have what I call 'career assets'—their earning capacities and the benefits and entitlements of their employment* (such as their pensions, medical insurance, and social security). These assets are at least as valuable, and are often much more valuable, than the tangible assets they have acquired in the course of their marriage. In fact, in less than a year the average couple can earn more money than all of their tangible assets are worth together. This fact underscores the value of earning capacity, which is only one of the many forms of what is now called the 'new property.'

A major thesis of this chapter is that the nature of property is changing in Western societies. Instead of investing in land or the family farm, people today invest in human capital and careers. The new property that results from these investments includes enhanced earning capacities, pensions and job-related benefits. Since these new forms of property are often the major assets acquired during marriage, I argue that the law should recognize them as part of the marital property that is divided at divorce (see also Weitzman 1974, 1981*b*, 1985). There is a discernible trend in this direction in the United States.

But before examining the treatment of the new property, it is important to look at how the courts have handled *traditional* property upon divorce. This is the subject of the first half of this chapter. After a brief review of the legal tradition, it examines the empirical research on the amount and type of conventional property that divorcing couples own, and how it is currently divided upon divorce.

Two issues are of importance in this first section. First, how equal is the current division of marital property? Secondly, how are courts treating the family home and to what extent are they giving priority to the needs of minor children?

The second half of this chapter looks at the new property of career assets, which the courts have only recently begun to consider as property. In particular, I trace recent developments in the law with respect to retirement benefits, professional degrees, and medical insurance.

Throughout the United States judges, lawyers, and policy-makers are wrestling with the complexities of defining and valuing the new property. The major definitional problem is whether career assets should be recognized as marital property to be divided at divorce.

The major valuation problem is how to calculate their worth. while the courts know how to value a family home by relying on its market value, there are no equally simple formulas for valuing the new property. Since one cannot sell one's pension or earning capacity, there is no market to establish the value of the new property. In addition, many forms of new property are contingent. For example, a worker may not live long enough to receive a pension. Despite these complexities, the courts in the United States are developing procedures both to value and to divide these assets at divorce.

Underlying the discussion of both types of marital property is a more basic theoretical issue concerning the aim of the law. What is the purpose of dividing property at divorce? Traditionally property awards were used to reward the 'innocent spouse' and to punish 'the guilty' spouse. But with the widespread adoption of no-fault divorce laws, fault is becoming increasingly irrelevant. (Freed and Walker (1990: 532–3) report that marital fault has been explicitly excluded as a factor in property distribution and/or maintenance in seventeen states while it remains (one of many factors) in twenty-two states. In three states it is excluded from property awards but not from alimony.)

A second goal in dividing property at divorce is to recognize each spouse's contribution to the acquisition of marital property. In the past, contributions were defined almost exclusively in monetary terms. Each spouse's entitlement was based on his or her earnings or other financial contributions. Under this scheme, since husbands were the primary wage-earners, most of the property acquired during marriage was defined as 'his'. But today courts are more likely to recognize the equal importance of home-making and child-rearing and to assume that marriage is an economic partnership. Under this partnership theory of marriage, it is assumed that each spouse makes an equal (but not identical) contribution to the acquisition of marital property. Thus, the assets of the marital partnership are 'theirs'.

A third goal in allocating property at divorce is to provide a remedy for marriage-based dependency and need. For example, if there are minor children, and if the only marital property at divorce is the family home, the need-based theory might lead to an award of the home to the custodial parent and children. Along the same lines, if an older home-maker does not have the earning capacity to support herself, the major share of the property might be used to ensure her basic needs.

It is easy to see how these two later goals might appear to be in conflict. If the only tangible asset is the family home, the partnership standard would lead to an equal award to each partner, while the need-based standard would lead to an award to the custodial parent or older home-maker. As Martha Fineman (1989) observed, since there is no consensus about what constitutes justice, it is difficult to agree on the rules for dividing property upon divorce.

Thus, the dilemma of which theory—an entitlement theory or a need-based theory—best serves the interest of justice is discussed in the last section of this chapter. I suggest that the apparent conflict between these two theories is the result of an erroneous and limited definition of property. It is argued here that both goals may be achieved by recognizing career assets as marital property.

The impetus for many of the policy suggestions in this chapter comes from empirical research. In the United States, as in England, Belgium and Australia (see chapters by Maclean, van Houtte and Maddens, Ingleby and Funder), empirical research has played a critical role in stimulating a rethinking of the law. For it is research and 'hard data' that have revealed the inequities of the old rules, and it is research and 'hard data' that have underscored the economic importance of the new property.

For example, in California, a state where the law required an equal division of property, courts were found to be violating this mandate because they often allowed one spouse, typically the husband, to keep the couple's career assets for himself (Weitzman 1985). They were also allocating post-divorce income so that many wives and children suffered severe economic hardships. These findings, and the public debate they stimulated, led the 1985 California Senate to establish a blue ribbon Task Force on Family Equity. The Task Force was charged with reviewing *The Divorce Revolution* and making appropriate recommendations (California Senate 1987; Kay 1990). By 1987 the Task Force had proposed twenty-three pieces of new legislation (on child support, custody, alimony, and judicial education, as well as those on property). By January 1990 thirteen of these bills had become law.

But before turning to specific reforms, this chapter outlines the marital property laws in the United States (in the following section) and then reviews the empirical research on the division of traditional property at divorce.

Marital Property Regimes in the United States: Common-Law and Community-Property States

Until twenty years ago there were two distinct legal systems governing the property of married couples in the United States (Kay 1990: 11). Forty-two states had a separate-property system, based on the English common law, which recognized each spouse's individual ownership of the property he or she acquired during marriage. Under this system property was segregated into two categories, 'his' and 'hers'.

The remaining eight states were community-property states,[1] which considered all property acquired by either spouse during marriage as joint property. Property was merged into a unified 'community' as 'theirs.' Since the community-property states recognized the contribution both spouses had made to the economic assets of their marriage, whether by home-making or by earning a salary, each spouse owned one-half of the community property. In this system the starting-point for the division of property at divorce was a 50 : 50 division—half to the wife and half to the husband.

Although the community-property states routinely divided marital property at divorce, close to half of the common-law states did not. In 'strict title states' the courts could not transfer the property of one spouse to the other. Writing in 1986, Blumberg notes that 'as recently as ten years ago many states, including New York, Pennsylvania, Maryland and Virginia, did not have equitable distribution' (Blumberg, 1986: 1251). Thus, in a traditional separate-property system, the full-time home-maker had no right to any of the property her husband had acquired. In contrast, in community-property states, a full-time housewife was entitled to an equal share of the property.

While the states in the United States are still divided into common-law and community-property states, the stark contrast between the systems has blurred in recent years. This is a result of two legal developments. First, many common-law states have adopted Equal Rights Amendments to their state constitutions, which have been interpreted to give housewives

[1] Arizona, California, Idaho, Louisiana, Nevada, New Mexico, Texas and Washington.

access to the property that their husbands have acquired during marriage (Avner and Greene 1982).

Secondly, in recent years most separate-property states have abandoned strict title rules. As noted above, under strict title rules, the divorce courts could not invade the husband's title and could not award any of 'his' property to his wife. The title system favoured employed spouses who earned incomes, and disadvantaged home-makers. Most states abolished strict title rules in the 1970s and 1980s, and instituted 'equitable-distribution' rules that allowed the courts to distribute all property acquired during marriage (which could include transfer of title) (Kay 1990: 12).

In a majority of these states the court is authorized to divide only 'marital property', not 'separate property.' (Separate property is either property acquired before marriage or property acquired by gift or inheritance during marriage.)

Nevertheless, there is still a critical difference in the perspective with which commmunity-property and separate-property systems approach the division of assets at divorce. In many separate-property states the courts start with the underlying assumption that the property *really belongs to the husband* because he was the one who earned it. Drawing on the common-law legacy of dower rights for widows, they assume that one-third of the husband's property is an 'equitable portion' for the wife, with two-thirds left for the husband. Grace Blumberg (1986: 1251 n. 4) sees a movement towards equal division in the common-law states but, to date, only nine of the (current) forty-one common-law states have adopted either a presumptive or an absolute 50 : 50 division rule .

In the community-property states, in contrast, since the basic premiss is that all property acquired during marriage is 'earned' by the joint efforts of the two spouses, regardless of who receives the pay cheque or signs the deed, the starting-point for an 'equitable distribution' is a 50 – 50 division of marital assets. Thus six of the eight community-property states have a presumptive or mandatory equal-division rule (Freed and Walker 1990: 523–34).

The empirical research, though limited, supports the persistence of these different perspectives. Examining the equitable-distribution law in New York, Cohen and Hillman

(1984) found that, 'with few exceptions, the courts are not treating the wife as an equal partner'. In contrast, in California, a community-property state, my research reveals that a 50:50 division of property is the norm (Weitzman 1985).

The debate over whether an 'equal'-division rule is preferable to an 'equitable'-division rule is part of a larger debate about fixed versus discretionary rules. For example, Mary Ann Glendon (1982: 254) criticizes equitable-distribution rules because they give judges too much discretion and increase the likelihood of unfair and inconsistent awards. In addition, discretionary rules increase litigation and thereby advantage the partner with greater resources. It is for these reasons that many feminists have expressed concern about the adverse effects of the discretionary rules on women. On the other hand, Martha Fineman (1989) argues that judges need discretionary flexibility to award the family home, which is often the family's only asset, to the custodial parent. Fineman's position is challenged by the data reported below in the section on the family home; there it is noted that judges are 'reluctant' to make awards that seem to favour the wife, when they have discretion, even though such awards are in the interests of minor children. For these reasons, this chapter and others in this book (Chapters 3 and 4) argue for clear directives to judges in the form of fixed rules such as an equal-division rule.

Traditional Property

The Empirical Research

My research on the impact of no-fault divorce in California was the first systematic empirical study of the legal process of divorce in the United States (Weitzman 1980, 1981*b*, and 1985). Following its publication, researchers in five other states began similar studies to examine comparability across state lines. This section draws on the results of all of these studies to provide an overview of knowledge about the division of property at divorce in the United States.

The California study was designed to measure the impact of

California's no-fault divorce law, the first no-fault divorce law in the United States, which was instituted in 1970. [2] Data were collected from the following sources:

1. random samples of 2,500 divorce cases drawn from court records in San Francisco and Los Angeles in 1968 (two years before no-fault divorce), 1972 (two years after no-fault divorce was instituted), and 1977 (five years later);[3]
2. in-depth interviews with a stratified random sample of 228 recently divorced men and women;[4] and
3. structured interviews with 44 family law judges and 169 attorneys who specialized in divorce cases in 1974–5.[5] (See also Weitzman 1985: pp. xvii–xxi.)

After the preliminary results of my research were published (Weitzman 1981), Heather Wishik set out to gather similar data in Vermont (Wishik 1986). She examined divorce cases in four Vermont Superior Courts in 1982–3. Out of 277 divorce cases, she took a random sample of forty-eight cases for follow-up interviews.

Following Weitzman and Wishik, James McLindon (1987)

[2] I would like to acknowledge my debt to Professor Ruth Dixon, with whom I collected these data.

[3] Approximately 2,500 divorce cases were randomly drawn from court records in San Francisco and Los Angeles, the two major cities in California: 1,000 cases in 1968, two years before the no-fault law was instituted, and 1,000 cases in 1972, two years after the no-fault law was instituted. The third sample of 500 divorce cases was drawn from court dockets in 1977 to examine the extent of the change seven years after no-fault was instituted. Since few inter-city differences were found in the earlier sample, the 1977 sample was limited to Los Angeles (where one-third of all California divorces are granted).

[4] Structured in-depth interviewed with 228 recently divorced men and women (114 men and 114 women) were conducted approximately one year after the legal divorce in 1978. A stratified random sampling procedure was used to obtain respondents of all socio-economic groups and all lengths of marital duration. Since most divorcing couples are relatively young and do not have much property to divide, couples in longer marriages and couples with property were oversampled to provide enough couples in these groups for analysis. In reporting on these data below the interview responses have been weighted—i.e. adjusted so that the data reflects a normal sample of divorced persons—such as the 1977 docket sample.

[5] Structured interviews were conducted with virtually all of the judges who heard family law cases in San Francisco and Los Angeles counties in 1974 and 1975 (a total of 44 judges). During these same years in-depth interviews were conducted with 169 matrimonial attorneys in San Francisco and Los Angeles. The 77 attorneys from San Franciso comprised most of the family law bar in that area. In Los Angeles, where more than 1,400 attorneys identified themselves as matrimonial attorneys, the interview sample was restricted to an élite subsample of 92 'experts'.

undertook a similar study in Connecticut. He drew a random sample of one hundred cases from New Haven court records in the 1970s, along with one hundred cases from the 1980's, to compare settlements before and after no-fault was instituted. The Connecticut sample included a disproportionate number of longer married and more well-to-do couples, who also had more than the average amount of property. McLindon studied only court records. He did not interview.

In Oregon, Barbara Rowe and Alice Milles Morrow (1988) looked at divorce cases from three urban counties in 1983–4. Rowe's and Morrow's sample was limited to 116 individuals who had been married at least ten years. Thus their research also focussed on a more propertied sample.

In Alaska, Barbara Baker (1987) and the Alaska Women's Commission randomly selected subjects from court files in 1984–5. They interviewed 139 subjects.

Finally, in New York, Marsha Garrison (1990) examined three hundred divorce cases in three regions in 1978 and 1984, selecting one hundred cases each of contested, consensual, and default cases. Garrison's analysis was limited to court records. She did not conduct interviews.

The Amount and Value of Marital Property

In most states, marital property subject to division at divorce is limited to the income and property acquired by either the husband or the wife during marriage (excluding gifts and inheritance). For example, *community property* is defined by the California Civil code ss. 687 (1982), 5107–8 (1983) as *all property* acquired by husband and wife, or by either, *during marriage* with the exception of property acquired by gift, bequest, devise, or descent (and their rents, issues, and profits)'.

The first and perhaps most important finding in the California study is that the average divorcing couple have relatively few assets, and those assets are typically of relatively low value. This is reflected in all of the random samples of California court records, and in the property reported by the divorced men and women in the interviews. For example, in the Los Angeles court records, divorcing couples listed household furnishings (89 per cent), cars (71 per cent), and some savings in the form of money in bank accounts, stocks or bonds (62 per cent). But only half (46 per cent) of the couples owned or were buying a family home, and even fewer said they had a pension (24 per cent), or a business (11 per cent), or other real estate (11 per cent).

In addition, most divorcing men and women in California did not have any separate property (i.e. property acquired before marriage, or by gift or inheritance during marriage). Only 14 per cent of the financial statements listed separate property, and those that were listed were quite modest. In the 1978 interview sample the median value of separate property claimed by the husband was $10,000, while the wife's was $2,000.

The relatively low value of the community property owned by divorcing couples is evident in the statistics on the 'net worth' of the 1978 interview sample (weighted to represent the total population of divorcing couples in Californa in that year). Nine per cent of all the divorcing couples had a *negative* net worth: their debts were greater than their assets. Another 39 per cent had less than $10,000 net worth. Cumulatively, close to 60 per cent of the divorcing couples had less than $20,000 net worth, in 1978 dollars.

How do these data compare with those from other states? While the data from other states are not strictly comparable, in general they support the conclusion that divorcing couples have relatively little property to divide. The first report of the scarcity of marital property at divorce is found in William J. Goode's classic study of divorce in Detroit, Michigan, in 1948 (Goode 1956). In interviews with 425 divorced mothers, Goode found that 40 per cent of the families had 'no property' to divide (i.e. had only a few household items). Only 18 per cent of the families had property worth $4,000 or more (Goode 1956: 217). Similarly, in a 1978 survey of court records in Cleveland, Ohio, McGraw, Sterin, and Davis (1981–2: 470) reported that only 'a small portion of all cases have a house and other property'.

Only two of the five other research studies described at the beginning of this section included data on the total value of marital assets. In the McLindon study of court records in urban Connecticut the median value of assets appears, at first glance, to be higher than those in California. But the discrepancy may be explained by the disproportionate number of upper-income couples in his sample (McLindon 1987). When we eliminate the wealthiest couples who earn over $50,000 a year (who, McLindon notes, are over-represented), his figures are consistent with the California samples.

Similarly, the median value of assets reported by Rowe and Morrow in Oregon is high because their sample is restricted to couples who were married for more than ten years. Since marital duration is positively correlated with the amount of property, these longer-married couples naturally have significantly more property to divide at divorce. When this sample bias is controlled, the Oregon figures are comparable to those in the other studies (Rowe and Morrow 1988: 470).

The best available data on the small amount of 'traditional property' owned by divorcing couples in the United States are provided by the US Census Bureau. A 1978 survey conducted by the Census Bureau found that less than half of the divorced women reported having any marital property to divide upon divorce (US Census 1981: 1). In fact, if there is any discrepancy between the research studies in individual states and the data collected by the Census Bureau, it is that the couples in the court studies appear to have slightly *more* property than the national average. In the 1978 census study, the divorced women who reported having received any property got an average (median) award of $4,648. Since most of these awards were in separate-property states, it is likely that these women received less than half of the marital property. If so, then the total amount of marital property might be estimated at two to three times the amount of their award, or between $9,000 and $14,000. (the higher estimate is only slightly less than the California median of $15,000 when couples with no property are excluded from the sample, as they were in the census study.)

One should be extremely cautious about generalizing from the census data because they do not control for the number of years since the divorce. They therefore include property awards made at different points in time which have not been adjusted for inflation or converted into 1978 dollars. The Census Bureau reports that it decided to remove the question on the value of property awards from its later surveys because of these difficulties (US Census Bureau 1983: 5).

Nevertheless, divorcing couples have, on the average, a lower net worth than married couples in the United States. A 1984 study by the Federal Reserve Board calculated the typical family's net worth as $20,752 in 1977.

The conclusion that most divorcing couples do not have substantial property to divide is also evident in the English data reported by Todd and Jones (1972), and the Scottish data reported by Manners and Rauta (1981).

The Amount of Property by Marital Duration and Income

As might be expected, both amount and value of property increase with marital duration. In California couples married less than five years had, on average, only $3,000 net worth in 1978 dollars. This increased to an average of almost $50,000 net worth among couples married eighteen years or more.

In a parallel way, the value of marital property increases with family income, as shown in Table 5.1. Couples with family incomes of between $10,000 and $20,000 a year had, on average, property with a net worth of less than $5,000. This increased to nearly $22,000 among couples with family

TABLE 5.1. *Value of property by family income (dollars)*

Family income (yearly)	Value of property		
	Median income (in group)	Net value of assets* (including debts)	Gross value of assets* (excluding debts)
Less than 10,000	5,000	300	1,000
10,000–19,999	16,000	4,100	6,800
20,000–29,999	23,000	21,800	24,600
30,000–49,999	35,000	61,500	62,700
50,000–or more	55,000	85,600	115,300

Notes:
This table is based on weighted data from interviews with divorced men and women, Los Angeles County, California, 1978.
* Median value, rounded to nearest $100
Source: Weitzman 1985: 59.

incomes between $20,000 and $30,000. and to more than $85,000 among couples with yearly incomes of $50,000 or more.

Table 5.1 shows two important relationships between income and property. The first is the expected correlation between the two: income and property increase together, so that higher-income families have more property. The second relationship, which is more surprising, concerns the relative importance of income when compared with property. This is one of the most important findings of the California research: *in just one year, the average divorcing couple can earn more than the value of their total assets*. It would take the median family with a yearly income of $20,000 less than seven months to earn as much as the net value of their property (which is $10,900). This indicates that *the spouses' earning capacity is typically worth much more than the tangible assets of the marriage*.

The value of earning capacity is evident at all income levels. For example, a couple earning between $10,000 and $20,000 a year has accumulated about $4,000 worth of property. With a median yearly income of $16,000, it would take them only one-quarter of a year to earn $4,000—the value of their total community property. Similarly, a couple in the next higher income bracket, with a median yearly income of $23,000, would take less than a year to earn the value of the property they accumulated during the marriage.

It is only in families with incomes over $30,000 that the value of marital property is greater than yearly family income. Yet even there it takes the average family less than two years to earn as much as their property is worth. *Since property is divided once, but earning capacity continues to produce income year after year, the latter is clearly of greater cumulative value in the long run.*

A similar analysis reveals the relatively greater value of the earning capacity of the husband alone when compared with the tangible assets acquired during the marriage. It only takes the average divorced man about ten months to earn as much as the entire net worth of the community property.

Policy Implications: the Importance of Career Assets

The data in Table 5.1 have important policy implications. One implication is that support awards (i.e. awards of alimony and child support) tend to be more valuable in the long run than property awards. This is because support awards redistribute future income, which is where the real wealth of most families lies. In addition, since property can be divided only once, but income continues to be earned every year, the cumulative value of support awards is likely to be much greater. This suggests that as long as the traditional definition of property is retained, support awards that divide income, especially future income, are the most valuable entitlements awarded at divorce. (But if the courts were to recognize and divide the new property, then property would again become the pivotal issue at divorce.)

A second and related implication is that the courts cannot be dividing marital property equally. If one partner builds his or her earning capacity during marriage, while the other stays out of the labour force to be a home-maker and parent, the earning partner has acquired the major asset of the marriage. If that person's earning power—or the income it produces—is not divided upon divorce, the two spouses are left with very unequal shares of their family assets. Thus, the courts cannot divide marital property 'equally' if they do not recognize and divide these career assets as marital property.

In the discussion that follows, the traditional definition of marital property is used (i.e. career assets and earning capacity are omitted) so that we may examine the distribution of traditional assets at divorce.

The Value of Homes and other Assets

For those couples with traditional forms of property, the family home was typically the couple's most valuable asset. National data show that 72 per cent of all US families own or are buying their own homes (Statistical abstract, of the US 1990: 47, table 59). Since divorcing couples are more likely to be younger and poorer than married couples in general, they are less likely to own houses. Nevertheless, about half (46 per cent) of the divorcing couples in California owned homes, with a median equity of about $53,000 in 1984 dollars. Only 11 per cent of the divorcing couples owned a business and only 11 per cent owned other real estate. Surprisingly, in 1978 only 24 per cent of the California men and only 11 per cent of the women said they had pensions at the time of divorce.

Once again, we note the relatively low value of most of these assets. While most divorcing couples owned household furnishing (89 per cent) and cars (71 per cent), the mean monetary value of these assets was less than $14,000 together in 1984 dollars. Similarly, even though most (61 per cent) of the divorcing couples had some savings in the form of money in bank accounts, stocks, or bonds, these assets had a median value of only $1,800.

Dividing the Property: The Decline in the Wife's Share with No-fault Divorce

During the past two decades most states in the United States have undergone major changes in the rules for divorce. The Divorce Revolution, which was launched with California's no-fault divorce law of 1970, has not only brought no-fault grounds for divorce; it has also altered the rules for dividing property and awarding support.[6] Since different reforms were adopted in different states at different times, it is impossible to cover the array of changes in the entire United States in this chapter. Instead I shall focus on California as the point of departure, and note the parallels (and differences) in other states.

Before 1970, under California's traditional fault-based divorce law, the 'innocent party' had to receive more than half of the property. This was typically the wife, both because her husband was more likely to want a divorce and because prevailing norms of chivalry dictated that he would let her file for the divorce as the 'innocent party'. After 1970, when the no-fault divorce law took effect, judges were instructed to ignore fault and to divide the community assets and liabilities *equally*. The court could make an unequal division only if the total of the community property was under $5,000 and one spouse's whereabouts were unknown, or if the debts exceeded the assets. (The judge could also adjust property in the unusual event of deliberate concealment or misappropriation

[6] According to Professor Herma Hill Kay, fifteen states have 'pure no-fault' divorce laws in the sense that they have abolished all fault-based grounds for divorce and established instead the principle of marriage breakdown as the exclusive basis for dissolution; twenty-one states have added a no-fault provision of the marriage breakdown variety to their existing fault grounds; and fourteen states and the District of Columbia have combined fault grounds with a no-fault provision based on voluntary separation or incompatibility (Kay 1987*a*: 5, 6; nn. 19, 20, 22).

of community property by one party.) In addition, a husband and wife could agree to a non-equal division, either in writing or orally in court.

The equal division no-fault law had a dramatic effect on marital property awards. In 1968, under the old law, the wife, as the 'innocent' plaintiff is most cases, was usually awarded the lion's share of the property. She received more than half (i.e. 60 per cent or more) in four out of five divorce cases in San Francisco, and three out of five cases in Los Angeles. Many of these unequal awards were the result of awards of the family home and furnishings to the wife.

By 1972, under the new law, the percentage of wives who were awarded most of the community property dropped. For example, in Los Angeles county, where wives were awarded close to 80 per cent of the property under the old fault law, they were awarded closer to half (54 per cent) under no-fault. By 1977 equal division was the norm.

These results parallel those reported by Karen Seal (1977: 11). Seal found a significant decline in the assets awarded exclusively to the wife in San Diego California.

One might ask how it is still possible, under a strict equal-division rule, to have cases in which property is not divided equally. As noted above, husbands and wives may agree to an unequal division and these agreements may reflect property-support trade-offs. For example, a wife may accept more than 50 per cent of the tangible property in exchange for a lower support award.

One of the justifications for the equal-division rules in California was the reformers' belief that property was usually divided in roughly equal proportions under the old law. (A 51 : 49 per cent division of the property was in technical compliance with the rule that 'more than one-half' of the assets be awarded to the innocent party.) An equal-division rule, the reformers asserted, would merely codify the common practice of roughly equal property splits.

These data strongly contradict the reformers' assertions. They indicate that property was *not* being divided equally under the old law, and certainly not in the expected 51 : 49 per cent ratios. Rather, in three-quarters of the 1968 cases there was a substantially unequal division, presumably to assist a dependent wife (and children). Thus, these findings challenge the widespread myth that the no-fault divorce law merely codified existing practice. They indicate, instead, that the new law has dramatically altered the division of property at divorce.

In practical terms, the major impact of the equal-division rule has been to force the sale of the family home.

The Family Home

Traditionally, the family home was awarded to the wife, both because it was assumed to be hers—in the sense that she had organized, decorated, and maintained it—and because she was usually the 'innocent' party and therefore entitled to a larger share of the community property. In addition, if she had custody of the children, which was most often the case, she needed the home to maintain a stable environment for them.

In California the treatment of the family home changed dramatically under the equal-division requirement of the no-fault divorce law. The number of homes being divided equally rose from less than a quarter (23 per cent) of the homes in 1968, to more than a third (35 per cent) in 1977, and explicit orders to sell the home rose from about one in ten in 1968, to about one in three in 1977. By that year, selling the house was the typical means of dividing it equally.

This trend is disturbing because of the harmful social and economic consequences of dislocation to minor children and older home-makers. In fact, many of the attorneys and judges interviewed expressed concern about a forced sale of the family home, especially in families with minor children.

Other researchers, observing similar trends, echoed these concerns about the loss of the family home for minor children. In San Diego, California, Karen Seal (1977: 12) found that 66 per cent of the wives were awarded the home in 1968 before no-fault, but that by 1976 the percentage had dropped to 42 per cent. As Seal noted, the minority of wives who were able to keep the family home under no-fault 'paid' for their husbands' share by 'buying him out', or by relinquishing their claims to other assets, such as their husbands' pension.

In Connecticut, attorney Robert McLindon (1987) observed an even more dramatic shift in home disposition after the implementation of no-fault. During the 1970s 82 per cent of the women were awarded the family home outright. By the 1980s, under no-fault, that number fell to 37 per cent (McLindon 1987: 376). McLindon argues that these figures signal an erosion in the two principles which governed property awards in the fault era: the principle that wives receive the home and the principle that the home follows the children.

This theory is consistent with the data that show no correlation between disposition of the home and child custody in the no-fault era. In California, the presence of minor children did not increase the likelihood that the wife would be awarded the family home. In fact, 66 per cent of the couples who were forced to sell their homes had minor children (Weitzman 1985: 79). Similarly, in Vermont, even though the overwhelming majority of wives received physical custody of the children, Wishik reported that only 41 per cent of the wives were granted possession of the home (Wishik 1986: 90).

While the principle of the house following the children has obviously eroded for women, it is surprising to find that it still holds when the father gets custody. In both Vermont and Alaska, father custody almost guaranteed that the father would be awarded the marital home. In Alaska, fathers with custody received the home in 93 per cent of the cases (Baker 1987: 9) and in Vermont men with custody were granted the house in every case studied (Wishik 1986: 91). In contrast, wives with custody were awarded the home in only 68 per cent of the cases in Alaska (Baker, 197: 9), and only 52 per cent of the cases in Vermont (Wishik 1986: 91).

Despite these general trends, there is still wide variation in the disposition of the family home in different states. For example, in the Oregon sample of longer married women, Rowe and Morrow (1988: 473) reported that women received the home in 55 per cent of the cases, while in the New York (Garrison 1990: 19), they were awarded the home in only 35 per cent of the cases.

Since wives with custody can no longer count on being awarded the family home, the only way the California women we interviewed managed to keep the home was to trade it for an asset of equal value, such as the husband's pension or a vacation home. However, such trade-offs are possible only in the small percentage of divorcing families that have other assets, and, as we already know, most families do not.

Since couples in longer marriages are more likely to have pensions, an older home-maker is more likely to be in a position where she can give up her pension rights in return for the family home. But foregoing pension rights is a serious risk for an older woman. Thus, even if other property exists, it may not be in the woman's (or her children's) best interest to trade it in order to keep the home. Another possibility for the custodial mother who is determined to maintain the home for her children is to accept a smaller amount of spousal or child support or to forgo support entirely. But, once again, few women can 'afford' to forgo support. For example, one 38-year-old California housewife pleaded with her husband, and then with the court, to work out some arrangement to allow her to keep the family home for her fourteen-year-old son who was experiencing 'a lot of emotional turmoil'. But, since she had no job, she could not 'afford' to accept her hsband's offer of a mere $100 a month in child support in exchange for the home. The judge ordered it sold and gave her three months to vacate it. As she said:

> I begged the judge . . All I wanted was enough time for Brian [her son] to adjust to the divorce . . . I broke down and cried on the stand . . . but the judge refused. He gave me three months to move—three months to move 15 years—[of my life]—right in the middle of the school semester . . . It was a nightmare . . . The most degrading and unjust experience of my life'. (Weitzman 1985, 81)

In a qualitative study of divorced mothers in California, sociologist Terry Arendell (1986: 42) observed the 'catch-22' of women having to choose between their homes and adequate support. Those who chose support had to sell their homes, but those who chose their homes were in equally dire straits because they often did not have the income to maintain them.

One way of maintaining the family home for minor children without violating the rule that requires an equal division of property is to keep the home in joint ownership and to delay its sale until the children reach 18. But the California judges we interviewed resisted this 'solution' because they were concerned about the husband's loss of his capital. As one judge said, 'it unfairly deprives the husband of the use of his share of the equity in the home'. While some judges were willing to leave the home in joint ownership for 'a few years', very few were willing to let it remain unsold until all of the children attained their majority. Even fewer were willing to make an exception for an older woman, who, they asserted, did not 'need' the home anymore (even if her college-age children considered it their home as well).

Inspired by the 'child-first' principle in England, whereby the needs of the children have priority over those of the husband or wife, I recommended 'a legislative directive to require judges to delay the sale of the family home in the interests of stability for minor children and their custodian'. I also proposed a delayed sale 'to assure an older housewife continued use and possession of the family home' (Weitzman 1985: 384–7). The California Senate Task Force (that was established in response to *The Divorce Revolution*) proposed two bills to accomplish this, noting that interviews with judges had revealed that they were reluctant to delay the immediate sale of the family home without a law that directed them to do so (California Senate 1987: IV–4). The first bill created a presumption in favour of deferring the sale of the family home in the interests of minor children. This bill, with many specifications (including a list of ten factors for the court to consider in ordering a deferred sale) was passed by the California legislature and became law in 1988. (California Civil Code §4700.10(b) 1989).

The Task Force also supported the recommendation that long-married economically dependent wives be given the right to retain the family home, regardless of the presence of minor children, but this bill failed in the legislature.

Because the home is typically such a large part of the tangible property, its allocation takes on a great deal of importance. Unfortunately, for the same reason, there is a great deal of resistance to delaying the sale of the home, because most people assume that marital property cannot be divided equally unless the home is sold. (A more cynical interpretation is that the sale of the home generates money to pay lawyer's fees—which may help explain why the California bar opposed the bills to delay the sale of the family home.) It is only when we recognize the importance of the new property that we see that many families have other assets that may be as valuable as the family home, and that it may be possible to divide marital property equally—or, at least equitably—without selling the home.

The New Property of Career Assets

'Career assets' are the tangible and intangible assets that are acquired as part of either spouse's career or career potential (Weitzman 1974 and 1985). The term includes a large array of specific assets such as pensions and retirement benefits, a professional education and licence, enhanced earning capacity, medical and hospital insurance, and goodwill value of a business, entitlement to company goods and services, and government benefits such as social security.

This section examines the changing legal status of these new forms of property. It argues that if they have been acquired in the course of a marriage, they should be included in the pool of marital property to be divided upon divorce.

This conclusion is based on two premisses. The first is that career assets are joint property. Most married couples acquire career assets in the same manner that they acquire the other property that the courts currently recognize as marital property.

The second premiss is that it is impossible to have an equal or equitable division of marital property if these assets are not divided. Since the major wealth of most divorcing families lies in these assets, to exclude them from the pool of marital property is to skew the apportionment in favour of the primary working spouse—usually the husband—and to produce an inequitable and unfair division of marital property.

The first rationale for recognizing career assets as marital property is that most married couples acquire them in much the same manner as they acquire tangible assets. Consider, first, a family in which the husband is the sole wage-earner. It is likely that this family will devote time, energy, and money to build the husband's career. The wife may abandon or postpone her own education to put him through school or help establish his career; she may quit her job to move with him; or she may use her own job skills—skills that would command a salary if she were working for someone else—to help advance his career. Whether she types his papers, entertains his clients, writes the payroll cheques for his employees, or keeps the children from disturbing him, she is performing services that contribute to his career. This couple has invested their joint resources in the 'human capital' of the bread-winning spouse.

The issue is often no less significant in two-income families. Even though both spouses work, it is common for them to give priority to one spouse's career in the expectation that both will share the benefits of that decision (Prager 1977). Even dual-career professional couples seem to follow this pattern. For example, in one study of 107 dual-career couples with Ph.D.s in psychology, the couple most typically moved to advance the husband's career, despite their strong commitment to an egalitarian ideology (Wallston, Fost and Berger 1978).

There are many reasons for the common pattern of putting the husband's career first, even if the couple endorse egalitarian ideals. Most couples have been socialized to think of his occupation and his career as more important. In addition, since women are more likely to assume responsibility for child-rearing and home-making in the early years of marriage, young couples may fall into a division of labour that 'seems natural'. An economic reason for giving the husband's career the first priority is that husbands typically earn more money than their wives—even if they have the same occupational qualifications. If the husband is also older, he is already a year or two ahead in his career and his career seems like 'the better investment'.

A career developed in the course of a marriage is just like the income that is earned or the real property that is accumulated, because it is a product of the couple's joint efforts and resources. As a result of the couple's united efforts, the husband may obtain a valuable education or training, a licence to practise a trade or profession, job experience and seniority, a network of professional contacts, a track record and reputation, and professional or business goodwill.

If a spouse enters a marriage with a pre-established career, that person's career assets should be regarded as his or her separate property. But, if a career is partially or wholly built during marriage, it seems reasonable to view that career (and the assets that are attached to it) as a product of the marital partnership. If only part of a career is developed during marriage, courts should recognize both the separate and joint interests in it, just as they do with tangible property. And if both spouses' careers have been developed during marriage, the assets of both careers should be calculated and the difference adjusted.

The second rationale for recognizing career assets as marital property is that many of them are a form of deferred compensation for work performed during marriage. Many career assets are benefits that employees earn, even though they may not be paid directly to the worker and may not be used immediately. For example, compensation packages include such career assets as life, health, hospital, and disability insurance; the right to unemployment and social security benefits; entitlement to discounted or free goods and services; the right to paid sick leave and vacation benefits; and the right to a pension and other retirement benefits.

The third, and one of the most persuasive arguments for recognizing career assets as marital property comes from the concept of a marital partnership articulated by the divorcing couples themselves. Consider, for example, the folowing quote from a 51-year-old woman who was married to a college professor for thirty years:

> We married at 21, with no money . . . When he was a graduate student I worked as a secretary then typed papers at night to make extra money. When he became an assistant professor I 'retired' to raise our children but I never stopped working for him—typing, editing, working on his books . . . My college English degree was very useful for translating his brilliant ideas into comprehensible sentences . . . My name never appeared on the title page as his co-author, where it belonged, only in the dedication or thank you's . . . There's more, lots more—the hours mothering his graduate students, hosting department parties, finding homes for visiting professors . . . I was always available to help . . .
>
> I got $700 a month for three years. The judge said, I was 'smart and healthy enough to get a job.' I am to 'report back like a school girl' in 3 years. Never mind that I am 51 . . . Never mind that I *had* a job and did it well and am old enough to be entitled to a pension . . . It's not that I regret my life or didn't enjoy what I did. *But it was supposed to be a partnership*—a 50 : 50 split. It isn't fair that he gets to keep it. It isn't fair for the court to treat it as his . . . I earned it just as much as he did'. (Weitzman 1985: 193).

Sharing and supporting one's spouse's career may be equally important to younger couples. For example, in a parallel case, a young woman explained that, instead of taking a job, she 'invested in her husband because they were partners in his career':

> I spent the last seven years of my life doing everything I could to help him get tenure . . . and deferring all of my own needs and goals . . . I edited his papers, worked as his unpaid research assistant and his all-around go-fer . . . I spent two vacations reading galleys instead of the trips to Europe he promised—and there are three hundred examples like that. Every day, every week, every year we put off something *for us* in order to do something for *his career* . . . Well, now that he has tenure I think I should share the results of my work, I earned it'. (Weitzman 1985: 158)

Recent years have brought increased social recognition of the joint efforts that go into building a career. The pages that follow look at the increased legal recognition of three types of career assets: pensions and other retirement benefits, a professional education and licence, and medical insurance benefits. These are highlighted as representative examples, but the type of career assets will vary with the occupation. For example, members of the United States armed services have access to the PX and commissary privileges; airline employees and their families are entitled to free and discounted travel; doctors and members of their families receive 'professional courtesy' from other doctors and are not charged for medical treatment; corporate executives may benefit from company planes, apartments, expense accounts, meals, and vacations; professors are entitled to reduced tuition for their children; writers receive royalties for books and articles they have written that continue, hopefully, for years to come; and the employees of some companies are given discounts on company products and are entitled to use company goods, services, and facilities that range from cafeterias and day-care centres to executive dining-rooms and villas in Europe. Thus, even though this chapter focuses on the most common career assets, the concept of new forms of property in employment-related benefits extends far beyond the scope of this discussion.

I believe the law in the United States is on the brink of a critical expansion in the definition of marital property, which is reflected in the trends noted below.

Pensions and Other Retirement Benefits*

This is one of the most rapidly changing areas of family law in the United States. In a mere ten years, between 1980 and 1990, most states in the United States moved to recognize pensions as marital property to be divided at divorce. This trend reflects the dual realization (1) that these assets are of great value, and (2) that they are a form of defered compensation for work performed during marriage.

Both the value of the pensions and the marital interest in them are reflected in a typical decision by the Minnesota Supreme Court:

> The pension was one of the major assets of the marriage, and only the house ranked with equal stature. To award one party this asset would ignore the (statutory) presumption that each spouse contributed to the acquisition of proprty while they lived together as husband and wife. (*Janssen v Janssen* 331 NW 2d 752 (Minn. Sup. Ct. 1983))

A number of the critical pension cases have involved long marriages in which the pension was the couple's most important asset. Consider, for example, the facts in the frequently cited Colorado case *In re Marriage of Grubb* (745 P. 2d 664 (Colo. 1987)). Leisa and William Grubb had been married for thirty-four years. Leisa, who was 58 at the time of divorce, was a mother and home-maker during the marriage. William, who was 60, was employed by a large company and was earning approximately $92,000 a year (a salary about five times the average male income in the United States).[7] He was entitled to receive a life-time pension of about $35,000 a year. The Colorado Supreme Court held that his pension was marital property, reasoning that 'retirement benefits, far from being a mere gratuity deriving from the employer's beneficence, are nothing less than a form of deferred compensation . . . earned by the employee'.

---

* I am indebted to Tracy Higgins for superb research assistance with the second half of this chapter.

[7] The median male income in 1988 was $18,908; the median female income in 1988 was $8,884; the median household was $27,332 (US Census Bureau 1989*a*).

Vested and Non-vested Pensions

The courts have traditionally distinguished between two types of pensions. A *vested* pension is one that is secure. If an employee's interest in a pension or retirement plan is vested, the employee is entitled to collect the pension even if he or she leaves the job (or is fired) before retirement age. A *non-vested* pension is not secure; it is a contingent right that is subject to forfeiture if the employee relationship terminates before retirement.

The major trend in divorce law in recent years has been to recognize non-vested pensions as marital property to be divided upon divorce. California was the first state to adopt this view and its rationale is instructive.

The traditional California rule was similar to the traditional law in many states: non-vested pensions were not marital property because they were 'mere expectancies' and not 'truly property'. This rule was changed by a 1976 California Supreme Court decision *In re Marriage of Brown* (544 P. 2d 561 (Calif. 1976)). The Court reasoned that the right to future benefits, even though not guaranteed, is a *property right* none the less. If assets have been acquired with community funds (and community efforts) during marriage, they should be recognized as part of the community property.

One of the major justifications for the *Brown* decision is particularly relevant to our subsequent discussion of other career assets, because it focuses on the inequity between husband and wife. The *Brown* court pointed to the practical unfairness that resulted from allowing the working spouse, who was typically the husband, to retain all of the pension and retirement benefits for himself. As the California Supreme Court said, the old rule compelled 'an inequitable division of rights acquired through community effort'. (*Brown* 1976: 562). The court also explicity acknowledged that the exclusion of non-vested pensions from marital property 'skewed the division of property towards the working spouse' and therefore did not divide property equally (Brown 1976: 506).

It is evident that a parallel argument could be made for all career assets: the major inequality in property awards in California today is that the wage-earner, who is typically the husband, is allowed to retain the benefits of a career and earning capacity (that were built during marriage) for himself.

The importance of pensions in California was underscored by a highly publicized case in which a wife successfully sued her divorce attorney for malpractice because he neglected her interest in her husband's pension. In *Smith* v. *Lewis* (13 Cal. 3d 349 (Calif. 1975)) the California Supreme Court affirmed a malpractice judgment of $100,000.00 against an attorney who failed to assert a wife's claim to a share of her husband's military retirement benefits.

In the 1980s other states followed California's lead and began to recognize non-vested pensions as marital assets. As a 1983 Pennsylvania court reasoned, 'it makes no difference whether a pension plan is vested or not vested since we find that any pension plan is a marital asset to the extent that it was first acquired during marriage' (*King* v. *King* 9 FLR 2273 (Pa. Ct. C. P. 1983)).

The state of the law on pensions as of June 1990 is summarized in Table 5.2. As it indicates, most states in the United States now include vested pension benefits in the marital estate. However, there are still five states that continue to distinguish between vested and non-vested pensions and two states that refuse to recognize any pensions as marital property.

Private and Military Pensions

Military pensions have received a great deal of attention in recent years because of the publicity and outrage that followed a 1981 US Supreme Court decision in the case of *McCarty* v. *McCarty* (453 US 210 (US Sup. Ct. 1981)).

The case involved a California doctor Richard McCarty, and his wife Patricia. In a nineteen-year marriage Pat had followed Richard to the University of Oregon for four years of medical school, then on to Hawaii, California, Texas, and the nation's capital, thinking she was his partner for better or for worse. In 1976 the couple separated when Richard was a Colonel in the United States Army and the Chief of Cardiology at an army hospital in California. Under California's community-property law, Pat claimed and was awarded her share of Richard's pension—a 45 per cent interest. Richard appealed the decision and the case went up to the US

TABLE 5.2. *States that recognize pensions as marital property (at divorce)*

All pensions recognized	Only vested pensions recognized	No pensions recognized
Alaska	Florida	Alabama
Arizona	Indiana	Mississippi
Arkansas	New Hampshire	
California	North Carolina	
Colorado	Oregon	
Connecticut		
Delaware		
Georgia		
Hawaii		
Idaho		
Illinois		
Iowa		
Kentucky		
Louisiana		
Maryland		
Massachusetts		
Michigan		
Minnesota		
Missouri		
Montana		
Nebraska		
Nevada		
New Jersey		
New Mexico		
New York		
North Dakota		
Oklahoma		
Pennsylvania		
Rhode Island		
Texas		
Utah		
Virginia		
Wisconsin		
Wyoming		
Washington DC		

Supreme Court. He argued that a military pension from the federal government was not community property.

Shocking both women and men across the country, the US Supreme Court sided with Dr McCarty. The Court found that the treatment of military pensions as community property 'threatened grave harm' to the government's interest in providing for retired military members, and that it would frustrate the military's efforts to attract recruits. The Court decided that the military intended the pension as a reward for 'him'—not 'them'.

The outrage that followed the McCarty decision led to the formation of EXPOSE (Ex-Partners of Servicemen for Equality) to lobby for federal legislation that would guarantee divorced wives an equitable share in the assets accrued during a military marriage. Doris Mozley (1982), the wife of a military doctor, and one of the founders of EXPOSE, argued that military wives served their country along with their husbands and were entitled to share their military pensions:

[We need legislation] to reduce the unfairness of a system that says that a wife who served our country for years earned nothing in her own right . . . The law should recognize the special sacrifices of the military spouse and the lack of security which former spouses of service members face as they approach retirement years . . . What the military wife must have in order to serve best is the security of knowing that, if her marriage ends, the country will reward her service by giving her what she has *earned* . . . What military wives want is the same type of law to protect us that Congress has already passed for the Foreign Service wife, and that is a presumption that the long-term military wife is entitled to a pro-rata share of the pension . . . (Mozley 1982)

EXPOSE members picketed military facilities to protest the 'throw-away military wife system' with signs saying 'I served my country 20 years with my military husband'. Newspaper articles chronicled their stories:

Sue, married thirty years ago when women were raised to believe that marriage was forever, followed her air force officer husband and raised three children, moving 20 times during their 30-year marriage . . .

Military wives are like Sue: they don't know how much their husband earns, and they develop no career of their own as they regularly uproot themselves to follow a husband to a new assignment. They can't work in one place long enough to build up a pension of their own and—like Sue—they assume they don't need to, that their husband's pension will always be there to fall back on. (Turnquist 1983)

These efforts led to the 1982 Uniformed Services Former Spouse's Protection Act. Although the Act did not provide the 50 per cent guarantee that EXPOSE had lobbied for (i.e. half of the pension after twenty years of marriage), it did overturn the *McCarty* decision by explicitly permitting state courts to treat retirment pay as community property. Since then the court can award up to, but not more than, 50 per cent of the disposable retirement pay. As Fran Leonard (1980: 9) points out, this leaves many military wives subject to state laws and does not assure them the pro-rata share of their husbands' pensions that is now provided to wives of foreign service officers.

The pioneering legislation for other federal employees, introduced by Democratic Congresswoman Pat Schroeder, was the Foreign Service Act of 1980. While the foreign service retirement system covers only a few thousand workers and their spouses, it provided the first formula for pension-sharing at divorce and has been the model for proposed changes in other federal pension systems. The Act entitles the divorced wives of foreign service officers to a share of their ex-husband's retirement benefits if they were married for ten or more years. The wife's share is pro rata according to the years of the marriage and is 50 per cent after a twenty-year marriage. It is also possible for a divorced wife to receive her share of the pension directly from the government (Women's Legal Defense Fund 1983: 10).

In 1984 the US Congress passed the Retirement Equity Act which requires private pension plans, such as company and union plans, to comply with court orders in a divorce decree. Under the Act all or part of a participant's benefits in a pension plan may be paid to an alternative payee if the court orders it. California courts, for example, issue orders for private pension plans to mail monthly cheques directly to both the spouse and the employee. The courts also issue orders directing plans to pay benefits to the spouse on the death of the employee.

Social Security

The major retirement benefit in the United States is provided by the social security system, a national old-age/retirement programme that provides workers and their dependents with benefits upon retirement, disability, or death of the worker. All wage-earners pay a social security tax, which is deducted from their earnings by their employers. When they retire at 65 for men, 62 for women, they or their families receive a monthly benefit.

The social security system allows a divorced spouse to receive social security benefits from the earnings of a working spouse if their marriage lasted for more than ten years. (A spouse is not entitled to any benefits if the marriage ends before the ten-year threshold.) Under the present system, a divorced woman is entitled to half of her ex-husband's benefit, which is based on his earnings record, unless she would get more on the basis of her individual earnings (Peer 1984). Working women who are married often get little or no return on the social security tax they pay, according to a 1984 study of social security benefits (Peer 1984: 1, 11). That is because they typically earn lower wages and are entitled to lower benefits than they can claim as the wife of their higher paid husbands. For example, in 1989 the average monthly benefit for a retired woman worker was $373, while women survivors received $493 (based on their husband's earnings) (*Social Security Bulletin* 1989: 2).

Since 1983 social security rules have been gender-neutral in theory, but in practice they still reflect the outmoded work and family patterns of fifty years ago. The social security programme is designed for a family with a continuously employed wage-earning husband and a non-employed home-making wife. In less traditional family situations, women are disadvantaged by the programme, which is not tailored to their work patterns or family needs (Older Women's League 1990: 4). Since women tend to make less money, have more care-giving responsibilities, and live longer than their male counterparts, when they do collect social security, their total average benefits are less. In 1989 the average benefit for a retired male worker was $604 a month, but only $373 a month for a retired woman worker (*Social Security Bulletin* 1989: 2).

This is virtually the same ratio as it was twenty years ago, despite major changes in women's work patterns.

Most divorced women would be eligible for higher benefits under a proposed 'shared-earnings' system advocated by women's activists (Women's Legal Defense Fund 1983: 10). Under this system each spouse would be credited with half of the couple's total earnings in each year of marriage. This means that the earnings of a husband and wife would be split equally for the pupose of computing benefits. For example, if a married woman left the paid labour force to care for her children, she would get credit for one-half of her husband's earnings. If both spouses worked, their combined earnings would be split 50 : 50. These credits would be added to any wages the individuals earned before or after marriage. This earnings sharing system was still being studied by the Congress of the United States as of January 1991).

Pension Ownership: Why Men Predominate

In California 24 per cent of husbands acquired pension rights during marriage, compared with only 11 per cent of the wives. This 2 : 1 ratio is evident in Oregon and Alaska as well.[8] In Vermont the gender difference is even more extreme. Wishik (1986: 92) found that 25 per cent of the husbands had pensions compared with only 2 per cent of their wives.

Among 65-year-olds in the United States as a whole, less than a quarter (23.5 per cent) of the women are entitled to pensions as a result of their own wage-earning work, compared with nearly half (46.0 per cent) of the men (Older Women's League 1990: 8). In 1987 the average pension income for women over 65 was $4,723, only 60 per cent of men's average of $7,907 (Older Women's League 1990: 8).

Pension ownership is positively correlated with both income and length of marriage in all states. For example, in California pension ownership rises from 12 per cent of those married ten years or less, to 56 per cent of those married eighteen years or more for men with yearly incomes under $20,000.

[8] In the sample of longer married divorce cases in Oregon there were more pensions, but the sex difference remained: 63 per cent of the men and 29 per cent of the women had acquired pension rights (Rowe and Morrow 1988: 470–474). Similarly, in the higher-income sample in Alaska, Baker (1987: 9) found 54 per cent of the husbands and 33 per cent of the wives had pensions (The variation in pension ownership reported in different states may be explained by the socio-economic characteristics of the samples).

Married women are much less likely to acquire pensions, regardless of their age or the marital duration. In fact, in the California sample, only the high-earning women, those with incomes of $20,000 or more a year, had pensions—and less than 5 per cent of the divorced women earned that much yearly income in 1978.

The striking difference in pension ownership among married men and women deserves a brief explanation. Since 54 per cent of married women are in the labour force in the United States (Reskin and Hartmann 1986: 3), why don't more married women acquire pension rights during marriage? The answer lies in the structure of female work patterns (Quadagno 1988). Pension eligibility requires long-term, continuous, full-time work for one employer. Women's family responsibilities often prevent them from meeting these requirements. Despite changes in recent decades, married women are still more likely to be the primary care-takers and the secondary wage-earners in their families. If they give priority to their family roles, and if they move from job to job to accommodate their husband's careers, they do not build a continuous employment record with one employer. (Most pensions require five years on the job before vesting: in 1990 the mean tenure for men on their current job was 5.1 years, while it was 3.7 years for women (Older Women's League 1990: 9).

Women are also penalized because they are more likely to leave the workforce to care for children. Women average 11.5 years out of the workforce during their working years, compared with men's 1.3 (Older Women's League 1990:). These gaps drastically diminish women's pension entitlements.

Even when women are in the labour force, they are much more likely than men to make work arrangements that accommodate their family responsibilities. In 1983, only half of the women workers worked full time year-round, compared with approximately two-thirds of men (Bianchi and Spain, 1986: 157). Since many companies restrict pension benefits to full-time workers, part-time work severely limits women's access to pension benefits. Woods (1989: 6) found that the gap narrows when one looks only at full-time workers. There, 51 per cent of the men and 44 per cent of the women are covered.

There are also structural features of the labour market, such as the high degree of sex segregation, that disadvantage women. For example, women are under-represented in manufacturing jobs, in which 50–60 per cent of workers have pension coverage, and are over-represented in trade and service jobs, in which only 20–40 per cent of employees have pensions (Quadagno 1988: 542).

Women also tend to work for smaller companies than men do, and the smaller the company, the less likely it is to offer pension benefits. Only 25 per cent of employers with less than twenty-five workers offer pension coverage to their employees, compared with 89 per cent of employers with more than 1,000 workers (Older Women's League 1990: 9). Thus women are less likely than men to work for companies that offer pension coverage to their employees.

Finally, women are concentrated in the lower-paying sectors of the labour force, where there is less pension coverage. Less than half of the workers who earn less than $1,000 per month have pension benefits, compared with more than three-quarters of those who earn more than $1,000 per month (Older Women's League 1990: 9).

In summary, both private and public pension systems penalize work patterns which are more often female, and benefit those which are more often male. As a result, women are less likely than men to acquire pension benefits. This difference underscores the importance of recognizing the marital interest in the husband's pension, since both his work advantages and her work disadvantages are influenced by the result of their family arrangements.

Division of Pensions at Divorce

Beyond the threshold question of whether or not pension benefits constitute marital assets, the court must determine how pension benefits will be valued and divided. On a general level there are two basic approaches.

One approach is to 'buy-out' or 'cash-out' the interest of the non-employee spouse at the time of the divorce. This is typically done by awarding her (or him) a lump-sum settlement—or a marital asset of equivalent value, such as the home. The second approach is the future share method, where the division is delayed until the pension benefits are paid. Each spouse is awarded a percentage of a benefit that will be paid in the future.

The preferred method depends on the age of the parties, the extent of their assets, and each spouse's alternative prospects for retirement income. Most of the California attorneys we interviewed favoured the cash-out method for younger couples with other assets, to achieve a 'clean break' at the time of divorce. In contrast, the future-share method was typically favoured for older and longer-married couples, especially if they had minimal assets and no additional sources of retirement income. This method calculates the *percentage* of the pension owned by the marital partnership and awards each spouse half of the community's percentage when the pension is paid.

What Part of the Pension is Marital Property?

Given that pension rights are a form of deferred compensation earned throughout the employee's career, the marital interest derives from the period during which the emloyee was both married and working. If the emloyee was married throughout the employment period, the pension rights will be totally marital property. If the employee worked before marriage or will work after marriage, his or her pension rights will be part marital property and part separate property. The method of division must, therefore, take into account the marital share of the total pension.

To calculate the percentage of the pension that is considered marital property, the courts typically use a simple 'time rule'. For example, let us say a man has worked for twenty years and is entitled to a pension of $1,000 a month. Assume he was married for fifteen of the twenty years. Three-quarters of his twenty-year pension, or $750 a month, would then be marital property. Half of the marital share, or $375 a month, would be awarded to his spouse. The worker would be entitled to $375 for his half of the marital property plus $250 for the quarter of the pension which is his separate property.

The future-share approach sidesteps these calculations at the time of the divorce. The court simply retains jurisdiction until the worker retires. There are several advantages to this approach. First, it avoids the court's having to speculate about the value of the pension for a cash-out. Secondly, both spouses bear the risk that no retirement benefit will be received. Thirdly, both spouses may share in the cost-of-living increases and other benefits that are granted to pension-holders after the divorce. Perhaps the most important advantage of the future-share method is that it avoids the difficult and costly calculations of expert witnesses at the time of the divorce.

On the other hand, the advantage of a cash-out is a 'clean-break' settlement at the time of the divorce. Once the present value of the employee spouse's pension rights is computed, the employee is typically awarded those rights with an offsetting award of other property to the non-employee spouse. The complexity of this approach depends upon the type of plan involved.

If the employee has a *defined contribution plan*, the calculations are simple. Under such a plan, a separate retirement account is maintained for each employee. Periodic contributions are made to the account according to a prescribed formula, such as a percentage of the employer's profits or the employee's salary. Because a separate account is maintained for each employee, the value of the benefits at the time of divorce is simply the amount in the employee's acount at that time. (When an employee retires, the benefit received is the annuity that can be purchased at that time with the amount in the employee's acount.)

But if the worker belongs to a *defined benefit plan*, the calculations are more difficult. Under a defined benefit plan there is no separate account for each employee. One large retirement fund is maintained by the employer. The pension benefits due to any employee are based on a formula. Normally, the formula contains several variables, such as the length of service and the highest monthly salary. A court may use the formula to calculate the 'value' of the monthly payment the employee has earned during the marriage. However, to calculate the aggregate value of the pension the court must estimate both the date of retirement and the life expectancy of the employee. Once this amount is determined, the court must discount it to its present value.

Under most defined benefit plans, the employee's estate will receive no benefits if the employee dies before retirement, even if the rights are vested or matured. Thus, the value of these rights must be discounted for the possibility that death may occur prior to receipt of the benefits. In contrast, with most defined contribution plans the employee's estate will receive the amount in the employee's retirement account if the rights were vested. Thus defined contribution plans need not be discounted for mortality.

Finally, if the employee worked before marriage, that portion of the pension is the employee's separate property and the calculation must be adjusted to account for only the 'coverture fraction' of the pension.

It is ideal if the present-value method results in a lump-sum cash payment at the time of the divorce or an equivalent property award. But if the marital assets are not sufficient to cover the value of the pension, the total sum may be paid over time.

There are several advantages of the present-value/cash-out method. First, the non-employed spouse will receive existing assets at the time of divorce, when these assets are most needed. Secondly, the non-employed spouse avoids the risk of adverse financial consequences if the employed spouse quits, is fired, dies, or becomes disabled. Thirdly, the present-value method avoids the continuation of an acrimonious relationship. Finally, present valuation simplifies the terms of the judgment and avoids the administrative burden of retaining jurisdiction over the parties.

Whether or not an immediate cash-out takes place, the present-value method *precludes* the non-employee spouse from sharing in post-separation promotions or increases in pay which generate high pensions. Because many courts consider this the separate property of the employee spouse, many prefer the present-valuation method.

Control Over Pension Options

A divorced person who has been awarded a share of his or her spouse's pension may still face problems in collecting the benefit. One problem occurs if the worker elects to forgo survivor's coverage. Under most pension plans a worker can opt for full monthly cheques during his life-time, or can opt for a reduced pension that will provide a survivor's benefit for his widow. In the past many workers elected to 'opt out' or waive survivor's coverage, and the choice was typically theirs alone (Porter 1980).

As of 1979, more than 64 per cent of the federal civil service, 31 per cent of the foreign service, and 95 per cent of the military had opted out of survivor's benefits (Leonard 1980). As a result, millions of older women, most of whom were married, but some of whom were divorced, learnt for the first time upon their husbands' deaths that they had been 'elected out' of any interest in future pension benefits. This problem was dealt with by the Retirement Equity Act of 1984. This law prevents workers from opting out of survivor's benefits without the written consent of their spouses (or ex-spouses, in the event of a court-ordered pension split at divorce).

A recipient spouse may face other difficulties in collecting court-awarded pension benefits. If the employee spouse dies before retirement age, his equity in the pension may be lost. As Sylvia Porter noted, there is a provision called the widow's blackout in most pensions that denies a survivor's benefit to the spouse of a worker who dies before 'early retirement age', usually 55. What the husband intended and expected for his widow simply does not count. The Retirement Equity Act of 1984 eliminates this problem by guaranteeing the pension rights of spouses of workers who die before retirement age.

Another barrier may arise if the worker chooses to delay retirement—and thereby delays both his and his former spouse's benefits. In many states there is nothing a dependent spouse can do: she must simply wait until the worker decides to retire before she can collect her share of the pension (Leonard 1980). But in some states, like California, the non-employed spouse may elect to begin receiving benefits at any time after the employed spouse becomes eligible to retire. Similarly, on a national level, as of 1985 a divorced spouse may collect social security benefits even though her former husband has not applied for them himself (as long as the husband is eligible to collect social security and as long as the wife is entitled to benefits as a spouse of ten or more years).

A Warning on Awareness of Pension Entitlements

Although this section has focused on the law, it is important to note the ever-present gap between the law and social reality. This is not only because most of the legal changes governing pensions were passed in the 1980s. There may also be a lingering belief among divorcing men and women—as well as among their attorneys—that the husband's pension is 'really his'. Thus, while California attorneys were aggressive in seeing that pensions were included in the divorcing couples' property (perhaps as a result of the malpractice case cited above), in other states there is a gap between the law on the books and the law in practice. In Vermont, for example, Wishik found that 85 per cent of the pensions were not even valued at the time of divorce—let alone divided (1986: 93). In Alaska, almost half of the pension's were not valued (Baker 1987: 9) and in Oregon 61 per cent of the pensions were not valued (Rowe and Morrow 1988: 471). In over 80 per cent of the divorce cases in these studies the pensions were retained by the worker. As Rowe and Morrow note (1988: 471), 'few couples had an idea as to the value(s) of their pension funds, despite the fact that Oregon courts have been dividing the value of pensions at divorce since 1976'. As Wishik observed (1986: 93), the pattern reflects a dangerous omission for divorcing women:

> In view of the fact that pensions may represent a large portion of the accrued capital in a marriage, such naivete about the present value of existing rights to future pension benefits probably means that men, who are the ones likely to have such rights, are leaving marriage with an asset which has been undervalued by the spouses and/or their attorneys in their discussions about property division.

During the 1980s in the United States courts have moved toward a widespread recognition of pension rights as part of the marital estate to be divided at divorce. Courts no longer ask whether the pension benefits are property. Rather, they assume that they are marital assets and must be included in the marital estate. In the 1990s the cutting-edge issues will be those of valuation and division. This recognition of pension benefits represents an important step towards the inclusion of non-traditional types of property in divorce settlements and, consequently, greater economic equality between divorcing spouses.

Education and Professional Degrees as Marital Property

A less well-recognized but equally important career asset is the acquisition of a professional degree during marriage. In the United States, unlike many countries in Western Europe, a university education is extremely expensive. Most under-graduate colleges and professional schools are private institutions that charge tuition. For example, for a resident student at a private college like Harvard, expenses for the 1990/1 academic year totally approximately $23,000 (*Harvard & Radcliffe: Official Register of Harvard University 1990–91*: 33). (That is more than the average male salary in the United States each year.)

The Official Register of Harvard University lists the expenses for resident students as: tuition $14,450, college facilities fee $1,080; room and board $5,125; books and supplies $1,545; and medical insurance $600. In addition students pay for their travel to and from the university (and for vacations), which could easily bring the total yearly cost to over $25,000.

While there are state universities with lower tuition and fees, nevertheless most students (or, to be more accurate, their parents) pay for higher education with a combination of savings and loans. Full tuition scholarships and grants are much less common than in Europe, and most students graduate with sizable debts. For example, the average graduate of Harvard College in 1990 owed between $10,000 and $12,000 in student loan debts (*Harvard & Radcliffe: Official Register 1990–91*: 35).

Most professional schools are even more expensive. Expenses at the Harvard Law School are $25,500 a year and exceed $30,000 a year at the Harvard Medical School. With a law degree requiring three years of postgraduate education, and a medical degree four, almost all professional school graduates have substantial loans and substantial debts. (The average student graduating from Harvard law school had a debt of more than $50,000 in 1990).

Nevertheless, most students consider these debts worth the financial investment, because professional degrees typically lead to significantly increased earnings over the career of the degree-holder. While a graduate of Harvard College with a bachelor's degree earned, on average, $24,000 in 1990, starting salaries for graduates of the Harvard Law School averaged more than $50,000 that year—and those graduates who chose (and were chosen) to work in Wall Street law firms in New York City received starting salaries of $90,000 in 1990. Clearly, an investment of one's time and resources on a graduate degree is an investment in one's 'human capital' that is likely to yield a valuable return.

Although it does not fit a traditional conception of property, a professional degree or licence that is acquired during marriage represents a marital investment in the human capital and earning capacity of one spouse. The fruits of that investment, just like the fruits of an investment in the stock market, should be included in the pool of marital property that is divided at divorce.

In the United States, disputes over professional degrees typically arise when one spouse, most often the wife, agrees to support her husband through his professional studies in the expectation that both will enjoy the benefits of the degree. If the couple divorces soon after the acquisition of the degree, the couple is likely to have very few tangible assets because most of their resources will have been used to finance the husband's education. Unless the wife's contribution is considered in the divorce settlement, the husband would receive a 'windfall' of the entire benefit of the couple's joint investment. The wife, on the other hand, would receive no return on what is typically a very substantial investment of her time and financial resources.

In the United States today men still earn the majority of the professional degrees. In 1986 women earned only 13 per cent of the engineering degrees, 31 per cent of the medical degrees, and 39 per cent of the law degrees (US Census Bureau 1989*b*: 158).

Legal Treatment of Professional Degrees

In a summary of family law in the United States, Freed and Walker (1990: 535) noted that

> the trend toward considering the value of professional degrees and licenses as divisible property upon divorce continues to grow. . . . Most states seem to be moving toward a specific type of postmarital payment in lieu of alimony, regardless of whether it is characterized as divisible property or alimony.

In this section I will review the ways the courts in the United States are approaching professional degrees, and then discuss the problems of valuation and remedies.

The Traditional Approach The traditional treatment of professional degrees and licences in marital dissolutions has been to deny their divisibility as marital property. Because educational assets lack traditional property traits, many courts have been unwilling to include them in the property settlement. Pointing to the lack of a market or exchange value, to the uncertainty of future earnings, and to the personal quality of a degree, these courts have reasoned that the degree cannot be treated as property.

A brief look at two cases that are typical of the traditional approach is instructive. The first case is one of the most frequently cited cases supporting the traditional view, *In re the Marriage of Graham* (574 P. 2d 75 Colo. 1978)). Mrs Graham worked as a flight attendant and contributed 70 per cent of the family's support. Mr Graham was employed part time; however, most of his efforts were devoted to acquiring both a bachelor's degree in engineering and a master's degree in business administration. The Grahams were married for six years, and they accumulated no other marital assets during their marriage. Holding that Mr Graham's degrees were not part of the marital estate, the Colorado court argued that

> [a]n education degree, such as an M.B.A., is simply not encompassed even by the broad views of the concept of 'property'. It does not have an exchange value or any objective transferable value on an open market. It is personal to the beholder . . . It cannot be assigned, sold, transferred, conveyed or pledged.

The court, therefore, denied Mrs Graham any interest in her husband's two degrees. The court did suggest, however, that the fact that one spouse had contributed to the education of the other could be considered in the equitable division of other marital assets, or in the award of maintenance.

In the second case, *Hoak* v. *Hoak* (14 *FLR* 1370 (W. Va. 1988)), the wife had supported her husband throughout medical school. While recognizing that she had 'made personal financial sacrifices . . . and postponed her own career plans', the West Virginia Supreme Court of Appeals held that the degree was not subject to distribution. The court reasoned that 'a degree of any kind results primarily from the effort of the student who earns it. Financial and emotional support are important, as are homemaker services, but they bear no logical relation to the value of the resulting degree.' Noting that the value of the degree was highly speculative, the court held that the degree did not fall within the statutory definition of marital property because it represented money or assets earned after dissolution of the marriage.

Degrees as property Just as the courts began to recognize the unfairness of excluding intangible but highly valuable pension rights in the division of property upon divorce, some courts have similarly begun to realize the unfairness of excluding the intangible but highly valuable assets of an education, degree, and professional licence. New York led the way in recognizing degrees as marital property in *O'Brien* v. *O'Brien* (489 NE 2d 712 (NY 1985)). The court's reasoning illustrates the rationale for the propertization of career assets.

John and Loretta O'Brien were married in 1971. At the time of the marriage Loretta worked as a grammar school teacher and held a bachelor's degree and a temporary teaching certificate. She needed eighteen months of additional study to obtain her permanent certification, but she gave up her plans to support John's education. John had finished three-and-a-half years of college at the time of the marriage, but had quit before obtaining his degree. Loretta (and her parents) encouraged him to finish college and to apply to medical school because he said he had always wanted to be a doctor.

After they were married, John returned to college and received his bachelor's degree. In 1973 the couple moved to Guadalahara, Mexico, so that John could attend medical school. They returned to New York in 1976, where John completed his training and obtained a licence to practice surgery. Two months after obtaining his licence, he filed for divorce.

While her husband attended school, Loretta O'Brien held several teaching and tutorial positions. She contributed all of her income to the marriage. As a result of John's educational expenses, they had accumulated few tangible assets at the time of the divorce.

The trial court granted Loretta O'Brien's claim to a share of her husband's medical degree, which the trial court valued at $472,000. To determine the value of the degree the court calculated the difference between the expected income of the average college-educated white male of John's age, and the average income of the same man with a licence to practice surgery. After valuing the degree as worth $472,000, the court granted Mrs O'Brien 40 per cent of the degree, $188,000, payable in eleven annual instalments.

John immediately appealed the decision, claiming the licence was his personal attainment. Although the intermediate court agreed with him, the New York Court of Appeals upheld the original verdict and issued a strong opinion holding that the medical licence constituted marital property.

The reasoning of the highest court of New York is instructive. After noting that 'the parties' only asset of any consequence is the husband's newly acquired license to practice medicine (*O'Brian* v. *O'Brien* 1985: 580), the court pointed out that New York statutes recognize that 'spouses have an equitable claim to things of value arising out of the marital relationship . . . Those things acquired during marriage and subject to distribution (at divorce) have been classified as "marital property"' (O'Brian 1985: 583). The Court then cited its own decision, recognizing unvested pensions as marital property, and concluded, by analogy, that 'marital property (also) encompasses a license to practice medicine to the extent that the license is acquired during marriage' (O'Brien 1985: 584).

The New York Court explicitly acknowledged the importance of a partnership theory of marriage in its 1980 divorce law: 'Equitable distribution was based on the premise that a marriage is, among other things, an economic partnership to which both parties contribute as spouse, parent, wage earner or homemaker' (O'Brien 1985: 585). It then concluded that recognition of a licence as marital property was not only consistent with the economic partnership theory; it provided one of the best examples of that partnership theory in practice:

> As this case demonstrates, few undertakings during a marriage better qualify as the type of joint effort that the statute's economic partnership theory is intended to address than contributions toward one spouse's acquisition of a professional license. Working spouses are often required to contribute substantial income as wage earners, sacrifice their own educational or career goals and opportunities for child rearing, perform the bulk of household duties and respons-

ibilites and forgo the acquisition of marital assets that could have been accumulated if the professional spouse had been employed rather than occupied with the study and training necessary to acquire a professional license.

In this case, nearly all of the parties' nine-year marriage was devoted to the acquisition of plaintiff's medical license and defendant played a major role in the project. She worked continuously during the marriage and contributed all of her earnings to their joint effort, she sacrificed her own educational and career opportunities, and she travelled with plaintiff to Mexico . . . these contributions represent investments in the economic partnership of the marriage and that the product of the parties' joint efforts, the professional license, should be considered marital property. (O'Brien 1985: 585–6).

The O'Brien decision is important in one additional respect. The court explicitly rejected maintenance or alimony as a way of compensating Loretta O'Brien, because her claim was based on *property*, not on need. As the court stated:

Limiting a working spouse to a maintenance award, either general or rehabilitative, not only is contrary to the economic partnership concept underlying the statute but also retains the uncertain and inequitable economic ties of dependence that the Legislature sought to extinguish by equitable distribution . . . [t]he function of equitable distribution is to recognize that when a marriage ends, each of the spouses, based on the totality of the contributions made to it, has a stake in and right to a share of the marital assets accumulated while it endured, not because that share is needed, but because those assets represent the capital product of what was essentially a partnership entity. (O'Brien 1985: 587)

The Intermediate Approach Most states have settled on an intermediate approach that recognizes the value of the spouse's contribution and tries to compensate her. In *Mahoney* v. *Mahoney* (453 A. 2d 946 NJ 1982)) the New Jersey Supreme Court refused to treat the husband's degree as marital property, but it also wanted to avoid the harsh result of denying the wife any recovery whatsoever, so it introduced the concet of 'reimbursement alimony'.

In *Mahoney* the couple were married for seven years. During that time they generally shared the household expenses, except for a two-year period in which the husband attended the Wharton School of Business and received his degree.

During this period, Mrs Mahoney contributed about $24,000 to the household. While Mr Mahoney was a student, he made no financial contributions. Upon divorce, the wife sought reimbursement for the amount of support she had given her husband while he obtained his degree.

The New Jersey Court expressed concern about the speculative nature of the value of the degree, explaining that it had 'never subjected to equitable distribution an asset whose future monetary value is as uncertain and unquantifiable as a professional degree'. The Court was also disturbed by the fact that the degree did not easily fit traditional notions of property. The Court's conclusion that the amount of future earnings would be 'entirely speculative' seems unresponsive to the request made by the wife for reimbursement. She did not ask that the degree be valued according to the future earning capacity of the husband; she merely wanted restitution of the amount she had contributed towards it. Responding to this request, the Court said that 'valuing educational assets in terms of their cost would be an erroneous application of equitable distribution law', and therefore refused the wife any property claim.

While noting that 'marriage is not a business arrangement in which the parties keep track of debits and credits', the Court realized that it would be unfair to ignore the wife's contribution. Thus, it introduced the concept of reimbursement alimony, suggesting that there will be circumstances where a supporting spouse should be reimbursed for the financial contributions he or she has made to the spouse's successful professional training. It is unclear from the opinion how this 'reimbursement alimony' differs from conventional alimony payments. If it is based upon the need of the non-working spouse and terminable upon remarriage, it does not represent a significant move towards recognizing a real interest for the supporting spouse in the degree. If, however, it is to be awarded solely in recognition of the spouse's contribution towards the degree and is not terminable upon remarriage, a reimbursement alimony award looks less like alimony and more like a property award. This restitutionary notion may, in fact, have been what the court intended to convey. Use of the term alimony rather than property may have been a way for the court to retain jurisdiction to adjust the amount of the award, should the husband's professional career turn out to be less lucrative than originally anticipated.

In *Hubbard* v. *Hubbard* (603 P. 2d 747 (Okla. 1979)) the Supreme Court of Oklahoma provided explicitly for restitution of the supporting spouse's contribution to the acquisition of the professional degree. Mrs Hubbard had worked to support the family for over twelve years while Mr Hubbard attended pre-medical and medical school and completed his internship and residency training. While the court agreed explicitly with the *Graham* court's conclusion that a professional degree is not property, it nevertheless recognized an equitable claim for repayment on the part of the wife.

The court reasoned that allowing Dr Hubbard to retain the entire value of the medical degree and licence would constitute 'unjust enrichment'. Thus, an award of restitution was required by principles of equity. The court wrote, 'There is no reason in law or equity why Dr Hubbard should retain the only valuable asset which was accumulated through joint efforts, i.e. his increased earning capacity, free of claims for reimbursement by his wife'. This conclusion, it should be noted, is not based on notions of property but on an implied contract between the husband and wife to advance the husband's medical career.

The three approaches to the treatment of professional degrees and licences are summarized in Table 5.3, which shows how the states in the United States line up as of June 1990. While twelve states have rejected the concept of a degree as property, twenty-one states take the intermediate approach that attempts to compensate the supporting spouse. New York stands alone in treating the degree as property and in dividing it at divorce.

Valuation and Remedies

Courts have typically used two approaches to calculate the value of a professional education: one focuses on the costs incurred, the second on the gains received (in future earning capacity). A third approach seeks to achieve equity or parity between the parties through an alimony award, or by providing the non-professional spouse with an equivalent opportunity for educational advancement.

TABLE 5.3. *States that recognize degrees as marital property at divorce (as of June 1990)*

Degrees recognized	Intermediate (reimbursement/ restitution	Degrees not recognized
New York	California	Alabama
	Connecticut	Alaska
	Illinois	Arizona
	Indiana	Colorado
	Iowa	Florida
	Louisiana	Kentucky
	Minnesota	Maryland
	Nebraska	Massachusetts
	New Jersey	Michigan
	North Carolina	New Hampshire
	Ohio	South Carolina
	Oklahoma	South Dakota
	Oregon	
	Pennsylvania	
	Tennessee	
	Utah	
	Vermont	
	Virginia	
	West Virginia	
	Washington	
	Wisconsin	

Cost Incurred: The Reimbursement Approach The approach that focuses on the cost of an education is evident in many of the cases discussed above. This method calculates the financial cost of the education at the time it was acquired. Simple estimates focus on the direct, out-of-pocket expenses for tuition, books, lab. fees, bank loans, and living expenses—plus whatever interest that money would have earned if it had instead been invested. More complex calculations include indirect costs such as forgone opportunies.

Benefits Gained: Enhanced Earning Capacity The second approach involves ascertaining the capacity of the professional education to produce a future stream of income. Once such a value is established, the total sum can be divided, or a percentage awarded to each spouse over time. This is the approach the New York Court accepted in the *O'Brien* case.

Equity and Parity: Alimony or an Equivalent Opportunity The third approach does not rely on formulas or calculations. Rather it allows the judge to 'do justice' and create parity. The judge may award some other property to the supporting spouse, or may use an alimony award, or may provide her (or him) with an equivalent educational opportunity. Although the last remedy may be limited to younger and highly motivated spouses, it demonstrates how a judge can provide equity with a creative solution.

A New York court fashioned this type of remedy in the 1975 case of *Morgan* v. *Morgan* (366 NYS 2d 977 (New York 1975)), in which a wife who put her husband through college and law school asked the court to award her support so that she could attend medical school. The case presented a difficult issue, because Mrs Morgan was a skilled executive secretary with 'the ability to be self-supporting'. Yet her husband, a Wall Street attorney at the time of the divorce, was earning three times her current salary.

The judge concluded that 'self-supporting' does not imply that the wife should be compelled to take any position available when her obvious potential in life would be greatly inhibited. Further, the judge recognized that any possible short-term economic cost would be far outweighed by the potential benefit, economic, emotional and otherwise, of her pursuing her education. He decided she should have an opportunity to achieve a professional education comparable to the one her husband had received as a result of her assistance, and he awarded her enough support to complete medical school.

The difficulty of successfully asserting a claim to an equivalent educational opportunity is suggested by the fact that *Morgan* was reversed on appeal. The higher New York court focused on Mrs Morgan's ability to be self-supporting and concluded that, 'although the wife's ambition is most commendable, the court below was in error for including in the alimony award monies for the achievement of that goal'.

Ten years later the highest court in New York changed its mind and recognized a professional degree as marital property in the *O'Brien* case discussed above. If Mrs Morgan had been divorced ten years later, her fate would have been very different.

Medical Insurance

For European readers who assume that one's basic medical needs are covered by national health insurance, it is hard to imagine the crisis that one faces in a society in which most medical insurance is linked to employment, and divorced spouses, who were previously covered as dependents on their husband's policies, suddenly find themselves with no medical insurance coverage at all. In the United States 37 million people (about 15 per cent of the US population) have no medical insurance, either because they are not employed, or because they are employed part time or in industries which do not provide medical benefits (National Center for Health Statistics 1988: 171).

During a marriage in which only one spouse is employed outside the home, the members of the employee's family are covered as his or her dependents and share in the benefits for doctors' fees, medicine, hospital care, and other health and accident protection. Upon divorce, the non-employed spouse (typically the wife) and minor children generally lose this coverage because of the traditonal assumption that the rights to insurance belong only to the worker.

Increased awareness of the value of these entitlements, and an influential article by Yale Law School Professor Charles Reich arguing that the new property in our society is the property of entitlement—i.e. the right to government and private benefits such as medical insurance (Reich 1964–5)—led to claims that this new property should be divided upon divorce. There are really two issues here, and they parallel those for pensions and educational degrees: whether insurance rights are 'assets' or 'property', and whether they should be, and can be, divided upon divorce. There is a very slow but steady trend to answer both questions affirmatively.

The assertion that insurance rights are a form of property is most convincingly put forth by those who experience the results of losing these rights at divorce. For example, consider the story told by one 52-year-old woman we interviewed in California:

> Since I had always been covered by Bill's policy at Lockheed I never thought about insurance, and no one mentioned it when we drew up the divorce settlement. We agreed to have Bill keep the kids on his policy, but since he was going to remarry I couldn't be covered as his wife. About two years before the divorce, I [had] found a lump in my breast and they removed it and said it was benign.
>
> After the divorce, when I applied for individual Blue Cross they wrote in a cancer exclusion because of my history. There was nothing I could do, it was take it or leave it . . . Then, when I discovered the other lump about eight months later, I went into a total panic. I had to have a radical [mastectomy] and chemotherapy, and there was no way I could possibly afford it. I just wanted to die . . . I did think of suicide—but I couldn't leave the kids. (Weitzman 1985: 136)

A similar experience led Tish Sommers, president and founder of the Older Women's League (OWL), to successful advocacy of insurance conversion laws (Klemesrud 1980). These laws permit a divorced woman who was once covered by a group or family policy to be able to convert to an individual policy without new proof of eligibility. When Sommers was divorced at the age of 57, she lost her health insurance under her husband's policy and was subsequently refused coverage 'by one carrier after another' because she had a history of cancer. Then, six months before she became eligible for Medicare, she suffered a recurrence of cancer and faced expensive radiation treatments with no medical or hospital insurance whatsoever.

'In today's medical economy, health coverage is a must', argues Frances Leonard, legal counsel for the Older Women's League. 'It is no longer possible for an individual to pay his or her own medical expenses' (Leonard 1984: 1). Yet access to medical care is almost entirely through employment-related health plans. Since women are often covered as dependents of employees, they are especially vulnerable at divorce, when they may lose their dependency status and their insurance coverage. Women between the ages of 45 and 65 are most severely affected, because they are often unable to secure individual coverage if they lose their group coverage. They are too young for Medicare, the national medical programme for those over 65, and they are too old to be 'good risks' for private coverage.

As of January 1990 twenty three states had statutes providing for the conversion of insurance upon divorce (Freed and Walker 1990: 555). In some states the statutes provide that accident and health-insurance policies which terminate upon divorce *must* contain a conversion privilege for divorced spouses without proof of insurability. This means that the insurer must offer a conversion policy to a dependent spouse without regard to whether he or she would normally qualify, and must bypass the physical examination and doctor's report normally required to obtain coverage.

Even these laws may not go far enough in providing divorced wives with adequate medical and hospital insurance. Many of the conversion policies afford far less coverage than the original policy and require the beneficiary to pay costly premiums to maintain them. For example, one of the women we interviewed found, to her dismay, that her conversion policy cost over $5,000 a year.

Dental insurance is another valuable asset that is often lost at divorce, as one 53-year-old woman we interviewed discovered:

> It was always my dental health that could wait . . . There is a yearly ceiling on each family's bill under the company dental insurance plan, so Andy and the kids went first . . . I never intended to do without it, but it was always to be next year . . . and then next year . . . Last year, my turn finally came, after the divorce, and it cost me $6,000. His teeth, of course, were paid for, as a community expense. (Weitzman 1985: 137)

The loss of medical and dental insurance is particularly troubling for long-term wives who feel that they are being pushed out to make room for new wives (who are more likely to be employed and to have insurance in their own right.) The Older Women's League has pressed for legislation to guarantee long-married wives the right to remain a member of their ex-husbands' group plans (which typically provide better coverage and lower premiums than conversion policies). In 1986 the Older Women's League won a partial victory when the US Congress passed Public Law 99–272, a group health insurance continuation law. This law requires employers to allow divorced spouses and children (as well as widows and children) to remain members of the group, as long as they pay their own premiums, for a period of three years.

The same principle was used by 55-year-old Edith Curtis, who applied for state unemployment compensation after her thirty-five-year marriage to a college professor ended in divorce (Bernard 1984). Although Curtis had never been employed, and had not contributed to the unemployment insurance fund, she claimed that all of the fringe benefits and assets of her husband's career were community property in Idaho, and that she was entitled to share them (Chase 1985). Although Edith Curtis lost her suit, the case for an expanded definition of career assets as marital property, including unemployment benefits, is certainly not closed. Some claims to unconventional assets have fared better. For example, courts have been willing to consider claims for a share of personal injury awards as marital property if they were compensation for lost earnings or medical expenses borne by the marital community. (See Blumberg 1986 for an extensive discussion of these assets.)

Finally, in some states, life and disability insurance policies, whether privately owned or company financed, are treated as marital assets to be divided at divorce. Even if a policy has no cash surrender value, the court may order the wage-earner to maintain payments on the policy to keep his children or former wife listed as the beneficiary; this also provides some protection against the loss of support payments if the wage-earner dies or is killed in an accident (Freed and Walker 1985).

Conclusion

What does this discussion of the new property reveal? How does it affect our conclusions about the extent to which property is being divided equally or equitably upon divorce?

We have seen that the career assets analysed in this chapter are typically acquired during marriage in the same manner that other marital property is acquired. These assets are, along with the family home, often the most valuable assets a couple owns at the time of the divorce. If courts do not recognize some or all of these assets as marital property, they are excluding a major portion of a couple's property from the pool of property to be divided upon divorce. In addition, if the courts treat these assets as the property of only the major wage-earner, they are in most cases allowing the husband to keep the family's most valuable assets.

Obviously, any conclusions made about the *de facto* equality or inequality of current divisions of property will rest on whether career assets are defined as 'marital property'.

If we accept the current limited definition of property used by many US courts, we are led to two (erroneous) conclusions: first, that the property of most divorcing couples is relatively modest; and, second, that their property is being divided equally.

On the other hand, if we adopt an expanded definition of property that includes the intangible assets of a marriage, such as the career assets discussed in this chapter, we are led to two very different conclusions: first, that most divorcing couples have accumulated property of considerable value; and, second, that the husband typically leaves the marriage with most of their assets.

As the second set of conclusions gains acceptance in the US, we see growing dissatisfaction with the law and a rise in claims to share the new property. Increasingly, divorce courts are being asked to recognize and divide pensions, professional degrees, goodwill, medical insurance, and a range of other career assets. This is one of the most innovative and rapidly changing areas of family law, and the changes are visible in both legislative and case-law developments throughout the United States.

Legal decisions about the new property that will be made in the next decade will have profound long-term consequences, and be critical in defining and redefining the nature of the marital partnership in our time.

Research support from the Rockefeller Foundation's Program on Gender Roles, the German Marshall Fund, and the National Science Foundation is gratefully acknowledged.

References

Arendell, T. (1986), *Mothers and Divorce* (Berkeley, Calif.).

Avner, J., and Greene, K. (1982), 'State ERA Impact on Family Law', *Family Law Reporter*, 8: 4023–35).

Baker, B. (1987), *Family Equity at Issue: A Study of the Economic Consequences of Divorce on Women and Children* (Alaska Women's Commission, Achorage, Alaska).

Bernard, K. (1984), 'Her Day in Court: Divorce Takes "Benefits" Fight to High Court', *Lewiston Morning Tribune*, 11 Oct.

Bianchi, S. M., and Spain, D. (1986), *American Women in Transition* (New York).

Bissett-Johnson, A., and Newell, S. (1988), 'Professional Degrees in Marital Property: Canadian Developments', *Community Property Journal*, 15: 63–77.

Blumberg, G. (1986), 'Marital Property Treatment of Pensions, Disability Pay, Workers' Compensation, and Other Wage Substitutes: An Insurance, or Replacement Analysis', *UCLA Law Review*, 33: 1250–1308.

California Civil Code (1982–90) (St Paul Minn.).

California Senate (1987), *Final Report of the Task Force on Family Equity* 1 June (Sacramento, Calif.).

Chase, M. (1985), 'Single Trouble: The No-Fault Divorce has a Fault of its Own, Many Women Learn', *Wall Street Journal*, 21 Jan.

Clark, H. (1988), *The Law of Domestic Relations in the United States* (St Paul, Minn.).

Cohen, H. N., and Hillman, A. S. (1984), *Analysis of Seventy Select Decisions after Trial under New York State's Equitable Distribution Law, from January 1981 through October 1984* (1 Nov.) (New York Women's Bar Association, New York).

Ellman, I. (1989), 'The Theory of Alimony', *California Law Review*, 77: 1–77.

Fineman, M. (1989), 'Societal Factors Affecting the Creation of Legal Rules for Distribution of Property at Divorce', *Family Law Quarterly*, 23/2: 279–99.

Foster, H. H., jun., and Freed, D. J. (1984), 'Law and the Family: Politics of Divorce Process—Bargaining Leverage, Unfair Edge', *New York Law Journal*, 19217: 6, 11 July.

Freed, D. J., and Walker, T. B. (1985), 'Family Law in the Fifty States: An Overview', *Family Law Quarterly*, 18/4: 426–7.

————(1989), 'Family Law in the Fifty States: An Overview', *Family Law Quarterly*, 22/3: 1–115.

————(1990), 'Family Law in the Fifty States: An Overview', *Family Law Quarterly*, 23/4: 495–608.

Garrison, M. (1990), 'The Economics of Divorce: Changing Rules,

Changing Results', in S. D. Sugerman and H. H. Kay (eds.), *Divorce Reform at the Crossroads* (New Haven, Conn.).

Gilligan, C. (1983), *In a Different Voice* (Cambridge, Mass.).

Glendon, M. A. (1982), 'Property Rights upon Dissolution of Marriages and Informal Unions', in N. E. Eastham and B. Krivy (eds.), *The Cambridge Lectures 1981* (London).

——(1987), *Abortion and Divorce in Western Law* (Cambridge, Mass.).

Goode, W. J. (1956), *After Divorce* (later: *Woman in Divorce*) (New York).

Harvard & Radcliffe: Official Register of Harvard University 1990–91 (1990) (Cambridge, Mass.).

Holstrom, L. (1972), *The Two-Career Family* (Cambridge, Mass.).

Kay, H. H. (1987*a*), 'Equality and Difference: A Perspective on No-Fault Divorce and its Aftermath', *University of Cincinnati Law Review*, 56: 1–55.

—— (1987b), 'An Appraisal of California's No-Fault Divorce Law', *California Law Review*, 75: 291–319.

——(1990), 'Beyond No-Fault: New Directions in Divorce Reform', in S. D. Sugerman and H. H. Kay (eds.), *Divorce Reform at the Crossroads* (New Haven, Conn.).

Klemesrud, J. (1980), 'New Focus on Concerns of Older Women', *New York Times*, 13 Oct.

Krauskopf, J. (1980), 'Recompense for Financing Spouse's Education: Legal Protection for the Marital Investor in Human Capital', *University of Kansas Law Review*, 28: 379–417.

Leonard, F. (1980), 'Older Women and Pensions: Catch 22', in T. Sommers and L. Shields, (eds.), *Gray Paper No. 1* (Washington DC).

——(1984), 'Access to Health Insurance for Mid-life Women: An Overview', memo, Older Women's League (Washington DC).

Levy, R. (1969), 'Uniform Marriage and Divorce Legislation: A Preliminary Analysis', 'internal document prepared by the Reporter of the Special Committee on Divorce of the National Conference of Commissioners on Uniform State Laws' (Chicago, Ill.).

Manners, A. J., and Rauta, I. (1981), *Family Property in Scotland* (Edinburgh).

Marcus, I. (1989), 'Locked In and Locked Out: Reflections on the History of Divorce Law Reform in New York State', *Buffalo Law Review*, 37: 375.

McGraw, R. E., Sterin, G. J., and Davis, J. M. (1981–2), 'A Case Study in Divorce Law Reform and its Aftermath', *Journal of Family Law*, 20/3: 443–87.

McLindon, J. (1987), 'Separate but Unequal: The Economic

Disaster of Divorce for Women and Children', *Family Law Quarterly*, 21: 351–409.

MOZLEY, D., 'The Other Side of the Ex-Spouse Coin', *Navy Times*, 12 July 1982, p. 21.

National Center for Health Statistics (1988), *Health: United States 1988* (US Department of Health and Human Services, Rockville, Md.).

OLDER WOMAN'S LEAGUE (1990), *Heading for Hardship: Retirement Income for American Women in the Next Century* (Washington DC).

PAPANECK, H. (1973), 'Men, Women, and Work: Reflections on the Two-Person Career', *American Journal of Sociology*, 78: 852–72.

PEARSON, J. (1984), 'Summary of Research', paper prepared for the Wingspread Conference on Child Custody, sponsored by the Women's Legal Defense Fund, Mar. (Wingspread, Wisconsin).

PEER, R. (1984), 'Study Challenges Pension Proposal: Effect upon Women of Social Security Formula Disputed', *New York Times*, 30 Dec.

POLIKOFF, N. (1983), 'Gender and Child-Custody Determinations: Exploding the Myths', in I. Diamond (ed.), *Families, Politics and Public Policies: A Feminist Dialogue on Women and the State* (New York).

PORTER, S. (1980), 'New Older Women's League Helps that Invisible Group', *Boston Herald*, 13 Oct.

PRAGER, S. (1977), 'Sharing Principles and the Future of Marital Property Law', *UCLA Law Review*, 25:1: 6–11.

QUADAGNO, J. (1988), 'Women's Access to Pensions and the Structure of Eligibility Rules: Systems of Production and Reproduction', *Sociological Quarterly*, 29/4: 541–58.

REICH, C. (1964–5), 'Individual Rights and Social Welfare: The Emerging Legal Issues', *Yale Law Journal*, 74: 1245–57.

RESKIN, B. F., and HARTMAN, H. I. (1986) (eds.), *Women's Work, Men's Work: Sex Segregation on the Job* (Washington DC).

ROWE, B. R., and MORROW, A. M. (1988), 'The Economic Consequences of Divorce in Oregon after 10 or More Years of Marriage', *Willamette Law Review*, 24: 463–85.

SCHULMAN, J., and PITT, V. (1982), 'Second Thoughts on Joint Custody: Analysis of Legislation and its Impact for Women and Children', *Golden Gate University Law Review*, 12/3: 539–77.

SEAL, K. (1977), 'A Decade of No-Fault Divorce', *Family Advocate*, 1/1: 10, 11, 14, 15.

Social Security Bulletin: Annual Statistical Supplement (1989) (Washington DC).

TODD, J., and JONES, L. (1972), *Matrimonial Property* (London).

TURNQUIST, K. (1983), 'Military Injustice: Ex-Wives Are Casualties—

Divorce is a Raw Deal for Wives of Servicemen', *Willamett Week*, 18 Jan.

United States Bureau of the Census (1981), *Child Support and Alimony, 1978* (Current Population Reports Series P–23, No. 112); Washington DC).

——(1983), *Child Support and Alimony, 1981* (Current Population Reports, Series P–23, No. 124; Washington DC).

——(1989*a*), *Money, Income, and Poverty Status in the US, 1988* (Current Population Reports, Series P–60, No. 166; Washington DC).

——(1989*b*), *Statistical Abstract of the US 1989* (109th edn., Washington, DC).

——(1990) *Statistical Abstract of the US 1990* (110th edn., Washington DC).

WALLSTON, B. S., FOSTER, M. A., and BERGER, M. (1978), 'I Will Follow Him: Myth, Reality or Forced Choice—Job Seeking Experiences of Dual Career Couples', in J. Bryson and R. Bryson (eds.), *Dual Career Couples* (New York).

WEISBERGER, J. (1985), 'The Wisconsin Marital Property Act: Highlights of the Wisconsin Experience in Developing a Model for Comprehensive Common Law Property Reform', *Wisconsin Women's Law Journal*, 1: 5.

——(1981*a*), *The Marriage Contract: Spouses, Lovers and the Law* (New York).

——(1981*b*), 'The Economic Consequences of Divorce', *UCLA Law Review*, 28/6: 1181–1268.

——(1985), *The Divorce Revolution: The Unexpected Social and Economic Consequences for Women and Children in America* (New York).

——and DIXON, R. B. (1980), 'The Alimony Myth: Does No-Fault Make a Difference', *Family Law Quarterly*, 14/3: 141–85.

WEITZMAN, L. J. (1974), 'Legal Regulation of Marriage: Tradition and Change', *California Law Review* 62: 1269–88.

WISHIK, H.R. (1986), 'Economics of Divorce: An Exploratory Study', *Family Law Quarterly*, 20: 79–103.

WOMEN'S LEGAL DEFENSE FUND (1983), *Your Pension Rights at Divorce: What Women Need to Know* (Washington DC).

6. Australia: A Proposal for Reform

Kathleen Funder

In Australia, as in many Western countries (OECD 1990), the economic hardship of marriage breakdown falls heavily on women with dependent children. Recognition of this economic burden, and of its unequal division, can be seen in recent inquiries and reviews, including the Maintenance Inquiry (1986), and the Social Security Review (1986*a*). Actual and proposed reforms appear to have three main objectives: the alleviation of poverty, a reduction in public costs associated with the support of lone-parent families, and a more equal distribution of the hardship of divorce.

The Dimensions of hardship

The Australian Family Law Act 1975 introduced non-fault divorce and marked a watershed in marriage dissolution, with the rates in the 1980s plateauing at a very much higher level than would have been predicted a decade before. By 1987 the crude divorce rate in Australia was 2.4 divorces per 1,000 population, a figure which has been fairly stable in recent years. The Australian Institute of Family Studies (AIFS) estimates indicate that 30–3 per cent of marriages contracted in the 1970s will end in divorce, with a small decline predicted in the future, based on a tendency towards later marriage and a lower marriage rate. The divorce rate in 1987 was 11 per 1,000 married women, with the highest rate of 18.7 per cent applying at ages 25–9. In that year 39,700 divorces were granted, involving 44,100 dependent children.

In 1985 Australia had about four million families, 2.18 million (54.6 per cent) of which were families with dependent children. Of these families with dependent children 315,000 (14.4 per cent) had only one parent, and 261,000 (83.0 per cent) of the lone-parent families were receiving some social security payments (Social Security Review 1986*b*). Most lone-parent families (278,000 or 88.2 per cent) are female-headed, and these women and their children are more likely than male-headed families to be in receipt of pensions or benefits.

Lone-parent families are more likely to be poor. In 1981–2, 56.2 per cent (177,000) of female lone parents were in the lowest decile of unit incomes, compared with 17.2 per cent (6,200) of their male counterparts and 3.5 per cent of married couples. Thus being female increases by almost thirtyfold the chances of being a very poor lone parent. Most (63.2 per cent) female lone parents received their main income from social security/welfare sources (Social Security Review 1986*b*). In the decade 1978–88 the number of beneficiaries had more than trebled, with a commensurate growth in costs.

The Family Law Act—Provisions for Financial Settlements

Three means of achieving just and equitable financial outcomes are available under the Family Law Act. First, property can be reallocated between the parties. Secondly, adjustment may be made through the award of spousal maintenance, subject to the twin conditions of the needs of one spouse and the capacity to pay off the other. Thirdly, child maintenance orders may transfer money from the non-resident parent to the resident parent on the basis of continuing shared responsibility for the financial support of children of the marriage. A major difference between the property and maintenance orders is that maintenance orders may be adjusted according to changing needs and capacities to pay, while property settlements are immutable.

Under the Australian Family Law Act 1975 marriage does not change the property rights of the individual. Without an assumption of community of property, no base line for its division applies. In Mallett's case, the High Court rejected a 50 : 50 baseline for property division, leaving judges with wide discretionary powers in allocating property in order to arrive at a just and equitable outcome. Two broad sets of considerations are applied in reaching such a settlement: the contributions each party has made to the economy of the marriage and their respective needs after the dissolution. Contributions to the economic partnership of the marriage may be both financial and non-financial, direct and indirect. Thus home-making and child-rearing, as well as contributions from the money economy, are included in assessing how much each has invested. (Family Law Act, s. 79 (4)). A list of possible sources of need may also be weighed by the court in arriving at a fair and equitable settlement (FLA s. 75 (2)). Basically, needs are assessed in terms of post-separation circumstances, whereas contributions concern the efforts of the parties during the marriage. Such a neat division serves a useful purpose in dividing the law into manageable segments for reference; it is rarely so easy to divide life circumstances into pre- and post-separation phases, or into contributions without consequences or needs unrelated to marriage.

Under section 81 of the Family Law Act the court shall, as far as practicable, make such orders as will finally determine the financial relationships between the parties to the marriage and avoid further proceedings between them. This section is an endorsement of the clean-break framework. Whether by design or by accident, spousal maintenance orders, as they are currently used, fit more or less well within the clean-break principle. Orders are relatively rare and ongoing orders are commonly complied with only until property settlements are finalized (Harrison 1986).

Child maintenance orders are made on the basis of the needs of the children and the responsibility of both parents to provide care and support for them. Orders are not final in intent, since they are meant to be responsive to children's changing needs and parents' changing circumstances. In practice, however, the AIFS survey data show that such orders, when made, were commonly not varied and thus remained at their original level, or were simply not complied with (Harrison and McDonald 1988). The new Child Support Scheme, introduced in 1988, is designed to increase both compliance with orders and the amount of child maintenance paid.

Problem Areas of the Law under Review

Criticisms of the operation of the law received by a Joint Select Committee of the Federal Parliament (1980) were that wide discretion resulted in uncertainty, inconsistency, and excessive legal costs. In 1983 the Attorney-General referred the issue of Matrimonial Property to the Australian Law Reform Commission. An AIFS survey, designed to provide a representative picture of the economic consequences of marriage breakdown and the role of the law, showed that for families with dependent children economic hardship fell disproportionately on women (Weston 1986).

Women living alone or as lone parents experienced a drastic fall in living standards three to five years after separation. Their average household income was just over 50 per cent of the pre-separation income; men who had not repartnered had about 80 per cent of their pre-separation household income. However, as in this study most women who had not repartnered were caring for two children, over half still ended up living in poverty in spite of any maintenance paid. Only 13 per cent of single men were similarly poor, and many were better off on an income-needs ratio than before separation. Contrary to the myth, women were 'asset rich and income poor', since 92 per cent of the group received a property allocation below the limit which entitles a woman to full social security benefit.

Rules for the systematic allocation of property between spouses, many of whom bargain in the shadow of the law, were difficult to find, and many respondents reported divisions of property outside the 60 : 40 range. Outcomes which are so variable may indicate the flexibility of the law to deal with individual circumstances, though such an interpretation was not supported in a survey of disputed cases before judges and registrars (Schwartzkoff and Rizzo 1985). Although Family Court judges and registrars reported weighing up contributions of spouses to the marriage, they cited property-settlement outcomes at about 50 : 50. The AIFS study, however, showed that the needs of the custodial parent for housing appeared to be an important factor, weighing shares in the property in favour of the custodian. When businesses or farms were part of the property, however, shares were more variable, with valuation of these assets posing a problem (McDonald 1986). Contributions made to the business and ownership were important in deciding how much each party received.

In addition to documenting the inequitable distribution of property, the AIFS study showed that some property, such as superannuation benefits, were omitted or inconsistently treated in property settlements, although they were often of significant value (McDonald 1986). The implications are that the law must consider both the definition of property and the rules for its division.

Systematic inequalities in outcome, resulting in serious hardship for many, were redressed neither by property settlement nor by spousal maintenance payments, which were very rarely reported by the surveyed men and women. Moreover, child maintenance was not regularly ordered or paid, and when paid was at an almost uniformly low level. Thus property settlements, spousal maintenance, and child maintenance appear ineffective in achieving a fair distribution of the financial burdens of divorce.

Gender Gap and Opportunity Costs of Children

The disparity in standard of living between men and women is largely due to their different earning capacities, which does not appear to be offset by maintenance paid, or property transferred, and to the woman's disproportionate burden of financial and care responsibility for the children of the marriage. There are two components to the disparity in income. The first concerns the gender gap in earnings which exists in Australia; the second is related to the differing effects of marriage, child-bearing, and child-rearing upon the income-earning capacity of men and women (Funder 1986).

It is unrealistic to expect individuals, and the legal system, to attempt to redress structural inequalities (i.e. gender differences) in employment and earnings. Thus, discussion of the impact of the present law on the economic circumstances of men, women, and children after divorce must distinguish between the general social and economic influences on income, which account for continuing differences between average earnings for men and women, and those factors which are particular to marriage and the law relating to its dissolution.

In Australia, in spite of legislation phasing in equal pay since the mid-1960s, by 1984 adult women's full-time, ordinary hours' earnings were still only 80 per cent those of men (Australian Bureau of Statistics (ABS) 1987). Causes of this discrepancy include sex differences in education (particularly in science and technology), sex segregation in the job market, and associated differences in opportunity for on-job training and career advancement. Moreover, although the importance of sex discrimination is debated, there is strong evidence that gender, net of credentials, years of experience, and hours worked account for some of the income differential (Jones 1983).

Differences in men's and women's earnings are also influenced by family-related interruptions to work, which are reflected in the broken-work histories of married women with children (less than 1 per cent of the women in the AIFS study had uninterrupted work histories compared with 96 per cent of men), and their common return to work part time. In the clerical, sales, and service occupations, women make up 65 per cent of the workers, but almost half are part time. Time out of work depreciates human capital measured by earning capacity (Mincer 1980), and tailoring work to children's needs seems to involve downward occupational mobility, further depressing earnings (Funder 1986; Joshi 1984).

Marriage-related effects on women's earnings were described in the AIFS study of divorced women (Funder 1986). Lone mothers who had spent more than two-thirds of their married life out of the workforce were $50 per week (25 per cent of the average net income for this group) worse off than those who had been out of the workforce less than one-third of the marriage. This difference persisted when other factors such as education, occupational level, and time since separation were statistically controlled and all income transfers between the partners included. Women withdrew from the workforce almost exclusively to bear and rear children, and it is to this that their lower earnings are attributable. Although it seemed plausible that property transfers made under the Family Law Act, section 8, might have offset some or all of this imbalance, no evidence for such counter-balancing transfers was found.

Past and continuing care of children was a powerful influence on earnings, yet couples chose to reduce the wife's participation in the paid workforce to give her more time to care for the home and children—an arrangement confirmed in an AIFS national study of maternity leave (Glezer 1988). Women rarely indicated that lack of job opportunity or child-care provisions was the most important hindrance to their employment. The high value put on the quality of parenting for young children clearly runs counter to economic independence for women. Within marriage, however, partners make their priorities, including the child-rearing conditions for their children, and share the benefits and costs of their decisions.

The balance between paid work and work in the home is a powerful determinant of the inequities observed in the settlement of the economic aspects of the marriage partnership. Time, tasks and resources, and the location of residence are commonly organized as part of a strategy to maximize the security and earnings of the husband usually the higher earner. The wife will normally be an integral part of the productive unit, giving precedence to employment obligations, assuming major responsibility for the children and home-making. The cost and benefits of these arrangements are shared during the marriage.

It is evident, however, that the benefits of investing in the husband's career—his security of employment, his increasing earning capacity based on continuous employment, experience, and efforts in the work place—are not to the wife's advantage after separation. Conversely, the costs borne by the marriage partnership of the depreciation of the wife's earning capacity through interrupted participation, downward occupational mobility, and part time participation (which tends to be in sectors without career paths) are not passed on to the husband after separation.

Opportunity Costs and Family Law

The fact that financial settlements under the Family Law Act, 1975, in Australia systematically leave women with dependent children bearing the greater burden was acknowledged by the Australian Law Reform Commission (1986). A major cause of this inequality was seen in the discrepancy in income-needs ratios between men and women which derived in part from the division of labour—past and present—in the care of children.

Two avenues for redress are possible under the Family Law Act: first through spousal and child maintenance provisions, and second through property division. At first sight, the maintenance approach appears logical and direct. Under section 77(2)(k) one of the matters to be taken into account in awarding spousal maintenance is 'the duration of the marriage and the extent to which it has affected the earning capacity of the party whose maintenance is under consideration'. Women who have reduced earnings associated with having assumed primary responsibility for the care of children during the marriage could claim a transfer from the spouse, thus equalizing or at least sharing the deficit as they had done during the marriage. Moreover, the earning decrement which is associated with the ongoing care of children after the separation might be seen as part of the costs of maintaining children, albeit indirect costs, and be taken into account in calculating periodic child maintenance.

Objections to using the maintenance provisions to share the opportunity and direct costs of children relate to the violation of the clean-break principle which is widely espoused. Moreover, at a pragmatic level, the court's record for enforcing any sort of maintenance order has been so poor that this course has been largely eschewed; lawyers frequently recommend 'a bird in the hand' approach. In the new Child Support Scheme the assumption has been made that the indirect costs of children are a component of the resident parent's support of the child. In general, however, the notion of open-ended or very long-term spousal support is commonly rejected by both men and women (Harrison 1986). Alimony cuts across the psychological meaning of divorce as the severence of interdependent spousal relationships at all possible levels.

In practice, clean break has come to mean settlement day, whether in court, a lawyer's office, or elsewhere; any continuing transfers are seen as a violation of the principle. In some cases, however, because of the complexity of business, or the lack of liquid assets, payments are made over time in order to reach a fair financial settlement. Thus there are precedents for the clean break being achieved over a limited period of time. The principle of severence of interdependencies is thus observed, but not at the expense of an equitable settlement. The door is open for finite spousal maintenance—not recurrent—as a means of obtaining fair outcomes in some cases where to insist on a settlement-day approach would risk injustice to one of the parties.

The unequal burden may also be redistributed through the property settlement. Precedent exists for this, in that custodial parents tend to receive more of the basic assets than non-resident parents (McDonald 1986). This often secures the children's home and may well represent a lump-sum child maintenance component (although legally it is not seen as such). Securing housing for children and their resident parents is important psychologically, socially, and economically, and has been shown to accelerate re-entry into the paid workforce (Wulff 1988). Where hardship is unequally shared and there is sufficient property, a component might be transferred to the party who bears the greater burden of past and future child-care responsibilities. Where insufficient property exists, periodic payments could be made over a specified time.

If family law is to play any part in redressing the inequalities which currently exist, that component of inequality which derives from structural features of the Australian workforce must be distinguished from that part which derives from the marriage. It is only the latter which may fairly be considered the responsibility of the parties to the marriage, and hence come under the domain of family law.

Differences in earnings between men and women reflect a variety of causative factors, but are none the less consistently described. Some differences exist even when education, occupation, and continuity in the workforce are held constant. Fig. 6.1 shows a schematic representation of the lifetime earnings of men and women who have had continuous work experience. The 'gender gap' in earnings is represented by the difference between the two lines. This gap, although a serious inequality, cannot be attributed to the marriage. Children are, however, part of the business of a marriage. Their care and financial support are the responsibility of the two partners who must allocate time and effort to children's needs. The way in which they do this, although constrained by gender differences in wage rates, is a private matter. It is part of the conduct of the marriage and is assumed to be a joint decision, maximizing the benefits of the partnership. The usual pattern is for the mother to withdraw from the paid workforce to bear and rear children, returning part time as their needs diminish.

When women withdraw from the workforce to care for

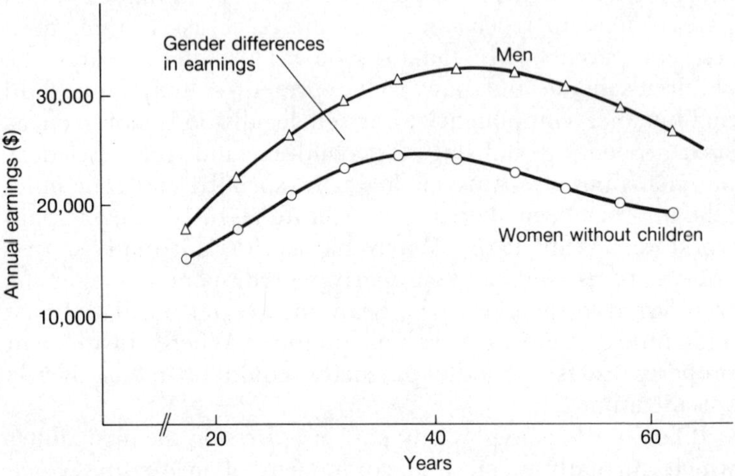

FIG. 6.1. Average earnings of men and of women without children

children, the opportunity costs they incur from child-rearing may be expressed in terms of lifetime earnings *vis-à-vis* women of similar background who have had continuous work experience. It would not be appropriate to count these costs in comparison with the earnings of men, since there are structural differences which explain at least some of the differences in earnings between men and women, shown in Fig. 6.1. Opportunity costs of women who withdraw from the workforce to care for children may be calculated by comparing the earnings of women who have children with those of like women who have uninterrupted work histories. Fig. 6.2 shows how these opportunity costs are defined. Fig. 6.2 shows a hypothetical comparison between the lifetime earning streams of women with similar educational and occupational backgrounds. The gap between the two reflects the wage losses attributed to the efforts and time devoted to children and resulting in loss of earnings. This loss is referred to as the opportunity costs of children.

Some of these costs are shared in the marriage partnership, and losses of income are counted against the quality of life for all family members and the parents' investment in the children. The benefits of children and quality of life are

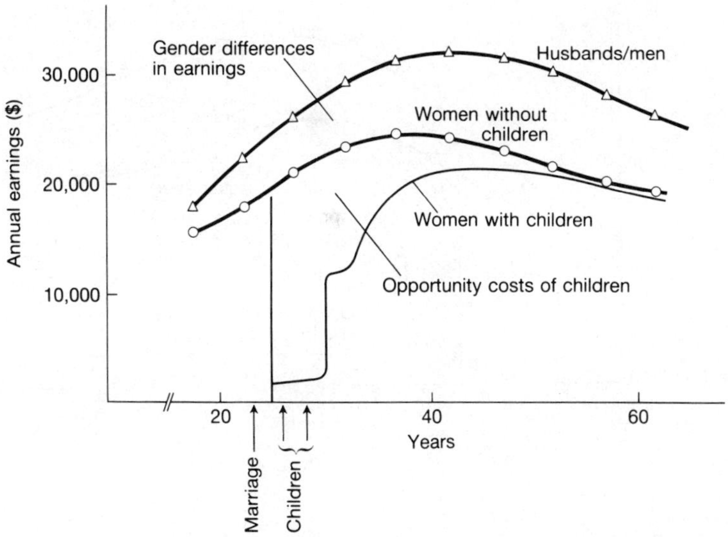

FIG. 6.2. Average earnings of men, women without children, and women with children

shared, as are the loss of all or part of one spouse's income. This is not the subject for reallocation. These costs, however, continue in the future in two ways which are relevant to the financial settlement of the marriage partnership. First, the depreciation of earnings originating in the care of children of the marriage continues to be felt in the post-separation period. Secondly, this is commonly exacerbated by the demands that dependent children continue to make on the custodial parent, who is most often the same parent who has taken prime responsibility for them during the marriage. Although it is recognized here that these two components are separate, and that the continuing indirect costs of children after separation might be treated as a factor in calculating child maintenance, they are considered together at this point.

Fig. 6.3 shows how opportunity costs, calculated against the lifetime earnings expected for like women, may be estimated. Also shown is the allocation of these opportunity costs into two categories: those which were shared during the marriage and those which were borne solely by the woman, who took

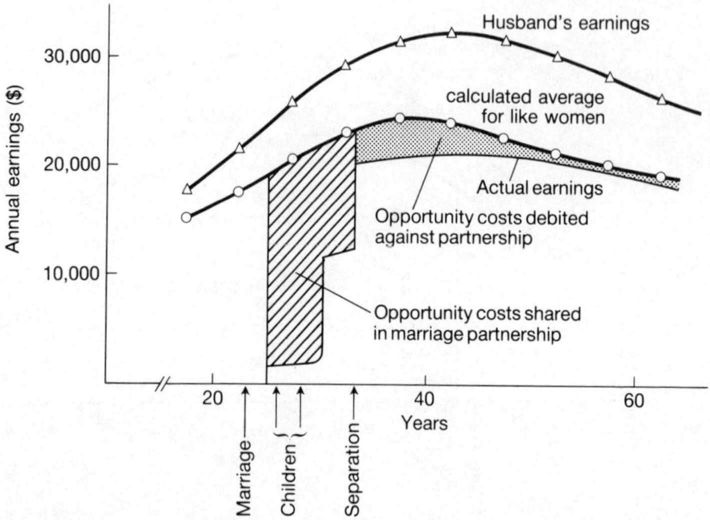

FIG. 6.3. Estimated opportunity costs

the primary role in rearing the children. As the lost earnings during the marriage were shared by the partnership, they are not the concern of settlement. Only the deferred costs borne solely by the wife are considered as a debt against the marriage partnership.

An Alternative Approach

Any alternative approach to settlement of the marriage partnership should conform with a number of principles:

1. it should produce just and equitable outcomes;
2. it should be consistent with the principle of marriage as a partnership of equals which does not exploit one partner at the expense of the other;
3. it should be predictable and accountable, making public the principles and means of calculating the shares;
4. it should include a means of putting a money value on one of the most significant determinants of present inequalities—the depreciated earning capacity of women who have assumed the primary responsibility for

rearing children and who have withdrawn or modified their workforce participation to fulfil this role;

5. it should cover most cases in a fair and equitable way but allow the right of appeal against the application of the system to unusual cases where outcomes would be unjust.

At the heart of this proposal is the concept that labour invested in raising children and making a home detracts from present or future efforts in the paid workforce. The withdrawal from the workforce has immediate costs to the marriage partnership in terms of lost earnings which are shared during the marriage, as are the attendant advantages of having happy children, a secure income, and a certain quality of life. As with the whole working economy of the marriage and the various contributions of the parties, this loss is not the subject of the settlement.

When a marriage ends, the costs of the depreciated earnings which were previously absorbed by the partnership are carried by the partner whose paid work has been interrupted and whose individual earnings are reduced. The partner who has stayed in the workforce, usually the husband, has typically increased his earning capacity through experience, extra training, earning increments which come with years of service, reputation as a worker, goodwill in business, etc., all of which can only be earned with years of uninterrupted service to a profession. This means that, instead of the assets (increased earning capacity) and the losses (depreciation in earnings) being shared, since they were in part or whole acquired during the marriage, the husband is left with the assets and the wife with the loss.

Fairness demands that the debt of continued depreciated earnings be claimed against the total assets of the partnership and by virtue of contributions to it. The debt should not be claimed against the husband, in as much as both parties decided to apportion their roles on the tacit understanding that the benefits and costs be shared. It is thus a debt to be claimed against the marriage partnership at the time of settlement. The principle suggested here differs from the current thinking in several important ways.

It assumes that ex-wives, among whom are many poor and

welfare recipients, have earned the right to some deferred payments against the losses they incurred in making their contributions to the marriage. They are thus reclassified as debtors asserting their claim against the marriage partnership, rather than as being in need of support (either from the ex-spouse through maintenance or from the government through public benefits). This approach is a powerful endorsement of the notion of marriage as a partnership between equals.

It does not require a tallying of contributions during the marriage, but assumes that the partnership was a shared enterprise. When the partnership is dissolved, however, debts which were carried in unison cannot be allocated to one party. Similarly, the whole orientation of the approach is retroactive, and not directed to guessing at future needs and circumstances; the debt once assessed and paid cannot be claimed again. The approach is thus consistent with the desire of people for the swiftest severing of financial ties.

Calculating the Debt against the Marriage Partnership

There are several econometric models for calculating the opportunity costs of children. Opportunity costs may be broadly defined as 'the earnings that a woman might have had, but had to forgo, because of the need to care for her children' (Reed and McIntosh 1971). Costs are estimated by comparing the lifetime earnings of groups of women who have had no children, and no child-induced interruptions to their workforce participation, with those of women who have borne children.

The bases for these estimates are large nationally representative samples of women and the collection of statistics on their workforce participation, earnings, and fertility. Calhoun and Espenshade (1986) in Australia have calculated the costs of having children. All conclude that the presence, age, and number of children have estimable effects on women's earnings. The availability of national scales for these costs means that estimates can be made of the costs for a woman of particular socio-economic, fertility, and labour force characteristics. Joshi (1984) demonstrates that interruptions to women's work are primarily associated with children and that the cost of these interruptions, measured by gross cash earnings forgone as a result of family formation, is about double the loss of actual woman-years in the labour force.

Although there are differences in methods and estimates, these approaches provide statistical estimates of the opportunity costs of children which lessen women's earning capacity in comparison with childless women of similar educational, occupational, and regional characteristics; both suffer from a number of limitations. Any extrapolations made from a group to an individual will contain errors. Observations of particular cohorts of people will not take account of changes in, for example, women's workforce participation rates. This is a weakness shared, however, by all insurance tables and compensation estimates. For example, recent estimates of the life expectancy for young Australian men aged 18 in 1985 were revised upwards to 73.6 years from 72 years, the estimated life span in 1970–2 (ABS 1987).

Beggs's and Chapman's (1988) estimates provide a base for calculating opportunity costs of children and generating tables of costs under a range of demographic, socio-economic, family formation, and family dissolution circumstances. Such tables could then be made available to the public and used by the court as standards against which to assess the outstanding opportunity-costs estimates to be borne by the carer of the children. As with all insurance and compensation tables, each set of circumstances would be assessed within a band of values. The band would be set to cover about 95 per cent of cases, outside of which there could be a system of appeal. Negotiations would be possible on the basis of individual variations, but the parameters would be set.

Allocation of Opportunity Costs to the Partnership

To be both effective and equitable the following principles in compensating for lost earning capacity from the net property of the marriage might be considered:

1. that the compensation is for prospective loss of income post-separation, to compensate for the cumulative loss following the lowered point of entry back into the workforce. It is *not* for the retrospective losses during the

marriage; where losses during the marriage and the prospective cumulative loss post-separation are similar, however, is that they are a charge on the joint economy of the marriage;
2. that the compensation is calculated and finite, since ideally the compensation should be levied as a once-and-for-all debit against the net joint property of the marriage at the time of separation.

An outline of the procedures for the payment of compensation for opportunity costs might be as follows:

1. Determine the net property of the partnership after all other liabilities have been accounted for.
2. Deduct from that net amount another debt—that of the opportunity costs, payable in this case to one partner.
3. Divide the remaining property equally between the partners.

An example of this process, constructed for an average case in the AIFS study, might be as follows. Average net property value before calculating opportunity costs was $50,000. Time out of the workforce for a woman married ten years with two children aged 7 and 9 at the time of separation was about five years. Future opportunity costs of a clerical worker from the time of separation through the normal working life (we have no scales, but would estimate this on the basis that these costs would be diminishing over the working life between 34 and 60). Let us set this at $20,000. On the assumption that these costs be based on the difference between her full-time earnings and those of a matched woman without children, the calculation would be as follows:

Total net assets	$50,000	
Less opportunity costs	$20,000	
Remaining net assets	$30,000	
50 : 50 shares of remainder	husband	wife
	$15,000	$15,000
Final settlement of matrimonial property	$15,000	$35,000

In the AIFS study the average net annual income differential between men and women after tax and maintenance payments was $7,800 in favour of the man at the time of interview, three to five years after separation. This difference comprises both an amount attributable to the general income differences between men and women, and an amount attributable to support in the workforce by the marriage partnership, as well as the opportunity costs of children on the career. In this hypothetical case, the man would recoup in under sixteen months (through the earnings differential) the net amount paid out of 'his' share of marital property to compensate the wife for her lowered earnings. In this example, as in most cases, there are clearly resources to pay the compensation entirely out of assets or to charge some of the debt against the husband's earnings in the years immediately following separation.

Further Questions

Although the Australian Family Law Act of 1975 includes specific recognition of the opportunity costs of children, and national scales of costs have been developed, there are several further questions to be addressed. Possible conflicts between compensation claims and child maintenance responsibilities must be explored. There is very poor evidence for earning advantages of married men over single men (Calhoun and Espenshade 1986); similarly Joshi (1984) reports that marriage *per se* has little effect on women's lifetime earnings. Thus, in spite of the US cases exploring the value of wives' efforts in augmenting husband's human capital, the evidence is not strong for specifically marriage-related costs and benefits for either sex.

Reforms confront a complex array of economic, social, and legal structures which embody social norms of the past and present. Social values are not, however, unified and harmonious. They are a pastiche of carry-overs from previous generations and recent additions. Not surprisingly, reforms relating to marriage and divorce highlight, as they confront, the many inconsistencies which are the very fabric of Australian social mores. Contentious issues include the division of labour in managing the marriage economy, equality of opportunity in paid employment, and the role of the state in supporting lone-parent families which result from divorce. As Ellwood (1987) has argued, reforms will only come about if they can resolve value conflicts.

This proposal endorses marriage as a partnership of equals. Its focus is on settling debts, not on establishing dependency needs. Much of this rhetoric is commonplace in Australia; it remains to be seen if its practical expression will be accepted by the decision-makers within the community and by the community as a whole.

References

Australian Bureau of Statistics (ABS) (1987), *Lifetables: The Labour Force in Australia* (Canberra).

Australian Joint Select Committee on the Family Law Act (1980), *Family Law in Australia*, Report (Canberra), vol. i.

Australian Cabinet Sub-Committee on Maintenance (1986), *Child Support: A Discussion Paper on Child Maintenance* (North Ryde, NSW).

Australian Law Reform Commission (1987) *Matrimonial Property*, Report No. 39, (The Hambly Report) (Camberra).

BEGGS, J., and CHAPMAN, B. (1988) 'The Forgone Earnings from Child-Rearing in Australia', paper commissioned by the Australian Institute of Family Studies, Australian National University Centre for Economic Policy Research, Discussion Paper No. 190 (Melbourne).

CALHOUN, C. A., and ESPENSHADE, T. J. (1986), 'The Opportunity Costs of Rearing American Children', Projects report, The Urban Institute (Washington, DC).

ELLWOOD, D. T. (1990), 'Valuing the United States Income Support System for Lone Mothers', in OECD, *Lone Parents: The Economic Challenge* (Paris).

FUNDER, K. (1986), 'Work and the marriage partnership', in P. McDonald (ed.), *Settling Up: Property and Income Distribution on Divorce in Australia* (Sydney).

——(in press), 'The Value of Work in Marriage: Options for Compensation after Marriage Breakdown', in D. Ironmonger (ed.), *Households Work* (Sydney).

GLEZER, H. (1988), *Maternity Leave in Australia* (Melbourne).

HARRISON, M. (1986), 'Maintenance, custody and access', in P. McDonald (ed.), *Settling Up: Property and Income Distribution on Divorce in Australia* (Sydney).

——and McDonald, P. (1988), 'Parents and Children after Marriage Breakdown: The Price of Child Maintenance', paper presented to *Bicentenary Family Law Conference*, Melbourne, 16–20 March, Business Law Education Centre.

Jones, F. L. (1983), 'Income inequality', in D. H. Broom (ed.), *Unfinished Business: Social Justice for Women in Australia* (Sydney), ch. 5.

Joshi, H. (1984), *Women's Participation in Paid Work: Further Analysis of the Women and Employment Survey* (Department of Employment Research, Monograph No. 45; London).

McDonald, P. (1986), 'Property Distribution: The Shares of Each Partner and Their Determinants', in P. McDonald (ed.), *Settling Up: Property and Income Distribution on Divorce in Australia* (Sydney).

Mincer, J. (1980), 'Human Capital and Earnings', in A. B. Atkinson (ed.), *Wealth, Income and Inequality* (2nd edn., Oxford).

Organization For Economic Co-Operation and Development (OECD) (1990), *Lone Parents: The Economic Challenge* (Paris).

Reed, R. H., and McIntosh, S. (1971), 'Costs of Children', in E. R. Morse and R. H. Reed (eds.), *Economic Aspects of Population Change* (Washington, DC).

Schwartzkoff, J., and Rizzo, C. (1985), *A survey of Family Court Property Cases in Australia* (Matrimonial Property Law Research paper No. 1: Sydney).

Social Security Review (1986*a*), *Income Support for Families with Children*, Background Paper No. 1 (Canberra).

Social Security Review (1986*b*), *Australian Families' Current Situation and Trends: 1969–1985*, Background Paper No. 10: (Canberra).

Weston, R. (1986), 'Changes in Household Income Circumstances', in P. McDonald (ed.), *Settling Up: Property and Income Distribution on Divorce in Australia* (Sydney).

Wulff, M. (1988), 'Demographic Change and Housing Policy; An Analysis of a Government Home Ownership Scheme on Female Sole Parents', paper presented at the 4th National Conference of the Australian Population Association, 31 Aug.–2 Sept. (Brisbane).

7. Property Division and Pension-Splitting in the FRG

Wolfgang Voegeli and Barbara Willenbacher

In the nineteenth and early twentieth centuries family law in Germany stressed the importance of family property administered by the head of the family. The main objective was to protect family property as an entity against the individual claims of family members, especially in the case of entailed family estates, family enterprises, and family farms. For that reason the law of succession and of matrimonial property discriminated against wives and especially widows.

As their relatives were often not able to support them and as the income of small family enterprises declined, widows accounted for the majority of the poor. In the big cities one-third were supported by welfare (Schallhofer 1987). Survivor benefits were instituted through insurance, at first only for civil servants, then for salaried employees, and finally for workers.

The diminishing importance of family property after the First and Second World Wars has favoured changes in matrimonial-property law, and the laws of succession have begun to be centred around the surviving spouse. In the FRG, in contrast to common-law countries, freedom to dispose of property is limited and heirs in the first degree cannot be disinherited except through restrictive exclusion clauses (mainly following the violation of maintenance obligations by the deceased) (Meulders Klein 1988).

Nearly all pension plans include survivor benefits, including 90 per cent of all private pension plans. There is no provision for opting out of survivor-benefit clauses, nor can third parties benefit. Only private insurance systems do not automatically include survivor benefits, and require additional payments for surviving spouses, and only life-insurance systems include the possibility of benefiting third parties. The economic situation of widows has improved as a result of the addition of different pension assets (mainly derived and personal pensions assets). But the economic situation of divorced women in old age is still critical, with the great majority receiving incomes below the poverty level (Der Bundesminister für Arbeit und Sozialordnung 1985).

The Legal History of Property Division

In the FRG until 1953 matrimonial property was nominally separate property. But in law the husband had sole control of his wife's property and the income from it. In Prussia, however, after 1974, women could hold separate property, which they could control autonomously if the marriage contract provided for this. But income from employment, whether earned as wages or in an owned business, was reserved for the husband. This system of exploitation was legitimized with the argument that it was the husband's duty to pay for the family expenses. The law stated that he had to use the income from the wife's property to pay for the maintenance of wife and children. The legal position, therefore, was that women with considerable property effectively supported the whole family in kind as well as in money. Furthermore, wives were compelled by law to work in their husband's business—an obligation which was not mutual.

This regime had barely been enacted when it became increasingly labelled as outdated by the legal profession. The German Civil Code of 1896 was not an attempt to create a law geared to modern developments in family structure in an industrialized society. Instead it preserved the privileged position of men.

The legal profession favoured a system of deferred community of property, which already existed in some Scandinavian states. This regime provided for separate property during marriage, with a compensation claim upon dissolution of the marriage.

But, in contrast to Swiss compensation claims, which assign one-third of the assets acquired during marriage to the wives, the German legal profession, influenced by the bourgeois women's movement, favoured an equal division of property assets. The reason given for this was idealistic, referring to the 'essence of marriage', and, although there was almost unanimity on this question of matrimonial property, even during the Nazi-period, it was not enacted in the FRG until 1957.

This matrimonial-property regime was seen as the only one which took account adequately of the marital partnership, while at the same time respecting individual economic rights. The argument against separate property was that it disadvantaged women who for some time during marriage gave up employment, at least in part, or who worked in their husband's business. The alternative of counterbalancing this by giving the courts discretion to alter property titles was never seriously discussed in the FRG. Such a power would extend the powers of the judiciary considerably, and create a high degree of uncertainty about the outcomes. Community of property was rejected, as it would integrate property acquired before marriage into the matrimonial property, even though it was not the product of the joint effort of the spouses.

Joint ownership of property acquired during marriage was also rejected, on the grounds that debts and the risks of business transactions should be excluded to protect the wives' interests. In a system of deferred community property, the compensation claim only affected the property acquired during the marriage, including any rise in the value of property already held at the beginning of the marriage. The increments in the property of both spouses were compared, and the spouse with the lesser increment was awarded compensation to the value of one-half of the difference of the respective values. The interesting aspect of this regime was that its unifying effect took place at the time of the dissolution of the marriage. Indeed, its main social importance was that it rounded off the process of developing individual independence for married women in property matters.

Whilst there was no opposition to the new matrimonial-property regime, the proposal to include social security insurance and other pension assets into the marital property to be divided was stiffly opposed. It was argued that pension assets were not vested property, the claim to an old age pension being open to discriminate variation by new legal provisions. Furthermore, they could not be treated as vested property, as the actual value of the assets was incalculable. Moreover, these assets were seen as resulting from the individual activity of the employed spouse and not from the joint marital effort.

All these arguments are no longer accepted, although the introduction of pension-splitting systems in 1977 produced a fierce legal battle before the Federal Constitutional Court. But since the court decided in favour of the constitutionality of the pension-compensation system in 1980, the system has become widely accepted. There was only one major attempt at a decisive change to the system in 1984, which tried to block the whole instrument by procedural means while avowing to uphold the principle, but this was warded off. In fact, the splitting of pension assets is the aspect of the reformed divorce law which has had the greatest impact on family policy.

It was the Divorce Reform Act of 1977 which introduced for the first time an independent social security claim for divorced women, while the reform of the social security pension scheme in 1985 failed to change the derived character of pensions for surviving spouses.

The Legal Dictum of Equal Contributions

The legal division of matrimonial property is based upon the mutual obligation to contribute to family maintenance. The bread-winner and home-maker roles are treated as equal in family law. Even in the case of a two-wage-earner family the different incomes of wives and husbands are seen as equal contributions to family income. In contrast to the Canadian law reform, which differentiated between a partnership and a separate two-wage-earner pattern (Baxter 1987), the matrimonial-property regime in the FRG treats two-wage-earner families as an entity.

It is a standing dictum of the Federal Constitutional Court that the equal entitlement of the spouses in all marital property forms part of the constitutionally protected essence of marriage, and that this equal entitlement transcends separation and divorce and affects the relationship between the ex-spouses with respect to maintenance and provision in old age (Bundesverfassungsgericht JZ 1980: 267 ff.).

This notion of equality has also been introduced into maintenance law. The German Civil Code (Burgerliches-gesetzbuch (BGB) s. 1360) states that both spouses have an equal obligation to contribute to the family maintenance, and that the wife's work in the house is seen as a consequence of a joint marital decision. The law regarding child maintenance defined child-care as maintenance in kind: child-care is, therefore, generally seen as equal to the monetary maintenance paid by the other parent. Unlike the common-law countries, therefore, a monetary assessment of the contribution of wives to the family property has never been discussed. It was not only the notion of unity and equality that prevented this, but also the argument that the complex exchanges between spouses can never be properly assessed. They constitute a mixture of material and non-material exchanges which can only be valued by the parties involved, and whose personal value is largely dependent upon the time and situation in which they were exchanged.

The legal dictum of equal marital contributions, regardless of different economic contributions, is based upon the philosophical concept of marital solidarity. But nevertheless the economic reality of marriage and family life shows that husbands and wives have equal earning capacity in only a minority of cases. Part-time work and the reduced earning capacity of wives as a result of discontinuous employment are still typical in the 'modern' family.

Property Definition

Property is defined by the courts as every object and obligation with a monetary value. Property has to be vested to be considered. It is sufficient, though, that the property is conditionally attached to a person if the occurrence of such conditions hinges on the actions of the title-holder or the lapse of time. However, the courts have made one exception. A title to recurrent payments is not viewed as present property when they are due. For this reason, claims to pensions, be they to the social security insurance system or to private pension plans, were not deemed property before 1977. It follows from the aforesaid definition that career assets, indeed all forms of human capital, are not considered property.

The standard matrimonial-property regime is commonly referred to as a deferred community of property. However, the label of 'community' is misleading. It is rather a system of separate property whilst the marriage is intact, with provision for compensation on divorce, the spouse with the smaller increase of property acquired during marriage being entitled to 50 per cent of the difference in the value of the respective property increments (BGB ss. 1372–8). Transactions between the spouses during the marriage are not taken into consideration. This may cause hardships in the case of one spouse having paid the debts of the other. Also, existing debts are only considered in so far as they reduce the value of the respective spouse's property to nought. If there are more debts than assets, this is not taken into account as a negative property for the purpose of calculating the compensation claim.

The property regime of deferred community of property includes all forms of property acquired during the marriage, with a few exceptions, such as inheritance, and severance payments for soldiers, which are treated as the product of purely individual efforts and thus treated as the property of the individual who has earned them. But compensation payments for pain and suffering, severance payments for employees, and lottery winnings have to be considered if matrimonial property is divided at divorce (Schwab 1984).

With respect to the marital home, the rule of inalienability of title applies and the courts have no power to alter titles. But, if both spouses are joint owners, the rules of joint ownership allow one spouse to force the sale of the property. If only one spouse is the owner, the monetary compensation claim might force him or her to sell in order to meet these demands. A hardship clause has been introduced, however, to enable the owner-spouse to defer the sale. The same clause previously protected the owners of businesses. Furthermore, the parties may enter into agreements with respect to the property of the marital home, though these have to be notarized—as do all property contracts.

As for the household chattels, the judge may allocate any item to the spouse who is most in need of it. If titles are altered thereby, the judge may order compensation. The value of these transactions is considered in the calculation of the overall property compensation claim, according to their value at that time.

Exclusion and Reduction of Property Division

The individual claims of spouses after divorce to monetary compensation are irrespective of any fault. The only exclusion clause holds the same reasons valid for the exclusion of succession and maintenance claims between other relatives. This occurs only rarely, usually in cases where legal maintenance obligations have been violated. The High Court practice interprets this exclusion clause very restrictively.

For this reason, compensation for career assets is ruled out, because the pursuit of higher or university education cannot be treated as violation of marital obligations. The spouse who has financed the career asset has no claim to payment in the case of property division after divorce (Schwenzer 1988). Contrary to the common-law practice, the courts do not consider marital circumstances or the interests of children. The principle of equal marital contributions requires an equal division of property, even though the statutory matrimonial-property regime is not based upon community property.

The Socio-Legal Practice of Property Division

According to our data, marriage contracts with the purpose of excluding the statutory matrimonial-property regime amount to only 5 per cent of our sample. But compensation payments are made in only 15 per cent of divorces, in half of the cases of up to DM 5,000, the average being DM 20,000. The division of matrimonial property generally favours women: they are the recipients of 80 per cent of compensation payments.

But compensation payments do not fully compensate the economic disadvantages caused by household activities and child-caring. The number of childless women, employed full time, who receive compensation payments exceeds the number of mothers with minor children. This is because two-wage-earner families naturally have higher savings than one-wage-earner families with small children. In the latter families, small savings are generally already used up during the separation period to cover the additional cost of two households. In contrast to Anglo-Saxon countries, the matrimonial home is rarely the object of property division. This occurs in less than 5 per cent of the cases studied.

The practice of compensation payments has not changed since the enactment of no-fault divorce, because property division did not depend on fault.

The division of household chattels and other objects of property (cars, small estates, etc.) as well as of debts exceeds the number of compensation payments. In 30–40 per cent of cases household chattels and other objects of property are divided; in 10–30 per cent debts; in 25–50 per cent the right to stay in the rented marital home or apartment; and in 35 per cent the division of divorce litigation costs. In these cases a change in private-settlement criteria is obvious: before 1977 women had usually been favoured, whereas after 1977—the enactment of no-fault divorce—only a minority of women have profited from divorce settlements. The division of debts still follows the traditional pattern: the majority of men take over responsibility. But private credit settlements are not compulsory; if the ex-husband is or would be insolvent, the ex-wife is jointly and severally liable.

Property division before and after 1977 can be differentiated by the acceptance of creditor liabilities. Since the enactment of no-fault divorce, beneficiaries of legal property division have had to go to court more often to realize their claims.

But property division has not improved the economic situation of the majority of divorced women. With the wage-earner family constituting 80–90 per cent of all families, the importance of the old property has greatly diminished. Generally, property in these families will consist of consumer goods, a small savings account, and, varying from area to area, a modest house, very often mortgaged. As most divorces occur during the early years of marriage, the divorcing couple will be at the beginning of their careers, while at the same time debts for the purchase of the consumer goods necessary to set up a household will still be high. In most cases debts rather than assets will have to be shared out.

The insignificance of property division at divorce is aggravated by the following factors:

1. divorced men have lower earning capacities than married men;
2. divorced men use their earning capacities less well than married men;

3. the income level of divorced couples is lower than the income of married couples (Giesecke 1987);
4. divorced couples have higher rates of indebtness and lower rates of savings than married couples;
5. in the small group of higher-income couples, separate property settlements were more common, and women rarely know about the property acquired by their husband

But there are forms of new property, which in most cases will have been accumulated during marriage: in particular, assets in social security insurance systems or private superannuation plans; in short, all work-related benefits.

Women will have acquired less of these entitlements during marriage because the traditional division of labour in the family still prevails, in that they take over child-care responsibilities and thereby partly or wholly retreat from the workforce, or have reduced earning capacities, on account of the sex-segregated labour market.

The Division of Pension Assets and Marriage Policy

The reason for accepting the pension-splitting scheme is that it is incorporated in maintenance and matrimonial-property law.

The argument that pension assets are a product of purely individual efforts runs counter to the reasoning behind the matrimonial-property regime of deferred community of property which—with very few exceptions— includes all forms of 'old property', however acquired during marriage. The ethical reason for the splitting of marital property is that marriage is a unity in which the couple share equally whilst they live together. At the end of such a union one may not treat the spouses as if they had been unrelated individuals all the while. The economic reason put forth is that housewives and mothers contribute to the family well-being and thus set their husbands free to earn an income outside the home. The political reason is that, by treating women's contribution to the family well-being as equal to men's, the constitutional equal-rights clause would be implemented without having to change the traditional division of roles within the family and thereby the family structure. The notion of equality between household and paid work serves to reinforce the conservative family doctrine under the cloak of equality. Today it constitutes an element of the constitutional protection of marriage as interpreted by the Federal Constitutional Court.

The legal argument for not including pension assets in the division of property, which was put forward in the debate before the enactment of the new marital-property regime in 1957—that such assets were not property but mere expectations—has crumbled as gradually the Federal Constitutional Court has recognized social security pension assets as property protected by the constitution against government intervention. The final recognition came in the case in which the constitutionality of the pension-splitting scheme was challenged. As pension assets are acquired through individual contributions, and as their accumulation is destined to be for the individual social security member's profit, and as the individual is entitled to the pension payments, all elements of private property protected by the constitution are included. The fact that the individuals generally can only make dispositions regarding their social security pension claims at the time they fall due, and then only regarding the monthly payments and not the capital value, was not seen as a negation of the still-existing individual entitlement. Neither was the fact considered relevant that the amount of the pension assets can finally only be determined at the time the claim falls due. The law governing the pension-splitting scheme calls for a fictitious calculation of old age pension at the time divorce proceedings are instituted, and with respect to the assets acquired during marriage. The problem that these assets might be valued differently at the time the claim to a pension falls due is seen as secondary and solvable. The law has been amended to allow for later adjustments if there are relevant differences in valuation.

The Function of the Pension-Splitting Scheme

Old age pensions are acquired by more than 80 per cent of the population through the social security insurance system. Apart from this system there are also pensions for civil servants, and several private pension plans which operate instead of social security insurance or as complementary systems. The social security system is a contributory insurance scheme into which, at present, 18.5 per cent of gross wages are paid. The percentage changes are regulated by statute. Of these contributions, employer and employee pay half each. For each member of the social insurance scheme there is an account; but this does not record the actual sum paid in; instead these sums are transferred into percentages of the average contributions. Thus, over a working lifetime, the percentage of each member's contribution in relation to the average contribution may be calculated. This percentage, together with the number of months of contributions made, determines the amount of the old age pension. The current average income is decided by statute, and is regularly updated. Thus, the scheme provides for individual claims to a certain percentage of the national average income from employment. In other words, it has an inherent dynamic which links the development of pensions to the development of real wages, and thus protects the members against inflation and lets them participate in the rise of productivity to the same degree as wage-earners do.

The pension system for civil servants is dynamized in a similar manner. Pension systems that offer an alternative to the social security system generally operate in much the same way. Complementary systems, on the other hand, often lack the social security system's dynamics and mostly function in the same way as a capital fund or a life insurance.

Due to the highly formalized and legally fixed calculation of social security old age pensions, the notional old age pension of each member may be calculated at any time for any period. Hence, upon divorce the assets acquired during the marriage are calculated and added to assets acquired in complementary schemes recalculated to make them comparable to the dynamic assets in the social security system. This is done with the help of conversion tables issued by statute and regularly updated. Then, just as the system of deferred community property prescribes, the total assets of each spouse are compared and one-half of the difference is transferred to the account of the spouse with the lesser assets. The general rule is that compensation has to take place by way of transferring assets to a social security account or by opening such an account through a court decree, where it did not previously exist.

The spouses do not have to institute proceedings for the compensation of pension assets. This is done *ex officio* by the family court. As compliance with an ensuing court order does not involve any action on the side of the spouses, the enforcement of court orders is 100 per cent effective. The whole procedure is an administrative act in which the main participants are the family court and the pension organizations.

The parties may agree, however, not to have their pension assets split. Such agreement is subject to judicial approval if entered into within one year before divorce proceedings were instituted. The family court will approve, if during the marriage the spouses have earned approximately the same amount or if during a short marriage only very few assets have been acquired, so that the difference could not be substantial.

As long as the spouses have acquired assets only in social security insurance, or in the civil service pension scheme, the application of the law is not beset with major problems, despite frequent litigation. Serious concern has been aroused, however, about the compensation for assets in private pension plans. The first problem is that these pension plans lack the dynamics of the social security systems. In addition, the private systems vary between themselves. The problem has been solved like the Gordian Knot. The government has issued statutory conversion tables. But the values given in these tables are only rough approximations. In individual cases they could be unjust. If undue hardship may ensue, then a general clause allows the court partly to dismiss the compensation claim or to find a more equitable solution. This problem, however, is not yet fully dealt with.

The second problem is that originally the law provided for the debtor spouse to pay a lump-sum contribution to the social security insurance fund in order to compensate for assets in private pension plans. This has caused serious economic hardship, as a claim to a monthly pension of DM 100 in the social security system represents a capital value of approximately DM 20,000. Here the Federal Constitutional Court has ruled that the law was unconstitutional in requiring such a lump-sum payment without allowing for other possible ways of making compensation. This has since been remedied with a variety of methods of compensation.

If the regulations of the pension plan permit, the assets can now be split directly and the creditor spouse can become a new beneficiary of the pension plan, or the pension plan invests these assets to be transferred in life insurance for the benefit of the recipient spouse. To enable a comparison between different pension plans, the assets in the social security system are used as a *tertium comparationis*, and the amount to be transferred is then reconverted into the respective pension plan.

If the regulations of the pension plan do not permit such direct splitting, and if it is a public corporation pension plan outside the civil service, then a quasi-splitting takes place. The court will calculate the amount to be transferred, if necessary with the help of the aforesaid tables, and transfer it to the social security account of the creditor spouse. Later on, when the old-age-pension claim of the creditor spouse falls due, the pension plan reimburses the social security insurance scheme for the monthly payments to the creditor spouse resulting from the assets transferred at the time of divorce. If a relatively small claim against the social security system is to be established, the pension plan pays a lump-sum contribution to the social security system immediately.

If, after all these operations, some pension claims remain uncompensated, then transferable pension assets may be divided differently. Transferable assets include those in the social security system, the civil servants' pension system, pension plans for public corporations, and private pension plans that allow a direct splitting. Generally, assets in private pension plans that do not allow a direct splitting will then be balanced against assets in the social security system. To protect the creditor spouse against a depletion of his claims against the social security system the law has set a ceiling at a claim of approximately DM 60 per month against the social security system. That represents a capital value of DM 12,000. Furthermore, if the economic situation of the debtor permits, the court may order a lump-sum contribution to the social security system.

If these operations leave any pension claim uncompensated, then this claim will be compensated at the time when the pension claim of the debtor spouse falls due, provided that the creditor spouse also has a current claim to a pension at that time. The compensation is then made in the form of monthly payments from the debtor spouse to the creditor. If the debtor dies, the divorced spouse has a claim against the pension plan of the debtor. The law gives the divorced spouse the status of a quasi-dependent relative. In case the pension plan provides for any payments to dependent relatives on the death of the member, then a divorced spouse with a still uncompensated compensation claim against the deceased is treated as such a relative.

These paragraphs have given a rough description of the compensation mechanism provided by the divorce law of the FRG. In reality, everything is much more complicated and intricate, as this section of the law covers probably the most complicated matters ever legally regulated.

Exclusion, Reduction, and Waiving of Pension Assets

In contrast with property division, private settlements concerning pension assets are generally controlled by the family court. In cases of property division, however, the splitting of family assets is nearly totally regulated by the family court. Marriage contracts which aim to exclude the splitting of pension assets concluded one year before the divorce petition are extremely rare, and may even be declared to be violating moral principles if they underprivilege the socially weaker party, that is, the wife (Becker 1983). Private autonomy is reduced: the majority of private settlements are submitted to the control of the family court. The buying-out of pension-asset claims, lump-sum payments, or other forms of compensation payments is restricted and only authorized in a few cases by the courts in contrast to common-law practice. The main focus is centred on the preferential treatment of pension assets.

In the first years of the new divorce law the legal profession favoured waiving claims and excluding pension-splitting schemes. But, since the Federal Constitutional Court confirmed pension-splitting, the legal practice has changed and has treated exclusion and waiving very restrictively. Not even the waiving of DM 10 is accepted (Schmidbauer 1986).

The most important reason for exclusion is the incalculability of non-vested assets at the moment of divorce (on the side of the debtor or the creditor). In contrast to common-law practice, these claims may be executed when the pension claim of the debtor spouse arises. As additional pension assets for employees in private firms which amount to 30–50 per cent of the employed male population are often not-vested at the time of divorce, and private pension funds refuse pension-splitting in favour of the social security system, they will be important in the future, when divorced women reach pension age. At the moment we do not know if divorced women will use these pension-asset claims. The same phenomenon can be observed in the Netherlands, where the constitutional court included private pension assets into the definition of community property in 1981 (Pintens 1985). Data will not be available for another 10–20 years to evaluate this splitting scheme. The legal profession is still critical *vis-à-vis* delayed pension claims, and favours waiving or inactivity in cases where claims are not bureaucratically institutionalized and calculable by the statutory calculation schemes. Also older women are less apt to initiate action against ex-spouses, as required in cases of delayed compensation claims.

The second most important reason for exclusion is the length of marriage: in the case of a childless marriage which ends after not more than two years of marriage, neither the splitting of pension assets nor spousal maintenance is available. And in the majority of cases where the creditor spouse has financed the career development of the debtor spouse pension-splitting is not available (Lefevre 1984), contrary to the legal practice in property cases.

Since 1983 the ratio of waiving and exclusion has declined to 30 per cent. In half of the cases childless couples after a short duration of marriage waive their claims, and in the remaining cases many were incalculable as well as being not-vested (Glockner 1985).

These figures will change when the required periods of insurance for women are altered, as the number of married women with no vested pension assets at the time of divorce will increase.

The Socio-Legal Reality of Pension-Splitting

The overwhelming majority of the divided pension assets result from splitting social security assets (see Table 7.1).

TABLE 7.1. *Splitting of pension assets (%)*

	Splitting of social security	Quasi-splitting and lump-sum payments	Splitting of other assets
1978	21	4	–
1979	60	8	1
1980	60	10	1
1981	60	10	1
1982	50	9	1
1983	67	10	1
1984	73	2	3
1985	73	2	1
1986	69	1	–

	Payments of the debtor spouse to the creditor spouse	Waiving of claims	Exclusion
1978	–	26	48
1979	1	18	26
1980	1	14	21
1981	1	14	21 *
1982	–	18	23
1983	1	11	21
1984	12	14	10
1985	12	15	11
1986	2	18	12

Note

* addition more than 100 per cent.

Source: Stat. Bundesamt, Fachserie 10, Reihe 2, Zivil- und Strafgerichte 1978–1988.

Other forms of pension assets are of no importance. Ninety five per cent of women benefit compared with 5 per cent of men (Knoedel 1984). In contrast with the division of matrimonial property, the splitting of social security assets compensates child-caring women to a greater extent. The compliance rate increases with marriage duration and the number of children. But the compensation margin naturally depends on the earning capacities of the husband. The amount of pension assets split varies according to the workers', employees', or miners' pension scheme. The average amount transferred to the wife's pension accounts runs to DM 130 in the workers' pension scheme, to DM 180 in the employees' pension scheme, and to DM 182 in the miners' pension scheme. But the civil servants', public corporation, and private pension schemes favour women on average with DM 348. The compliance rate for pension-splitting obligations is higher in the low-earning capacity groups and decreases in the high-earning capacity groups.

The average sum of transfer payments of pension assets to divorced women evens out the difference in income levels for divorced and widowed women in old age. But it will not balance the income differences between men and women in old age caused by the segregated labour market, as women have still lower earning capacity than men, resulting in lower pension assets. Widows with a survivor benefit of 60 per cent of the matured pension assets of their deceased husband receive higher incomes than single women who were continuously engaged in the labour market (Kohleiss 1987). These effects are due to the post-war policy of compensating the war generation, especially the men, for the loss of insured time due to the Second World War (Bruckner and Meyer 1987).

General Evaluation

The aims of the policy behind the pension-splitting scheme were to ensure an independent old-age-pension claim for divorced women, to lay the basis for a pension for divorced women that would be above the poverty line, and to let women partake equally in the 'new property' acquired during marriage. In the latter two aspects the system is worth criticizing, despite its apparent smooth functioning. Men still profit more from social security insurance, as some benefits are linked to the continuous payment of contributions, for which a transfer of accounts upon divorce has no impact. The question of whether time in school, tertiary education, and unemployment was valued as times of contribution hinges upon the fact that more than half of the time between entering the insurance system and becoming eligible for a pension is covered with contributions from employment. A housewife, even if she was a voluntary member of the scheme, will very often not be able to fulfil this requirement, as voluntary membership does not count in this respect. These prerequesites which underprivilege women will be abolished by the social security reforms which will increase the number of women eligible for their own pension, as well as improving counting time spent in child-care.

Furthermore, this scheme does not provide an old age pension for women at a level that, by itself, would guarantee an income above the poverty line. For most divorced women, however, even if they were housewives during marriage, it forms a solid base for building up their own assets in an ensuing working career. As the average duration of marriage ending in divorce is 10–11 years, and therefore considerably shorter than a working life, the prospect of being able to acquire an adequate old age pension is fairly good. It is not so for women who get divorced after a long period of marriage during which they were not employed.

Comparison of the claims of widows to surviving dependents' pensions shows that divorced women are suffering discrimination. Whilst the system treats married and divorced couples equally during their lifetime, it does not do so when one of the spouses dies. For a married couple, the widow then receives a widow's pension of 60 per cent of the deceased's pension claim, if she is over 45, or if she has to care for a child, regardless of how long the marriage existed. That is, all the assets of the deceased are taken into account, regardless of whether they were acquired during or before the marriage. The divorced spouse, on the other hand, never receives more than 50 per cent of the assets acquired during marriage, even though she might have been married for a long time and have raised a number of children.

The system obviously has a strong bias towards the institution of marriage and does not consider the contribution of wives and mothers to the social security system. Their contribution lies in the fact that they forgo income in order to raise the future working generation, whose job it will be to pay the contributions to the social security system that are necessary to cover the considerably higher claims of women with an uninterrupted working career, who usually have not raised any children. Social security law at the time of writing recognized child-care time as one year's contribution to the social security system, and this may be extended to three years.

It is also important that divorced women should have an independent claim to social security insurance which they would not lose on remarriage. The overall picture, then, is that, whilst in individual cases the instrument of a family law might ensure the economic security of divorced women in old age, in general it does not. The transfer of pension assets can only supplement individual assets acquired through participation in the workforce. Here women who have raised children are generally disadvantaged, compared with men. Treating social security pension assets as a fixed amount of property cannot be a solution. Instead the bias towards marriage should be eliminated, and the work invested in child-rearing recognized as beneficial to the community of insured members. Moreover, the reintegration of divorced mothers into the labour market should be of utmost public concern, as only in this way can women acquire pension claims that will guarantee an economic status above the poverty line.

Summary

Division of property and pension assets on divorce is controlled by the family court only in the case of the low-income groups. High-income groups, who are under-represented in divorce cases, especially self-employed persons, minimize litigation costs by private settlements and reduce the number of regulated divorce consequences. The legal profession favours a clear, calculable, and bureaucratic frame of reference for the division of property and pension assets. But only the low-income groups conform to the expectations of the legal profession, whereas the property situation of the high-income groups is less clear. The highly differentiated German social security system, and the institutionalized statutory calculation schemes for transfer payments, lead to successful implementation of splitting pension assets at the moment of divorce in 95 per cent of the divorce cases for the employed population. Lump-sum payments (outside the social security system) amount on average to a monthly value of only DM 34 pension assets (Knoedel) and are paid in only 20 per cent of the cases where payments were awarded. The institutionalized implementation rules discourage division of pension assets for high-income groups by the family court. These claims are delayed to pension age and then depend on the private initiative of the creditors. They may be counterbalanced by the ideology of the legal profession favouring a clean break at the moment of divorce.

Regardless of the institutional divergence of FRG pension plans on the one side, and US plans on the other, there is nevertheless a striking convergence on the low level of basic social security system claims for pension assets by divorced women. The additional pensions safeguarding the standard of living, however, depend either on delayed claims against the ex-husband (in the FRG and the Netherlands) or on divergent calculation schemes for lump-sum payments (in Anglo-Saxon countries).

The implication of the old and the new property (Glendon 1981) for women supports the conclusion that the economic needs of divorced women are neither fully covered by property- or pension-asset claims, nor by integration into the labour market. The importance of the new property is valid only for men on account of the segregated labour market.

References

BAXTER, I. (1987), 'Family Law Reform in Canada', *American Journal of Comparative Law*, 35: 801–8.

BECKER, F. (1983), *Versorgungsausgleichsvertrage* (Konigstein).

BRUCKNER, E., and MEYER, K. U. (1987), 'Lebensgeschichte und Austritt aus der Erwerbstatigkeit im alter' Working Paper No. 228; Sonderforschungsbereich 3 (Frankfurt and Mannheim).

DER BUNDESMINISTER FÜR ARBEIT UND SOZIALORDNUNG (1985), *Daten zur Einkomenssituation im Alter* (Munich), iii.

GLENDON, M. A. (1981), *The New Family and the New Property* (Toronto).

GLOCKNER, R. (1985), 'Ergebnis einter statistischen Erhebung zum Versorgungsausgleich', in *Deutsche Rentenversicherung*, 195–200.

GIESECKE, D. (1987), 'Erwerbsverhalten, Scheidungsrisiko und Wohlfahrtsniveau von Frauen', dissertation (Hanover).

KNOEDEL, P. (1984), 'Aus der Statistik der deutschen gesetzlichen Rentenversicherung', in *Deutsche Rentenversicherung*, 140–67.

KOHLEISS, A. (1987), 'Frauenrechte in der gesetzlichen Rentenversicherung', in U. Gehard *et al.*, *Auf Kosten der Frauen* (Weinheim).

LEFEVRE, J. (1984), *Versorgungsausgleich* (Dusseldorf).
MEULDERS KLEIN, M. T. (1988), 'Famille, stat et securité économique d'existence dans la tourmente', in M. T. Meulders Klein and J. Eekelaar, *Family, State and Individual Economic Security* (Brussels).
PINTENS, W. (1985), 'Die durchfuhrung des Versorgungsausgleichs im Rahmen des Sozialrechts', in H. Zacher (ed.), *Der Versorgungsausgleich im internationalen Vergleich und der zwischenstaatlichen Praxis* (Berlin).
SCHALLHOFER, P. (1987), 'Frauen als Sozialhilfreempfangerinnen', in U. Gerhard *et al.*, *Auf Kosten der Frauen* (Weinheim).
SCHMIDBAUER, W. (1986), *Der Versorgungsausgleich bei Ehescheidung* (Berg).
SCHWAB, D. (1984), 'Newe Rechtsprechung zum Zugewinnausgleich', in Bielefeld, *Zeitschrift für gesanite Familienrecht*, 429–36.
SCHWENZER, J. (1988), 'The Medical Student Syndrome', in Bielefeld, *Zeitschrift für gesanite Familienrecht*, 1114–21.

Part Four
Income Support

8. Introduction

Mavis Maclean and Lenore J. Weitzman

As the arrangements to be made at the end of a marriage become less concerned with the change in legal status and focus more clearly on financial arrangements and provision for children, a marked division has developed since the 1970s between approaches to wife support and those to child support.

Child support has gradually become the focal point of attention, as research has revealed the economic vulnerability and attendant problems experienced by children after divorce (discussed in the following chapters). The need for child support is now accepted, even though it rarely provides enough income for the post-divorce mother-headed family. Nevertheless, there is widespread agreement that children need a 'meal ticket', at least during their minority. The main area for debate is how the responsibility should be shared between custodial parent, non-custodial parent, and the state or society as a whole.

Spousal support, however, still largely in practice support for ex-wives, evokes a more complex response. On the one hand, with the development of no-fault divorce and increased participation of women in the labour market, some policy-makers assume that there is no reason for ex-spouses to have any continuing financial relationship after divorce. If women are seeking equality with men in the labour market, they argue, then wives should no longer expect financial support from an ex-husband after divorce. Scandinavian divorce laws gradually incorporated this view during the 1970s, and the current law (Swedish Marriage Code, Ch. 6 s. 7, amended 1987) now states that 'Following a divorce each spouse shall be responsible for his or her own support.'

This approach is reflected in the evolution of policies in other Western countries as well—a response to the strong pressure from groups of divorced men and their second wives, such as the Campaign for Justice on Divorce in the United Kingdom and the Fathers' Rights groups in the United States.

The UK Matrimonial and Family Procedings Act 1984 emphasizes the clean break, making the case for spousal support one which must be justified. While older homemakers who have not participated in the labour market throughout their marriage receive special consideration, they are typically treated as exceptions to the rule. Even they are held up to the ideal of rehabilitative maintenance to be paid for a limited period during which the ex-wife retrains or re-establishes herself in the labour market (see Chapter 17 below).

On the other hand, there is a growing awareness of the impractical nature of these expectations and the impossibility of the clean break. This awareness is the result of three factors. First, social scientists point to the fact that most divorced women retain responsibility for their children; this not only limits their labour-force participation, but also suggests the inappropriateness of a clean break which might further undermine the father's relationship with his children. Secondly, feminists have argued that it is unjust to change the rules of marriage in the middle of the game. If women are expected to put their 'earning capacities' on hold while they care for their children during marriage, it is unfair not to recognize and compensate them for the impairment and dependency that creates.

Thirdly, and perhaps most importantly, the clean-break scenario does not apply to the majority of divorcing couples. The ideal clean-break couple have never had children and at the time of the divorce, have only to divide their property (a tiny minority of divorcing couples). For this 'ideal' couple, a clear-cut division of property allows each spouse to leave the marriage without entangling obligations and allows each to pursue his or her own life-course. But this works only if the couple do not have any children. Children require continuing parental support that limits the earning capacity of the custodial parent—and necessitates continuing financial assistance from the non-custodial parent.

In most countries approximately two-thirds of divorcing couples currently have children of school age. If we also include all couples with children who are not yet economically independent (e.g., in the United States many 'children' between 18 and 21 are in college and are financially still dependent on their parents, and in the United Kingdom there are high rates of unemployment among the school-leaving population), and if we include all couples where a child of the marriage who is now independent has affected the earning capacity of the mother, it becomes evident that the conditions for a clean break cannot be met by the vast majority of divorcing couples.

As Mary Ann Glendon has pointed out, support laws that start from the principle that no spousal support should be available treat as exceptional what is in fact statistically the most frequent case—that of a spouse whose capacity for self-support is impaired because of her child-care responsibilities (Glendon 1989).

How, then, does a woman put together an income package after divorce? If we take out the direct cost of child-rearing and deal with this through child support, what is the ex-wife's situation? Her standard of living, unless she remarries, is likely to be lower than her ex-husband's (unless he leaves the labour market, or makes several more child-producing relationships) for three reasons. First because her earnings as a woman are low. In Leviticus 27: 1–8 it is laid down that the labour of men aged between 20 and 60 years is worth 50 shekels, but that the labour of a woman of the same age is worth only 30 shekels. Little has changed. Secondly, as a wife she is likely to have altered her job to fit in with her husband's needs, and rarely to her own career advantage. Thirdly, on having children her earnings are likely to have been interrupted by time out of the labour market and by some years of part-time work. In addition, her earning capacity will have been permanently reduced through loss of promotion and fringe benefits, particularly pension entitlements, affected by career interruptions and part-time work. She may also have contributed to increasing her husband's earning capacity—but that is a separate issue. A wife's total earnings by the time of divorce and her capacity to earn in future are reduced directly as a result of marriage. She is in difficulty, even if she works full time and relatively continuously.

This difficulty arises from the premature ending of a relationship contracted for life, which would, if it had continued over a lifetime, have yielded an acceptable economic return through a share in the husband's lifetime earnings and pension entitlements. It is important to focus here on disrupted income flows, not on property. The wife loses an anticipated stream of income that she relied on when she interrupted or altered her employment.

One counter-argument is that women should now realize that marriage is not permanent, and should plan their lives accordingly. For today, marriage is a rational economic choice only if the relationship is thought to be lifelong. With a high divorce rate, women may be dissuaded from marrying and risking divorce when they come to realize the likely future losses. And men may be reluctant to marry and risk divorce when they realize that they may have to share the full economic costs. As William Goode (1984) observed, such rational economic calculus leads to declining investments in the family collectivity.

But what if we want to counter these trends and encourage women and men to continue to invest in the family and in marriage? We could decide that society as a whole should share the responsibility for increased divorce rates, and should therefore share the economic costs from public funds. Or we could suggest that it is time to rethink the premature abandonment of alimony and other forms of income transfer from husbands to wives after divorce.

What, then, should be the role of wife support? We suggest that what alimony does is compensate the woman for the loss sustained through marriage which becomes visible, and falls on her shoulders, when the marriage ends. Rehabilitative fixed-term alimony is not a satisfactory solution, because it is seldom possible for women, even with this help, to recover their former earning capacity or achieve a new and satisfactory level of earned income. Periodical payments from ex-husband to ex-wife may be the only way to compensate for loss of earnings due to marriage and motherhood both during the marriage and thereafter. A cash sum sufficient to yield this level of income over time is unlikely to be available, although the use of annuities in the United Kingdom suggests a broader applicability to middle-income men than previously assumed.

Thus we reject the practicability of the clean-break solution. While the logic and ideology of the clean break seem attractive—it is easy to implement and looks forward not backward—it is likely to lead to disastrous outcomes, creating more problems than it solves. Given the present labour market and family conditions, where women take the major responsibility for domestic life and child-rearing, and suffer the major economic disadvantages resulting from this, a clean break, simply put, creates great hardships for many divorced women. The rhetoric has outstripped the reality. We suggest that policy-makers need to think again about the need for long-term alimony (until there are more major changes in women's opportunities). If men (and society in the pressures and expectations it has for men) require women's dependency during marriage in the form of putting the male career foremost, they may have to accept a degree of continuing female economic dependency after marriage ends.

While it is widely assumed that the full-time home-maker is disappearing, the woman who interrupts or subordinates her career for her family is still quite common. These low-earning working mothers show no signs of disappearing. Nor are their families becoming equal partnerships in which husbands and wives fully share domestic responsibilities. These realities have led to a rethinking of the role and importance of alimony in the United States (see Krauskopf 1989). In contrast, claims for periodic spouse-support payments seem to be increasingly dismissed in the United Kingdom and off the agenda altogether in Sweden (where, interestingly, there is growing pressure from young women demanding the right to choose to become housewives and mothers).

The question of alimony and the wife's situation after divorce will be considered further in Chapter 14. The intervening chapters focus on four recent developments in child support, bringing together empirical work that reflects the international concern with developing ways to assess and enforce the child-support obligation. The final chapter of Part Four highlights the need for great care in methodology in approaching these issues.

The four case studies of child-support policies describe the most recent policy initiatives in this area at the time of writing. All these studies have led to renewed government interest in assuring adequate and equitable levels of child support. They also indicate the importance of administrative decisions and procedures, instead of individual negotiation or private ordering with judicial arbitration. This line of development is familiar to students of social policy, where a newly identified need must first be energetically claimed by individuals, either through pressure-group activity or legislation. As it becomes established, it is regarded as an unquestioned and customary right.

The first study reported in Chapter 9 by Karel Maddens and Jean van Houtte from Belgium describes state involvement in guaranteeing that the custodial parent receives the child-support payments agreed to by parents and authorized by court orders. This programme was initiated in the context of low birth-rates, particularly among the higher socio-economic groups, and reflects the government's goal of easing the burden of bringing up children.

In Chapter 10 Irwin Garfinkel describes the child-support-assurance system developed in Wisconsin, whereby a fixed proportion of the non-custodial parent's income is allocated (as a right) to each child, with payment guaranteed by the state. Any non-custodial parent is at liberty to be more generous—but the state lays down the minimum standard. Wisconsin has gone further than most other states in the United States, which still use guidelines for judges in setting child support. Some of these establish a basic minimum amount, or a fixed proportion of income. Others try to achieve parity between the living standards of the household of each of the biological parents of the child.

All these methods of calculation are beset by problems. For example, if a minimum standard is used, it is unlikely to be exceeded; a mathematical formula is open to argument and depends on accurate disclosure of income; an equalization formula will need to cope with remarriage and new dependency and resources on either side. But, while failing to solve all problems, the introduction of state guidelines throughout the United States, while not approaching a solution to poverty in mother-headed households, has raised child-support levels (see Tjaden, Thoeness, and Pearson 1989 for Hawaii, Colorado, and Massachusetts) by about 15 per cent.

In Australia state involvement has gone one stage further, in that the child support, set at a fixed proportion of the non-custodial parent's income, is now collected by the tax authorities together with other deductions from the payroll. There may still be arguments about, for example, a farmer's level of income, but these are familiar to the Taxation Office which is well equipped to deal with them. Margaret Harrison describes the new scheme in more detail in Chapter 11. This kind of administrative approach should offer certainty after the introduction process is complete. Even if it cannot, for political reasons, provide a particularly high payment to the recipient, it confronts the issue of which family of a repartnered man should take precedence by taking the matter out of the individual's area of choice. Any woman joining a man who has children elsewhere will enter that relationship knowing his obligation to them is firmly in place—just as she would if he had children living with him.

These three chapters concentrate on income support for children, as the area where exciting though frustrating developments are happening. On the one hand, guidelines and federal enforcement procedures are being set up in the United States, but most lone-parent mother-headed families still live at or below the poverty level. On the other hand, generous lone-parent payments in Sweden are causing problems, because these families are now better off than two-parent low-waged families. The debate of the next decade will be about sharing the financial responsibility for children between custodial parents, non-custodial parents, and society (Krause 1990). In apportioning this responsibility we begin with the premiss that there can be no clean break between parents and children. In contrast, Chapter 12 describes the civil-law tradition of child support in the FRG, under which levels of support for children after divorce increased to keep pace with support for children whose parents never married.

The next two chapters in Part Four, by Maclean and Eekelaar and Weitzman, return to the issue of wife support, which the editors believe has been too easily dismissed as anachronistic and/or unnecessary. Since we are not optimistic about attempts to solve women's income problems after divorce through property division (unless property is redefined), we think it is crucial to keep wife support on the public agenda until women are no longer financially disadvantaged by marriage itself.

After the alimony drone, the next myth to demolish is that of the financially secure working mother. The majority of divorced women work in sex-segregated, low-paid, insecure jobs, with limited sick pay and pension entitlements, and carry the twin burden of the direct and opportunity costs of child-care. Compensation for these deficits is usually only available over time, as periodic payments. Even the appealing clarity of the Australian 'settling-up' approach, as it stands, can deal with events only up to the point of divorce. Unfortunately the problems are longer-lived for those women who remain divorced, and do not repartner. The challenge for the next decade is that of improving the standard of living of these women and their children—through child support, alimony, and the public purse—so that we do not force yet another generation to experience the economic impoverishment of divorce documented in Chapter 15.

References

GLENDON, M. A. (1989), *The Transformation of Family Law* (Chicago).

GOODE, W. J. (1984), 'Individual Investments in Family Relationships over the Coming Decade', *Tocqueville Review*, 6: 51–83.

KRAUSE, H. D. (1990), 'Child Support Reassessed', *University of Illinois Law Review*, 1989 (2): 367–98.

KRAUSKOPF, J. (1989), 'Theories of Property Division, Spousal Support', *Family Law Quarterly*, 23/2: 253–78.

TJADEN, P., THOENESS, N., and PEARSON, J. (1989), 'Will these children be supported adequately?', *Judges Journal*, 28/4: 4–10.

WEITZMAN, L. J. (1985), *The Divorce Revolution: The Unexpected Social and Economic Consequences for Women and Children in America* (New York).

9. Child Support in Belgium

Karel Maddens and Jean van Houtte

This Chapter reports on an inquiry into the socio-economic problems of child support in Belgium and investigates the effectiveness of the legal duty of support after divorce. The support system aims to offer a solution to the financial problems which may result from divorce. Even though divorce has been pronounced, both spouses are required to make a financial contribution towards the support of their children and, if necessary, of the needy partner.

It appears, however, that the support system does not guarantee effective performance of the duty of support. It seems that the amounts of support awarded are very low, and, in addition, they are paid irregularly. This impression, however, was not based on empirical data until recently.

In 1987 the Secretary for the Environment and Social Emancipation commissioned two university study centres, the Centre for the Sociology of Law of the University of Antwerp (UFSIA) and the University of Liege, to collect quantitative data concerning the duty of support.

The First Phase of the Inquiry

The first phase of this inquiry was a case study in two judicial districts, intended to trace, on the basis of content analysis, information concerning court decisions awarding child and/or spousal maintenance in the case of fault-based divorce, as well as maintenance agreements entered into by the spouses as a result of divorce by consent.

The researchers sought to discover the extent to which the inefficiency of the maintenance system could be traced back to the judicial decision: and to investigate whether problems in compliance could be predicted, on the basis of the data available from the court files.

The first-instance courts of Ghent and Liege were selected as the location for the study. In both cases 1984 was chosen as the study period. The study looked at the temporary measures decided upon at the beginning of the case, and during proceedings, for fault-based divorces. It also examined the maintenance arrangements made by partners in the case of divorce by consent.

From the results of this preliminary research the researchers concluded that payment of maintenance would be more problematic in the case of fault-based divorce. There were two reasons.

Firstly, maintenance was often a source of dispute in fault-based divorce and could give rise to a legal battle, whereas in the case of divorce by consent (no-fault divorce) an agreement had been reached. Secondly, a comparison of the two types of divorce populations at the time of payment suggests that the group of fault-based divorces included proportionately fewer men with higher professional qualifications. This group was therefore more likely to be restricted financially, and to have more difficulty in paying maintenace.

For the women, the number of housewives involved in divorce by consent was far smaller, which meant that those involved were financially more independent. This explains the small number of cases of spousal maintenance.

When the income-variable was incorporated into the analysis, it became possible to trace a number of vulnerable groups, both among those entitled to maintenance and among those with a duty of support. Among those entitled to maintenance was a large number of women with no income at all (or only a small income). These women would, in view of the amounts of the maintenance, have a hard time financially.

On the other hand, the distribution of income of those with a duty of support also suggested that subsequent payment of maintenance would be difficult. Apart from financial constraints and the degree of conflict in the divorce, in other countries non-payment is associated with various factors: a low level of parental co-operation and lack of support from fathers in raising the children during the marriage; traditional role-patterns; short duration of marriage; a lack of or infrequent contact between the children and their father; and the remarriage or repartnering of the divorced father.

All this suggested that the problems related to child and spouse maintenance are affected by factors which come into play after the legal decision has been made. The award of maintenance by consent or through the adjudication of the court does not guarantee its subsequent payment.

The Second Phase of the Inquiry

The second phase of the study was a national inquiry organized to investigate to what extent maintenance was paid, and the financial position of divorced women with dependent children.

The sample consisted of 593 divorced women with dependent minor children from a previous marriage entitled to receive maintenance.

The study paid special attention to the general financial position of divorced women with dependent children, as well as to receipt of maintenance. The failure of a marriage plays an important part in causing financial difficulties, and generally leads to the impoverishment of one or both partners. Single divorced women with dependent children are in a particularly weak position.

This is closely related to societal norms governing role patterns in the family. Women more readily give up their professional, and thereby their financial ambitions to perform a number of tasks within the family. Marriage offers them sufficient guarantees to accept this position of dependence. Divorce, however, does away with these guarantees and places them in a weak position. The crucial question is whether the maintenance system offers them sufficient and reliable support.

Divorce is not the only cause of financial difficulties. But it is a catalyst which brings to the forefront structural factors which were present before and during the marriage.

Financial Position of Women

Special attention was paid to the financial position of divorced women with dependent children in relation to certain socio-economic variables.

First we compared the financial position of the population of divorced women with that of the general population in Belgium. The lives of divorced women with dependent children are a great deal more insecure than those of the general population.

The population of divorced women, however, is not a homogeneous group. Crucial factors affecting their financial position are the present family situation, the number of dependent children, and participation in paid work. However, elements from the past were also taken into consideration; these included the level of education, the number of dependent children from a previous marriage, paid employment before and during the marriage, and the level of conflict in the divorce procedure.

The analysis identified a typical financially weak group: professionally inactive, single, divorced women with large families.

In this respect, it is not divorce alone but divorce combined with a number of handicaps which was decisive: these handicaps included a low level of education, a low level of professional activity, and a large number of dependent children from a previous marriage. These were the structural factors determining women's poor opportunities in life, which caused some women to end up in a position of marked and irreversible dependence, for which they pay very dearly if they divorce. This hidden inequality was revealed by divorce, especially for one-parent families.

One way out of this financial impasse is to start a new relationship (remarriage or cohabitation) which will result in the ex-spouse's lost income being replaced. However, this does not change the pre-existing position of dependence.

As in the first phase, the study also looked at the kind of divorce procedure followed. The dichotomy between fault-based divorce and divorce by consent was confirmed. Women in a weak position, with low levels of education and professional activity, and with low or no income during marriage, needed to have recourse to a conflict-laden divorce procedure (divorce on the grounds of certain facts) in order to get something out of it. Divorcees by consent had fewer dependent children, had enjoyed a better education, and were professionally more active with a higher income; their lives were therefore more secure.

Measures Relating to the Children

The first phase of the study showed that in over 80 per cent of cases custody was awarded to the mother. Visiting rights were often reported as a source of dispute. Nearly 30 per cent of ex-spouses no longer exercised the visiting rights agreed upon or awarded to them. Only half of them kept to the access arrangements made. There were special difficulties connected with access in the case of fault-based divorce.

Child support was agreed or ordered in 80 per cent of families with dependent children, in 95 per cent of cases to be paid by the ex-husband to the divorced wife. Irrespective of the number of children, divorced women with dependent children received an average of FB 6,000 per month. Flemish divorced women received the lowest child maintenance, FB 5,800. In Wallonia they received FB 6,800, and in Brussels the average amount was FB 9,100.

The average support allowance for children was FB 4,250 per child per month. This amount decreased with the number of dependent children. A woman with one dependent minor child received FB 4,556; with two dependent children FB 8,290 or FB 4,145 per child; for a woman with three children this amount was FB 10,150, a decrease to FB 3,383 per child.

Were these amounts high enough to cover costs? In order to evaluate the level of support, we took as a basis for comparison the level of subsistance minima, as calculated by the UFSIA Centre for Social Policy. The 'cost' of child support was calculated as the difference between the subsistence minima for an active couple without children, and those for an active couple with dependent children. The figures date from 1985, and so the amounts may be rather low. Using this method, it cost a family FB 5,600 per month to support one child, FB 8,900 two children, and FB 10,500 three children.

The average child-support payments awarded were clearly below these minimal cost estimates. Furthermore, we should not forget that educating a child produces heavy indirect costs, such as the need for a larger home, child-care, and so on.

For amounts of child support there was also a difference between fault and no-fault cases. In divorce by consent the amount of child support appeared to be higher at FB 4,600, compared with FB 3,700 in fault-based divorce.

TABLE 9.1. *Compliance (%)*

Payment made	Child-support payments (N=593)	Alimony (N=65)
Every month without delay	58.3	43.1
Every month but with a delay	11.4	6.2
With a delay of between one and three months	4.2	1.5
Occasionally	8.0	7.7
Non-payment	18.1	41.5

Apart from child support, a needy partner can also be awarded alimony support in her/his own right, either by the decision of the court or on the basis of an agreement.

Only 15 per cent of the divorced women with dependent children studied were entitled to personal alimony at the conclusion of the divorce procedure, and only 5 per cent of the women interviewed reported receiving it regularly. On average, they received FB 7,100 alimony per month, and in total (i.e. child support plus alimony) an average amount of FB 7,500 FB.

At the time of the study four out of five women were receiving some support, but this amounted on average to 17 per cent of the total household income. As a result of their low income, divorced women remarrying were more dependent on support allowances than remarried or cohabiting people. For the former group this made up 20 per cent of the household income, compared with 11 per cent for the latter.

Compliance

Of the divorced women interviewed, 70 per cent reported receiving child support sometime within the month, 4 per cent received it with a delay of up to three months, 8 per cent received occasional payments, and 18 per cent received nothing at all.

Payment of alimony to a needy partner was more unreliable. Only 50 per cent received their allowance regularly, within the month; about 2 per cent reported a delay of up to three months, 8 per cent occasional payments, and 41 per cent no longer received any alimony at all. Compliance problems with alimony began in half of the cases immediately after the award was made, and only just over half of the child-support agreements ever got under way.

The figures in Table 9.1 apply to the situation at the time of the inquiry. However, this does not imply that women had not experienced problems previously. In total over a third (about 35 per cent) of the sample population reported financial problems due to irregular payment of child support and/or alimony.

The group most vulnerable to non-receipt of maintenance was that of women in a lone-parent situation who had several dependent children. In addition, they had a low level of schooling, they were less active professionally, both during and after the marriage, and were less able to cope with poor maintenance payment than those who collected it regularly. The profile resembled the typical financially insecure divorced woman.

Divorced women with financial problems resulting from non-payment of maintenance often bear the responsibility for raising the children and performing household tasks alone. Women not experiencing difficulties with receiving child support or alimony had been less subject to traditional role patterns during the marriage, and had shared responsibility with their partners for child-care and household tasks. All the factors associated with financial difficulty after divorce (i.e. low level of education, more dependent children, professional inactivity, and no sharing of household and child-care tasks during marriage) contributed to placing these women in a position of marked dependence on their marriage partner during married life. The divorce therefore was more conflict-laden and fault-based, which in turn affected the payment of maintenance in a negative way. After fault-based divorce only 57 per cent of ex-wives reported receiving child support regularly, compared with 87 per cent of ex-wives after divorce by consent.

The ex-husbands of the vulnerable women also showed characteristics which might have had a negative impact on the payment of child support or alimony: lower professional status, higher levels of unemployment, and lower incomes. All these factors negatively associated with regular payment were over-represented in the fault-based divorce group. There were also factors associated with poor compliance: these included lack of or low frequency of contact between the children and the father, short duration of marriage, and a traditional role pattern concerning child-care (i.e. leaving it to the mother). Repartnering or remarriage by the ex-father or mother appeared to have no effect on whether child support was received regularly or not.

To overcome the financial problems resulting from poor payment or non-payment of maintenance most divorced women (45 per cent) turned to family or friends. Only 26 per cent appealed to social welfare agencies, such as the Public Welfare Agency, and 29 per cent had not sought financial support. Seventeen per cent of the sample population had taken legal action to secure attachment of earnings.

Conclusion and Policy Recommendations

Research into the socio-economic problems of the duty of support must go beyond a strictly quantitative analysis of compliance with maintenance-payment awards. The award and payment of maintenance, and the financial consequences of non-payment, can only be approached in a comprehensive analysis.

Only in this way can we demonstrate that the present financial insecurity and the poor level of compliance have structural causes which were present during and even before the marriage: namely the level of education and the position of the woman in the labour market, the income differences between men and women, and role patterns in marriage.

The problem calls for an overall approach. Long term and more far-reaching initiatives have to deal with the structural causes for the financial problems in which many women with children find themselves. This means improving women's position on the labour market, well-organized child-care, and development of the parental skills of men and women.

Since completion of the study more short-term initiatives with regard to the duty of support have been taken. Firstly, the subsistence income for single mothers with unmarried dependent minor children was increased. Secondly, a Bill introduced by the Secretary for the Environment and Social Emancipation attributes a new dual task to the Public Welfare Centres: on the one hand, paying advances on unpaid support for children; on the other hand, claiming unpaid alimony on behalf of and for the account of the person entitled. This measure can help divorced women with dependent children to overcome financial problems due to divorce and non-payment of maintenance.

Reference

BAWIN, B., VAN HOUTTE, J., GAUTHIER, A., GUILLAUME, J. F., and MADDENS, K. (1989), *De socio-economische problematik van de onderhondsuerplichtingen in Belgie* (Brussels).

10. Child-Support Trends in the United States

Irwin Garfinkel

Public alarm over family break-up has grown with the rise in the welfare rolls. Aid to Families with Dependent Children (AFDC, formerly ADC, for Aid to Dependent Children) was enacted as part of the Social Security Act of 1935 to provide for the needs of poor fatherless children, most of whose fathers had died. It was expected that Survivors Insurance, to be enacted in 1939, would support children whose fathers had a work history, and in the interim—until all families were covered by this insurance—AFDC would fill the gap.

Since the 1930s, however, the caseload has changed dramatically. Now the vast majority of the cases, close to 90 per cent, are on welfare because the fathers are absent from home—divorced from, separated from, or never married to the mothers of their children. That the state should support children who have able-bodied fathers who have deserted them has never been a very popular idea. Though such children were covered by AFDC from the outset, whether they should have been covered was controversial. Enthusiasm for supporting such children was further eroded with the change in women's work patterns. By the early 1970s nearly half of all middle- and upper-income mothers, even those with young children, were working outside the home at least part time, and the proportion of married mothers who earn wages has continued to grow since then.

Government's response has been, belatedly, to foster the traditional means of support for children: contributions from both parents. Private child support is moving from individual determinations in the court room to the routinization associated with taxation and social insurance. At the same time, the public child-support system, welfare, is changing. No longer are government benefits expected to substitute for parental earnings. Rather they are coming to be viewed as a supplement to the earnings of both parents.

The remainder of this chaper is organized as follows: it first describes the structure, weaknesses, and changes in the private and public parts of the United States child-support system. It then introduces the new child-support-assurance system, towards which the US and other countries are moving (Garfinkel and Wong 1987). The following section describes the 1984 and 1988 federal legislation, and the last section is a conclusion.

Private Child Support

Historically, the private child-support system in the United States has been a state prerogative implemented through the judicial branch. In most states the obligation to pay child support is explicitly stated in statute, although in some the obligation is only implied (Krause 1981).

Under the traditional family court system, three steps are involved in obtaining private child support: (1) the identification and location of the non-resident parent; (2) the determination by a court of the amount of child support to be paid; and (3) the payment of child support to the resident parent. Each step is potentially problematic.

When the mother of the child is unwed, courts must first establish the paternity of the father before a child-support obligation can be imposed. Some men who are named as fathers acknowledge paternity, while others contest the allegation. Blood tests play an increasingly important role in resolving these paternity disputes.

The second stage in the child-support-enforcement process is the establishment of the child-support award. Under the traditional system, the courts were given wide latitude in determining child-support amounts. In some jurisdictions, judges used numerical standards for determining child-support obligations. For example, nearly every county in Michigan used a standard in which the non-resident parent's obligation depended only upon the income of that parent and the number of children owed support (Chambers 1979). But before 1984 such child standards were the exception rather than the rule.

Although in principle child-support orders could be modified in response to changes in circumstances, legislation and judicial practice made it extremely difficult to do so. The explicit intention was to discourage 'unwarranted harassment of the supporting parent by the custodial parent and wasteful use of court facilities' (Krause 1981).

The third stage of the child-support-enforcement process is the payment of support. The standard procedure has been for the court to order the non-resident parent to pay, with the actual collection left to the beneficiary of the order—the resident parent. This meant that, if the non-resident parent failed to pay, the resident parent had to initiate a legal action, usually by citing the non-resident parent for contempt of court. This proceeding was fraught with difficulties for the resident parent. It required legal counsel—a substantial financial burden for a parent already not receiving support—and often involved difficult fact determinations because of the lack of adequate records of direct payments to the resident parent.

Jail is the ultimate sanction for those who do not pay. Thousands of non-resident parents have been jailed each year in Michigan for failure to comply with child-support orders. There have been no systematic studies on the prevalence of jailing elsewhere. According to Chambers (1979), jailing works. That is, when combined with an effective monitoring system, it deters non-payment. His conclusion is based on the strong association between performance and utilization of jails across counties in Michigan.

The old child-support-enforcement system condoned and therefore fostered parental irresponsibility. It was rife with inequity, and it contributed to poverty and welfare dependence.

Of women with children potentially eligible for child support—women whose children have a living non-resident father—only six out of ten even have a child-support award. The proportions vary with the marital status of the mother. Slightly more than eight out of ten divorced and remarried mothers have child-support awards. About 50 per cent of separated mothers have awards. Less than two in ten never-married mothers have awards. Of those with child-support awards, only half receive the full amount to which they are entitled and over a quarter receive nothing. All told, more than half of the women potentially eligible for child support receive nothing.

Child-support awards are also considered to be inadequate. As yet, however, we do not have good evidence about how much of the problem is due to initial awards being low and how much to the failure to update awards to reflect changes in the earning ability of the non-resident parent or changes in the cost of living. A preliminary analysis of Wisconsin court record data indicates that, on average, child-support orders during the years 1980–3 were nearly identical as a percentage of the non-resident parent's income to the percentages called for by the Wisconsin percentage-of-income standard, which was published in 1984. This suggests that the initial awards in Wisconsin were not too low and therefore that the failure to update was the source of low awards. However, the Wisconsin court records have missing data on income in about half the cases. A preliminary examination of national data suggests that the failure to update awards may account for no more than half of the difference between the observed level of awards and the Wisconsin standard.

When the number of broken marriages and paternity cases was small, perhaps greater equity was achieved by the old individualized system. In small communities, the judge knew the parents and their circumstances, so justice was better served by taking account of all particulars. But when the number of cases is large, and the system impersonal, this method breaks down. In practice, judges now do very little to tailor child support to particular circumstances. The case-by-case determination treats equals unequally.

Numerous studies have documented that the child-support system treats equals unequally (White and Stone 1976; Yee 1979). Data from Wisconsin divorce cases indicate awards that range from zero to over 100 per cent of the non-resident father's income (Nichols-Casebolt, Garfinkel, and Wong 1988). Every year, millions of non-resident parents fail to pay any child support. A few thousand are thrown in jail; but the vast bulk of those that do not pay suffer no consequences.

In addition to treating equals unequally, the child-support system is regressive. That is, child-support obligations represent a greater proportion of the incomes of low-income non-resident parents than of the incomes of those who are well off.

Finally, the child-support system contributes to the economic insecurity and welfare dependence of single mothers and their children. Nearly half of all single mothers with children are poor. Another quarter have incomes which are only a few thousand dollars above the poverty line (Garfinkel and McLanahan 1986). Furthermore, although the most fortunate half of mothers who divorce are unlikely to fall into poverty, they do suffer from huge income drops upon divorce—on average about 50 per cent (Duncan and Hoffman 1985). This pervasive economic insecurity in turn leads to widespread welfare dependence. Although the proportion of single mothers who receive welfare has dropped steadily since the mid-1970s, when it was over 50 per cent, the proportion remains over 40 per cent (Garfinkel and McLanahan 1986).

Federal interest in child support grew as the caseload of the AFDC programme grew and shifted from orphans to children with living absent parents. Although the first federal legislation to enforce collection of child support was enacted in 1950, and there were further bills in 1965 and 1967, the 1975 legislation was particularly significant because it established the Federal Office of Child Support Enforcement; required all states to establish state offices of child-support enforcement; and provided federal reimbursement for about three-quarters of each state's enforcement costs. That is to say, the 1975 Act created the public bureaucracy to enforce the private child-support obligation. The initial purpose of this bureaucracy was to collect child-support payment from non-resident parents of welfare recipients. The payments were to be made to welfare departments to reimburse them for their welfare outlays.

Some states already had relatively strong public agencies charged with enforcing private child support. Michigan and Wisconsin, for example, along with five other states, already required that all private child-support payments be paid to and thereby monitored by an administrative arm of the courts. As noted above, the courts in Michigan also used a simple numerical standard for establishing child-support obligations as a percentage of the non-resident parent's income. By 1979 Wisconsin had enacted a wage-assignment law, which required county courts to require employers to withhold child-support obligations from wages and other sources of income in the event that the obligers became delinquent in payment of child support.

By 1985 national collections reached $2.7 billion, including $1 billion for AFDC recipients. This represented an increase of 282 per cent in collections for AFDC families between 1976 and 1985. Census Bureau statistics indicate that real child-support award levels fell rather sharply during the early 1980s, and overall payment rates of child support relative to what is owed have increased only slightly. The decline in the real amount of child support owed seems attributable to the erosion of the real value of awards with inflation, to the changing composition of those getting awards (i.e. more never-married and fewer divorced women), and to the increase in the relative earnings of mothers *vis-à-vis* fathers (in many states, child-support awards decline as the earnings of the resident parent—usually the mother—increase (Beller and Graham 1988; Robins 1989).

Still, there is good reason to believe both that the system is getting better and that child-support collections will continue to grow, as the 1985 figures do not reflect the strongest federal child-support legislation to date. That legislation, passed in 1984 and 1988, will be discussed below.

Public Child Support

Public child support is a significant feature of the US child-support system. The AFDC programme is the largest public programme that provides cash benefits to children potentially eligible for child support. In 1988 the average monthly caseload in the AFDC programme consisted of 3.7 million families with 7.3 million children. Although the programme aids children of widows and children in two-parent families when the father is unemployed or disabled, altogether these represent only 13 per cent of the families aided. The overwhelming majority of families receiving AFDC consist of mothers with children who are living apart from their fathers. Indeed, the children aided by AFDC represent over one-third of all children living with their mothers who are potentially eligible for child support. This is a crude, conservative estimate. The denominator comes from US Bureau of the Census (1987), which indicates that there are 15.2 million children who live with their mothers who are potentially eligible for child support. (The four-or-more-children category was treated as if there was an average of five children in the category.) The Census report includes children up to age 21, whereas only those of up to age 18 are eligible for AFDC. This is why the estimate is conservative. The numerator comes from United States House of Representatives Committee of Ways and Means, *Background Material* (1989: Tables 21, 22, and 23, pp. 560, 563, and 569). Table 21 indicates there were 7.1 million child recipients of AFDC in 1985. Table 22 indicates that, in 1984, 3.6, 8.6, and 1.9 per cent of cases were eligible because of, respectively, incapacity, unemployment, or death of the parent. Table 26 indicates another 9.9 per cent of the cases in 1987 had no adult present. Thus 76 per cent of AFDC cases are headed by mothers potentially eligible for child support. Multiplying 7.1 million by 76 per cent yields 5.4 million children, which is about 36 per cent of the total number of children eligible for child support.

Resident parents who receive AFDC benefits must assign their rights to child support to the state and co-operate with state officials to help locate, establish the identity of, and secure child support from the non-resident parent of their children. The family is entitled to receive up to $50 per month of the child support paid by the non-resident parent. All additional child support paid is kept by the state to offset the AFDC benefit.

In the fiscal year 1988 the cost of the AFDC programme was $17 billion. Of this, $9.3 billion, or a bit more than half, was paid for by the federal government. The states paid for the rest. States, however, determine benefit levels and administer the programmes.

Families eligible for AFDC are also automatically eligible for medical assistance benefits through the Medicaid programme. In addition, nearly all AFDC families are eligible for food stamps, which may be used in lieu of money to purchase food. Finally, about 20 per cent of AFDC families also live in public housing or receive public rent subsidies.

Public transfers substantially exceed private child-support transfers. Whereas slightly over $7 billion in private child support was paid in 1985, expenditures for single-mother families in AFDC, Medicaid, Food Stamp, and housing assistance programmes equalled $24 billion, or more than three times private child support. Estimates of private child support are taken from US Bureau of the Census (1987). Estimates of public child transfers were derived by Garfinkel and McLanahan (1986: Table 11, p. 140).

All of the public transfer programmes discussd above have one thing in common: they provide benefits only to families with low incomes. To be eligible, families, for the most part, must have incomes below the poverty line. In a few states, because of work-related expense deductions, it is possible to remain on AFDC with incomes slightly above the poverty level. Despite all the attention such cases have received, however, they are rare.

In order to confine eligibility for these programmes to low-income families, benefits are reduced as other income increases. Benefits in the AFDC programme are reduced by one dollar for each dollar of unearned income. (As noted above, however, the first $50 per month of child support does not result in a reduction in AFDC benefits.) Earned income is treated somewhat more generously. Work-related expenses of up to $70 per month, plus up to $160 per month for child-care expenses, plus an additional $30 per month, are first subtracted from earnings. Benefits are then reduced by one dollar of earnings in excess of these deductions. In addition, for the first four months of work, one-third of all earnings are ignored in calculating benefits. Benefits in the Food Stamp programme are reduced by about 30 cents for each dollar of other income. Taken together, the benefit reduction rates in the AFDC and Food Stamp programmes average about 75 per cent. What is more, if a mother on AFDC can earn enough to leave welfare, she will lose not only her AFDC benefits, but after a one-year period her Medicaid benefits as well.

As mentioned above, dissatisfaction with AFDC has grown along with costs and caseloads. On a number of occasions regulations have been changd in an effort to reduce the welfare population. The first government programme explicitly to aid AFDC mothers in finding employment was the Work Incentive programme (WIN), established in 1967. WIN required all non-exempted persons aged 16 or older who applied for or received AFDC to register for work and training. The programme was supposed to assess job skills and provide job training and employment placement, but it has furnished little assistance of this nature. It has not had much impact on either work or caseloads.

In 1981 the Reagan administration sought to cut off benefits to recipients with substantial earnings and to require those who received benefits to work for them. Congress agreed to much, but not all, of this strategy. By 1987 almost every major welfare reform proposal contained both work requirements and·the provision of services such as training and day care to facilitate work, and the 1988 Family Support Act enacted this new philosophy into law.

Nevertheless, as it is currently structured, AFDC encourages welfare dependency. After four months on a job, a woman on AFDC faces a reduction in benefits of a dollar for every dollar of net earnings. It is not surprising, therefore, that the vast majority of mothers on welfare do not work.

Even if they were fully employed, however, one-half of welfare mothers could earn no more than the amount of their annual welfare grant, and another quarter could earn only up to about $3,200 more (Sawhill 1976). How many more could not earn enough to cover the costs of their Medicaid benefits has not been established. But surely the numbers are large. Finally, this estimate takes no account of the necessity of some of these mothers to work less than full time, full year (Ellwood 1986). This evidence suggests that transfers are necessary to provide an adequate standard of living for these families. The only way to alleviate the poverty of single parents without creating total dependency is to supplement rather than replace their earnings. This is what a child-support-assurance system is designed to accomplish.

A Child-Support-Assurance System

Under a child-support-system, all parents living apart from their children are obliged to share their income with their children. The sharing rate is specified in law and, apart from exceptional cases, depends only upon the number of children owed support. In Wisconsin this rate, known as the percentage-of-income standard, is equal to 17 per cent of the non-resident parent's gross income for one child, and 25, 29, 31, and 34 per cent respectively for two, three, four, and five or more children. The obligation is collected through payroll withholding when that is possible, as are social security and income taxes. In other words, child support is akin to a proportional tax on non-resident parents. Children with a legally liable parent are entitled to benefits equal to either the child support paid by the non-resident parent or a socially assured minimum benefit, whichever is higher. Should the non-resident parent pay less than the assured benefit, the difference is paid by the state. The extra costs of the assured benefit are financed from AFDC savings that result from increased child-support collections.

The state of Wisconsin, following the recommendation of the Institute for Research on Poverty 1982 study report (Garfinkel and Melli 1982), is implementing the child-support-assurance system in stages. The percentage-of-income standard became the presumptive child-support obligation as of July 1987 (i.e. judges may depart from the standard only if they construct a written justification which can be reviewed by a higher court). The percentages, however, are still being used to arrive at fixed-dollar child-support orders rather than orders expressed in percentage terms. Immediate withholding became operational state-wide in July 1987. The assured benefit was scheduled to be piloted in two counties in January 1990, but has been postponed.

The plan has a number of advantages over the traditional court proceedings. A percentage-of-income standard for child support would reduce inequities and is easy to understand. A fixed sharing rate provides automatic indexing of child-support awards, so that, as the income of the non-resident parent increases, the award increases. Since very low child-support payments are related to lack of adjustment for increased earnings as well as to low court orders, indexing should increase payment amounts. Also, if the earnings of non-resident parents decrease owing to unemployment or illness, their obligations will also drop.

Automatic withholding, rather than withholding in response to delinquency, will increase both the size and timeliness of child-support payments. Non-resident parents who have defaulted for a few months may have spent the money for other purposes and often cannot pay back the arrearage. Most important, Wisconsin's recent experience with withholding in response to delinquency shows that 70 per cent of non-resident parents became delinquent within three years. No society profits by making so many into lawbreakers. Uniform automatic withholding removes any element of stigma and punishment from the collection process, while enhancing children's economic security.

The assured benefit insures children from middle- and upper-middle-income families against the risk that their non-resident parent's income declines. When the percentage-of-income standard is fully implemented and child-support orders are expressed in percentage terms, a sudden decline in the non-resident parent's income caused by illness or unemployment would result in a precipitous decline in child support if it were not for the assured benefit.

The assured benefit also enables those with low earning ability and low child-support entitlements to escape poverty. A large proportion of welfare mothers would still be poor even if they worked full time and received all the private child support to which they were entitled in the absence of an assured benefit.

The assured benefit will encourage work and reduce welfare dependence, because, unlike welfare, the assured benefit will not be reduced by one dollar for each dollar of earnings.

Finally, the assured benefit is an effective means of reinvesting the savings of increased child-support collections. Sharing the gains of increased collections with poor resident-parent families who have child-support awards is an investment, because it gives the resident parents an incentive to co-operate in establishing paternity and locating the non-resident parent.

A cost-neutral federal child-support-assurance system could, according to my crude estimate, reduce the poverty gap—the amount by which a family's income falls below the poverty line—and AFDC caseloads by, respectively, 40 per cent and 50 per cent. This estimate is an upper bound in that it assumes child-support awards, upon which eligibility for benefits depends, are obtained in all cases.

This estimate both indicates the potential of a child-support system to reduce poverty and dependence, and reveals its limits. For it tells us that, even if all the welfare savings resulting from increased private child support to AFDC families were used to finance an assured benefit, over half of the poverty problem for this group would remain. In short, child support can play a large part in solving the nation's poverty and welfare problems for single mothers and their children. But, by itself, it is insufficient.

Federal Child-Support Reforms of 1984 and 1988

After a series of minor reforms in the late 1970s and early 1980s, major federal child-support legislation was enacted in 1984 and 1988. These reforms move the nation a considerable distance on the collection side and a tiny distance on the benefit side towards a child-support-assurance system. They require states to adopt expedited procedures for establishing paternity and child-support awards; provide for increased federal assistance for establishing paternity; mandate performance standards for state programmes to establish paternity; and require states to obtain social security numbers from both parents when issuing birth certificates and to use these numbers in establishing paternity.

The states are required to adopt numeric child-support guidelines that courts must use in determining child-support obligations. While the 1984 legislation allowed the courts to ignore the guidelines, the 1988 legislation makes the guidelines the presumptive child-support award. Furthermore, states are required to review child-support awards at least every three years.

States are also required routinely to withhold child-support obligations from pay cheques. Whereas the 1984 legislation required withholding only in the event that payments were one month delinquent, the 1988 legislation requires withholding from the outset of the child-support obligation for all IV–D cases (those being handled by the Office of Child Support Enforcement) as of 1990, and for all child-support cases as of 1994. In order to carry out these requirements, states will be forced to develop the capacity routinely to monitor payments in all cases. Only seven states, including Wisconsin, had this capability by 1988.

Finally, 1984 and 1988 legislation gave Wisconsin and New York respectively the authority to use federal funds that would otherwise have been devoted to AFDC to help fund assured child-support benefits. New York State commenced a demonstration of a variant of an assured benefit in autumn 1988, but the Wisconsin plan to do so in 1990 was postponed.

Conclusion

The old systems of private and public child support in the United States are inadequate. The private system condones and thereby fosters parental irresponsibility, is rife with inequity, and contributes to the poverty and welfare dependence of single mothers and their children. The public system does too little to reduce economic insecurity and dependence.

The new child-support-assurance system in Wisconsin has become a model for the nation. State standards of child support and routine income-withholding of child-support obligation move child support away from the judicial model of treating each case uniquely towards a more bureaucratic model characteristic of taxation and social insurance programmes. With respect to an assured child-support benefit, the federal government has proceeded more cautiously by giving New York and Wisconsin authority to use federal funds that would otherwise have been devoted to AFDC to help fund an assured child-support benefit.

Although a fully implemented national child-support-assurance system could reduce poverty and welfare dependence respectively by as much as 40 per cent and 50 per cent, equally substantial poverty and welfare dependence would remain. Better child-care and health-care services, along with cash benefits, like child allowances, would complement and enhance the anti-poverty effectiveness of a child-support-assurance system.

References

BELLER, A. H., and GRAHAM, J. W. (1988), 'Child Support Payments: Evidence from Repeated Cross-Sections', *American Economic Review, Papers and Proceedings*, 78: 81–5.

BUMPASS, L. (1984), 'Children and Marital Disruption: A Replication and Update', *Demography*, 21: 71–82.

CHAMBERS, D. (1979), *Making Fathers Pay: The Enforcement of Child Support* (Chicago).

DUNCAN, G. J., and HOFFMAN, S. D. (1985), 'A Reconsideration of the Economic Consequences of Marital Dissolution', *Demography*, 22: 485–98.

ELLWOOD, D. (1986), 'Working Off of Welfare: Prospects and Policies for Self-Sufficiency of Women Heading Families',

Institute for Research on Poverty Dicussion Paper No. 803–86 (University of Wisconsin-Madison).

GARFINKEL, I., and MCLANAHAN, S. (1986), *Single Mothers and their Children: A New American Dilemma* (Washington).

——MELLI, M. (1982), *Child Support: Weaknesses of the Old Features of a Proposed New System*, i, Institute for Research on Poverty Special Report No. 32A (University of Wisconsin-Madison).

——WONG, P. (1987), 'Child Support and Public Policy', paper presented at the Conference of National Experts: Lone Parents: The Economic Challenge of Changing Family Structures, 15–17 Dec. OECD (Paris).

KRAUSE, H. D. (1981), *Child Support in America: The Legal Perspective* (Charlottesville).

NICHOLS-CASEBOLT, A., GARFINKEL, I., and WONG, P. (1988), 'Reforming Wisconsin's Child Support System', in S. Danziger and J. F. Witte (eds.), *State Policy Choices: The Wisconsin Experience* (Madison, Wis.).

ROBINS, P. K. (1989), 'Why Are Child Support Awards Declining?' (IRP Discussion Paper No. 885–89; University of Wisconsin-Madison).

SAWHILL, I. (1976), 'Discrimination and Poverty among Women who Head Families', *Signs: Journal of Women in Culture and Society*, 2: 201–11.

UNITED STATES BUREAU OF THE CENSUS (1987), *Child Support and Alimony, 1985* (Current Population Reports, Series P-23, No. 152; Washington, DC).

UNITED STATES DEPARTMENT OF HEALTH AND HUMAN SERVICES, Office of Child Support Enforcement (1986), *Child Support Enforcement Statistics, Fiscal Year 1985*, ii (Rockville, Md).

——*Child Support Enforcement, Fifth Annual Report to the Congress for the Period Ending September 30, 1980* (Rockville, Md).

UNITED STATES HOUSE OF REPRESENTATIVES, Committee on Ways and Means (1989), *Background Material and Data on Programs within the Jurisdiction of the Committee on Ways and Means* (Washington, DC).

WHITE, K., and STONE, T, (1976), 'A Study of Alimony and Child Support Rulings, with some Recommendations', *Family Law Quarterly*, 11: 75–85.

YEE, L. (1979), 'What Happens in Child Support Cases', *Denver Law Journal*, 57: 21–68.

11. Child Maintenance in Australia: The New Era

Margaret Harrison

Since 1985 Australian family law has seen increasing amounts of energy devoted to the issue of child maintenance. The early years of the Family Law Act of 1975 were dominated by discussion about the introduction of no-fault divorce, arguments about the effectiveness of the informal procedures of the Family Court, its closure to the public, and the role of the court counsellors in custody and access application. There were complaints about the Family Court's apparent inability to enforce maintenace orders, and calls for a reintroduction of jailing for failure to pay; but such issues were not in the forefront until the early 1980s.

At that time several concerns, which have continued to drive the reform movement, converged. These included mounting disquiet over the burgeoning social security budget, related anger at the ability of non-custodial parents to avoid financial responsibilities for their children, and the obvious relationship between lone-parent pensioners and poverty: One perceived cause of the increasing numbers of lone-parent pensions was the Family Law Act provision, which allowed a custodial parent's social-security entitlements to be taken into account when child maintenance was being assessed. This appeared to result in pensions being treated as the major source of support for many, with the non-custodial parent, almost invariably the father, 'topping up' the pensions amount, if his income permitted, to the maximum level permitted by the income test. In 1985 nearly 90 per cent of all lone parents were pensioners, and less than 20 per cent of them received income, from any source, which exceeded the free area.

Thus, social security, not known for its generosity, was being relied on to raise children, and private support was seen merely as an addition to public support. As the stringent income test is seen by many as a work disincentive, there was concern that a generation of women with the care of dependent children were being locked into a cycle of poverty. The reliance on benefits was accentuated by the failure to activate provisions in the Social Security Act which required pension applicants to seek maintenance from their child's other parent before their pension entitlement was assured.

Compliance has always been a serious problem for those who actually have orders or approved agreements in place. In 1983 the Attorney-General's Department investigated the possibility of establishing a national maintenance agency for the collection and enforcement of orders. Only two states—Western Australia and South Australia—had centralized agencies in place. The report of the Department's inquiry team included an estimate that 40 per cent of all parents with maintenance orders received *no* payments, and a maximum of 40 per cent of orders were fully complied with. In response to these figures, the team recommended the setting up of a separate enforcement agency with a large administrative structure similar in size to that of the Family Court itself. Not surprisingly, this found little government support.

The inquiry was criticized for its restricted terms of reference, which had resulted in an almost total failure to address: (1) the issues of the low amounts being awarded as child maintenance, and (2) the failure of the existing enforcement agencies to increase the proportion of eligible parents who were actually receiving maintenance. One outcome of the discussion at that time was a suggestion that a child-support tax should be considered, with a levy being placed via the taxation system on the gross income of the non-custodial parent (Harrison, Harper, and Edwards 1984). While this had already been considered in several overseas jurisdictions, it was a new concept for Australia, and was treated initially with considerable scorn.

The Economic Consequences of Marriage Breakdown Study

In 1985 the Australian Institute of Family Studies (AIFS) began publishing results from its Economic Consequences of Marriage Breakdown study which had been conducted the previous year (McDonald 1986). One striking finding from that study was that there was a 'going rate' of $20 per week per child for maintenance orders and agreements, which operated irrespective of the income of the liable parent, and resulted in lower proportions of income being paid by higher earning fathers. The AIFS costs-of-children study (Lovering 1984) had estimated the expenditure needed to raise children of different ages at different socio-economic levels, and the discrepancy between these figures and the amounts being paid in child maintenance was considerable.

An additional finding, already foreshadowed in the Californian context by Weitzman (1985), was that marriage breakdown had different economic impacts on men and women. Women (who had custody of children in nearly 90 per cent of cases) were generally worse off than they had been just before separation. This was particularly noticeable in the case of female lone parents, three-quarters of whom were, on average, $78 per week worse off, whilst three-quarters of the men were better off by a similar amount (Weston 1986). The data also showed that women whose husbands were earning the highest amounts of income before separation were most likely to be financially dependent on them, and consequently were the most likely to have been in receipt of social-security payments since the separation.

The Economic Consequences study was composed of divorced parents, who comprise about one-third of all those eligible for child maintenance. In 1986 McDonald and Weston calculated from a variety of data sources that 24 per cent of *all* potentially eligible custodial mothers were receiving regular maintenance payments in 1982. Divorced women were the most likely recipients (36 per cent), the never-married the least likely (9 per cent).

Administrative Assessment Proposals

During 1985 the Family Law Council published a report which endorsed the need for maintenance to be set by way of administrative formula, and suggested several models for its accomplishment. The government's response was to set up a Cabinet Sub-Committee, which examined a variety of reform options and set out issues for community discussion. The Committee's report (1986) paved the way for reform by way of administrative assessment, but left unanswered its exact nature and application. The report stated the necessary objectives of any reform as being that:

- non-custodial parents share in the cost of supporting their children according to their capacity to pay;
- adequate support is available for all children not living with both parents;
- Commonwealth expenditure is limited to the minimum necessary to ensure these needs are met;
- work incentives to participate in the labour force are not impaired; and
- the overall arrangements are non-intrusive to personal privacy and are simple, flexible, and efficient.

The next official move was an announcement in early 1987 that major reform was imminent, but that it would be phased in over two stages. The first stage would ensure collection of maintenance specified in existing court orders and court-registered agreements through a Child Support Agency which would be part of the Australian Taxation Department. The second stage would address the issue of amounts by providing for administrative assessment by way of a formula. With this move the government presumably sought to diffuse opposition, and to acquire some time in which staff expertise and major administrative structures could be built up, whilst helping those whose orders had been deliberately flouted or had petered out.

Stage One

Major Characteristics

Ultimately, the stage-one reform package involved amendments to the Family Law Act and Social Security Legislation, and passage of the Child Support Act. The latter Act passed effortlessly through both Houses of Parliament with bi-partisan support and came into operation on 1 June 1988. The Family Law Act amendments (which were effective from 1 April 1988) had the effect of removing the provision which had previously allowed social-security entitlements to be taken into account in determining maintenance, gave priority to child support over other commitments of separating parents, and required the court to consider a non-custodial parent's capacity to pay periodic maintenance before considering other forms of payment. Where non-periodic payments *were* specified, the court had to specify exactly what the maintenance component was, so that the financial circumstances of pensioners or potential pensioners were known for the administration of the income test.

The revenue aspects of the reforms were made clear with the amendments to the Social Security Act. These introduced an additional income test for money received as maintenance. The effect of this is that pensions are reduced by 50 cents in the dollar where maintenance in excess of $15 per week for the first child and $5 for each subsequent child is received. Pensioners are still able to earn $40 per week and $12 for each child in their care before their pensions start to be reduced. The various amounts involved in non-periodic payments (most commonly made for clothing, extra lessons, or school fees) must be calculated and converted into weekly sums, once again for the purpose of assessing whether, and to what extent, the income test applies. The amendments involved a reactivation of the provision that parents in receipt of lone-parent pensions were required to take 'reasonable steps to obtain maintenance'.

One measure of the anticipated savings is to be found in the financial-impact statement in the explanatory memorandum to the child-support legislation, where net gains of $120 million in the 1988/9 financial year were predicted.

The Child Support Act was the central feature of the stage-one reforms. It established the Child Support Agency within the Australian Taxation Department, and created the office of Child Support Registrar (held by the Commissioner of Taxation).

Once an order or court-approved agreement is registered, the amount owing becomes a debt due to the Commonwealth and payable to the Registrar. The custodial parent is no longer a party to the transaction, and therefore cannot take any proceedings for late payment or default. All payees are required to register with the Agency within fourteen days of their order being made or their agreement being registered, and must indicate whether they want their maintenance collected by the Agency or not. Pensioner payees *must* so indicate. Non-pensioner payees may opt in or out of the system at any time, but payers have no choice. The Act also contains a variety of financial penalties for late registration or payment.

Payment may be made directly to the Child Support Agency or, where possible, the maintenance will be collected directly at source by the payer's employer and transferred to the Agency. Where this automatic withholding occurs, no garnishee order is required. The money is finally transferred from the Agency's trust account to the Department of Social Security, which transmits it monthly to the custodial parent, after any necessary pension adjustments have been made.

Overall, the stage-one reforms have achieved an integration of the social security, taxation, and family-law systems. One obvious advantage of including the Taxation Office in the procedures is its ability to trace and locate liable parents, and involve employers in the payment process. The Family Law Act and Social Security Act now have complementary (instead of sometimes conflicting) provisions for, for example, the identification and quantification of non-periodic payments. All stage-one-related legislation has a strong and consistent theme that financial support of children is primarily a two-parent responsibility.

Operation

The AIFS is carrying out an evaluation of the effectiveness of the stage-one procedures. To date data have been collected and analysed from (1) a sample of parents eligible to pay or receive child maintenance before the scheme came into operation, and (2) a sample of respondents from the first 6,000 Agency registrants (Harrison, Snider, and Merlo 1990). This latter sample was drawn in order to assess any 'teething problems' experienced by Agency non-custodial and custodial parents, and is the forerunner of a representative sample which will be approached in 1991, when numbers have built up sufficiently.

The pre-scheme data show the accuracy of earlier estimates of the coverage of custodial parents by maintenance awards. Only 34 per cent of the 3,500 custodial parents surveyed were receiving regular payments; 12 per cent had once received it, but payments had stopped; 7 per cent said maintenance arrangements had been made but no money had ever been paid; 23 per cent had never managed to have orders or agreements put in place; 24 per cent said specifically that they had never sought maintenance from their child's other parent. Where maintenance *was* paid, it averaged $23.98 per child per week. This information provides a baseline from which the effectiveness of the reforms may be measured subsequently.

The early data on Child Support Agency registrants, complemented by information from the Agency itself, from welfare groups, and from family-law practitioners, are already providing some clear indications of the operation of the stage-one procedures. One immediately obvious finding is that so far only a very small proportion (approximately 5 per cent) of all those eligible to receive maintenance for children in their care have been affected, with about 30,000 cases being registered out of an estimated potential population of 500,000 to 600,000 (Harrison, Snider and Merlo 1990). Estimated savings for the 1988/9 financial year are about $18 million—a small fraction of the original estimates.

Overall client satisfaction is not easy to judge, as those with complaints are probably more likely to express an opinion than are those who are satisfied or unconcerned. However, in general, custodial parents are happy with the new procedures, and non-custodial parents are not. The major grievance of custodians is that the initial post-registration payment takes approximately eight weeks to be transmitted to them, a delay which angers parents whose money was received more speedily under previous arrangements. For those whose former partners had refused to pay, had paid irregularly, or in incorrect amounts, or were simply untraceable, the reforms appear to be an improvement. However, custodians who were on full pensions and had no earned income have found their pensions reduced where the amounts paid pursuant to their orders exceed the amount permitted under the maintenance-income test. Although their incomes remain the same, some are angered (perhaps unreasonably) by this, possibly expecting that their financial positions would actually improve under the reforms; others are quite bewildered and unable to understand the adjustments. Because two departments plus the courts are involved in the administration of the scheme, there are several opportunities for both custodial and non-custodial parents to find themselves in, or be directed to, the wrong department, or to be shunted from one to the other.

Non-custodial parents' major complaints centre around the perceived lopsided nature of the system, which pursues payment of child maintenance but cannot guarantee access.

Another 'hiccup' is the slow introduction of the automatic deduction arrangements. These were publicized as one of the strengths of the scheme when it was introduced. However, at the time of writing, only a small percentage of cases involve employer-transmitted payments.

In terms of amounts being paid, the Agency has been registering a large number of 'old' orders, and consequently average payments are still low—about $25 per week per child. Analysis of maintenance payments *vis-à-vis* cost-of-living figures for 1988 and 1989 suggests that orders made since the stage-one reforms came into effect are $4.65 and $6.78 respectively per week higher than would otherwise be expected.

Opposition

When the reforms were announced, there was immediate opposition from several disparate sources. Feminists were quick to object to what they described as the reinforcement of the 'eternal biological family' (Graycar 1989) and of women's dependence on men. The privatization of child maintenance was seen as being of no particular assistance to women who, if their job prospects are poor and child-care facilities unavailable or too costly, are unable to improve their long-term opportunities. Welfare groups were concerned that women would be obliged to seek maintenance via the courts before their pension entitlement was guaranteed, and were unimpressed by government assurances that the obligation would not be enforced where there was fear of violence or harassment. The maintenance income test was also criticized for its stringency, lending weight to concerns that the reforms were driven more by the desire to contain public expenditure than by a determination to improve the poor financial circumstances of lone-parent families. Lawyers were happy enough with the collection aspects of stage one, but began to lobby intensively against the administrative assessment proposals, as did lone-father groups. The latter were worried that amounts payable would increase considerably. Lawyers argued that 'the interests of justice require each case to be assessed individually rather than being subject to a broad formula approach. [This] derives from the basic and traditional concept of access to the courts for enforcement of an individual's rights' (Lanteri 1989).

Stage Two

Once the decision was made to adopt a formulaic approach to maintenance assessment, a number of important decisions still had to be made about the precise nature of the formula. These included: to whom it would apply; what percentages of either gross or net income should be allocated for child maintenance; whether the formula could be avoided by those with income under or over a certain level; whether custodial-parent income should be taken into account; how non-periodic payments should be treated; in what circumstances appeals or variation should be permitted; and how amounts might be reviewed. As part of this process the government appointed a Child Support Consultative Group, under the chairmanship of a Family Court judge, to advise on a formula which the Child Support Agency would ultimately apply. The Group's report was published in 1988 and many of its recommendations were subsequently translated into the Child Support (Assessment) Act which came into operation on 1 October 1989. This Act only applies to maintenance of children who were born or whose parents separated after that date. There was concern that retrospectivity might work unfairly where parents had made arrangements on the basis of a completely different set of principles. This would be most obvious in cases where a larger portion of the matrimonial home had been transferred to the custodian, and new maintenance calculations ignored or called for a recalculation of its value.

Maintenance assessment under the Act is based on the taxable income of the non-custodial parent (and in some circumstances the custodial parent). The non-custodian is permitted to have an amount of formula-free income (called the self-support component), which is deducted from the taxable income. The remaining sum is multiplied by the appropriate child-support percentage. The amount of the self-support component varies with the number of natural or adopted children for whom the non-custodial parent has ongoing care, the principle being that neither the first nor the second family should benefit at the expense of the other. Where there are no such children, the exemption is approximately \$6,500 per year; where a new child is born, the amount increases to \$12,000. The component is not adjusted to take into account the need to support a financially dependent wife, or step-children.

The child-support percentages vary according to the number of children eligible for support. Where they are in the sole or primary care of the custodial parent, they are: 18 per cent for one child and 27 per cent for two, ranging to 36 per cent for five or more children. Where custody is shared between parents, or with a third person, different percentages apply.

The percentages were determined by using evidence which showed the proportion of family income normally spent on children in a two-parent family, together with a number of additional factors which would apply in the case of separated families. They included a recognition that child-rearing costs are higher where parents do not live together, that custodial parents bear the indirect costs of child-rearing, while non-custodial parents incur costs associated with access visits.

As an example of the way in which maintenance is assessed administratively in a 'normal' situation, the following example is provided.

The separating couple (married or *de facto*) have two children who they agree, will live primarily with their mother. The father has a taxable income of \$25,000 per annum (an average income in Australia in the late 1980s) and no new children to support. The mother is earning \$18,000 per annum.

The father's liability is worked out by deducting the self-support component from his taxable income, and multiplying the remaining sum by 27 per cent.

With the figures in this example this translates as:

(\$25,000 – \$6,500) × 27 per cent

or \$4,995 per annum (\$96 per week) for the two children. The discrepancy between amounts commonly ordered by courts before the reforms and the amounts payable under the administrative assessment provisions is obviously significant.

Using the same basic example, and assuming incomes remain unchanged, if subsequently the non-custodial father has a new child, his payments to his first family will be reduced, as the self-support component will double. The formula in that case would be:

($25,000 – $12,00) × 27 per cent

giving a total annual liability of $3,510 ($67.50 per week).

The legislation adopted the Consultative Group's recommendations about the treatment of custodial parental income, which was a controversial topic. It acknowledges that the custodian is already involved in direct and indirect income-sharing with the children by providing items such as clothing and entertainment, and taking her income into account immediately would be blatantly unfair. The solution is to disregard earnings unless they exceed a total of the average, plus an allocation for child-care expenses (for children aged less than 12). Custodial parents' income is, on current figures, therefore only of relevance to the formula when it exceeds approximately $28,000 per annum. At or above that level it reduces the custodial parent's liability in the following way: the non-custodial father in the earlier example is earning $25,000 per annum and the custodial mother is earning $30,000. The father has no new children, so the self-support component is $6,500 per annum. This is adjusted by the amount the mother's income exceeds the permitted amount. The father's maintenance liability is:

($25,000 – ($6,500 + $2000)) × 27 per cent

This translates as $4,455 per annum, or $85 per week.

The formula and its permitted variations were intended to be uncomplicated and to enable separating parents to have a clear understanding of their financial responsibilities towards their children. However, already family lawyers are complaining vociferously that the mathematics involved make it difficult for them to explain to clients what their assessed amounts will be.

One important characteristic of the administrative assessment procedures is that the assessed liability is reviewed annually. The AIFS Economic Consequences of Marriage Breakdown study showed that, before 1988, amounts paid as child maintenance usually remained constant over a period of several years, despite the impact of inflation on original amounts, and regardless of changes in custodial or non-custodial parental incomes. Thus, unless the parents were able to come to a private arrangement, or the custodian had the tenacity or wherewithal to return to court (as very few appeared to do), the value of maintenance awards was eroded over the years.

Once the maintenance assessment has been made, the collection process already established for stage one applies.

Obviously the intention of the stage-two legislation is to remove the function of quantifying maintenance from the courts in an overwhelming number of cases. As with stage-one provisions, pensioners have statutory limitations on the arrangements they may make, and their ability to make private arrangements is limited. Non-pensioners may contract out by lodging consent agreements with the Agency. Provided these satisfy formal requirements, they will be binding and enforceable, and may be varied by later agreements. Unregistered child-support agreements may also be entered into, but it is too early in the life of the scheme for the extent of their usage to be known.

The Role of the Legal System

It is also too early to know how frequently the appeals provisions of the Child Support (Assessment) Act will be relied on. Practitioners have given dire warnings of the frequency with which the formula will be shown to be inappropriate, and a number of interesting test cases are anticipated. But by December 1990, from over 25,000 administrative assessments made, only 169 appeals had been lodged or heard.

The appeal provisions are based on the existence of special circumstances, the proof of which will allow the administrative assessment to be departed from in specific instances. These include the fact that the child has special needs, that the liable parent has a duty to maintain another person (including another child), that there are high costs associated with access, and that an inequitable determination would result from the application of the formula because of the income, earning capacity, property, and financial resources of either parent.

This last point would include the case where a non-custodial parent has a high taxable income. A cap was imposed on the formula, on the basis that child-raising expenses are not directly proportional to incomes over a certain level, and that expenditure on children by high-income families is largely discretionary. Therefore, maintenance liability for all non-custodial fathers, regardless of their incomes, cannot, under the formula, exceed the amount that would be payable by a liable parent earning two-and-a-half times average earnings (approximately $65,000 per annum).

The Australian Prime Minister pledged in 1986 that no child in the country would be in poverty by the year 1990. While it is a promise he has probably lived to regret, the new maintenance system (both stages one and two) is one of the Labor Party's planks in its platform to improve the financial position of children. As such, it has been and will continue to be closely monitored.

Having been in operation since October 1989, the effectiveness and impacts of the more radical stage-two provisions cannot yet be gauged. There is a good deal of rhetoric and apprehension that the payment of much higher amounts of maintenance will create a backlash against custodial parents, and lead to an increase in custody and access disputes. (The contrary view is that more non-custodial parents will become involved in their children's lives in a positive way, and that access battles will be reduced as the non-payment argument will no longer apply). Other, more fanciful, speculations include the hope that men will only have additional children when they can afford to. Non-custodial parent groups have been as relentless in their opposition as the lawyers have been, using both the 'no-access–no-payment' argument, and the objection that the formula and its variations will lead to ridiculously high payments. However, the reforms have come into practice with little publicity. Various attitude surveys have shown that the average taxpayer supports the containment of public spending, on the basis that he is 'tired of supporting other people's children'.

Obviously for those directly affected by the new procedures, attitudes will take some time to change, remembering that for many years payment was virtually an elective act, and amounts paid were often pitifully small. The different eligibility requirements for stage one and stage two have complicated the picture, producing several simultaneous 'generations' of separated and divorced parents who are paying (or not) according to different legislative provisions. While there will be some interesting challenges to the legislation, and probably some minor amendments to it over the next year or so, Australia has departed from its previous maintenance assessment, collection, and payment procedures in a bold and substantial way.

References

Attorney-General's Department (1984), *A Maintenance Agency for Australia: The Report of the National Maintenance Inquiry* (Canberra).

Australian Cabinet Sub-Committee on Maintenance (1986), *Child Support: A Discussion Paper on Child Maintenance* (North Ryde, NSW).

Child Support Consultative Group (1988), *Child Support: Formula for Australia* (The Fogarty Report) (Canberra).

Family Law Council (1985), *Report of the Maintenance Sub-Committee* (Canberra).

Graycar, R. (1989), 'Family Law and Social Security in Australia: The Child Support Connection', *Australian Journal of Family Law*, 3/1: 70–92.

Harrison, M., Harper, P., and Edwards, M. (1984), 'Child Support—Public or Private?' paper presented at the Family Law in 84 conference of the Law Council of Australia (Hobart).

——and McDonald, P. (1988), 'Parents and Children after Marriage Breakdown: The Price of Child Maintenance', in *Bicentary Family Law Conference* (Business Law Education Centre, Melbourne).

——Snider, G., and Merlo, R. (1990), *Who Pays for the Children?* (Australian Institute of Family Studies, Monograph 9; Melbourne).

Lanteri, A. (1989), 'Child Maintenance: The Child Support Agency Scheme', unpublished paper presented at the Third Australian Family Research Conference (Ballarat).

Lovering, K. (1984), *Cost of Children in Australia* (Australian Institute of Family Studies, Working Paper No. 8; (Melbourne).

McDonald, P. (ed.) (1986), *Settling Up: Property and Income Distribution on Divorce in Australia* (Sydney).

——Weston, R. (1986), 'The Data Base for Child Support Reform', in P. Troy (ed.) *Child Support* (Canberra).

Weitzman, L. (1985), *The Divorce Revolution: The Unexpected Social and Economic Consequences for Women and Children in America* (New York).

Weston, R. (1986), 'Changes in Household Income Circumstances', in P. McDonald (ed.), *Settling Up: Property and Income Distribution on Divorce in Australia* (Sydney).

12. Child Maintenance in the FRG

Barbara Willenbacher and Wolfgang Voegeli

In contrast to the common-law tradition, the German Civil Code has always treated claims for child maintenance as the individual claims of the children themselves. Child maintenance, therefore, is seen as meeting the individual needs of the child, and not as part of the household income of the custodial parent. This chapter refers to the provision in the FRG at the time of writing, 1989, according to the German Civil Code (Burgerlichesgesetzbuch (BGB)), but this formed the basis for provision throughout Germany after unification, in 1990.

Relations in the ascending and descending line have an obligation to maintain each other in case of need (BGB s. 1602). This obligation is normally limited to the extent that the debtor's own needs are met, but this limitation does not apply to the claims of minor children against their parents (BGB s. 1603). Parents, therefore, have to share their income with their children, even if this means poverty for themselves. The law does not distinguish between children living in the same household with their parent(s) or living elsewhere, and the amount of the maintenance due is not clearly defined. The German Civil Code states that the levels of adequate maintenance vary with the economic status of the recipient (BGB s. 1619 para 1). Every child may demand the payment of maintenance from his or her parents until he or she has received vocational training or academic education commensurate with his or her abilities. If the child is unemployed after such training, the parents have to provide maintenance for a time. But the child then has to take any available job, even if the job is not appropriate to the training and qualification achieved.

There have been numerous attempts in the past to create formulas by which the courts would be able to set a maintenance payment so that they could determine a disputed maintenance obligation without litigation. These efforts were successful after a law on the minimum maintenance ('Regelunterhalt') for ex-nuptial children was passed in 1969

(BGB s. 1615). Since then the federal government has fixed and regularly adjusted the minimum maintenance for three age groups (0–6, 7–12, 13–17 years) by statutory instruments ('Regelunterhaltsverordnung' of 27 June 1970, *Bundesgesetzblatt*, i. 1010). The adjustment is based on the recommendation of the Federal Bureau of Statistics. In addition to these standard amounts, the debtor parent has to cover any special need that might arise. In any event, though, the minimum living wage of DM 1,100 may not be undercut.

Procedure

To facilitate child-maintenance claims, the law provides procedures giving these claims a privileged status over other monetary claims. For ex-nuptial children the law does not provide for legal title to a specific sum, but rather the parental obligation to pay the current statutory minimum, plus, if appropriate, a supplement specified as a percentage of the statutory minimum (Civil Procedural Code (Zivilprozessirdnung (ZPO), ss. 642, 6642d)). On that basis there is a simplified procedure for setting and updating the amounts of maintenance in the orders made. If the child moves into a higher age group, or the 'Regelunterhalt' has changed, a junior officer of the court fixes the new amount without a hearing. The whole procedure is more administrative than judicial in character, as the respondent cannot oppose the increase as he is already bound to pay the 'Regelunterhalt', whatever its amount. This simplified procedure is applicable to orders from court decisions, settlements in court, and enforceable deeds with the consent of the paying parent.

On the basis of the 'Regelunterhalt' for ex-nuptial children, a table was prepared by the Supreme Court in Dusseldorf for the calculation of maintenance for children of divorcing parents, which the court regularly adjusts whenever the statutory minimum is adjusted. Though it has no legal status, this table, known as the Dusseldorf Table, has effectively structured child maintenance claims, as it has been almost universally adopted by the other supreme courts with minor discrepancies here and there. The statutory minimum maintenance for the three age groups is also the minimum of the Dusseldorf Table. Only the non-custodial parent has to pay monetary maintenance, related to this income, as the custodial parent regularly provides maintenance in kind by way of care and education. Only in exceptional cases, if the custodial parent has a substantially higher income, or if the child has special needs, or if for any other reason it would be a special hardship for the non-custodial parent to provide the full monetary maintenance, do the courts extend a monetary maintenance obligation to the custodial parent. The same holds true if the child does not live with the custodial parent. The table of amounts is devised for a standard family with two children. The supreme courts differ in their way of varying the table if there are fewer or more than two children. There are several systems of deductions and supplements, in which the difference between the next higher or lower income group is normally the maximum variation.

The 'Regelunterhalt' and the 'Jugendamt'—that is, the rule and the simplified procedure—did much to indirectly improve the enforcement of maintenance for divorcing parents. The Maintenance Reform Law of 29 July 1976 (*Bundesgesetzblatt*, i. 2029) subsequently introduced similar regulations for nuptial children. The 'Regelunterhalt' for ex-nuptial children was also declared to be the minimum level of maintenance for nuptial children who were living with a separated or divorced parent (BGB s. 1610 para. 3). The ZPO contains a simplified procedure for altering maintenance, which functions in much the same way as the procedure described for ex-nuptial children, the only difference being that nuptial children may not obtain a title to the payment of 'Regelunterhalt', but have to state specific amounts. By statutory rules the Federal Government only changes the levels for maintenance if the cost of living or real wages change considerably. Then, on application, a junior court officer will change a maintenance order accordingly without a hearing. Only after moving into a higher age group do nuptial children have to institute formal proceedings in case of non-co-operation of the paying parent. A further handicap for nuptial children exists in so far as their custodial parent has to take the initiative individually, as the 'Jugendamt' has no right to represent them legally. But it can set up enforceable orders at the request of both parents. The cheapest way of obtaining an enforceable title is to have an order set up by the 'Jugendamt'. The notary public is more order set up by the 'Jugendamt'. The notary public is more expensive, and the costliest way is a court decision. The cost of settlements in court are not much of an obstacle for most parents. Ex-nuptial children are represented by the 'Jugendamt' and so do not need professional legal representation. Separated mothers are likely to institute proceedings for divorce at some time anyway, and on application the court will hear maintenance claims together with the divorce suit. Usually, though, the question of maintenance arises during the period of separation. If the non-custodial parent refuses to pay, the custodial parent has to institute proceedings. Even if she turns to the welfare agencies for help, the latter would grant benefits only on the condition that the custodial parent institutes proceedings; otherwise the welfare agencies would decree the transfer of maintenance claims of the child to the welfare agencies and institute proceedings themselves. The latter procedure is not often chosen, as the welfare agencies do not seem to be competent to handle civil maintenance claims. Properly staffed these agencies could form effective enforcement agencies. Aid is liberally awarded and 70 per cent of child-support claims (before and after divorce) are financed by legal aid.

Enforcement

Once an order is made, enforcement is relatively easy if the debtor's address is known and he has a regular income. The former does not pose much of a problem in the FRG, where every person has to register his address, and 80 per cent of the working population do have a regular income. If, however, someone intends to dodge enforcement by constantly changing addresses and jobs, he may be quite successful, though at the price of his own economic downfall. Garnishment of wages or bank accounts only requires an application to a junior officer of the court, who will issue a garnishment order. It is not necessary for the debtor to have a hearing before the order is issued (s. 834 ZPO). He can himself institute formal proceedings to try and stop the garnishment.

In addition there is the child-support advance payment scheme ('Unterhaltsvorschussgesetz' of 23 July 1979, *Bundesgesetzblatt*, i. 1184), which offers minimum child support to every child under 6 for a maximum of three years. This law was originally meant to improve enforcement. Normally, the child must already be in possession of an enforceable title. The agency advances the 'Regelunterhalt' and tries to recover from the debtor parent. But it became apparent that 50 per cent of the children receiving advance payments are not in possession of an enforceable title and that recovery is therefore limited.

The law now also provides (1) for children who have instituted maintenance proceedings but after three months still do not have an enforceable title in their hands, (2) for chidren whose fathers or whose fathers' addresses are unknown or outside the FRG, and (3) for those cases in which litigation appears pointless (i.e. whose fathers are unable to pay).

This agency mainly serves two purposes. The first is to secure child maintenance in periods of transition. Twenty seven per cent of the payments go to children of separated parents, only 13 per cent to chidren of divorced parents. The second is to offer maintenance where private law claims are ineffective. The low-recovery quota of 20–30 per cent does not give any reason to believe that enforcement is the major impact of the law. On the contrary, it seems that, once a period of uncertainty or transition is over (i.e. fatherhood is established, or maintenance title secured during separation), then the civil-law claims and their individual enforcement are comparatively effective. There is no longitudinal study yet of child-maintenance claims over time. Compliance with the formula stated above (the Dusseldorf Table) is very high only in the higher income groups. One factor accounting for the lower actual payments is the system of deductions mentioned above. A second factor is the incidence of spousal maintenance. Where it competes with child maintenance for a share of a low male income, both are reduced proportionally in order to leave the debtor spouse/father his minimum living wage. It is clear, however, that the compliance rate for child support has increased over the last ten years. Child support is paid regularly and in full in 75 per cent of cases. Child support is regulated by court judgements in 50 per cent of the cases, and in the other 50 per cent is arranged by private settlements, just as for spousal maintenance. Since the enactment of the no-fault divorce law, the number of child-support actions has risen with spouse maintenance actions. Maintenance payments are now more often enforced by the court, and the figure for private settlements has fallen. Either the number of women willing to enforce maintenance payments has increased, or the number of men willing to pay maintenance has decreased.

13. Child Support, Wife Support, or Family Support?

Mavis Maclean and John Eekelaar

During the 1980s concern about the economic problems of lone-parent households has been expressed mainly in terms of concern about the low levels of child support awarded (together with low levels of compliance or enforcement of orders made). The measures taken in Europe, the United States, and Australia, described above (see Chapters 9, 10, and 11) have been concerned with enforcement and levels of child support and seem to be achieving some success in improving both. At the same time income support for ex-partners (usually ex-wives) seems to be disappearing with relatively little protest, though there is a resurgence of interest in alimony in the United States. Perhaps this is because the resources formerly divided between child support and spousal support may to some degree have remained similar in amount but have been renamed as child support.

Payments from parent to child carry less ideological 'baggage', are more acceptable to both parties, and fulfil the role of linking absent parent and child while side-stepping the marital conflict. The new Australian Child Support Agency, for example, is based upon the expectation of a low incidence of spousal support, the adjustment between ex-partners being achieved through property arrangement when resources permit. The wife, who is usually looking after the children, takes the house, which benefits both her and the children, and compensates for her interrupted earning capacity and pension. The husband, whose earning capacity is unaffected by marriage (except perhaps positively to a small degree), or by divorce (except perhaps negatively for a short period), is therefore creditworthy and able to start again in the housing market, and keeps his own occupational pension. The English court-based approach, which in the past has been required to give the interests of the children first consideration at the end of a marriage, has used its discretion to seek a solution by making the best use of existing resources. The judges have tended to try to keep a roof over the heads of the first family and the second family, and to share out other remaining resources to best effect, sometimes bearing in mind (although this is contrary to the 'public interest') the welfare arrangements of the Department of Social Security.

What is the 'Cost of a Child'?

If financial adjustment on divorce is to concentrate on increased levels of child support, we need to think carefully about what is included under that heading and what the implications are for ex-wives. The literature on establishing levels of child support indicates that the concept of child support includes at least four separate but related elements. These are subsistence costs, actual expenditure, the costs of child-care, and the opportunity costs of child-rearing.

Subsistence Costs

These include the costs which must necessarily be expended on raising a child. For example, the *Interim Report of the US Office of Child Support Enforcement*, which produced the basis for developing the US guidelines, states:

> First a minimum cost of raising a child can be specified. This subsistence level expenditure is keyed to a basic diet that meets minimum nutrition needs. The requirements of such a diet have been established by the US Department of Agriculture. Additional minimum expenditures are estimated in relationship to the minimum adequate diet. (US Department of Health and Human Services 1985)

Such an assessment is used in setting levels of subsistence welfare payments, such as the child additions to income support in the United Kingdom. These figures tend to assume that housing costs are met.

Actual Expenditure

This element represents the expenditure necessary to sustain a certain standard of living for a child. The US report cited above continues:

> Above the minimum level there is no absolute cost of raising a child. Expenditures on a child within a household are inextricably

dependant on the level of total household expenditures. As overall household income increases, additional income is allotted to children as well as adults. Thus the average 'cost' of a child in a middle income household is considerably more than the average 'cost' of a child in a low income household! (US Department of Health and Human Services 1985)

These costs in the United Kingdom can be derived from the Family Expenditure Survey data used to establish Equivalence Scales (i.e. the proportion of income required to maintain households of different composition at a comparable standard of living as indicated chiefly by the proportion of household expenditure devoted to food). In the OECD countries the average extra amount of income required to maintain the standard of living of a two-adult household after a child arrives is 20 per cent of the previous income. These two costs are generally the main components of what is held to be the 'cost' of a child. There are, however, two other kinds of child-related costs (OECD 1990).

The Costs of Child-Care

In calculating actual expenditure on children, the costs of caring for children while parents enter the labour market are generally omitted. These costs tend to increase significantly after divorce, as during marriage the spouse is the most common source of unpaid child-care, particularly when wives work part time.

The Opportunity Costs of Child-Rearing

The major impact of a child on its parents' standard of living arises from the mother's loss of income when she leaves work. The average mother of two children in the United Kingdom spends three years out of paid work followed by four years in part-time work. It has been calculated that, if she has completed seven years of secondary education but has no further qualifications, she loses a total of £135,000 in lost earnings and promotion forgone over her working life, leaving aside loss of pension entitlement (Joshi 1984).

It is not always clear how far child-support formulas take all these elements into account. Sometimes a certain adjustment might be made for increases in child-care costs on separation (as in the case of the Australian formula). In many

American formulas child-care costs are treated separately, on the grounds that they are both variable in themselves—ranging from free care from friends and kin to expensive professional care—and that these costs are specific to a particular group of lone parents—i.e. working mothers of young children.

Usually no account is taken of the opportunity costs of having children. Most formulas try to seek as support the proportion of income which a parent would have expended on the child had that parent's total income still been available to the child's household. This principle underpins the American income-sharing schemes, and the Australian scheme.

By including in the definition of the 'cost' of a child the share of income which is actually spent on the child, this approach incorporates into the concept of 'cost' an element drawn from the actual standard of living of the family concerned. This, however, causes problems when used as a measure for determining what should be paid in child support after the family has divided into two households.

By setting the award above subsistence, and at a level determined by reference to what *would* have been allocated to the child *if* the absent parent's *entire income* was available to the family (even though it is not), the award is made on the basis of an hypothesis that the whole family is better off than it probably is. The danger of this is that, because the ultimate result is perceived to be one of keeping the benefits received by the child 'in touch' with the income level of the absent parent, and is not a mere 'subsistence' award, it may be thought that an award made on this basis is all that needs be done to ensure a 'fair' result between the absent parent and the child. But this need not be so. The level assumes that this is the proportion of income which would otherwise be coming into the family that would be allocated to the child. But that income is not coming into the family. Such income, which might be essential to meet such liabilities as housing costs, local taxes, and utilities bills, is absent. An award made on this basis does not exhaust the extent of a claim a child might properly make.

The second major problem is that income-sharing schemes are based on calculations of the proportion of *joint* income which is devoted to the children. They usually factor into the formula any income earned by the care-giving parent, and assess the absent parent's liability in accordance with the ratio between the two incomes. This is a process which can be undertaken by a court. Indeed, it must be one of the factors to be considered in arriving at an overall settlement between the two adults. But it will not necessarily be the only one. The care-giver's *potential* earnings may be relevant. So might be other resources available to the care-giver. Income-sharing formulas in the United States, where they are used as *rebuttable presumptions* within the context of court adjudication, take into acount these wider issues.

A third problem concerns housing. The child-support formula percentages were intended to include an element for housing costs. These are referred to in the development of the United States' guidelines, from which the Australian formula is ultimately derived (US Department of Health and Human Services 1985: 26, 48). A family's housing status is particularly relevant to its standard of living. But, as the report of the Australian Child Support Consultative Group (1989: 42)—the Fogarty Report—recognized, housing needs may sometimes best be met 'if the non-custodial parent is able to, and either agrees or is ordered to, finance the retention of the matrimonial home by the custodial parent by transfer of equity, continuing to meet the mortgage commitments, or continuing to pay the rent'. It accepted that non-custodial parents will often be able or willing to do these things only if they can obtain a commensurate reduction in current child-support obligations.

The solution in Australia has been to enact that either parent can apply to a court that child support be provided in a form other than that of periodic amounts; if the court grants the application, it must first quantify the proportion or value of the settlement which is to be attributable to the support of any child and then state whether the support it now orders is to be credited against the liable parent's obligation towards such child or children under the formula. Normally it should be so credited (Child Support (Assessment) Act 1989, ss. 123–5). The decision of the courts in these matters will be broadly discretionary.

The result of this amalgam of elements is that these formulas risk achieving both too little and too much. They could achieve too little if the legal framework in which they operate was structured so as to suggest that application of the formula deal exhaustively with all the issues that could arise on a claim of child support: i.e. both the actual cost of the child (which the formula is supposed to represent) *and* the standard of living at which it is fair the child should live. They could achieve too much if it was represented that the formula quantifies a sum which *only* represented the actual costs of bringing up a child and which should, therefore, be paid without other regard to issues of fairness between competing families.

Separating the Elements

It seems clear that 'primary' child-support and standard-of-living issues are both relevant to the issue of child support. The question is whether they can both be dealt with by a single formula and in a single process. Many advantages are to be gained by distinguishing between these elements.

In practice family law can allocate only available resources. In raising levels of child support we may simply see the money formerly termed wife support passing between households under a different label. The child-support label carries the advantage of surviving repartnering, but with this the disadvantage of ceasing when dependent children reach economic independence. While seeking and applauding more generous and more reliable child support, we would like to emphasize that this does not complete the need for financial readjustment after divorce. The former wife also needs recognition of her damaged earnings and entitlement to pension. Where property is available, compensation may be achieved. Where there is no 'house for pension', we may need to reconsider the role of periodic payments for the former wife as well as for the children.

References

Child Support Consultative Group (1988), *Child Support: Formula for Australia* (The Fogarty Report) (Canberra).

Joshi, H. (1985), *The Price of Parenting (London)*.

Organization for Economic Co-Operation and Development (OECD), (1990), *Lone Parents: The Economic Challenge* (Paris).

United States Department of Health and Human Services (1985), *Interim Report of the US Office of Child Support Enforcement* (Washington DC).

14. Alimony: Its Premature Demise and Recent Resurgence in the United States

Lenore J. Weitzman

Alimony, more than any other aspect of divorce law, exemplifies the transformation in the position of women under the US divorce reforms of the 1970s. Although alimony was never awarded in the frequency and abundance that many Americans believed, the implementation of the new divorce laws in the United States in the 1970s resulted in a reduction in the already small percentage of women who received spousal support. In addition, there was a shift from life-long awards to shorter-term transitional awards. It looked as if alimony was going to disappear: with a larger percentage of married women in the labour force, it was assumed that women were rapidly becoming capable of supporting themselves after divorce.

But the expected demise of alimony was premature. By the late 1980s appellate courts, legal scholars, and policy-makers were asserting the continuing need for income transfers to wives after divorce (California Senate 1987; Ellman 1989; Goldfarb 1987; Kay 1990; Krauskopf 1985; Weitzman 1985). This resurgent interest in alimony is based on two factors: a growing awareness of the economic consequences of divorce for older home-makers and mothers with continuing responsibilities for their children, and a commitment to honour the contributions and sacrifices that home-makers made to the welfare of their families.

This chapter reviews these trends. It first examines the empirical data on the distribution of alimony and its recent decline. It then explores the shifting legal climate, and points to the likely role of alimony in the near future in the United States.

The Alimony Myth

Until recently, folk wisdom in the United States led one to assume that nearly every divorced woman was awarded alimony. Newspapers sensationalized stories of seemingly exorbitant awards, while books and magazines warned men of the financial burdens they would endure following divorce. Women assumed that their husbands would continue to support them following a divorce, and men anticipated being saddled with heavy monthly payments.

This alimony myth—the belief that both sexes shared in the reality of alimony awards—was also prevalent among judges and lawyers. In California attorneys who specialized in divorce estimated that two-thirds of the divorced women received alimony (Weitzman and Dixon 1980: 143).

In reality, for over a century, the vast majority of divorced women in the US never received alimony. Census Bureau data reveal that less than 16 per cent of the divorces between 1887 and 1992 included provisions for permanent alimony (Weitzman and Dixon 1980: 180) and that percentage remained relatively stable until the 1970s. The women who did receive alimony were, not surprisingly, those most visible to judges and lawyers—they were the wives of middle- and upper-income men who could 'afford' to pay alimony.

The New Standards for Alimony

Although alimony awards were usually limited to the wives of men of means, for those women alimony was *not* a myth. It was assumed that a middle-class husband was responsible for, and continued to be responsible for, the support of his wife after divorce (unless she remarried and found a second husband to support her). It was these men who were active in reforming the divorce laws in the 1970s and it was their wives who were the targets of the reforms. The reformers pointed to women's increased participation in the labour force, and argued that the law could now assume that divorced wives would be capable of supporting themselves after divorce.

As the California Senate Task Force on Family Equity (1987: V–6) noted:

> the divorce reform laws brought sweeping changes in the theory and practice underlying the alimony or spousal support law. Under the fault system . . . wives were presumed financially dependent upon their husbands, and were entitled to alimony . . . The no-fault divorce reforms eliminated fault as a ground for alimony. The

primary standard for spousal support became 'financial need' of one spouse and 'ability to pay' of the other. . . . Courts have interpreted this to mean that wives are presumed to be capable of supporting themselves at divorce and are therefore not financially in need of spousal support.

However, as the Senate Task Force report observes, judicial interpretation and application of this standard resulted in economic hardship to women, because the courts presumed that wives were capable of supporting themselves and were not in financial need. Even women who proved financial need faced courts that presumed their need would be short lived because they could quickly become self-supporting (California Senate 1987: V–6).

The assumption of divorced women's self-sufficiency is reflected in three changes in the pattern of alimony awards under the new divorce laws of the 1970s: a decline in the overall percentage of women awarded alimony; a shift from permanent to short-term awards; and a shift from the assumption of dependency to the assumption of earning capacity among divorced women (Weitzman 1985: 143–214). These changes have had a dramatic impact on the two groups of women who were traditionally most likely to receive alimony: custodial mothers with pre-school children at home, and long-married older home-makers.

The Decline in Alimony Awards

The influence of the new divorce laws is illustrated by the drop in alimony under California's no-fault divorce law of 1970. In 1968, two years before no-fault, 20 per cent of divorcing wives in both Los Angeles and San Francisco were granted spousal support; by 1972 that number had fallen to 15 per cent, a statistically significant difference. Karen Seal (1977) reported a similar decline in the percentage of alimony awards in San Diego, California.

Similar trends have been reported by researchers in other states. In New Haven, Connecticut, James McLindon (1987) reported that the overall percentage of women awarded dropped by more than 30 per cent, from 61 per cent in the

1970s, to 30 per cent in 1982.* And the overall percentage of women receiving alimony was even less in other states. In New York, Marsha Garrison (1990) reported that only 12 per cent of nine hundred divorce settlements included alimony; in Alaska, Barbara Baker (1987) reported 10 per cent; and, in Vermont, Healther Wishik (1986) reported only 7 per cent. In 1983 Federal Census data reveal that only 14 per cent of divorcing women in the country were awarded spousal support, a percentage that had remained unchanged since 1978 (US Census Bureau 1985: 4).

The dollar amount of spousal support is also low. US Census data show an average spousal support award of less than $335 per month in 1983 and, as in 1978 and 1981, this amount averaged 22 per cent of the average male's income. These awards do not reflect either the standard of living established during the marriage or the husband's ability to pay. Nor do they provide an adequate standard of living. In fact, in 1983 the average spousal support award amounted to only 76 per cent of the poverty level income for that year (US Census Bureau 1985: 4).

The Shift from Permanent to Short-Term Awards

In accordance with the assumption that women could easily become self-sufficient after divorce, there was a shift from permanent alimony awards, awards based on the premiss of the wife's continued dependency, to time-limited awards. For example, in California, between 1968 and 1972, permanent alimony—awards labelled permanent, until death or remarriage—dropped from 62 per cent to 32 per cent of alimony awards in Los Angeles. By 1972 (and in subsequent years) two-thirds of the alimony awards were transitional awards for a limited and specified duration. The median duration of these fixed-time awards was twenty-five months, or about two years. Thus the average award carried an expectation of a short transition from marriage to self-sufficiency.

These trends are also evident in other states. In Connecticut, McLindon (1987) reported that permanent alimony was granted in all but one case in his 1970 sample; in contrast, in

* Both samples in New Haven were drawn from high SES families where alimony is more common.

1982, 40 per cent of the alimony awards were of limited duration. McLindon's figures are much higher than those from other states because of his high SES sample. In New York, Garrison found that 78 per cent of the awards in her 1978 sample were permanent, whereas only 37 per cent were permanent in 1984. In Vermont less than 2 per cent of the support awards granted in 1982 were permanent, with the majority of awards lasting only two or three years (Wishik 1986).

The Unrealistic Assumption of Earning Capacity

The standards of the new law have dictated a greater reliance on the wife's ability to support herself. Economic criteria, such as the wife's occupation and pre-divorce income, are therefore more important than the old standards of fault and innocence.

Although it is reasonable for courts to consider a wife's ability to support herself, it is shocking to see how little 'earning capacity' was necessary for California judges to decide that a woman was capable of self-sufficiency in the early 1970s. Our interviews revealed countless wives with low earning capacities and limited or marginal employment histories who were denied spousal support altogether because judges assumed they were capable of supporting themselves (Weitzman 1985: 178–80, 187–94).

Since few divorcing women have had full-time continuous careers, their 'employment histories' were often irregular. The judges tended to gloss over these irregularities and to assume that women with inadequate or obsolete skills were nevertheless employable and did not 'need' support. In fact, in 1978 Herma Hill Kay suggested to me that judges were affected by the feminist movement in the early 1970s, and were using women's demands for equality as a justification for denying and terminating alimony. This attitude is evident in the substantial earning capacity that one judge imputed to a woman who testified that she had not taught for twenty years and did not have California teaching credentials. As he said:

> Just because she's been married 20 years doesn't mean she can be a sponge for the rest of her life. If she was once a teacher, she can always get a job teaching . . . just because she hasn't taught in 20 years doesn't mean she can't teach. She is a teacher. (Weitzman 1985: 188)

But how realistic are these assumptions? For most of the divorced women who have been career home-makers and mothers, they are not realistic. Many employers do not recognize home-making skills as having a market value, and older women face both age and sex discrimination in the current labour market. As one older women observed: 'There is no way I can make up for 25 years out of the labor force . . . No one wants to make me president of the company just because I was president of the PTA' (Weitzman 1985: 209).

While judges believe 'that women are capable of self-sufficiency because they can easily find well-paid jobs to support themselves and their children, in actuality, the job market for women remains dismal and discriminatory, (California Senate 1985, V–2). Even the US Supreme Court noted that women are still struggling for 'the basic right to participate fully and equally in the workforce' (*California Federal* v. *Guerra*, 479 US 1987). Despite the rapid influx of women into the paid job market over the last two decades, women remain concentrated in a very small number of occupations, with low pay and limited opportunity for advancement (Bianchi and Spain 1986). Moreover, the disparity between wives' and husbands' earnings is still substantial. In 1982 wives' average earnings were only 42 per cent of what their spouses earned (US Census Bureau 1984: Table 31).

In theory, alimony is supposed to be available to those women who cannot support themselves, especially those with custody of young children and older home-makers. However, the gap between the theory and the reality is substantial.

The Response: The Inequities and Harsh Results

The resurgent interest in alimony may be traced to the growing awareness of the link between the new pattern of alimony awards and the economic hardships that women (and children) were suffering after divorce. Divorce is a direct cause of the increased poverty among women and children in the United States (Weitzman 1985: 351). As the California Supreme Court said, these results violate our notions of 'simple justice' (*In re Marriage of Brantner*, 67 Cal. App. 3d 416,

1977). Concern focused on the fact that judges were using the new standard of self-sufficiency to deny alimony to the two groups of women who were most in need of support: mothers with continuing responsibility for child-care and older homemakers.

This section examines the pattern of awards to these two groups of women and notes the mounting pressure to redefine alimony in response to these harsh results.

In many ways California has been the pioneering state in the resurgent interest in alimony. In response to the findings of *The Divorce Revolution* (Weitzman 1985) the California Senate established a blue ribbon task force to examine the economic consequences of divorce and to recommend new legislation to remedy the inequities. The Task Force was directed to develop proposals to 'equalize the effects of divorce especially as it affects older displaced homemakers, mothers and their minor children' (California Senate Resolution No. 28, 1986). The Task Force concluded that new legislation was needed to strengthen spousal support. The legislation it proposed, which has now become law, is discussed below.

Mothers with Dependent Children

The sharpest drop in alimony awards in the 1970s was the drop in alimony awards to mothers of children under 6. In California, 20 per cent were awarded alimony in 1968, under the fault law; by 1978, under no-fault, the percentage had dropped to 13 per cent (Weitzman 1985). The change is surprising because these women have the highest child-care costs (since their children are not yet in school) and are least able to work full time (California Senate 1987: V–2).

Why did the need to care for young children appear to have so little effect on alimony awards? Two-thirds of the Superior Court judges we interviewed in California said the goal of making the wife self-sufficient was more important than supporting the custodial parent. As they put it, it was 'good for a divorced woman to earn money instead of being dependent on her former husband' (Weitzman 1985). Although many of the young mothers we interviewed shared these sentiments and wanted to be self-sufficient, the economic reality of their low earnings and the need to support their children *compelled* their need for support from their former husbands.

Although there has been dramatic increase in the number of women in the labour market, most married women with children do not work full time outside the home. During marriage nearly two-thirds of mothers interrupt their careers and paid work for home-making and child-rearing (Besharov and Dally 1986: 11–13). Many more women say they would like to work outside the home but cannot afford the high cost of child-care on the wages they would earn (Bianchi and Spain 1986).

As a result of the wife's home-making and child-rearing responsibilities, a woman's earning capacity is often impaired during marriage, while her husband's earning capacity is typically enhanced. If she forgoes or delays education, training, and job opportunities, her future earning capacity is likely to be permanently impaired. Joan Krauskopf (1985: 261) notes that, for each year out of the paid labour market, a woman suffers a permanent lifetime reduced earning capacity of 1.2 per cent. For college-educated women, the decrease can be as much as 4.3 per cent for each year. A two-to-four-year break will permanently lower an average woman's earnings by 13 per cent, and a five-year break will lower earnings by 19 per cent (Economic Policy Council 1985: 53). At divorce, these women face serious financial difficulties, regardless of the length of their marriage. In addition, the demands of single parenthood after divorce lead to more discontinuous work patterns, part-time employment, and jobs with low promotional opportunities, and thereby further to curtail their earning potential (California Senate 1987: V–4). What is needed is generous and protracted support awards for young mothers to invest in their human capital and job skills to turn the cycle of disadvantage into a cycle of advantage.

While it is easier to see the need for spousal support when a woman has child-care responsibilities after divorce, the legacy of the years she devotes to child-care remain with her after her children are grown. If she has been working part time her earnings will be lower and she may not be entitled to a pension and other benefits. And if she was able to remain at home with her children, she is likely to face an even greater burden of entering the labour force in middle age. In short, she is cumulatively disadvantaged by having missed earlier opportunities to gain experience, acquire skills, and build her career.

The judges interviewed in California appeared to be oblivious of these economic realities. The focus of their concern was usually the father and his need for his income. They expressed great sympathy for the plight of divorced men and gave first priority to their needs. In fact, when the combined total of alimony and child-support awards were analysed, it was found that judges rarely ordered a husband to give up more than one-third of 'his income' to support his wife and children. He was, therefore, allowed to retain two-thirds of his income for himself, while his former wife and children, typically three people, were expected to survive on the remaining one-third.

Although one might consider these judicial decisions 'pure sexism', there is a more benign interpretation of what the judges thought they were doing. In their minds they were placing an 'equal' burden of support on men and women without realizing that the parties' earning capacities and parental responsibilities after divorce make that burden very unequal.

Responding to that unequal burden, the California Senate Task Force on Family Equity not only urged a reformulation of the standards for alimony; it also proposed compulsory judicial education to ensure that judges would be aware of the economic realities that divorced women faced. As the report states:

> Economic necessity, exacerbated by employment discrimination on the basis of age, sex, and family responsibilities, and equity itself require that spousal support be awarded in amounts that fairly compensate a woman for her contribution to her marriage, and for her child-rearing responsibilities both during marriage and after divorce. (California Senate 1987: V–5).

The Task Force then recommended new legislation to achieve this goal: it proposed a change in the primary standard for setting spousal support awards to the standard of living established during marriage (including opportunities forgone). In addition, it recommended 'comprehensive judicial education programs in family law to include instruction on gender bias and the economic consequences of dissolution' (California Senate 1987: ES–5). Both of these bills were passed by the California legislature (in 1987) and 1988) and are now the law.

Older Home-makers

The second group of women to be hurt by the divorce reforms of the 1970s were women who worked as full-time home-makers during the marriage. Looking only at the long married women who were housewives and mothers throughout their marriages, virtually all of them might be expected to be awarded spousal support. Surprisingly, one out of three is not (Weitzman 1985). These are the women who feel most betrayed by the current legal system of divorce—the older home-makers who are denied alimony. As one Californian woman said:

> You can't tell me there's justice if someone uses you for twenty-five years and then dumps you and walks out scot-free . . . It's not fair. It's not justice. It's a scandal . . . and those judges should be ashamed of themselves sitting up there in their black robes like God and hurting poor people like me. (Weitzman 1985: 190)

One of the greatest inequities in the current legal system of divorce is the punitive treatment of divorced wives after long-duration marriages. When we compare the post-divorce incomes of long-married husbands and wives, we find that wives are expected to live on much smaller amounts of money, and are economically much worse off, than their former husbands. For example, in California wives married eighteen years or more with pre-divorce family incomes of $20,000 to $30,000 a year had, on the average, median incomes of $6,300 a year after the divorce. Their husbands, in contrast, had median incomes of $20,000 a year—even if we assume that they were paying the full amount of alimony and child support the court ordered. The result is that the post-divorce income of these wives is 24 per cent of the previous family income, whereas the average post-divorce income from their husbands is 87 per cent of that standard (Weitzman 1985: 190).

Once again, the judges approach these cases mindful of the husband's need for 'his income' and his limited capacity to support two families. And, once again, it is clear that the judges simply misunderstand the economic reality of the wives' job prospects. In interviews, judges assured our researchers that most of these women would 'be able to find jobs'. But they did not interview these women a year later, as our researchers did, and did not hear about the frustrating experiences of women who applied for fifty jobs without success, or the devastation of being offered only minimum-wage jobs (after long marriages to professional men). As one woman said: 'The judge told me to go for job training—but no training can recapture twenty-seven years of my life. I'm too old to start from the beginning and I shouldn't have to. I deserve better' (Weitzman 1985: 210).

As this example suggests, women who have few marketable skills cannot make up for twenty or twenty-five years out of the job market. Most end up in low-paying jobs, living in greatly reduced circumstances, often on the edge of poverty (Leonard 1980). Since they cannot rely on social security, and since they do not have pension coverage (because they have not been employed), they are likely to experience extreme downward mobility and severe economic hardship after divorce.

It is no wonder that the older home-maker felt betrayed by the way the new divorce laws were being interpreted in the 1970s and 1980s. She was promised, by both her husband and our society—her contract, it could be said, both implied and expressed—that marriage was a partnership and that he would share his income with her. Instead, the courts changed the rules on her in the middle of the game—after she fulfilled her share of the bargain (and after she had passed the point where she could choose another life course).

Once the plight of older home-makers became evident, it evoked considerable sympathy and concern from both legal scholars and pólicy-makers. As the California Task Force on Family Equity wrote:

> In the absence of adequate spousal support awards, displaced home-makers may face a bleak financial plight. Divorce generally leaves these women with little or no source of support; their age and lack of marketable skills make self-support difficult (and sometimes impossible). When they attempt to enter the labor force, they face two kinds of discrimination: sex bias and age bias. (California Senate 1987: V–3

The Senate Task Force therefore focused on spousal support as the primary vehicle for remedying this unfairness and it recommended that it be strengthened. As it said:

> Spousal support is necessary to meet the economic crisis of the

displaced homemaker and other dependent spouses. It should be viewed as a form of legal insurance, protection, or pension for the spouse who has given priority to the other spouse's career and to child rearing instead of developing his or her own career or marketable skills. (California Senate 1987: V–4)

The Task Force therefore recommended two bills, which are now California law: the first, passed in 1988, states that support awards in marriages of long duration should serve to equalize the standards of living in the households of both parties after divorce; the second, passed in 1987, establishes a presumption of permanent support after a marriage of long duration.

It is evident that these bills attempt to do more than just equalize the economic inequities of the present legal system of divorce. They are also a statement of support for the underlying philosophy of marriage as an economic partnership. It is this underlying philosophy—and the role of the law in supporting the marital partnership—that this chapter now addresses.

The Resurgence of Alimony and the Theory of a Marital Partnership

The renewed interest in alimony as the vehicle for justice supporting the marital partnership has come from three sources: legal scholars, policy-makers, and the appellate courts. An example of the first is Joan Krauskopf's plea for the courts to recognize the social good of home-making and child-rearing and to 'follow the path of compensation rather than punishment for homemaking' (Krauskopf 1985: 320).

Among policy-makers, the forceful language and statutory changes from the legislatures of New York and California are noteworthy. In 1986 the New York legislature recognized the need for spousal support as a means of valuing home-making contributions and equalizing the economic burdens of divorce. It amended its maintenance (spousal-support) law to require courts to define 'reasonable needs' as the 'standard of living established during the marriage'. In enacting this law, the New York Legislature explained:

The maintenance provisions are being incorrectly interpreted by the court to deny indefinite (permanent) maintenance to divorced women who come away from long-term marriages or short-term marriages where there are young children to be cared for. Current interpretations . . . contribute to the 'feminization of poverty'. . . . There is something wrong with the way the court views what is 'reasonable' for women to have. In general it is not looking at her economic data in making maintenance awards. The court must be directed to maintain the parties at the same percentage of the standard of living they enjoyed together during the marriage, especially in long-term marriages and short-term marriages where there is a child or children to care for . . . (*'Memorandum in Support of Legislation* 1986)

Similarly, in 1987 the California Task Force (1987: V–7) recommended revising that state's law because:

This assumption of 'self-sufficiency' . . . ignores the fact that many of these wives have sacrificed their own career opportunities and earning potential because of tacit or express marital partnership agreements . . . Adequate spousal support awards are [not only] essential to equalizing the economic consequences of divorce between men and women, they reflect societal perceptions of the importance and value of homemaking and child-rearing contributions and sacrifices made during the marriage. (California Senate 1987: V–7)

The California Task Force also recommended establishing 'the standard of living established during the marriage' as the primary standard for spousal support awards. However, in marriages of long duration, it recommended an even stronger standard to provide for the sharing of post-divorce income. In long-duration marriages the goal of spousal support is to *equalize* the standard of living in the two post-divorce households.

The need for wife support to honour the partnership theory of marriage has also been advocated by feminists. For example, Sally Goldfarb of the National Organization for Women's Legal Defense and the Education Fund (1987: 2–3) argues that short-time alimony awards penalize women for adhering to the principle that an ongoing marriage is an equal partnership. As she notes, 'some 40 million American women are full time homemakers and the traditional allocation of gender roles has not died out even among young couples' (p. 12). In addition, employed wives restrict their job hours, and forgo opportunities for advancement, in order to be available for home-making and child-care services. Goldfarb argues that the result is that the home-maker frees her husband to concentrate on and enhance his earning power. But if the legal system supports the basic premiss of marital partnership theory—that the economic and non-economic contributions of the spouses are of equal value—then it cannot allow the husband to reap a windfall at his wife's expense. And if the legal system intends to encourage women to fulfil the socially valuable home-making role, then it must assure maintenance awards to support home-makers at divorce.

A final voice in this chorus comes from the appellate and Supreme Courts of several states chastising their lower court (trial) judges for their punitive treatment of older home-makers with short-term spousal-support awards. As the California Supreme Court put it, it was simply a matter of justice:

> A woman is not a breeding cow to be nurtured during her years of fecundity, then conveniently and economically converted into cheap steaks when past her prime . . . [T]he husband simply has to face up to the fact that his support responsibilities are going to be of extended duration—perhaps for life. This has nothing to do with feminism, sexism, male chauvinism, or any other trendy social ideology. It is ordinary common sense, basic decency, and simple justice. (*In re Marriage of Brantner*, 67 Cal. App. 3d 416, 1977: 419–20)

Although it is too soon to tell whether the new legislation in California and New York will dramatically alter the pattern of alimony awards, it is clear that predictions about the demise of alimony, at least in these states, were premature. Instead there is renewed interest in income support for wives as the legal mechanism that balances the equities in divorce and honours the partnership ideals of the marriage contract.

References

Baker, B. (1987), *Family Equity at Issue: A Study of the Economic Consequences of Divorce on Women and Children* (Alaska Women's Commission, Anchorage).

Besharov, D. and Dally, M. (1986), 'How Much are Working Mothers Working?', *State Report on Women's Rights*, 2:4 11–13.

Bianchi, S. M., and Spain, D. (1986), *American Women in Transition* (New York).

California Senate (1987), *Final Report of the Task Force on Family Equity* (June) (Sacramento, Calif.).

Cohen, H. N., and Hillman, A. S. (1984), *Analysis of Seventy Select Decisions after Trial under New York State's Equitable Distribution Law, from January 1981 through October 1984* (1 Nov.) (New York Women's Bar Association, New York).

Economic Policy Council UNA–USA (1985), *Work and Family in the United States: a Policy Initiative*, Report of the Family Policy Panel (Dec.) (New York).

Ellman, I. (1989) 'The Theory of Alimony', *California Law Review* 77: 1–77.

Garrison, M. (1990) 'The Economics of Divorce: Changing Rules, Changing Results', in S. D. Sugerman and H. H. Kay (eds.) *Divorce Reform at the Crossroads* (New Haven, Conn.).

Goldfarb, S. F. (1987) 'Rehabilitative Alimony, the "Alimony Drone", and the Marital Partnership', paper presented at the National Symposium on Alimony and Child Support, American Bar Association, 24 Apr. (Austin, Texas).

Kay, H. H. (1987) 'An Appraisal of California's No-Fault Divorce Law', *California Law Review*, 75: 291–319.

——(1990), 'Beyond No-Fault: New Directions in Divorce Reform', in S. D. Sugerman and H. H. Kay (eds.), *Divorce Reform at the Crossroads* (New Haven, Conn.).

Krauskopf, J. (1985) 'Maintenance: A Decade of Development', *Missouri Law Review*, 50: 259–320.

Larsen, (1979) 'Equity and Economics: A case for Spousal Support', *Golden Gate University Law Review*, 8: 443–51.

Leonard, F. (1980), 'Older Women and Pensions: Catch 22', in T. Sommers and L. Shields (eds.), *Gray Paper No. 1* (Washington, DC) (citing Fact Sheet issued by Congresswoman Pat Schroeder's office).

McLindon, J. (1987), 'Separate but Unequal: The Economic Disaster of Divorce for Women and Children', *Family Law Quarterly*, 21: 351–409.

Memorandum in Support of Legislation A.10567–A/S.8908–A (1986), amending New York DRL Section 236 Part B(1)(a).

Seal, K. (1977) 'A Decade of No-Fault Divorce', *Family Advocate* 1/1: 10, 11, 14, 15.

United States Bureau of the Census (1983) *Child Support and Alimony, 1981* (Current Population Reports, Series P–23, No. 124 (Washington DC).

——(1984), *Money Income of Households, Families and Persons in the*

United States, 1982 (Current Population Reports, Series P–60, No. 142, Washington DC).
——(1985), *Child Support and Alimony, 1983* (Current Population Reports, Series P–23, No. 141; Washington DC).
——(1990), *Money, Income, and Poverty Status in the US, 1988* (Current Population Reports, Series P–60, No. 166; Washington DC).
Weitzman, L. J. (1985), *The Divorce Revolution: The Unexpected Social and Economic Consequences for Women and Children in America* (New York).
——Dixon, R. B. (1980), 'The Alimony Myth: Does No-Fault make a Difference', *Family Law Quarterly*, 14/3: 141–85.
Wishik, H. P. (1986), 'Economics of Divorce: An Exploratory Study', *Family Law Quarterly*, 20: 79–103.

15. Estimating the Economic Consequences of Separation and Divorce: A Cautionary Tale from the United States

Annemette Sørensen

The high levels of separation and divorce that have been characteristic of American society since the late 1960s have forced the attention of social science, public policy, and the media on the economic consequences of marital dissolution. Several researchers have attempted to estimate what those consequences were, and most attention has been paid to the fact that women and children are much more likely to suffer economically from the breakup of a marriage than are men (Duncan and Hoffman 1985; Weitzman 1985). This testifies to the continuing economic dependence of women on men, and there can be little doubt that this is a major cause of the higher poverty rates among women (McLanahan, Sørensen, and Watson 1989). A review of the empirical research reveals, however, that, whereas researchers agree that women (and children) are more likely to experience a loss in economic status than men are, there is wide disagreement on how big the differences are. The estimates of change in economic status experienced by women in the United States range between declines of 9 per cent and 30 per cent, and the estimates of an increase for men show about the same degree of variation. Whereas one should expect some variation in estimates based on sample data, the variation in the estimates of the economic consequences of divorce seem uncomfortably large, and one must conclude that the degree of change in women's and men's economic status changes following the breakup of marriage is not fully understood.

This chapter presents a new set of estimates of the economic consequences of marital separation based on separations occurring between 1970 and 1983 to a random sample of US men and women who married sometime between 1969 and 1982. Whereas it is of interest to see what the economic consequences of marital dissolution are for recent marriage cohorts, the main contribution of this chapter will be to show how the choice of measures of economic status affects the estimates of change. The expression 'economic consequences' clearly refers to change in the economic situation following a separation, but what is meant by 'economic situation' is often unclear. It can refer to the total income available to a family, or it can refer to the standard of living that income confers on the family. If it is the latter, then one is confronted with the problem of deciding what the standard of living is for a given family, a decision that typically involves some adjustment of family income that somehow takes the size of the family into account. The results of the analysis presented later in this chapter suggest that any conclusion regarding how much men's and women's economic status change after a marital dissolution needs to specify what is meant by economic status. It is thus unwarranted to conclude, as was recently done (Hoffman and Duncan 1988), that US women experience a decline in economic status of about one-third. One really needs to ask, one-third of what?

The first section of this chapter covers previous research, and reviews four major studies of the economic consequences of separation and divorce in the United States, showing how diverse the estimates are. The second section describes the change in economic status following separation for younger US marriage cohorts, using four different measure of economic status before and after separation.

Previous Research

Cross-sectional Comparisons

The simplest way to assess how marital dissolution affects people's economic situation is to compare the economic status of the divorced and separated with that of the married. This comparison invariably shows that divorced women and men have lower family incomes than married women and men. Data for the United States in 1987 showed that divorced men had a mean household income that was 69 per cent of that of married men. Divorced women had only half the household income of married women.

Such differences in household income do not, however, tell us much about how economic well-being or standard of living differs for divorced and married men and women, since economic needs differ substantially as well. Men are much less likely to keep the children after a divorce; therefore, divorced men have lower needs for income than married men, whereas divorced women have only slightly lower needs than married women. Of the several ways to evaluate family income in terms of family needs, the simplest is per-capita income, and also on this measure divorced women fare substantially less well than married women; in 1980, for example, the per-capita income of divorced white women was 84 per cent of that of married women. The situation was very different for men; white divorced men had 47 per cent higher per-capita income than their married counterparts.

Based on cross-sectional evidence, men thus appear to benefit a great deal economically from being divorced, while women are better off married, both in terms of family income and per-capita income. However, we cannot simply view these differences between divorced and married individuals as differences brought on by marital dissolution. Lower-income women and men are more likely to divorce. They are also less likely to remarry, which means that a larger proportion of low-income people remain in the population of the currently divorced. The question is, then, how much of the difference between the married and divorced can be attributed to the divorce, and how much is due to selection into and out of the population of divorced individuals. To answer this question we turn to an examination of the evidence offered by longitudinal studies, comparing the economic situation of men and women before and after they divorce.

Longitudinal Evidence

Longitudinal studies support the conclusion that women experience downward economic mobility following divorce, while men tend to become better off economically. But this is where the consensus stops. As mentioned earlier, estimates of the magnitude of change vary a lot and they seem to depend quite heavily on the sample on which the results are based and on the way in which economic status is measured.

In this section I review the findings of four different studies using longitudinal data. Two of these (Duncan and Hoffman

1985; Weiss 1984) employed data from the Panel Study of Income Dynamics (PSID), a panel study begun in 1968 of a nationally representative sample; the third study (Nestel, Mercier, and Shaw 1983) used data for middle-aged women from another large-scale longitudinal study, the National Labor Survey (NLS); the fourth study is Weitzman's (1985) study of a sample of men and women who got divorced in Los Angeles County in California. All four studies focused on marital dissolutions that took place in the early 1970s, thus precluding the possibility that differences between them can be explained by historical changes in the consequences of divorce. Weitzman's study included individuals who had divorced during the year before she interviewed them, while the other studies included spearated men and women as well.

Each study used a somewhat different analytic strategy. Three of them estimated change by comparing the economic situation one year after the marital dissolution to that of the last year of marriage (Duncan and Hoffman 1985; Weiss 1984; Weitzman 1985), while the fourth study (Nestel, Mercier, and Shaw 1983) compared the economic situation one year after the marital dissolution (which could have occurred anytime between 1968 and 1972) to the situation in 1966. Therefore the base year may have been up to eight years before the divorce—years during which the couple's economic status probably improved. The economic loss after the divorce is therefore probably understated (Nestel, Mercier, and Shaw 1983).

There is also a great deal of variation in the measures of economic status. Three studies measured economic status by adjusting family income for economic need (Duncan and Hoffman 1985; Nestel, Mercier, and Shaw 1983; Weitzman 1985), but they used different standards of need. The needs standard used by Weitzman was the Bureau of Labor Statistics' (BLS) Lower Standard Budget for 1976 and 1977. The needs standard used by Duncan and Hoffman, and by Nestel, Mercier, and Shaw, was the official US poverty standard. Per-capita income was used by one study (Weitzman 1985), while one used only family income to measure economic status (Weiss 1984).

Family income tends to decrease for both men and women and the greatest decrease tends to be among those with relatively high pre-divorce family incomes. Estimates based on the PSID suggest that women who have not remarried on average experience a 30 per cent drop in family income in the year after separation or divorce (Hoffman and Duncan 1988; Weiss 1984). Weitzman's (1985) data from California suggest a decrease in family income for women married less than ten years ranging from 29 per cent to 71 per cent, with the typical level being about 50 per cent. Data for middle-aged women from the NLS (Nestel, Mercier, and Shaw 1983) suggest a decline in family income of about 50 per cent. Men's family incomes also decrease, but less than women's—according to the PSID estimate by 7 per cent; according to Weitzman by between 6 per cent and 25 per cent.

These changes in family income translate into very different changes in standard of living for women and men, because women tend to keep the children following a separation or divorce. For women, all studies show substantial decreases in economic status, measured either as per-capita income or income in relation to needs in the year after marital separation.

The NLS data for middle-aged women suggest a drop in per-capita income of about 30 per cent, while Weitzman reported changes in per-capita income ranging from a low of −58 per cent to a high of +16 per cent, with the typical figure being around −50 per cent.

Data from the PSID suggest an average drop of 9 per cent in women's family income in relation to needs; if one excludes women who have remarried, the decline is 13 per cent. Weitzman reports a decline of 73 per cent. In a recent re-examination of Weitzman's results, Hoffman and Duncan (1988) conclude that there must be a mistake in the figure of 73 per cent and that a more reasonable estimate for the Weitzman data would be around a 30 per cent decline in family income in relation to needs. It is clearly difficult to explain the wide range in the results—from a small 9 per cent decline (or 13 per cent if remarried women are excluded) in women's standard of living reported by Hoffman and Duncan (1988) to a 30 per cent drop in per-capita income for middle-aged women in the NLS data, to a 73 per cent drop in the standard of living for divorced women in California. While it is possible that the 73 per cent figure is too large in the light of the California data on the decline in per-capita income, the Hoffman and Duncan (1988) report of a 9 per cent decline seems very low. It is curious that Hoffman and Duncan (1988: 643) claim that the 30 per cent estimate they propose for the Weitzman data is 'similar to that found in our research and by Weiss'. Weiss does not report any results for income in relation to needs only for family income, and, as we have seen, it is women's family income, not their income in relation to needs, that declines 30 per cent during the year after separation or divorce.

The agreement on change in men's economic status is not much better. The PSID estimate suggests an increase in family income in relation to need of 13 per cent, while Weitzman estimates an increase of 42 per cent. It should be noted that the PSID estimate for men may be too high, because the attrition rate is higher among men with low income. Men with higher incomes are thus over-represented in the PSID sample, and, since their economic status tends to improve the most (Weitzman 1985), the overall estimate will be on the high side. The other two studies did not include men. One explanation for the large difference between the PSID and Weitzman may be the fact that the PSID sample includes both separated and divorced women, while the Weitzman sample includes only divorced women. The NLS study is the only study that compares the experiences of women who divorced and women who remained separated one year after the marital split. For whites there are not many differences, but among blacks the economic consequences of the marital dissolution are very much smaller for women who remained separated than they are for women who divorced. Per-capita income dropped by 34 per cent for divorced black women but only by 3 per cent for separated black women. Since the Weitzman sample excludes this group of women, she is apt to get a higher estimate of the change in economic status than the PSID, which includes separated women.

Individual Variations

The evidence discussed so far has focused on change in mean or median economic status, and this is what most studies tend to highlight. It is not clear, however, that the mean change is the most useful measure, because it may or may not conceal a great deal of variation. The rather modest decrease of 9 per cent in women's economic status might reflect a situation where a substantial proportion of women suffer severe economic setbacks following a divorce, while others are affected very little or benefit from it, or it may reflect a situation where most women will experience a rather modest reduction in standard of living.

Another problem is that it is difficult to say what it means to the individual woman that her economic status on average will drop by a certain amount in the year after a divorce or separation. For example, a 9 per cent decrease in the standard of living is not necessarily the same for the woman who was already poor while married as it is the upper-middle-class woman. This type of question is, however, beyond the scope of this chapter.

The research by Duncan and Hoffman (1985) provides some insights into these questions. They found that 23 per cent of all women experienced a reduction in economic status (measured as income in relation to needs) of more than 50 per cent; but they also reported that 27 per cent of all women experienced an increase in economic well-being following the divorce. Even among women who remained unmarried, 22 per cent were better off after the divorce, while 26 per cent of this group were among those who were in the group that experienced substantial downward mobility.

Among men, the majority (54 per cent) were better off and only 9 per cent had their economic status reduced by more than half. The majority of women, 73 per cent, were worse off economically after a divorce or separation, but a substantial minority was better off, even when women who remarried were not taken into consideration. These results showing that the economic consequences of divorce for both women and men are very variable are generally supported by Weitzman's research, which found that the change in economic status depended quite heavily on the economic situation before divorce.

Summary

This excursion into the world of longitudinal studies clearly shows that there are tremendous differences in the estimates of change in economic status following a marital dissolution, and it seems difficult to conclude from these studies, as did Hoffman and Duncan (1988), that women can expect an average decline of about 30 per cent in economic status, measured as the ratio between total family income and the annual needs of the family. Unless one completely discounts the evidence from the PSID (presented by Duncan and Hoffman (1985)), the 30 per cent figure seems too high, and a more reasonable guess would place the average change somewhere between a decline of 30 per cent and 10 per cent for women, and a somewhat smaller increase for men.

None of the studies reviewed based its estimates on a random sample of separations, a random sample of divorces, or a random sample of marriages. Each of them put various types of restrictions on the sample, which might well have affected the results. Weitzman (1985) studied only people who had legally divorced, while the other studies also included people who had not yet become legally divorced, and she restricted her sample to cases from the court records in a large city in southern California (Los Angeles). This is, of course, what all studies based on court records must do. They also typically are based on samples from one state (e.g. Wishik 1986) or from a county in a state (e.g. McLindon 1987). Using data from a representative sample, PSID, Duncan and Hoffman (1985), on the other hand, decided to select the subset of the separations or divorces that occurred to women between 26 and 55 years old and between the years 1969 and 1976. Why only women in this age group were selected is not made clear, and it is not clear what bias this may introduce. Clearly people who marry young and dissolve the mariage after a short time are excluded from the sample, as are people who separate after very long-lasting marriages. The other study using data from the PSID had as its major purpose to study change in consumption patterns of families with children. It therefore examined separations or divorces occurring between 1969 and 1974 to women who had children under 18 in the household the year of the marital breakup. This sample, therefore, was restricted to marital dissolutions involving children, a restriction which probably excludes a high proportion of separations after very short marriages, as well as a high proportion of separations after marriages of very long durations. Finally, the NLS sample consisted of separations and divorces recorded between 1968 and 1976 for mature women (between 30 and 44 years old in 1967), who had been married and living with their spouse in 1967. This sample of separations and divorces therefore resembles the one used by Duncan and Hoffman (1985), with the difference that the age range is somewhat more restricted, especially for younger ages. We might then expect rather similar results from the NLS data and the PSID results reported by Duncan and Hoffman. This does not come about, because the two studies measured change in different ways, with the latter comparing the year after to the year before the marital dissolution, while the former compared the post-separation situation with the economic status in 1966.

Finally, the most important reason for the confusion may be that each study employed a different measure of economic status: family income (Weiss 1984), per-capita income (Weitzman 1985), family income in relation to a needs standard implied by the Bureau of Labor Statistic's Standard Budget (BLS) (Weitzman 1985), and family income in relation to a need standard implied by the official US poverty line (Duncan and Hoffman 1985; Nestel, Mercier, and Shaw 1983). The BLS standard of need is somewhat higher than the one used for the US poverty line, or, to put it differently, the BLS standard assumes less economies of scale than the US poverty standard. While it has been generally recognized that change in family income will be different from change in per-capita income, no attention has been paid to the possibility that the use of different needs standards may also affect how much change one observes. The opposite was claimed by Hoffman and Duncan (1988: 644 n. 5), who stated that 'The needs standard using the BLS budget is about 25 per cent to 30 per cent higher than the poverty standard, although this should not affect the results.' As shown below, the use of different needs standards definitely does affect the results.

Given the array of differences in measures of economic status, in sample restrictions, and in the time period over which change is measured, it should in fact come as no surprise that the estimates are so different. It is beyond the scope of this chapter to pinpoint the exact role played by each factor. Instead it will focus on just one of these by demonstrating how the definition of economic status affects estimates of the economic consequences of divorce and separation.

Change in Economic Status for Younger Marriage Cohorts

The following analysis of the economic changes experienced in connection with marital dissolution is based on a representative sample of marriages formed between 1969 and 1982. The experiences should, therefore, present a reasonably good picture of the kind of economic changes experienced by a majority of the men and women who have been through a separation and divorce during the 1980s.

The Data

The data are from the 18th wave of the PSID, providing up to eighteen years' information about each sample member. The sample selected for this analysis consists of all sample members who married any time between 1969 and 1983 and whose marriage ended in separation between 1970 and 1984. A marital dissolution is detected by comparing the respondent's marital status in two adjacent years $t-1$ and t. If there is a change from 'married' to 'separated' or 'divorced', then the marriage is considered dissolved sometime between $t-1$ and t. This procedure counted 1,420 separations; of these 63 (4.4 per cent) had to be excluded from the analysis, because no income data for the first year of separation were available.

Change in economic status is assessed by comparing a given measure of the respondent's economic situation during the first year of separation with the situation during the last full year of marriage two years earlier. Income information is reported retrospectively for the past year. Thus, income data for the first year of separation, t, is reported in year $t+1$, while income data for the last full year of marriage is reported in year $t-1$. For individuals who were married for only one year, the pre-separation economic status refers to that year; that is, the change in economic status is measured over a one-year period rather than a two-year period. Since this may affect the estimates of change, all results are presented first for all separations, and then for separations occurring after more than one year of marriage.

Using the first year of separation to assess the post-separation situation leads to a somewhat high estimate of family income, and the results presented below are therefore probably somewhat optimistic; that is, the declines may be somewhat underestimated and the increases somewhat over-estimated by these data. From the way the post-separation measure is defined for the first year, we know about the separation year t. This has the advantage that the proportion of people who have remarried will be at a minimum, but the disadvantage that the post-separation estimate of total family income in some cases will be somewhat high, that is too optimistic. This is a consequence of the way the PSID reports family income for a year where there has been a separation. Some of those who were separated at the interview in year *t* actually separated in year $t-1$ (after the interview that year) and they will thus have been separated throughout year *t* (forgetting now for the moment about the possibility of remarriage), while others will have separated sometime during *t*, but before the interview that year. For the latter group the PSID estimated family income for the year *t* as the sum of the family income for the part of the year the couple were still together and the income for the part after they separated. One must therefore see the PSID estimate of total family income during the year *t*, the first year of separation, as a high estimate of an individual's family income after the separation. In contrast, the data for family size correctly reflects the family size *after* separation.

Measuring Economic Status

A given family income may give rise to very different standards of living, depending on how many people it has to support. If one is interested in the standard of living enjoyed by members of a family, family income therefore needs to be adjusted in some way. Per-capita income represents the simplest of these adjustments. The main problem with this as a measure of standard of living is that it assumes there are no economies of scale associated with living together with other people. This clearly is an unreasonable assumption. The problem is how large the economies of scale are. Many different answers have been given to this question. In a review of the literature on the equivalence scales that have been used to adjust family income (Bushman *et al.* 1988), it is shown that virtually all scales measure economic status by adjusting family income by family size raised to a power which ranges from 0.2 to 1 (the so-called size elasticity), with 1 representing per-capita income, and 0.2 representing an adjustment which assumes very large economies of scale. The equivalence scale underlying the US poverty line has a size elasticity of about 0.56, while the equivalence scale underlying the BLS standard (used by Weitzman 1985) has an elasticity of about 0.73 (Bushman *et al.* 1988: Table 2).

The choice of equivalence scale will affect the measures of change in ecomomic well-being following a separation. In general we shall expect that an adjustment of family income which implies greater economies of scale will reduce the amount of decline and in some instances turn a decline in family income into an increase in economic status. In order to demonstrate how important the choice of income adjustment is, the following analysis will use four different measures of economic status. The pre- and post-separation economic situation will be compared using unadjusted family income, per-capita income, family income adjusted by family size raised to the power of 0.56 (the US poverty standard) and to the power of 0.73 (BLS standard). Since post-separation family income is overestimated somewhat, all of these measures of the family's economic situation will provide estimates of the post-separation economic status which are somewhat optimistic. This in turn means that the estimates of the economic consequences of separation presented next should be seen as optimistic estimates; the increase for men will be somewhat exaggerated and the decrease for women somewhat underestimated.

Changes in Family Income

Some changes in total family income are, of course, to be expected when a couple decides to separate and live apart, simply because the potential number of earners in the family will go down. As shown in Table 15.1, the amount of change actually observed is relatively small for white men and somewhat larger for women and black men (and, as mentioned before, these figures are probably a little too optimistic). The mean income (measured in constant 1967 dollars) of white men and women during the last full year of marriage was well above $9,000. The post-separation average for white men was a little above $8,000, while the women's mean family income was only $5,859. White women thus experienced a substantially larger decline in mean family income than did men. The gender difference is substantially smaller among blacks, where men had on average 84 per cent and women 80 per cent of the pre-separation family income during the first year of separation. The ratio of the mean incomes is clearly smaller than the mean ratio of incomes for individuals. This is

TABLE 15.1. *Total family income before and after separation* (1967 $)

	White		Black	
	Men	Women	Men	Women
All				
Last year of marriage	9,637	9,478	7,714	6,376
First year of separation	8,169	5,859	5,491	4,208
Ratio of post- to pre-separation income				
Mean	1.00	0.74	0.84	0.80
25th percentile	0.59	0.37	0.49	0.34
50th percentile	0.82	0.58	0.70	0.53
75th percentile	1.06	0.89	0.97	0.90
N of cases	340	420	187	400
Married at least 2 years				
Last year of marriage	10,138	10,391	8,646	7,123
First year of separation	8,624	5,962	5,962	4,355
Ratio of post- to pre-separation income				
Mean	1.02	0.67	0.81	0.73
25th percentile	0.60	0.33	0.48	0.34
50th percentile	0.82	0.54	0.64	0.49
75th percentile	1.05	0.83	0.96	0.85
N of cases	252	295	135	281

because the distribution of ratios is skewed to the right. The ratio of the mean incomes for white men is, for example, 0.85, and for white women 0.62. The figures for men and women who had been married at least two years before separation show basically the same pattern, although the gender differences are somewhat greater for both whites and blacks.

The mean change in the ratio of post- to pre-separation family income tends to give a rather optimistic picture of the economic situation following a separation, because there are usually a few individuals who are much better off than was previously the case. This is reflected in the fact that the median ratio of post- to pre-separation income for all groups is substantially lower than the mean. The typical experience—for white men also—is that family income falls after a separation, and for substantial proportions the decline is quite severe. For 25 per cent of the women family income was about a third of what it used to be, while the 25th percentile for men was between 0.5 and 0.6. Looking at the other end of the distribution, the 75th percentile for all groups but white men was below 1, meaning that at least 75 per cent experienced a decline in family income.

These figures on change in total family income are instructive, because they demonstrate very clearly that the vast majority of all people who go through a separation will experience some decline in family income, and substantial proportions of women as well as of men will see their incomes reduced quite drastically. Women's loss of family income is a good deal greater than is men's, and this means that, taking into account that women usually have larger families to support after the separation, differences between women and men should increase.

Changes in Per-capita Income

Per-capita income is a simple and straightforward adjustment of income, which assumes that there are no economies of scale associated with sharing a household with others. As is clear from the data presented in Table 15.2, the mean per-capita

TABLE 15.2. *Per-capita income before and after separation* (1967 $)

	White		Black	
	Men	Women	Men	Women
All				
Last year of marriage	3,718	3,418	2,557	2,035
First year of separation	6,967	3,608	5,046	2,257
Ratio of post- to pre-separation per capita income				
Mean	2.38	1.18	2.51	1.36
25th percentile	1.24	0.56	1.29	0.47
50th percentile	1.75	0.88	1.90	0.80
75th percentile	2.73	1.44	2.75	1.56
N of cases	340	420	187	400
Married at least 2 years				
Last year of marriage	3,842	3,691	2,715	2,253
First year of separation	7,415	3,575	5,396	2,194
Ratio of post- to pre-separation per-capita income				
Mean	2.48	1.05	2.49	1.15
25th percentile	1.24	0.50	1.29	0.45
50th percentile	1.80	0.81	1.88	0.73
75th percentile	2.77	1.28	2.74	1.40
N of cases	252	295	135	281

income increased quite substantially for men, while there was a smaller mean increase for women. Men on average doubled their per-capita income, and half of those who had been married more than one year experienced an increase of at least 80 per cent. Women also on average had more income per person in the family, but the increase was quite modest, especially for those married more than a year. When we look at the median change in per-capita income for women, half of white women had 80 per cent or less than they used to, and the corresponding figure for black women was 73 per cent. The median change thus tells us that the most common experience for women is that per-capita income goes down after the separation, while the opposite is the case for men. Had we based our conclusion only on the mean change, the results would have been that both men and women on average have higher per-capita incomes during the first year of separation than they had two years earlier while they were still married.

Changes in Adjusted Family Income

The changes in per-capita income overestimate the gains experienced by many men and underestimate the decline experienced by most women, simply because it is assumed that there are no economic benefits from sharing a household with others. A more realistic assessment of change in economic status or well-being would be one that took economies of scale into account. Two such measures have been used here. One assumes relatively small economies of scale by adjusting family income by family size raised to the power of 0.73. This implies that a family of three is assumed to need 2.23 times as much income as a family of size one to maintain the same standard of living. The other measure assumes greater economies of scale by adjusting income by family size raised to the power of 0.56; this implies that a family of three needs only 1.85 times as much income as a single person. The results using these two measures of economic status are presented in full in Tables 15.3 and 15.4. The comments here will concentrate on a comparison of the median change in the two measures of adjusted family income. These figures are presented in Table 15.5. It is evident from Table 15.5 that the median change for men in

TABLE 15.3. *Adjusted family income (by size$^{0.73}$) before and after separation* (1967 $)

	White		Black	
	Men	Women	Men	Women
All				
Last year of marriage	4,761	4,448	3,418	2,733
First year of separation	7,189	4,006	5,134	2,572
Ratio of post- to pre-separation adjusted income				
Mean	1.85	1.03	1.84	1.15
25th percentile	1.01	0.52	1.05	0.44
50th percentile	1.44	0.80	1.35	0.72
75th percentile	2.10	1.29	2.03	1.30
N of cases	340	420	187	400
Married at least 2 years				
Last year of marriage	4,942	4,826	3,689	3,033
First year of separation	7,631	3,999	5,506	2,535
Ratio of post- to pre-separation adjusted income				
Mean	1.92	0.92	1.81	0.99
25th percentile	1.02	0.45	1.03	0.42
50th percentile	1.48	0.71	1.35	0.67
75th percentile	2.16	1.08	1.89	1.23
N of cases	252	295	135	281

adjusted family income is greater if economies of scale are assumed to be high. Fifty per cent of the white men experienced at least a 26 per cent increase in economic status according to the measure with low economies of scale. Using the other measure of adjusted income we find that half of the white men experienced an increase of at least 44 per cent. Similar results are observed for black men. For women, on the other hand, the decline in economic status is smaller the greater the economies of scale are assumed to be. The median loss for white women was 26 per cent and 20 per cent respectively.

Consider now all four measures of economic status. They can be ordered according to how great the adjustment for family size is, that is how great the economies of scale are assumed to be. Family income, then, comes at the top (no adjustment or infinitely large economies of scale) and per-capita income (full adjustment or no economies of scale) at the bottom. We see

TABLE 15.4. *Adjusted family income (by size$^{0.56}$) before and after separation* (1967 $)

	White		Black	
	Men	Women	Men	Women
All				
Last year of marriage	5,583	5,274	4,115	3,306
First year of separation	7,359	4,319	5,199	2,831
Ratio of post- to pre-separation adjusted income				
Mean	1.58	0.95	1.52	1.05
25th percentile	0.90	0.47	0.90	0.42
50th percentile	1.26	0.74	1.22	0.69
75th percentile	1.74	1.20	1.66	1.14
N of cases	340	420	187	400
Married at least 2 years				
Last year of marriage	5,812	5,737	4,484	3,675
First year of separation	7,800	4,332	5,592	2,818
Ratio of post- to pre-separation adjusted income				
Mean	1.64	0.85	1.49	0.91
25th percentile	0.60	0.43	0.84	0.40
50th percentile	1.27	0.66	1.19	0.61
75th percentile	1.05	1.01	1.50	1.09
N of cases	252	295	135	281

here that in general the improvement in men's economic status after a separation is much greater and the decline in women's economic status much smaller, if economies of scale are assumed to be large. From this it follows that the *difference* between men and women is greatest if one uses a measure of economic status which implies large economies of scale.

The differences brought on by the use of different measures are not trivial. For white women, for example, the median drop in economic status ranges from 42 per cent to 12 per cent, and excluding unadjusted family income from the comparison results in a range from 26 per cent to 12 per cent. For white men, the median change ranges from a decrease of 18 per cent (in family income) to an increase of 75 per cent, and excluding family income we get a range of increases from 26 per cent to 75 per cent. Differences of similar magnitude are observed for blacks, and for separations occurring after more than one year of marriage.

TABLE 15.5. *Median ratios of post- to pre-separation economic status, measured four different ways*

	White		Black	
	Men	Women	Men	Women
All				
Family income	0.82	0.58	0.70	0.53
Family income/size[56]	1.26	0.74	1.22	0.69
Family income/size[73]	1.44	0.80	1.35	0.72
Per-capita income	1.75	0.88	1.90	0.80
Married at least 2 years				
Family income	0.82	0.54	0.64	0.49
Family income/size[56]	1.27	0.66	1.19	0.61
Family income/size[73]	1.48	0.71	1.35	0.67
Per-capita income	1.80	0.81	1.88	0.73

Note:
The four measures of economic status are listed by decreasing economies of scale.

Discussion and Conclusion

In one sense this analysis has not clarified what the economic consequences of separation are. As shown by previous research it is clear that women on average lose economic status, although a sizeable proportion are better off separated than married, and it is also clear that men lose much less, and quite often gain a great deal economically. It has not been possible, however, to come up with a clear and simple answer to the question of the magnitude of the economic consequences of a marital separation. These were shown to depend heavily on the ways in which the family's economic status was defined. This should make it very clear that it is meaningless to ask the general question: 'What are the economic consequences of divorce?' The answer to that question can be almost anything, depending on what you mean by economic consequences. One therefore needs to ask more specific questions, such as how is family income affected by the separation, and how is the family's standard of living in relation to some specified standard of need affected.

Given the current practice where the children are much more likely to live with women after a separation, the decline in economic status experienced by most women will be smaller, the smaller the economies of scale are assumed to be;

and women's downward economic mobility will be much larger if one uses family income, for example, as the measure of economic status. Conversely, men, who tend to be better off under the current regime, will appear much better off if economies of scale are assumed to be small, and much less well off in terms of family income. The economic consequences of divorce for women and men, therefore, do not differ very much in terms of family income, but a great deal in terms of per-capita income. This means, of course, that an individual man or woman who compares his or her economic situation with that of the former spouse might quite legitimately come to very different conclusions about the differences in their situation, conclusions which could affect their view on the 'fairness' of their predicament. These differential effects for women and men clearly reflect the fact that the change in economic needs (as reflected in family size) is much greater for men than for women, because the latter tend to keep the children. Were men and women to divide children between them, then we would still find that the magnitude of the effects would depend on the measure of economic status, but the gender differential should be pretty much the same for all measures. A better understanding and description of the different meanings of the 'economic consequences of divorce' might thus not only improve the researchers' ability to come to some consensus about the matter; it might also clarify for individual women and men that former spouses might well be comparing apples and oranges when they compare their economic situations after separation.

References

Bushman, B., Rainwater, L., Schmauss, G., and Smeeding, T. (1988), 'Equivalence Scales, Well-being, Inequality and Poverty: Sensitivity Estimated across Ten Countries using the Luxembourg Income Study (LIS) Database', *Review of Income and Wealth* (June).

Duncan, G. J. and Hoffman, S. D. (1985), 'Economic Consequences of Marital Instability', in M. David and T. Smeeding (eds.), *Horizontal Equity, Uncertainty, and Well-Being* (Chicago).

Hoffman, S. D. and Duncan, G. J. (1988), 'What are the Economic Consequences of Divorce?', *Demography*, 25: 641–45.

McLanahan, S., Sørensen, A., and Watson, D. (1989), 'Sex

Differences in Poverty, 1950–1980', *Signs: Journal of Women in Culture and Society*, 15/1: 102–22.

McLindon, J. (1987), 'Separate but Unequal: The Economic Disaster of Divorce for Women and Children', *Family Law Quarterly*, 21: 351–409.

Nestel, G., Mercier, J., and Shaw, L. B. (1983), 'Economic Consequences of Midlife Change in Marital Status', in L. B. Shaw (ed.), *Unplanned Careers: The Working Lives of Middle-Aged Women* (Lexington, Mass.).

Weiss, R. S. (1984), 'The Impact of Marital Dissolution on Income and Consumption in Single Parent Households', *Journal of Marriage and the Family*, 46: 115–28.

Weitzman, L. J. (1985), *The Divorce Revolution: The Unexpected Social and Economic Consequences for Woman and Children in America* (New York).

Wishik, H. R. (1986), 'Economics of Divorce: An Exploratory Study', *Family Law Quarterly*, 20: 79–103.

Part Five
Societal Aspects

16. Intergenerational Consequences of Divorce: The United States Perspective

Sara McLanahan

Families headed by non-married women have increased dramatically since the early 1960s. Whereas in 1960 less than 7 per cent of all children in the United States were living in a female-headed family, by 1985 the proportion was over 21 per cent (US Census 1986). Indeed, if present trends continue, half of all children born in the past decade will live in a lone-parent family at some point before reaching 18 (Bumpass 1984). Given the importance of the family as a social institution, and given the high rates of poverty in families headed by single mothers, it is not surprising that researchers as well as policy-makers have responded to the change in family structure with interest and concern.

What happens to children who live in mother-only families? Do they perform less well in school? Do they exhibit more symptoms of psychological distress than children who live with two parents? Most important, what happens when they become adults? Are they more likely to be poor? Are they more likely to divorce and create mother-only families themselves? The answers to these questions are not simple, and the social-scientific literature reflects several changes of opinion since the early 1960s.

During the 1950s and early 1960s, the prevailing view was that divorce was indicative of individual pathology, and that parents would most likely pass their problems along to their children. Much of the research at this time was based on highly selective samples, such as children in treatment for psychological disorders or wards of the criminal justice system. Not surprisingly, personal failure rather than social

Support for some of the research reported here was provided in part by the Russell Sage Foundation and by the National Institute of Child Health and Human Development. Portions of this chapter are drawn from S. S. McLanahan and K. Booth, 'Mother-Only Familes: Problems, Reproduction, and Politics', forthcoming in *Journal of Marriage and the Family*; and from S. S. McLanahan, N. M. Astone, and N. Marks, 'The Role of Mother-Only Families in Reproducing Poverty', forthcoming in A. Huston (ed.), *Poverty and Children.*

factors was used to explain the fact that children from non-intact families exhibited more academic and social problems than children from stable families.

In the early 1970s the ideology began to change, as evidenced by Herzog's and Sudia's review of the research on children in 'fatherless families' (Herzog and Sudia 1973). These authors challenged earlier interpretations and showed that existing studies of mother-only families contained serious methodological flaws. They argued that many of the differences between stable and non-stable families could be explained by differences in family socio-economic status. In a changing political climate that viewed divorce and single parenthood more positively, interest focused on the 'strengths' of mother-only families and the ways in which single mothers successfully coped with poverty and stress. Despite Herzog's and Sudia's assertion that father absence *did* have some negative consequences for children, their critique of previous studies was taken by many as evidence that differences between intact and non-intact families were minimal or due entirely to income differences.

Since the late 1970s the pendulum has swung back again and researchers have moved beyond simplistic pathological and idealizing perspectives. More recent reviews of the literature have emphasized both that children in mother-only families are disadvantaged in a number of ways and that these disadvantages are outcomes of interactions among a variety of factors. Moreover, reviewers have noted that, while family socio-economic status is a major predictor of children's attainment, it cannot account for all of the problems associated with parental divorce and growing up in a mother-only family (Freeman and Shinn 1978; Hetherington, Camara, and Featherman 1983).

The new research indicated that children from mother-only families obtain fewer years of education and are more likely to drop out of high school than offspring from intact families (Garfinkel and McLanahan 1986; Krein and Beller 1988; McLanahan 1985; McLanahan and Bumpass 1988; Shaw 1982). They have lower earnings in young adulthood, they are more likely to be poor, and they are more likely to receive welfare when they become adults than their counterparts in two-parent families (Corcoran, Gordon, Laren, and Solon

1987; Hill, Augustyniak, and Ponza 1987; McLanahan 1988). Similar findings emerged from British studies using the Medical Research Council National Survey of Health and Development, a longitudinal study of 5,000 children born in 1946. In this study children who had experienced parental divorce showed lower educational attainment and lower socio-economic status in their mid-twenties than children whose parents had remained married and children who had lost a parent through death. The effect was mitigated but not removed by remarriage of the custodial parent (Maclean and Wadsworth 1988).

Children from mother-only families are also disadvantaged with respect to family formation and deviant behaviour. They are more likely to marry early and have children early, both in and out of wedlock (Abrahamse, Morrison, and Waite 1987; Hogan and Kitagawa 1985; McLanahan, Astone, and Marks 1988; McLanahan and Bumpass 1988; Michael and Tuma 1985), and those who marry are more likely to divorce (McLanahan and Bumpass 1988). In short, children who grow up in mother-only families are at greater risk of becoming single parents themselves, either through divorce or or non-marital child-bearing. Finally, offspring from non-intact families are more likely to commit delinquent acts and to engage in drug and alcohol use than offspring from two-parent families (Matsueda and Heimer 1987; Mott and Haurin 1987).

This chapter focuses on why children from mother-only families have lower attainment than children in two-parent families and what can be done to improve their life chances. In the discussion that follows, the terms 'non-intact family' and 'mother-only family' include children living with divorced mothers as well as children living with widowed mothers, never-married mothers, and stepparents. Much of the research on the intergenerational consequences of family disruption does not distinguish between divorce and other causes of disruption and single parenthood. Studies which have made this distinction usually find that the patterns are the same across all groups. Since divorce is by far the most common type of disruption, most mother-only families and non-intact families have experienced a divorce. First, income differences in one- and two-parent families are discussed, and estimates are made of the extent to which income accounts for differences in the attainment of children. Next the variation in parental socialization practices across different family forms is discussed. Children in mother-only families have less parental time than children in two-parent families, since the father is not living in the household and the mother is more likely to work outside the home. An important question, therefore, is whether the single mother is able to compensate for the loss of father's time in terms of helping her offspring with schoolwork and maintaining an effective level of communication. In addition to lack of income and parental time, children in mother-only families may be disadvantaged with respect to community resources: they may be more likely to live in poor neighbourhoods with high levels of crime and unemployment and to attend schools of poor quality. If this is true, it is important to know whether single mothers cope as well as married parents in such environments and, again, whether they are able effectively to control their adolescent children. The chapter ends by discussing the effects of social policy on single mothers, and by examining the current debate over welfare reform in the United States. Domestic programmes such as child support and child-care are discussed in terms of their potential to reduce economic insecurity and stress in mother-only families and thereby to improve the life chances of children.

Economic Insecurity in Mother-Only Families

Numerous researchers have argued that the lower socio-economic attainment of children in mother-only families is due to the fact that their families have less income. According to this view, single mothers have less money and invest less in their children, which in turn affects the characteristics of offspring as well as the quality of the parental household (Becker 1981; Weiss and Willis 1985). For example, family income has a strong influence on children's participation in extracurricular activities, travel experiences, and summer camps, all of which are positively related to school achievement. Economic necessity may also promote the premature assumption of adult responsibilities. Offspring from low-income families are more likely to leave school early to earn money for their families and to care for younger siblings than are offspring in middle-income families. They also may see marriage and parenthood as a means of escaping hardship and establishing an independent adult identity.

How substantial is the economic difference between one- and two-parent families? Is it large enough to account for differences in school achievement and family behaviour? The answer to the last question is yes. Approximately half of all mother-only families were poor in 1983, according to the official United States government definition of poverty, as compared with only 12 per cent of married-couple families (Garfinkel and McLanahan 1986). Trends in the poverty rates of mother-only families, married-couple families, and persons over 65 for the years 1967–85 are reported in Fig. 16.1. These numbers are based on the official definitions of poverty and include income from cash-transfer programmes such as Aid to Families with Dependent Children (AFDC), social security, and disability insurance.

Mother-only families have substantially higher poverty rates than other groups, and the gap between them and the

FIG. 16.1.

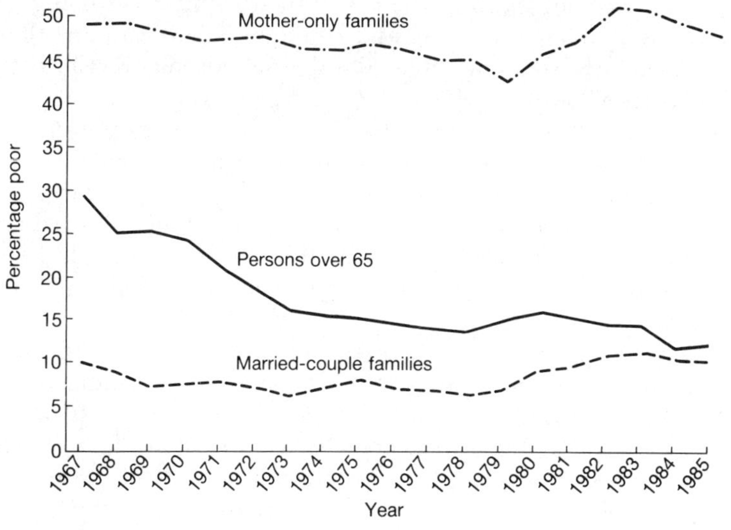

next poorest groups has increased since the early 1970s. The change in the relative status of mother-only families—often referred to as the 'feminization of poverty'—was due to the increase in the proportion of such families and to the decline in the poverty rates of other poor groups, primarily the aged.

Not only are mother-only families more likely to be poor than other groups, but the dynamics of their poverty are also different. Duncan and his colleagues found that nearly a quarter of the population was poor for at least one year during the decade from 1967 to 1978 (Duncan 1984). They also found considerable turnover in the poverty population, with most of the people who became poor remaining poor for less than two years. Among mother-only families, however, poverty lasts longer and is more severe. Bane and Ellwood (1983) have shown that during the late 1970s the average length of time in poverty for children in families headed by single mothers was seven years. This compares with 4.6 years for children in two-parent families. For black children the difference was even greater: twelve years for those in families headed by single women, compared with six years for those in two-parent families.

Poverty is not the only economic problem of mother-only families. Even families living above the poverty line are subject to income insecurity, and a large portion have experienced substantial declines in their standard of living as a result of divorce. Duncan and Hoffman (1985) estimate that the income of single mothers and their children one year after a divorce is only 67 per cent of their pre-divorce income. We would expect both partners to experience some drop in living standard after a divorce, since two separate households are more expensive to maintain than one. However, the drop for mothers is much greater than the drop for fathers. According to Duncan and Hoffman, the income of non-residential fathers one year after divorce is about 90 per cent of their pre-divorce income.

It is important to remember that poverty and income insecurity in mother-only families are not due entirely to marital disruption and non-marriage. A considerable proportion of single mothers were poor before their marriages ended or before they gave birth to a child out of wedlock. Mary Jo Bane (1986) uses the terms *event caused* and *reshuffled* to distinguish between the poverty that is a consequence of marital disruption or non-marriage and the poverty that exists before such events. She estimates that about 25 per cent of poor white single mothers and above 75 per cent of poor black single mothers were poor before forming mother-only families. Although these figures show that becoming a single mother does not *cause* all spells of poverty among mother-only families, they beg the question of whether such families would have escaped poverty sooner if the parents had remained married or married in the first place.

In sum, children in mother-only families are much more likely to be poor than children in two-parent families, in terms of both absolute income levels and income stability. Given these conditions, we would be surprised if they did not have lower socio-economic attainment than children who grew up with both natural parents. The question is, how great is the difference and how much is due to family income.

During the past several years my colleagues and I have been using longitudinal data to examine the relationship between family structure, income, and a series of young adult transitions, including high-school completion, non-marital motherhood and teen birth. Our analyses are based on three surveys: The Panel Study of Income Dynamics (PSID); the National Longitudinal Survey of Youth (NLSY); and the High School and Beyond Survey (HSB). Table 16.1 presents estimates of the effect of family structure based on these data. The numbers report the percentage increase in the risk of experiencing a particular event for children in mother-only and stepfamilies as compared to children in intact families. The family effects are reported both before and after income is taken into account (unadjusted and adjusted), which allows us to evaluate the importance of socio-economic factors in accounting for differences between one- and two-parent families. The HSB results are net of socio-economic status rather than income. This is because the HSB data contain a very bad measure of family income—30 per cent of the cases are missing. Analyses which use the faulty income measure in place of socio-economic status (SES) produce similar results, so we use SES. This variable is a composite measure of parental education, father's occupation, family income, and household possessions.

TABLE 16.1. *The effects of family structure on high-school graduation, pre-marital motherhood and teen birth (%)*

Family type	High-school drop-out (males and females combined)					
	PSID		NLSY		HSB	
	unadj.	adj.	unadj.	adj.	unadj.	adj.
Whites						
mother only	79*	55	133*	99*	159*	62*
step-parent	n.a.	n.a.	249*	215*	131*	103*
Blacks						
mother only	73*	30	57*	43*	93*	43*
step-parent	n.a.	n.a.	49	49	40	16
Hispanics[1]						
mother only	n.a.	n.a.	65*	57*	82*	42*
step-parent	n.a.	n.a.	73	64	68*	54
	Pre-marital and single motherhood (females only)					
	PSID		NLSY		HSB	
	unadj.	adj.	unadj.	adj.	unadj.	adj.
Whites						
mother only	122	84*	159*	138*	99	42
step-parent	n.a.	n.a.	209*	17*	103	82
Blacks						
mother only	139*	108*	62*	54*	166*	131*
step-parent	n.a.	n.a.	9	8	143*	120*
Hispanics						
mother only	n.a.	n.a.	158*	148*	111*	109*
step-parent	n.a.	n.a.	18	18	46	46

	Teen birth (females only)			
	NLSY		HSB	
	unadj.	adj.	unadj.	adj.
Whites				
mother only	52*	35	8	−24
step-parent	171*	141*	90*	72*

TABLE 16.1. Cont. *The effects of family structure on high-school graduation, pre-marital motherhood and teen birth (%)*

	Teen birth (females only).					
	PSID		NLSY		HSB	
	unadj.	adj.	unadj.	adj.	unadj.	adj.
Blacks						
mother only	60	46*		122*		90*
step-parent	24	24		103*		82*
Hispanics[1]						
mother only	65*	58*		52		33
step-parent	99	100*		155*		150*

Notes:
The effects are based on logit models and are expressed as the percentage increase in the risk of an event associated with each family type.

[1] The effect of family structure on high-school drop-out is significant for hispanic daughters but not for sons.

Sources: McLanahan 1985 and 1988; McLanahan and Bumpass 1988.

* $p < 0.05$

n.a. not available

Table 16.1 illustrates several important points. First, children from non-intact families clearly have a greater risk of experiencing each of the events examined here. The increase in risk (unadjusted) ranges from 50 to 150 per cent, with a few exceptions; and almost all of the effects are statistically significant. Secondly, living in a stepfamily appears to be just as risky as living with a single mother, and in some cases the risk is even greater. The latter is especially true of whites in the case of high-school drop-outs and non-marital motherhood. Thirdly, income accounts for a substantial portion of the difference between children in mother-only and intact families. A comparison of the unadjusted and adjusted percentages indicates that in some cases income explains more than half of the family difference. And, finally, income does *not* explain all of the variation across family types. Although the risk associated with living in a non-intact family is substantially smaller once income is taken into account, in most cases it remains statistically significant.

Parental Socialization in Mother-Only Families

If family income and socio-economic status do not account for all the differences in socio-economic attainment between offspring from intact and non-intact families, what else might explain the remaining difference? One possibility is that divorced parents adhere to a different set of values and expectations from married parents and therefore train their children to behave in different ways and to aspire to different goals. For example, divorced or never-married parents may have lower educational aspirations for their offspring or they may be more liberal with respect to non-marital sexual behaviour. The former could account for the higher incidence of dropping out of high school, whereas the latter might explain differences in family formation behaviour. On the last point, Thornton and Camburn (1987) found that divorced mothers, especially those who had remarried, held less restrictive attitudes about pre-marital sex than mothers who had been continuously married. In turn, mothers' attitudes were associated with the attitudes and behaviour of their offspring.

Alternatively, single parents may hold the same values as married parents but be less successful in transmitting these values to their children. Such a failure could be due to differences in the amount of time devoted to children or to less effective parenting styles. Successful socialization requires the development and maintenance of a stable parent–child relationship, and marital disruption may undermine such a relationship. Clearly, non-residential fathers spend less time with their children, which could undermine their ability to influence their offspring's behaviour. Frank Furstenberg and his colleagues (1983 and 1987) found that less than half of the children with divorced parents in their sample (ages 11–16) had seen their fathers during the past year. Not surprisingly, these children felt less close to their fathers than children living with both parents. Not everyone agrees about the value of a good relationship with the non-residential father. While theory suggests that fathers are an important influence on child development, Furstenberg's research (1983) indicated that contact with the non-residential father has no impact on children's well-being.

The mother–child relationship may also be altered by divorce. Whereas most studies report no difference in mother-attachment among children from intact and non-intact familes, at least two studies have found that the relationship between the mother and child may become closer and less hierarchical after a divorce. White, Brinkerhoff, and Booth (1985), and both Devall (1986) and Weiss (1979) report that the older daughters of divorced parents often become confidants of their mothers. Whether such a role builds responsibility or merely pushes the daughter into a premature adulthood, or both, is not clear. Since these studies are based on small convenience samples, their results cannot be generalized to the population of all disrupted families. However, their arguments are compelling and deserve further consideration.

A final way in which socialization practices may differ in intact and non-intact families is in the degree of social control single mothers exercise over their children. Hetherington and her colleagues found that divorced mothers were less consistent in their household schedules and discipline patterns than married mothers, at least during the first year after a divorce (Hetherington, Cox, and Cox 1978). Others have shown that adolescents in mother-only families are more susceptible to peer influences than those living with both natural parents (Dornbusch *et al.* 1985; Kellam, Ensminger, and Turner 1977; Steinberg 1987). Interestingly, the latter studies also show that grandmothers strengthen parental influence and control, whereas stepfathers have no positive effect in this regard.

As was the case with low income, parental socialization practices, such as lack of supervision or involvement, may not be a consequence of divorce. Rather, such characteristics may reflect pre-existing conditions that lead to marital instability as well as low attainment in children. If this is true, the children of divorced families would have exhibited the same problems even if their parents had stayed together. They (the children) might have been even worse off. The most impressive evidence in support of this hypothesis comes from Block and her colleagues (1986), who have shown that the personalities of children whose parents *eventually* divorce were different before the divorce.

Assuming that socialization practices and parent–child relationships are different in intact and non-intact families, the critical question is whether such differences can account for variation in child outcomes. My colleagues and I have attempted to answer this question in our analyses of the NLS-HSB survey. The former contains information on parents' educational aspirations, as well as parental behaviours such as supervision of social activities, helping with schoolwork, and general communication. We find that socialization factors account for *some* of the differences in school behaviour between children in intact and non-intact families. For example, parents in non-intact families provide less supervision and are less likely to help with homework than parents in intact families; and these differences account for some of the variation in children's grade-point average, school attendance, and deviant behaviour. However, they do *not* explain differences in high-school graduation or pre-marital birth, which were the outcomes we were most interested in explaining (Astone and McLanahan 1989).

Community Resources and Mother-Only Families

In addition to the economic and socialization arguments, some analysts believe that the negative consequences associated with divorce and single parenthood are due to neighbourhood or community characteristics. According to this view, children in non-intact families are more likely to live in socially isolated neighbourhoods than children in intact families, which in turn lowers their opportunity for economic mobility and raises the likelihood that they will drop-out from school and/or become teen parents. This argument, best and most recently articulated by William Julius Wilson, incorporates elements of both the economic-deprivation and socialization perspectives and raises the debate over family structure to a more macro-level of analysis (Wilson 1987). Whereas those who adhere to the economic-deprivation argument generally emphasize supply-side factors, such as household resources and parental investment, neighbourhood theorists stress demand-side factors, such as the quality of local labour markets and the extent to which information about jobs is readily available. According to this view, children from mother-only families have less access to jobs and therefore less incentive to invest in education or other human capital activities than children in intact families. Similarly, whereas socialization theorists focus primarily on parent–child relations and communication and control within the family, neighbourhood analysts stress the importance of community attitudes, local networks, and peer-group activities. The latter argue that mother-only families are isolated in 'underclass' neighbourhoods with high levels of poverty and disorganization, which, in turn, reduce parental control and increase the likelihood that offspring will be exposed to antisocial activities.

The neighbourhood hypothesis is distinct from previous arguments primarily in its emphasis on how social structure *constrains* family behaviour. According to this view, economic incentives and social norms within ghettos discourage socio-economic attainment and encourage early family formation. As was the case with the previous two hypotheses, the neighbourhood effect can be viewed as a cause or as a consequence of family disruption or non-marital births. In the version set forth by Wilson, school drop-out and single motherhood across the generations are both treated as consequences of the lack of jobs for men. Another version suggests that single mothers are less able than married parents to cope with life in ghetto neighbourhoods, where community controls are weaker and peer activities more dangerous. Sampson's (1987) study suggests that there is an interaction between living in a mother-only family and poor neighbourhood conditions. Delinquency rates are higher in areas with high unemployment and a high proportion of female-headed families.

Several researchers have found support from the neighbourhood argument. In their Chicago study, Hogan and Kitagawa (1985) were able to classify respondents according to census tract characteristics such as medium income, percentage poor, juvenile crime rates, marriage rates, and fertility rates. They found that neighbourhood quality has a significant effect on early pregnancy and is strongly related to parental supervision. Since then, Corcoran and her colleagues (1987) have shown that residential location is related to children's socio-economic attainment.

A major limitation of the neighbourhood hypothesis is that it applies to a relatively small proportion of all mother-only families. Whereas neighbourhoods may be important in explaining variation in the behaviour and attainment of many black adolescents, they cannot account for differences among most whites. Using information from the 1970 and 1980 census tracts of the hundred largest central cities, Garfinkel and McLanahan (1986) found that less than 5 per cent of white mother-only families were living in urban areas in which over 20 per cent of the population were poor, and less than 1 per cent were living in areas where over 40 per cent of the inhabitants were poor. Not surprisingly, the estimates for blacks were much higher, though, again, the majority of single mothers did not live in poverty neighbourhoods. About 35 per cent of black single mothers were living in areas where 20 per cent of the inhabitants were poor and about 10 per cent were living in areas where 40 per cent were poor.

Policy Recommendations

The studies described in the previous section indicate that income is the single most important factor, among those identified thus far, in accounting for differences in the socio-economic attainment of children from intact and non-intact families. Low income not only limits the amount of money available for college, travel, and other education-related goods; it is also associated with less effective parenting practices and with residence in neighbourhoods with poorer quality schools. Given the importance of income and given the fact that income can be manipulated by policy-makers, the last section of this chapter focuses on policies that have the potential to reduce poverty and economic insecurity in mother-only families.

Single mothers have three potential sources of income: individual earnings; private transfers, primarily child support from the non-resident parent; and public transfers, primarily welfare (AFDC) or Survivors' Insurance. Social policy can and does affect each of these income sources, not only for single mothers but for all families with children.

Increasing Individual Earnings

The most important source of income in mother-only families is earned income. Earnings account for about 60 per cent of the total family income in mother-only families in the United States as compared with 90 per cent of total family income in two-parent families. Garfinkel and McLanahan (1986) report that even in families headed by never-married mothers, which are more likely to rely on public assistance than other families, the earnings of the household head is the major source of income during any given year.

Despite the importance of earnings, however, single mothers earn only 35 per cent as much as the major bread-winner in two-parent families (i.e. the father). The lower earnings of single mothers are due to their gender as well as to their family status. Women who work full time, year-round, earn only about 60 per cent as much as men, a ratio that has remained relatively constant since the early 1960s. Whereas some of the gender gap in wages is due to differences in human capital (education, training, and work experience), a substantial portion is due to the fact that women are excluded from certain high-paying jobs and are concentrated in low-paying occupations. Corcoran and Duncan (1979) have shown that only 40 per cent of the wage gap between the sexes can be accounted for by differences in education, training, and work experience. The evidence indicates that, irrespective of the causes of segregation, policies such as affirmative action and pay equity, which are designed to increase the number of women in high-paying jobs and raise wages in low-paying sex-segregated jobs, could go a long way towards increasing the earnings and reducing poverty in mother-only families.

A second factor in accounting for the low earnings in mother-only families is labour supply. Not only do single mothers have lower wage rates; they also work fewer hours in the paid force than male bread-winners in two-parent households. Between 30 and 40 per cent of single mothers report no earnings at all during any given year, and, among those who do report earnings, many work less than full time. The importance of not working outside the home is profound. Ellwood (1986) has shown that only about 6 per cent of single mothers who work full time, year-round, are poor, as compared to more than 70 per cent of non-employed mothers. These findings should not be interpreted to mean that if all single mothers worked full time only 6 per cent of them would be poor. Rather, the apparent advantage of employed mothers reflects the selection process that channels women with higher wage rates into the labour force and those with lower wage rates into home-maker status. However, they do serve to show that single mothers who 'choose' to work full time, year-round, are much better off than their counterparts who are not employed or who work less than full time.

A major barrier to working is the cost of child-care. For mothers with the lowest wage rates, net earnings after paying for child-care are less than the income available through public assistance (Sawhill 1976). In effect, these women cannot afford to work outside the home. For others, wages are so low that the mother must limit her hours of paid work to the times when she can arrange for free child-care from a friend or relative. Thus, a second way that policy-makers can increase the earnings of single mothers is to subsidize child-care so that mothers can work more hours and take home more income.

At present, the government has two different mechanisms for providing child-care. For families in the lower half of the income distribution, there are income-tested child-care subsidies which cost less than $2 billion per year. For middle- and upper-middle income families, there is the child-care tax credit in the federal income tax, which costs over $3.5 billion (Garfinkel 1988). The current tax credit is of greater benefit to middle-income families than to low-income families, since the former have a higher tax rate than the latter. One solution is to combine the two mechanisms into a single programme, which would provide a refundable tax credit for those with very low earnings and declining credit for those with higher earnings. An alternative would be to provide child-care for all families and to charge a sliding-scale fee based upon income.

Increasing Private Transfers

A second source of income for single mothers is child support and alimony paid by the non-residential parent. In theory, both parents are responsible for the economic support of their children. When parents divorce, the non-residential parent bears an obligation to provide material support for his or her children. Unfortunately, the US child-support system has been a dismal failure, at least until the mid-1980s. In 1983 only 60 per cent of children with a living absent parent had a child-support award, and only half of those with an award received full payment. In addition, awards are rarely indexed to the cost of living and therefore their value declines over time. In 1983 child-support and alimony payments accounted for less than 13 per cent of total income in white mother-only familes and for less than 3 per cent of total income in black mother-only families (Garfinkel and McLanahan 1986).

Some have argued that non-residential parents cannot afford to pay child support and that requiring them to pay would push these parents, and their new families, into poverty. While this prediction is undoubtedly true for some cases, the evidence suggests that it does not hold for the majority of non-residential parents. First, as noted earlier, studies of the economic consequences of divorce show that the income loss experienced by the single mother is much greater than the loss experienced by the non-residential father. Moreover, estimates of the absent father's ability to pay indicate that on average the income of non-residential fathers is about $19,000 per year, only $3,000 less than the average for all prime-age males (Garfinkel and Oellerich 1990).

In response to this information, strong bipartisan support has developed for reforming the present child-support system and for increasing the income available to single mothers through private transfers. The new Wisconsin child-support-assurance system, discussed in Chapter 10, is an example of such a policy (Garfinkel 1985). The philosophy underlying this system is that parents are responsible for sharing income with their children, and government is responsible for assuring that children receive the child support to which they are legally entitled. The financial obligation of the non-residential parent is expressed as a percentage of income and is withheld from earnings, just as income and payroll taxes are withheld. In cases where the father is unemployed or has low earnings, the government makes up the difference, just as it does with social security pensions. Note that the third component of the child-support-assurance system proposal involves a public transfer in addition to governmental enforcement of private obligations. Garfinkel and his colleagues at the University of Wisconsin estimate that, if implemented at the national level, the system would reduce the poverty gap of mother-only families by about 40 per cent.

Public Transfers

The United States has always provided economic support to the most disadvantaged persons in society. During the colonial period single mothers were protected by policies patterned after the British poor-law system. Later, such policies were extended into programmes such as Widow's Pensions and Mothers' Pensions in the late 1800s and early

1900s, and Aid to Dependent Children (ADC) (since 1962 Aid to families with Dependent Children (AFDC)) and Survivors' Insurance (SI) in the late 1930s. While the latter two programmes both provide support to single mothers, they differ in one very important respect. AFDC, or welfare as it is commonly called, is a means-tested programme available only to poor single mothers, whereas SI is a universal programme available to all widowed mothers.

Although benefits were not high enough to support a family, at least when the policies were first implemented, both ADC and SI were originally designed to allow single mothers to behave as much like married mothers as possible, that is, to stay at home and raise their children. From the mid-1950s benefits began to rise and continued to increase throughout the 1960s and up to the mid-1970s. Ironically, just as benefits were becoming large enough to allow single mothers to stay at home, married mothers began entering the labour force in even greater numbers. Since the mid-1970s AFDC and other income-tested programmes for single mothers have declined by about 30 per cent. Initially, the decline was due to inflation and the failure of benefits to keep up with the cost of living. But in the early 1980s it was due to direct budget-cost legislation. SI has done much better than AFDC since the late 1970s because it is part of the social security system, whose benefits are indexed to the rate of inflation and less vulnerable to budget cutbacks. Although widows have always been treated more generously than other single mothers, they represent a decreasing proportion of all mother-only families.

AFDC—or Welfare—has come under considerable attack in recent years, and some analysts and policy-makers feel that the programme does more harm than good. A major criticism is that it discourages single mothers from entering the labour force by imposing a high tax rate on earnings. Welfare recipients lose nearly a dollar in benefits for each dollar earned. They also lose health care and other income-tested benefits. Given the high tax rate, their low earning capacity, and the cost of child-care, many single mothers would be worse off working full time than depending on welfare. The high tax rate implicit in welfare programmes is especially problematic, given the trends in labour-force participation of married women and the importance of earned income in all mother-only families.

In response to these concerns, many critics have called for replacing welfare with work. While such concerns date back at least to the early 1960s, there is a greater sense of urgency and bipartisan support in the 1990s than in the past. Many states are experimenting with different versions of work and training programmes, and others are planning to do so. Included under the 'work–welfare' rubric is a broad range of programmes which differ greatly in their intent and implementation. While some programmes simply impose a work requirement on the mother in exchange for her welfare cheque, many are aimed at providing resources that facilitate work: for example, child-care, transportation, training, and education (Gueron 1986). To date the evidence suggests that some states are spending a good deal of money on training and education, money that probably would not have been spent in the absence of a change in expectations regarding work.

Others are less optimistic about work–welfare programmes. Some argue that work and training programmes are simply strategies for reducing welfare costs and that single mothers and their children will be worse off than they were under the previous system (Handler 1988). In fact, if welfare benefits are simply replaced by work, children appear to be worse off in the sense that they have less time with the mother and no more income. Others note that, while single mothers appear to have benefited from previous employment training programmes, such benefits may not extend to all welfare mothers, since the earlier evaluations were based on voluntary participation and were restricted to mothers with children over the age of 6 (Garfinkel and McLanahan 1986). Finally, critics note that, whatever short-term benefits might accrue from welfare reform, income-tested programmes are inherently unstable and doomed to cutbacks because their political constituency is small and lacking in resources (Weir, Orloff, and Skocpol 1988).

For reasons such as these, developing and expanding universal programmes outside welfare as opposed to reforming the system from within may be the best long-term strategy for reducing poverty and income insecurity in mother-only families. Universal programmes, such as SI, treat all income groups in a similar fashion, and evidence suggests that they are more successful in reducing long-term economic insecurity than programmes aimed only at the poor. A recent comparison of six industrialized countries that rely on universal and employment-related income transfer programmes (e.g. Sweden, West Germany, and England), found single mothers doing better than in countries that rely on means-tested programmes (e.g. Australia and the United States) (Torrey and Smeeding 1988).

Two policies that fit the description of a universal programme are the child-care tax credit and the guaranteed minimum benefit in the child-support-assurance system. Both of these proposals benefit all mother-only families as opposed to only those who are poor or who fall below a given income level. Moreover, both programmes reinforce employment, in as much as they make working in the paid labour force a more attractive alternative than staying at home and receiving welfare. This is because, unlike welfare, benefits are not reduced dollar for dollar as earnings increase. In the case of the child-care credit, the subsidy decreases gradually as total income goes up; and in the case of the minimum child-support benefit, the subsidy is taxed at the mother's normal tax rate.

Two final examples of universal social policies are a children's allowance and universal health insurance. As is the case with the child-care policy, the current system has two mechanisms for helping families cover the cost of health care and child-rearing. For families at the bottom end of the income distribution, there are welfare and Medicaid. For those in the middle- and upper-middle income brackets, there is an income tax credit for dependent children and for medical care. In addition to a tax credit, health insurance provided through employers is not taxable, which represents a substantial public transfer to middle- and upper-income families. Replacing the child deduction with a smaller refundable tax credit that is more generous for those at the bottom of the income distribution, and requiring employers to provide health insurance to all employees, would greatly improve the living conditions of single mothers and their children without increasing the cost to society (McLanahan and Garfinkel 1989).

Together, the policies described above would go a long way towards increasing economic stability and reducing poverty in mother-only families. Moreover, they complement one another and therefore have important interaction effects.

Employment-related policies such as affirmative action and pay equity increase the wages of single mothers, as well as other women. Policies such as child-care, child support, and children's allowances supplement the earnings of single mothers and make working in the paid labour force a more viable alternative to welfare. Given that the well-being of children is essential to our nation's future, and given that over half of all children today will spend some time in a mother-only family, such policies deserve careful consideration.

Conclusion

Until the early 1980s many analysts as well as lay persons believed that divorce had no negative consequences for children, beyond the temporary stress associated with family disruption. This belief emerged during the 1970s, when divorce rates were at their peak, and legitimated the new ideology that children's interests are best served when their parents pursue their own personal happiness. Since 1980 a number of studies (see McLanahan and Bumpass 1988; Maclean and Wadsworth 1988) based on large, nationally representative surveys have challenged this view by showing that divorce is associated with a number of long-term negative outcomes in children.

While there is not definitive proof that divorce itself *causes* lower attainment in children, there are good theoretical reasons for believing that it reduces the quantity and quality of parental investment, which in turn reduces the children's well-being. The most important loss that comes with divorce, and the loss that is most strongly associated with child outcomes, is economic insecurity and income deprivation. The financial contribution from the non-residential parent (usually the father) to the child drops dramatically after the parents break up, and the residential parent (usually the mother) is rarely able to compensate for the income loss. Consequently, the child has fewer resources to draw on and must lower his or her expectations about the future.

There are also good theoretical reasons for believing that conflict between the parents and the erosion of parent–child relationships during and after divorce contribute to lower socio-economic attainment in children. However, the empirical evidence to support this hypothesis is much weaker than in the case of income. In fact, at least one national survey indicates that the father's involvement after divorce has no discernible benefits for the child (Furstenberg *et al.* 1983).

What, if anything, can society do to reduce the negative consequences of divorce for children? There are at least three possible answers to this question: we can try and reduce the incidence of divorce by tightening divorce laws and changing the tax code to make divorce more costly for parents; we can try and increase the financial contribution of the non-residential parent; and we can increase state support for children in mother-only families. The first strategy is preventive; the second and third are designed to reduce the costs of divorce for children by increasing private and public income transfer to non-intact families.

Changing the law as a means of reducing divorce is not likely to have a large effect, given the demographic and economic factors that underlie the long-term trend in divorce. To the extent that divorce reflects the growing economic independence of women over the last century, it is unlikely that changes in the law will have a strong impact on behaviour, although there would be some effect at the margin. To the extent that divorce reflects naïvety on the part of parents about the real consequences of their behaviour for children, and to the extent that children's well-being is part of the decision to divorce, a thorough dissemination of new information may alter the behaviour of some couples who are considering whether or not to end their marriage.

While social policy is probably not capable of reducing the divorce rate very much, it can do something to improve the income and economic security of single mothers and their children. With respect to the private commitment, the traditional system is grossly unjust with respect to the distribution of the costs of children between parents. In 1990 the mother, who is usually the parent with the lower earning capacity, still bears a disproportionate share of the costs of children after a divorce. Society can establish firm standards for child support and see that the non-residential parent pays what is owed. In addition to regulating and enforcing private child support, the state can also increase its share of the child-support burden by subsidizing child-care, guaranteeing a minimum child support, and providing a children's allowance. The United States is moving forwards vigorously in the area of private child-care and a minimum child-support benefit. All of these policies should improve the economic situation of mother-only families and reduce some of their long-term disadvantages for children.

References

ABRAHAMSE, A. F., MORRISON, P. A., and WAITE, L. J. (1987), 'Single Teen Mothers: Spotting Susceptible Adolescents in Advance', paper presented at the annual meeting of the Population Association of America (Chicago).

ASTONE, N. M., and MCLANAHAN, S. S. (1989), 'The Effect of Family Structure on School Completion', paper presented at the annual meeting of the Population Association of America, (Baltimore).

BANE, M. J. (1986), 'Household Composition and Poverty', in S. H. Danziger and D. H. Weinberg (eds.), *Fighting Poverty: What Works and What Doesn't* (Cambridge, Mass.), 209–31.

——and ELLWOOD, D. (1983), 'The Dynamics of Dependence: The Routes to Self-Sufficiency', report prepared for the Assistant Secretary for Planning and Evaluation, Department of Health and Human Services (Cambridge, Mass.).

BECKER, G. B. (1981), *A Treatise on the Family* (Cambridge, Mass.).

BLOCK, J. H., BLOCK, J., and GJERDE, P. F. (1986), 'The Personality of Children Prior to Divorce: A Prospective Study', *Child Development*, 57: 827–40.

BUMPASS, L. (1984), 'Children and Marital Disruption: A Replication and Update', *Demography*, 21: 71–82.

CORCORAN, M. R., and DUNCAN, G. (1979), 'Work History, Labour Force Attachment and Earnings Differences between the Races and Sexes', *Journal of Human Resources*, 14: 3–20.

——GORDON, R., LAREN, D. and SOLON, G. (1987), 'Intergenerational Transmission of Education, Income and Earnings', unpublished paper (Institute of Public Policy Studies, University of Michigan, Ann Arbor).

DEVALL, E. (1986), 'The Impact of Divorce and Maternal Employment on Pre-Adolescent Children', *Family Relations*, 35: 153–9.

DORNBUSCH, S. M., CARLSMITH, J. M., BUSHWALL, S. J., LITTER, P. L., LEIDERMAN, H., HASTORF, A. H., and GROSS, P. T. (1985), 'Single Parents, Extended Households and the Control of Adolescents', *Child Development*, 56: 326–41.

DUNCAN, G. J. (1984), *Years of Poverty, Years of Plenty* (Ann Arbor, Mich.).

——and HOFFMAN, S. D. (1985), 'A Reconsideration of the Economic Consequences of Marital Dissolution', *Demography*, 22: 485–98.

ELDER, G., jun., (1974), *Children of the Great Depression* (Chicago).

ELLWOOD, D. (1986), 'Working Off of Welfare: Prospects and Policies for Self-Sufficiency of Women Heading Families', Discussion Paper No. 803–86 (Institute for Research on Poverty, University of Wisconsin-Madison).

FREEMAN, W. H., and SHINN, M. (1978), 'Father Absence and Children's Cognitive Development', *Psychological Bulletin*, 85: 295–324.

FURSTENBERG, F., MORGAN, S. P., and ALLISON, P. (1987), 'Parental Participation and Children's Well-Being after Marital Disruption', *American Sociological Review*, 52: 695–701.

——NORD, C. W., PETERSON, J. L., and ZILL, N. (1983), 'The Life Course of Children of Divorce: Marital Disruption and Parental Contact', *American Sociological Review*, 48: 656–67.

GARFINKEL, I. (1985), 'The Role of Child Support Insurance in Antipoverty Policy', *The Annals of the American Academy of Political and Social Science*, 479: 119–31.

——OELLERICH, D. (1989), 'Noncustodial Fathers' Ability to Pay Child Support', *Demography* 26: 201–11.

——(1988), 'The Potential of Child Care to Reduce Poverty and Welfare Dependence', paper presented to Wingspread Symposium on the Economic Implications and Benefits of Child Care, 24–6 Jan. (Racine, Wis.).

——MCLANAHAN, S. S. (1986), *Single Mothers and their Children: A New American Dilemma* (Washington, DC).

GUERON, J. M. (1986), *Work Initiatives for Welfare Recipients: Lessons from a Multi-State Experiment* (New York).

HANDLER, J. F. (1988), 'Consensus on Redirection—Which Direction?' *Focus*, 11: 29–34.

HERZOG, E., and SUDIA, C. E. (1973), 'Children in Fatherless Families', in B. Caldwell and H. N. Ricciuti (eds.), *Review of Child Development Research* (Chicago), iii. 141–232.

HETHERINGTON, E. M., CAMARA, K. A., and FEATHERMAN, D. L. (1983), 'Achievement and Intellectual functioning of Children in One-Parent Households', in J. Spence (ed.), *Achievement and Achievement Motives* (San Francisco), 205–84.

——COX, M., and COX, R. (1978), 'The Aftermath of Divorce', in J. H. Stevens (eds.), *Mother–Child, Father–Child Relations* (Washington, DC).

HEYNS, B. (1985), 'The Influence of Parental Work on Children's School Achievement', in S. B. Kamerman and C. D. Hayes (eds.), *Families that work: Children in a Changing World* (Washington DC), 229–67.

HILL, M. S., AUGUSTYNIAK, S., and PONZA, M. (1987), 'Effects of Parental Divorce on Children's Attainments: An Empirical Comparison of Five Hypotheses', memeo (Survey Research Institute, University of Michigan, Ann Arbor).

HOGAN, D. P., and KITAGAWA, E. M. (1985), 'The Impact of Social Status, Family Structure and Neighbourhood on the Fertility of Black Adolescents', *American Journal of Sociology*, 90: 825–55.

KELLAM, S. G., ENSMINGER, M. E., and TURNER, R. J. (1977), 'Family Structure and the Mental Health of Children', *Archives of General Psychiatry*, 34: 1012–22.

KREIN, S. F., and BELLER, A. H. (1988), 'Educational Attainment of Children from Single-Parent Families: Differences by Exposure, Gender and Race', *Demography*, 25/2: 221–4.

LAMB, M. (ed.) (1981), *The Role of the Father in Child Development* (New York).

MACLEAN, M., and WADSWORTH, M. (1988), 'The Interests of Children after Parental Divorce: A Longer Term Perspective', *International Journal of Law and the Family*, 2: 155–66.

MATSUEDA, R. L., and HEIMER, K. (1987), 'Race, Family Structure, and Delinquency: A Test of Differential Association and Social Control Theories', *American Sociological Review*, 52/6: 826–40.

MCLANAHAN, S. S. (1985), 'The Reproduction of Poverty', *American Journal of Sociology*, 90: 873–901.

——(1988), 'Family Structure and Dependency: Early Transitions to Female Household Headship', *Demography*, 25: 1–16.

——ASTONE, N. M., and MARKS, N. (1988), 'The Role of Mother-Only Families in Reproducing Poverty', paper presented to the Conference on Poverty and Children, 20–2 June (Lawrence, Kan).

——and BUMPASS, L. (1988), 'Intergenerational Consequences of Family Disruption', *American Journal of Sociology*, 94: 130–52.

——andGARFINKEL, I. (1989), 'Single Mothers, the Underclass, and Social Policy', *Annals of the American Academy of Political and Social Science*, 501: 92–104.

MICHAEL, R. T., and TUMA, N. B. (1985), 'Entry into Marriage and Parenthood by Young Men and Women: The Influence of Family Background', *Demography*, 2: 515–44.

MOTT, F. L., and HAURIN, R. J. (1987), 'The Inter-relatedness of Age at First Intercourse, Early Childbearing, Alcohol and Drug Use among Young American Women', paper presented at the annual meeting of the Population Association of America (Chicago).

Rubin, L. B. (1976), *Worlds of Pain: Life in the Working-Class Family* (New York).

Sampson, R. J. (1987), 'Urban Black Violence: The Effect of Male Joblessness and Family Disruption', *American Journal of Sociology*, 93: 348–82.

Sawhill, I. (1976), 'Discrimination and Poverty among Women who Head Families', *Signs: Journal of Women in Culture and Society*, 1/2: 201–11.

Shaw, L. B. (1982), 'High School Completion for Young Women: Effects of Low Income and Living with a Single Parent', *Journal of Family Issues*, 3: 147–63.

Steinberg, L. (1987), 'Single Parents, Stepparents and the Susceptibility of Adolescents to Antisocial Peer Pressure', *Child Development*, 58: 269–75.

Thornton, A., and Camburn, D. (1987), 'The Influence of the Family on Premarital Sexual Attitudes and Behaviour', *Demography*, 24: 323–40.

Torrey, B. B., and Smeeding, T. (1988), 'Poor Children in Rich Countries', paper presented at the annual meeting of the Population Association of America (New Orleans).

United States Bureau of the Census, *Current Population Reports*, Series P–20, nos. 105 (1960), 106 (1961), and 423 (1988) (Washington, DC).

Weir, M., Orloff, A. S., and Skocpol, T. (1988), 'The Future of Social Policy in the United States: Political Constraints and Possibilities', in Weir, Orloff and Skocpol (eds.), *The Politics of Social Policy in the United States* (Princeton, NJ), 421–66.

Weiss, R. (1979), 'Growing Up a Little Faster: The Experience of Growing Up in a Single-Parent Household', *Journal of Social Issues*, 35: 97–111.

Weiss, Y., and Willis, R. (1985), 'Children as Collective Goods and Divorce Settlements', *Journal of Labor Economics*, 3: 268–92.

Weitzman, L. J. (1985), *The Divorce Revolution: The Unexpected Social and Economic Consequences for Women and Children in America* (New York).

White, L. K., Brinkerhoff, D. B., and Booth, A. (1985), 'The Effect of Marital Disruption on Child's Attachment to Parents', *Journal of Family Issues*, 6: 5–22.

Wilson, W. J. (1987), *The Truly Disadvantaged: The Inner City, the Underclass, and Public Policy* (Chicago).

17. The Relationship between Public and Private Financial Support following Divorce in England and Wales

Gwynn Davis, Stephen Cretney, Kay Bader, and Jean Collins

As long ago as 1974 the Finer Committee on One-Parent Families drew attention to the close links between the private law governing the resolution of marital and other family disputes and the welfare benefits system (HMSO 1974). As Kahn-Freund had earlier observed the private law of family maintenance and the public law of national insurance, taxation, and social security ought to be viewed as a single system regulating family finance (Kahn-Freund 1978). This is so despite the fact that each element has developed pragmatically from distinct historical sources and reflects a somewhat different set of underlying values.

The Finer Committee's proposals to integrate welfare benefits and the procedures of the 'private' family law have not been implemented. The relationship between public and private provision still lacks coherence, and this in turn exerts considerable influence upon the economic strategies which are adopted upon marital breakdown. For example, it has been observed that in Britain, where we have limited provision for substitute child-care, and social security policies which effectively discourage part-time employment, more lone parents are reliant on the social security system on a long-term basis than is the case in France, where the maintenance contribution from fathers tends to be lower (Bastard, Cardia Voneche, and Maclean 1989).

The lack of coherence to which we have referred is exacerbated by fiscal policies which are not specifically directed towards family breakdown. In particular, the policy of fiscal neutrality ('a dollar is a dollar') which has been in the ascendant since the emergence of Thatcherism as the dominant political philosophy remains subject to major qualifications in relation to the acquisition of ownership interests in domestic housing. This in turn has been a major factor in determining who emerges as 'rich' and who as 'poor' following marital breakdown.

Public-law provision also has a curious impact upon the effective jurisdiction of the divorce court. In theory, following the 1970 Matrimonial Proceedings and Property Act, virtually the whole of the parties' financial resources are at the disposal of the court: capital, property, and future income are placed in the melting-pot together. But divorce courts also have to contend with the availability of public resources of housing and income maintenance. In practice, the courts do their best to take these public resources into account. But the intermeshing of two decision-making processes—one judicial, the other administrative—can, as we shall see, produce very curious results.

Public Funding

This chapter begins with an overview of public funding, with reference to: (1) income maintenance under the welfare benefit system; (2) the allocation of housing, and the making of provision for its cost, by state agencies; (3) the tax treatment of payments made between parties to divorce proceedings; and (4) state funding of legal advice and representation in divorce

Income Maintenance

There are three benefits of particular significance: Income Support (formerly 'Supplementary Benefit'); Family Credit (formerly 'Family Income Supplement'); and Child Benefit (formerly 'Family Allowance').

Income Support is a means-tested benefit, calculated at subsistence level. At 1989 rates, the maximum sum payable to a lone parent over 18 is £34.90 weekly, to which is added (where relevant) the so-called 'family premium' of £6.50, and a 'lone-parent' premium of £3.90. Sums are then added in respect of each child—ranging from £11.75 for a child under 11 to £27.40 for a child of 18.

It is important to note that household income is aggregated for the purpose of calculating entitlement to Income Support.

If a divorced woman opts to co-habit, her entitlement is calculated on the basis of the *combined* income and child-care responsibilities of herself and her cohabitee. Only the first £15 of the claimant's weekly earnings is disregarded in calculating entitlement to Income Support. There is no tapering mechanism, which means that any earnings in excess of £15 per week, and *all* maintenance payments from a former spouse, lead to an equivalent loss of benefit. The practical consequence of this is to encourage divorced men to concentrate their resources on any current cohabitation, rather than on their former wife and children.

It is a general condition of entitlement to Income Support that the applicant should not be engaged in 'remunerative full-time work' (i.e. twenty-four hours or more per week in 1989), but that he or she should be 'available for work'—a condition which requires the applicant to show readiness to take any suitable work that is offered, and also to take active steps to seek work. However, in two important respects these conditions are varied for lone parents: first, a lone parent who is responsible for a child is exempted from the requirement of availability for work; and, secondly, a claimant who engages in (paid) child-minding is not to be treated as engaged in remunerative work.

Ownership of capital assets (£6,000 or more in 1989) is normally a complete bar to entitlement to Income Support; but the value of the claimant's home is totally disregarded for this purpose. Moreover, the amount of Income Support will be increased by the claimant's 'eligible housing costs', and, once the claimant has been on benefit for sixteen weeks, these will include the whole of the mortgage interest payments.

It can thus be seen that Income Support provision is maximized where the claimant has capital in the form of a dwelling-house, rather than cash; where the purchase of this dwelling-house is being funded by a mortgage; where the claimant has the care of at least one child; where the claimant is not cohabiting; and where she engages in paid child-minding.

Finally, it should be noted that in certain key respects Income Support is becoming even less generous than was formerly the case. First, the 'special-needs' payments which were formerly available to claimants on an occasional basis for the purchase of clothing and furniture are now being granted much more restrictively, and only on a 'loan' basis. Secondly, payments formerly available to cover special heating or dietary needs have been withdrawn. Thirdly, and perhaps most important, the cost of substitute child-care is no longer taken into account when calculating a claimant's income.

There are also changes at an administrative level which make the position of claimants less secure. One example concerns the system of 'diversion', whereby any private maintenance entitlement could in effect be assigned to the state, the claimant then receiving Income Support in full. To this extent, the state underwrote the private maintenance obligation in those cases where such payments, even if paid in full, would have placed mother and children below the state poverty line. The availability of this procedure is now being restricted, which means that these women will become vulnerable to the man's non-payment. These changes crucially affect the balance of advantage which has to be weighed by divorced women when calculating which sources of income (or combination of sources) offer the best return.

Family Credit is a means-tested benefit payable to those who are in work (at least twenty-four hours per week in 1989) but whose income falls below a certain level, which is calculated on the basis of family responsibilities. It is government policy to make employment supplemented by Family Credit an attractive alternative to unemployment financed wholly by Income Support. It has done this by, in effect, disregarding 30 per cent of earnings up to a certain level.

However, while Family Credit has undoubted advantages from the point of view of custodial parents who work, it does not fully give effect to the self-reliance philosophy supposedly embodied in the provisions of the Matrimonial and Family Proceedings Act 1984. This is because, as with Income Support, the cost of providing substitute child-care is not allowable in determining the amount of a claimant's income (*Parsons* v. *Hogg* [1985] 2 All ER 897). Accordingly, it will seldom be economically worthwhile for the mother of young children to seek low-paid work: she is likely to be better off on Income Support.

Another reason why Family Credit is not a viable option for many lone parents is that their housing costs will not be met.

Mortgage-holders, in particular, may have no choice other than to remain on Income Support. Other important differences between Family Credit and Income Support concern the relationship between the benefit and any maintenance payments from the former spouse. When on Income Support, any maintenance payment from the husband brings an equivalent reduction in benefit (which means that he has little incentive to make such payments: he is effectively paying the state). When in receipt of Family Credit, on the other hand, there is a tapering disregard of maintenance payments from the former spouse. A second difference is that, when a woman is in receipt of Income Support, the state is entitled to seek repayment of some or all of this money from the former spouse; but when the woman is in receipt of Family Credit, there is no attempt to recoup any part of this money from her ex-husband. So the principle of the 'liable relative' is applied in relation to one benefit, but not to the other. Hence Eekelaar's and Maclean's suggestion (1986: 30) that social policy in this area is somewhat unclear.

Child Benefit is a non-means-tested benefit payable as of right to all parents with dependent children. Its 1989 level is £7.25 per week, per child. As with all universal benefits, Child Benefit is expensive. This has led the Thatcher government to allow an erosion in its real value, there having been no increase to keep pace with inflation since 1986. As a result, the 1989 level of benefit bears little relation to the real cost of child-care. The issue of selectivity versus universality has been the subject of long-standing debate in the United Kingdom, as has the question of how much the cost of child-care should be borne by the community rather than by individual parents. The apparent wastefulness of giving money to the non-poor has to be set against the evidence that Child Benefit, in being paid to the woman, and in being non-means tested and therefore not giving rise to the problems of take-up associated with selective benefits, has had a significant impact upon the amount of money devoted to children within families (Hall *et al.* 1975: ch. 9). It is essential, therefore, when considering the appropriate balance between public and private support for families after divorce, to set this in the context of the *community*'s obligation to support the cost of child-rearing. Where this obligation is attenuated, as in the United

Kingdom, the children of divorced parents tend to be supported by means of a state benefit which provides, and is intended to provide, no more than subsistence income.

Housing

In recent years it has been the avowed policy of successive UK governments to encourage owner-occupation. The number of owner-occupied dwellings in the United Kingdom almost doubled between 1961 and 1986, from some 7 million to 14 million. The financial advantages of home-ownership have become even clearer under Mrs Thatcher. In the prosperous south-east, no less than 72 per cent of householders are owner-occupiers. (In Scotland, on the other hand, the level of home-ownership is much lower, with 60 per cent of householders living in rented accommodation in 1985.)

The trend towards owner-occupation has been reinforced by two specific policies. The first is based on the favourable treatment of mortgage interest. Mortgage interest on loans up to £30,000 attracts mortgage interest relief: the interest is deducted from the borrower's income for income-tax purposes. This is one of several tax concessions (another being the fact that Capital Gains Tax is not chargeable on disposals) which make ownership of a family home a significant tax shelter in English law. The second concerns the right of the tenant in public housing to buy the property. Before 1980 much rented accommodation was provided, generally at low cost, by local authorities, who generally operated a system of benevolent landlordism—for example, rarely exercising their legal rights to terminate tenancies. The Housing Act of 1980 transformed the position in two ways: First, tenants were given the right to buy the rented property at a substantial discount off its market value, and this right was extensively exercised. In 1985 over 200,00 houses were removed from the local authority housing stock in this way (*Social Trends* (1988), Table 8.11). Secondly, those who remained tenants were given legal security of tenure. As a result, local authorities are no longer able to reallocate tenancies informally when a relationship breaks down, against the wishes of one or other party, according to the authority's own criteria of housing need. Instead, they must await the decision of the court, following what may be protracted legal proceedings (Thornton 1989).

Tax Treatment of Maintenance Payments

Until 1988 divorce was, in theory at least, a most attractive option to tax-planners. It allowed the taxpayer to do what it was otherwise the consistent policy of the law to prevent—that is, to spread his income for tax purposes amongst those for whom he was obliged to provide maintenance. In particular, money paid to the parent who had the care of the children could be legally diverted for tax purposes from the the taxpayer to children. It would then be taxed only at the rate applicable to the child—generally nil. There is available to every individual, however young, a nil-rate tax band. In 1989/90 this was £2,785. This meant that reluctant husbands could be encouraged to pay maintenance on the basis that this favourable tax treatment meant that they were actually 'losing' less than they were contributing as maintenance.

The Finance Act 1988 marked a significant break with that practice: there is no longer the possibility of significant diversion of income to children for tax purposes. By way of partial compensation, however, a modest relief from taxation (with a top limit of £1,590 per annum) is now to be given to those making maintenance payments.

Legal Aid

Legal Aid (state funding for the payment of lawyers' fees) is available on a graduated basis, according to means, for the conduct of disputes relating to children, money, and property, and in supporting applications for an injunction. The means of husband and wife are assessed separately for the purpose of divorce proceedings, which means that some 70 per cent of the divorcing population are eligible for Legal Aid. In addition to Legal Aid, a more limited form of state funding, referred to as 'Legal Advice and Assistance', is available for preliminary work on the preparation of a divorce petition.

Parties to divorce proceedings who are granted Legal Aid obtain what is in effect a guarantee that their own legal costs will be met—or will not exceed a specified amount; and their lawyers equally obtain a guarantee that their fees will be paid—albeit at a rate lower than that often charged to 'private' clients.

However, if money or property is 'recovered or preserved' in the course of divorce proceedings (in practice, this applies whenever there is a dispute concerning the disposition of a privately owned matrimonial home), Legal Aid functions, in effect, as a loan rather than as an outright gift. Only the first £2,500 of money or property awarded to the legally aided person is exempt from the operation of the 'statutory charge'. If the eventual property share is greater than this, the costs disbursed by the Legal Aid Fund have in due course to be repaid.

The existence of the statutory charge reduces, to a great extent, the advantage which might otherwise be enjoyed by a legally aided person engaged in litigation against a privately paying spouse. However, the harshness of this rule is mitigated to the extent that, where the property 'recovered' is still needed as a family home, the enforcement of the charge may be postponed; likewise, if any money which is recovered can be shown to be needed for the purchase of an *alternative* home, the charge is again likely to be postponed. In either case there will remain a debt in respect of the legal costs incurred, but this will not in principle be repayable until the home (or any substitute) is finally sold—in many cases not until the death of the occupant. When the debt does fall to be repaid, simple interest (currently at 12 per cent per annum) will be added to the amount recoverable. The prospect of the eventual calling-in of this debt, with interest, is a matter of considerable concern to many low-earners and Income Support claimants.

The Relationship between Public and Private Provision

Having given this overview of certain key forms of public funding, this chapter now examines the financial circumstances of women and children post-divorce, paying particular attention to the relationship between public and private provision. These findings should of course be set in the broader context of women's role as the principal child-carers within marriage; and women's generally low earnings (the average wage for married women with dependent children being less than one-third that of men).

Research by Davis, Macleod, and Murch (1983) and Eekelaar and Maclean (1986) revealed that, at any one time, approximately one-third of divorced women with care of children are financially dependent on the state. Approximately two-thirds of these women had been dependent 'at some point' in the two years following separation (Davis, Macleod, and Murch 1983). These figures offer striking support for the argument that the distinguishing feature of lone-parent families is their poverty, but also suggest that some women find alternative sources of income once their situation has stabilized. This is an international picture. It is confirmed, for example, by Belgium (see Chapter 9), and by the analysis of Ermisch (1989).

Dependence on Income Support is reinforced by the so-called 'poverty trap', under which those who manage to lift themselves a little above the state poverty line may lose associated means-tested benefits such as free school meals, or rent and rate rebates. They may also be liable to income tax, all of which brings their net income down towards, or even, below Income Support level. The problem lies in a failure to develop a unified benefit system which is related coherently to earnings levels and tax policies. Only those very few women who are able to improve their incomes substantially following separation are in a position to lift their families out of benefit. This, again, is an international picture. For example, McLanahan (Chapter 16) demonstrates how, in the United States, the fact that eligibility for welfare also entitles lone parents to Medicaid and public housing acts as a disincentive to their seeking to become, in some measure, self-supporting. In the United States, as in Britain, there is no gradual tapering of the main welfare benefit against earnings: this means that low-paid work carries, in effect, a 100 per cent tax rate. At least in the United Kingdom there is an attempt, through Family Credit, to provide an alternative mechanism which offers some prospect of combining the woman's own earnings, maintenance payments, and state support—without these various elements cancelling one another out.

What part do maintenance payments pay in tipping the balance towards private rather than public support for post-divorce families? In most common-law countries, including the United Kingdom, the answer would appear to be that maintenance awards are pitched at a level below that of realistic child support, are not fully complied with, and lack effective enforcement. Indeed, the level of non-payment is one

one reason why many women *prefer* to rely on a simple, regular income from the state (Davis, Macleod, and Murch 1983). Although the amount may be small, at least it arrives regularly and they can control how it is spent.

Eekelaar and Maclean (1986: 90) discovered that maintenance was ordered—or paid voluntarily—in 65 per cent of divorces involving children. However, at the time of their interviews, money was actually changing hands in only 36 per cent of cases involving children. Where the custodial mother was not cohabiting or remarried, payment was being made in 54 per cent of cases. Even amongst those cases in which maintenance *was* being paid, the amount was often insufficient to lift the woman out of benefit—in which case these payments served to offset the state's contribution, rather than to increase the woman's net income. Comparable data from Australia (see Chapters 4, 6, and 11) suggest that, before the introduction of the new Child Support Formula, between a quarter and a third of custodial parents received some maintenance contribution—such payments as were made being well below the true cost of child-care. As in the United Kingdom, the problem would appear to be partly one of initial orders being made for very small amounts—a phenomenon which in turn reflects the new family responsibilities taken on by some men—and partly one of non-payment, the latter not assisted by a cumbersome and inefficient enforcement mechanism (McGregor 1981).

All this means that maintenance payments can be considered relatively insignificant in the context of post-divorce wealth transfer in the United Kingdom: we are a property country, rather than a maintenance country. What *really* matters, at least for couples who own their home, is the disposition of that home. The importance of the home as the repository of virtually the whole of these couples' transferable wealth has been exaggerated by rapid house-price inflation, particularly in the 1980s. As house prices have outstripped wages, many divorces are characterized by the transfer of large capital sums *and* by the woman's continued dependence on Family Credit or (more commonly) Income Support. She may own the roof, but she continues to live in near poverty. It should be noted that, despite the phenomenon which we are exploring here, divorced women are still under-represented amongst those who enjoy the benefits of owner-occupation (see *Social Trends* 1988: Table 8.24; Murphy 1989).

Meanwhile, the existence of the safety-net has been implicit in all maintenance calculations. Indeed, one of the most striking findings of our current research into financial arrangements on divorce in England is the extent to which the parties (independently of their legal advisers) understand the working of the social security system. For the woman, this means calculating the net financial benefit to be derived from her own employment, and determining whether it is worth pursuing her ex-husband for maintenance; for the man, there is the ever-present temptation to regard maintenance as a tax on his own earnings, rather than as a contribution to his former wife and children. In other words, we are finding that the existence of the safety-net is embedded in the thinking of most husbands, as well as being an (often unstated) element in any inter-lawyer negotiation or court adjudication. It is not so much that maintenance is calculated on the basis of the woman's entitlement to Income Support, but rather the other way round: the man's maintenance liability is assessed first. Nevertheless, the availability of the safety-net is understood by all. This explains why some of the amounts ordered are little more than tokens. It also suggests why attempts to pursue the man for non-payment can often appear so half-hearted. Recent judicial decisions reflect a growing appreciation of this reality. See, most notably, *Ashley* v. *Blackman* [1988] Fam. 85.

The 'diversion' mechanism whereby any maintenance payments from the husband go directly to the state can thus be seen to be of symbolic as well as practical significance: it is symbolic of the state's acceptance of its role as main provider for these families. Rather than the state 'topping up' the man's maintenance payments when these prove inadequate, the state is the main provider, with such payments as are made by the man being a contribution to the state coffers—in other words, a tax—which has no direct impact upon the financial circumstances of his former wife and children.

Earlier research revealed the complexity of the relationship between maintenance payments, social security, and the woman's own earnings. This is summarized in Table 17.1, based on interview data, which reveals there to be a positive

TABLE 17.1. *Maintenance, work, and receipt of benefit*

Work status	Receiving maintenance (n = 137)	Not receiving maintenance (n = 52)
Working full time	32 (23%)	11 (21%)
Working part time	52 (38%)	8 (15%)
Not working	53 (39%)	33 (63.5%)
Receiving state benefit	34 (25%)	29 (56%)

relationship between the payment of maintenance and the ex-wife being in employment (Davis, Macleod, and Murch, 1983). The pattern that emerges reflects a dual system of family support, comprising, on the one hand, the mother's employment coupled with maintenance payments from the ex-husband, and, on the other, dependence on state benefit. This pattern is itself strongly class-related, as measured by the employment category of the ex-husband. The likelihood of the woman being in employment—both during marriage and following divorce—varies across the social classes. Wives of husbands in social classes I and II are more likely than their working-class counterparts to be employed during marriage, and are better placed to *retain* their employment following separation.

It follows, therefore, that better-off male earners are more likely to have working ex-wives. Women whose ex-husbands are engaged in unskilled or partly skilled work are correspondingly more likely to be dependent on state benefit. We would suggest that the explanation for these patterns lies in the ability of relatively high-earning men to pay 'real' as distinct from 'token' maintenance: this, in turn, provides an economic incentive to their ex-wives to increase the family income through their own earnings, so lifting themselves and their children above the state poverty line (see, generally, Joshi 1989). But the ex-wives of low-earning men generally receive 'token' maintenance, if any, and are unable, themselves, to earn sufficient to lift their families out of benefit. The impoverished position of these Income Support families may be compared with the still relatively privileged private-maintenance or mother-employed families, although the latter have lost their pre-1988 tax advantages, and the former, it could be argued, are now offered an alternative escape-route through Family Credit.

In any consideration of the fairness of financial arrangements following divorce, there are always two comparisons to be made: first, the financial position of divorced parents compared with that of the continuing married (or the continuing cohabiting); and, secondly, the financial position of divorced women compared with that of divorced men (or of the custodian compared with the non-custodian). Underlying both comparisons is the disadvantaged economic position of women within marriage both as the principal child-carers, and as part-time workers and low earners. There is also the greater cost, post-separation, of maintaining two households, rather than one. And, thirdly, there is the greater likelihood, post-separation, of an inequitable distribution of resources *between* family members, with the man being well placed to retain the lion's share. The resulting inequalities—both between men and women, and between the continuing married and the separated—may in part be redeemed through access to state resources.

Dividing the Home

There are two other factors—strongly present in England, and seen at their most powerful in the late 1980s—which crucially affect the balance of economic advantage between men and women upon divorce. These factors operate in somewhat surprising ways. They also reveal the importance of considering the disposition of *homes* quite separately from the division of *wages*. The first is the very substantial financial advantage conferred by home-ownership; the second is the pre-eminence of child-welfare considerations in determining the disposition for the matrimonial home.

Home-Ownership

In England, many working-class families, with an income not much above state-benefit level, have been encouraged to buy their own homes. This they commonly do with the aid of a mortgage loan representing a high proportion of the equity value of the property. In this way there has become available to the poorer sections of society one of the traditional ways of amassing substantial wealth: the acquisition of an appreciating asset with the aid of a highly geared loan. When there is a divorce in such cases, it is common for the equity in the matrimonial home to be at least £30,000–£50,000, but for the couple's combined annual income to be less than £10,000. This represents a problem for the court. The Scottish Law Commission considered the possibility that the home might form the greatest part of a couple's property and yet not be susceptible to equal division; it expressed the view that equal sharing should, whenever possible, be sustained (Deech 1984). But English courts tend to cling to the principle that the home should be retained for the children's use. So, in those cases where there is substantial equity in the matrimonial home, and substantial income, the home can be sold, the proceeds divided, and both parties rehoused. But with low-income families, where there is insufficient equity in the matrimonial home to purchase two units of accommodation, 'welfare' considerations prevail. In these circumstances the home is treated as a 'roof' (rather than as an investment) and preserved intact for the children. In the former case, the proceeds of the sale of the home are likely to be divided 50 : 50; in the latter case, it is likely to be all or nothing. We should note, however, that courts have power to order that the wife and children enjoy the use of the property until the occurrence of some specified event, such as the youngest child becoming 18 (*Mesher* v. *Mesher* [1980] 1 All ER 126). There are numerous objections to such orders, but they are made in a significant number of cases (see Cretney 1984: 843). In this sense we now have two standards of justice; or perhaps it would be more accurate to say that the rich get 'justice', whilst the poor (or comparatively poor) get 'welfare'. In practice, this means that the home-owning, low-earning man is likely to lose up to 100 per cent of the value of his capital asset, although he is likely to be granted a rough-and-ready compensation in not being required to meet the true cost of maintaining his children.

The State's Willingness to Support the Home

As previously noted, where the Income Support claimant is a home-owner, the Department of Social Security (DSS) will pay the interest on any mortgage. This means that, whereas Income Support is denied if the claimant has capital in excess of £6,000, claimants with an asset (in the form of the home) worth far in excess of this figure can claim Income Support and have the bulk of their repayments met by the state, even as the home increases its capital value.

The state's willingness to support mortgages makes viable one of the most common financial settlements upon divorce—namely, that in which the woman has the home, the state pays, and the man makes no more than a token maintenance contribution, being then free to devote the bulk of his resources to trying to mount the property ladder once again.

The state's policy in maintaining homes is even more economically significant for many families than its contribution to income maintenance. Where the latter might be said to be parsimonious (despite Family Credit), the former is generous. The ability to support a mortgage has traditionally been related to earnings. But current DSS policy in dealing with the consequences of marriage breakdown leaves many unemployed single parents with one of the main advantages enjoyed by those with middle- to upper-range income. This, in turn, affects the balance of advantage between men and women on divorce. The woman is enabled to stay in the home; and, because the woman is enabled to stay, the man has to leave with little or nothing. There has been a windfall, through house-price inflation, but he does not get it. His economic prospects then depend upon his ability to acquire yet another mortgage-financed home. Even if realization of his share in the equity in the former matrimonial home is postponed, under the *Mesher* type order discussed above, that share may well be small because it is acknowledged that, when the children become independent, the woman will need to be rehoused.

From the woman's point of view, the DSS helps to preserve the economic advantage which is conferred, in the United Kingdom, by home-ownership. To this extent the combination of house-price inflation and statutory and judicial emphasis upon child welfare has contributed to the economic advantaging of at least some women, to be set alongside their wage disadvantaging. It also raises the intriguing prospect of a change in the economic balance of power upon the formation of any new union. Traditionally, remarriage has been seen as the most effective route out of poverty for divorced women. But our research reveals considerable anxiety on the part of some divorced men lest their former spouse secure the matrimonial home and then remarry, thus conferring a form of modern 'dowry' upon the second husband. This implies a change in the balance of economic advantage conferred by any new union. It is now possible to regard second husbands, not as economic saviours, but as economic predators, hunting separated wives and children in order to secure a roof.

All this suggests that, in what one might characterize as modest-income, single-asset divorces, the economic cost of divorce needs to be reassessed. The man will lose his windfall; but, on the other hand, he can begin again, relatively unencumbered, and at least he has his wages (provided, that is, he is in work). The woman may retain the home, but this is two-edged. First, she is likely to find herself trapped on Income Support: she cannot possibly earn enough to pay the mortgage, especially given the absence of any significant income disregard and the fact that she will have to meet her child-care expenses. Secondly, she may well have difficulty in paying for the upkeep of the property. And, thirdly, the DSS will meet the interest on the mortgage, but will not contribute to paying off the capital sum. This means that the mortgage will run into arrears, in which case the building society may seek repossession.

Perhaps the most surprising aspect of the picture presented here is the effective discouragement faced by these women should they wish to engage in economic activity. The 1984 Matrimonial and Family Proceedings Act aimed to promote economic self-sufficiency; and yet here we observe state policies which effectively lock divorced women into dependence upon Income Support.

On the other hand—and here we come to one of the central themes of this chaper—divorce can provide certain low-income groups with access to state resources which are not available to the continuing married. This being the case, it is possible to identify circumstances—against the conventional wisdom—where *both* parties emerge from their divorce as financial 'winners', rather than 'losers'. Certainly, an analysis in terms of winners and losers is one way of identifying the unlooked-for consequences of the present complex state provision. The cases referred to below are drawn from our research on financial negotiation on divorce in which we are involved at the time of writing.

Winners and Losers

Case One: Mr and Mrs Jenkins

There are two children of this marriage, and the divorce gave rise to a prolonged custody battle. The outcome is that the older child lives with Mr Jenkins and his cohabitee in her local-authority acommodation; the younger (handicapped) child lives with Mrs Jenkins in the former matrimonial home, which is privately owned. Mr Jenkins is a semi-skilled worker, on a modest wage (£7,300). Mrs Jenkins is unemployed, and receives Income Support (£55 per week). Mr Jenkins has continued to pay the mortgage, but does not pay any maintenance in addition. There is an equity of £51,000 in the matrimonial home. The settlement eventually reached is that Mr Jenkins will have a lump sum of £7,500. This is contrived to be paid immediately, because the building society will agree to Mrs Jenkins *increasing* the mortgage in order to release this sum to her ex-husband. The DSS will agree to pay the interest on the increased mortgage on behalf of Mrs Jenkins. Mr Jenkins and his cohabitee propose to buy her local-authority home. Mr Jenkins also agrees to pay maintenance of £10 per week for the child not living with him, although this does not result in any net gain for Mrs Jenkins, as she is on Income Support. Mr Jenkins is legally aided and will have to pay his costs of about £2,000 (largely spent on the custody battle) out of his settlement figure. Mr Jenkins was uncertain whether to accept this relatively modest lump sum. He fears that his wife may form a new relationship very soon, having walked off with 90 per cent of the equity in the matrimonial home.

It is possible to argue that both Mr and Mrs Jenkins are 'winners'. She is awarded the home, and most of her mortgage commitment will be met. On the downside, she is firmly locked into dependence on Income Support—unless and until she meets a new man, in which case she will become dependent on him. Mr Jenkins loses most of the value of the matrimonial home; but the state in effect provides him with a lump sum; his payments for his second child are little more than token; and he and his cohabitee will purchase her local-authority-owned home at 60 per cent discount. On the downside, although a low-paid manual worker, he has to pay all his legal costs.

Case Two: Mr and Mrs Bennett

Mrs Bennett lives in the former matrimonial home with the two children of the marriage (aged 6 and 8). The home is local-authority owned. Mrs Bennett was working half-time whilst the marriage subsisted, but has now increased her hours to thirty per week. She has made a claim for Family Credit. She is also in receipt of Housing Benefit, which means that she pays less than 50 per cent of the full rent. Mr Bennett earns approximately £10,000 per annum and the court orders him to pay £130 per month maintenance to his former wife for the two children. He is cohabiting, and shares the costs of his cohabitee's mortgaged home (somewhat unusually, she earns more than he does). The bulk of her substantial legal cost will be met by the state, but she had to make a contribution of £70. Mr Bennett declined Legal Aid, because he judged (wrongly, as it turned out) that the size of his required contribution made this not worthwhile.

In this case, state support (Family Credit and Housing Benefit) will supplement maintenance from the former husband, Mr Bennett being required to commit no more than 10 per cent of his net income to the support of his children. He is a 'winner' in that sense, as well as in securing the substantial economic benefit of being rehoused (and possibly even acquiring a financial interest in his cohabitee's property). On the downside, he has to pay his legal costs.

Mrs Bennett could not be characterized as a 'winner', but she retains the matrimonial home, whilst the combination of her own earnings, maintenance from her former husband, and state benefit lifts her above the poverty line. She controls her own income, and to that extent feels better off than when she was married.

Case Three: Mr and Mrs Coombes

Mr and Mrs Coombes lived in local-authority accommodation. They have two young children. He is a bricklayer, earning good money, but he pays no maintenance for his children, and Mrs Coombes has given up pursuing him. Immediately following her husband's departure, Mrs Coombes secured a part-time job as a shop-assistant. She was also granted Income Support. She has continued to live in the former matrimonial home and the DSS pays the rent to the local authority. Over the course of the research Mrs Coombes has increased her hours and her earnings. She is now eligible for Family Credit, and has applied. She does not know whether she will be better off until she sees the Family Credit figure, and also is told what Housing Benefit she will receive (the DSS no longer paying the rent once she comes off Income Support). The main reason that Mrs Coombes works is because she enjoys it—she wants to be out of the house. There is now a greater incentive to seek maintenance from her husband in that, once she is on Family Credit, only 70p in each £1 of maintenance payments is taken into account. Nevertheless, she sees no realistic prospect of getting money out of her husband—he spends all his money in the pub, and would rather go to prison than pay her anything.

This case is instructive in that it reveals one man's ability to revert *totally* to the single life—almost as if his wife and children had never been. He owned nothing, and therefore has lost nothing—except the liability to maintain. Whilst his former wife was claiming Income Support, Mr Coombes might have been pursued by the DSS under the 'liable relative' regulation, but, as is commonly the case, no attempt was made to do this. Now that Mrs Coombes has moved from Income Support to Family Credit, the DSS will take no further interest in Mr Coombes; he has effectively escaped the net. Mrs Coombes *might* pursue him, but she is an independent woman who prefers to control her own income. Mrs Coombes's legal costs were met in full from the Legal Aid Fund. Mr Coombes never troubled to consult a solicitor.

We have observed that parties to divorce proceedings—and especially custodial mothers—seek to arrive at workable financial solutions, determined pragmatically, and utilizing whatever public sources of income and accommodation are available to them. If the couple are able to co-operate, these same pragmatic considerations would seem to dictate that their private resources be divided in such a way as to maximize the state's contribution to one or both. Some manage this reasonably efficiently, but in the course of our research we have also come across many instances of couples who have failed to co-operate. In such cases, the final outcome has sometimes proved to be most inefficient, usually because it has failed to preserve 'the roof', thus denying access to public resources until the parties' own funds have been exhausted.

It is of course open to question whether it is the job of lawyers and courts to arrive at private distributions which most effectively tap state funds. In the FRG any waiving of maintenance claims which could result in the woman having to resort to welfare payments was deemed contrary to public policy and therefore void (see Chapter 7). It might, therefore, strike a continental reader as a little odd that, in the United Kingdom, the division of private income and property (and with it, the capacity to gain access to state resources) is in practice left so much to lawyer discretion.

Against this, it should be acknowledged that some registrars do see themselves as guardians of the public purse, although this varies considerably from court to court. Private negotiations can never oust the court's jurisdicitions; therefore, solicitors and barristers feel constrained, in varying degrees, when it comes to maximizing their clients' common interest in extracting money or accommodation from the state. One obvious tactic is to write off child maintenance in return for a favourable property settlement for the custodian. We see this happening, but not in such a blatant fashion as to suggest complete indifference to the public interest. Thus, most lawyer-negotiated settlements include a figure for child maintenance, even if this is so low that it only acts as a makeweight for Income Support and therefore as a 'cost' to the husband which confers no benefit upon the wife. This is a form of tokenism with which, for the reasons outlined, most lawyers collude. It is also possible that some solicitors (and some registrars) believe that divorced fathers *should* pay a modest tax to the state in return for having shuffled off most of the true cost of child-care.

Judicial and Administrative Decision-Making

This brings us to one of the key themes of this chapter, namely the curious way in which the interrelationship between public and private resources following divorce is mirrored by a pattern of dual decision-making: on the one hand, judicial; on the other, administrative. This is seen most clearly in relation to the allocation of local-authority housing. What we observe in these circumstances are two decision-making processes, conducted quite separately, but applied to the one resource. The local authority is not permitted to allocate the matrimonial home according to criteria which it has developed; it has to await the judicial decision (or the lawyer settlement). The local authority may then be handed a *fait accompli* which is expressly designed to circumvent the criteria which it, the authority, has developed. This is done with a view to forcing the authority to grant two units of accommodation to a separated family, where it would otherwise have granted only one. Thus, in the present state of English law, we have one system (lawyers and court) invited to manipulate another (the local authority). This certainly militates against there being any clear, consistent policy with regard to the allocation of local-authority housing stock upon divorce. It is also, as a process, time-consuming and expensive.

Case Four: Mr and Mrs Dewey

Mr and Mrs Dewey were married for nineteen years. Mr Dewey is 54, Mrs Dewey 53. There are three children of the marriage, none of whom is dependent. The couple live in local-authority accommodation. Both are in ill health: Mrs Dewey is assessed by the local authority as having a 63 per cent disability, Mr Dewey a 25 per cent disability. Both wish to remain in the matrimonial home.

Mr Dewey's solicitor tried to get a commitment from the local authority to rehouse her client, but was told that, if Mr Dewey relinquished the tenancy to Mrs Dewey, he might be considered to have made himself intentionally homeless, in which circumstances the local authority would be under no obligation to rehouse. In any event, the local authority would not promise to rehouse Mr Dewey, but appeared to accept that they would be under an obligation to rehouse Mrs Dewey.

Following thirteen months of negotiation, the court hearing was held in February 1989. This hearing was in turn adjourned when Mr Dewey's solicitor introduced a letter from the local authority which indicated that Mrs Dewey would be rehoused, should the court allocate the matrimonial home to Mr Dewey. However, the letter did not specify either the time or the location of this rehousing.

The hearing was adjourned for a further six weeks in order to call an officer from the housing authority as a witness. At the adjourned hearing a housing officer stated that Mrs Dewey would probably be rehoused within 6–8 weeks in a first-floor flat, or within three months in a ground-floor flat, which would be more suitable for her medical condition. The officer was less certain about Mr Dewey's chances of immediate rehousing, although she conceded his 25 per cent vulnerability. This evidence persuaded the registrar that the parties' interests would be best served by allocating the matrimonial home to Mr Dewey. Mrs Dewey appealed this decision. The appeal hearing was scheduled to be heard in two months' time. In the meantime, six weeks after the final hearing, the local authority offered Mrs Dewey a first-floor flat which, although only 100 yards from the matrimonial home, was not entirely suitable for her needs. However, Mr Dewey took a liking to this other flat. So the parties agreed between themselves that Mrs Dewey would stay in the matrimonial home and Mr Dewey would move into the new property. The local authority appear to have accepted this private arrangement, in spite of their unwillingness both before and at the court hearing to promise Mr Dewey alternative accommodation.

State-Supported Litigation: Money Well Spent?

Another remarkable feature of divorce litigation in the United Kingdom is our willingness to support, through the Legal Aid Fund, contested proceedings in cases where the private resources are minimal and the custodial parent is bound to remain state-dependant. We have observed several of these, all expensive as far as the Legal Aid Fund is concerned, with the division of assets being of no practical significance given the terms of the Income Support safety-net. In these circumstances we find one arm of the government expending considerable resources on pursuing a tiny amount of private maintenance, supposedly at the behest of another arm of government.

Case Five: Mr and Mrs Freeman

This couple married when Mr Freeman was aged 19 and Mrs Freeman aged 30—at which point she already had three children by previous relationships. They remained together for one year and it is acknowledged that Mr Freeman acted, albeit briefly, as the children's father. The couple separated in 1985, and Mrs Freeman continued to live in local-authority accommodation. She petitioned for divorce in 1987, and applied to the court for maintenance from Mr Freeman in June 1988. At the time when we first made contact, Mrs Freeman was on Income Support, plus £29 per week Child Benefit. She also received maintenance, with varying degrees of regularity, from the fathers of her three older children. This totalled £8 per week for the three, but it was paid, if at all, to the DSS direct, so Mrs Freeman never saw it. Her rent was paid by the DSS.

Mr Freeman has two children by a relationship which he embarked on following his separation from Mrs Freeman. That relationship has now ended, but he is required to pay maintenance for those children. At the time of Mrs Freeman's application to the court, Mr Freeman was in full-time employment, albeit on a low wage. He had a girlfriend, and was living with her in local-authority accommodation.

The final hearing in this case took place four years after the separation, two years after the divorce petition, and ten months after the application to the court on ancillary relief. Mrs Freeman was accompanied by her barrister and an assistant solicitor. Mr Freeman was unrepresented. He had had a bill from his solicitors for their services before the issue of a Legal Aid Certificate. He owes them £109 for their conduct of these proceedings. His wage-slip revealed him to be earning £20 a week net as a part-time barman. (He had, of course, been earning rather more than this at the point of Mrs Freeman's initial application.) Mr Freeman was due in court again a month later for a hearing concerning his failure to pay maintenance for the two children he had fathered following the breakdown of his relationship with Mrs Freeman.

The court was informed that Mrs Freeman was now living with the father of her fourth child. He was earning £80 a week net. She still received £8 per week maintenance (in total) from the fathers of her other three children, plus Child Benefit of £29 per week. She was having to pay rent of £40 per week. The registrar said that he must accept Mr Freeman's account of his earnings. He said that it might assist the parties to know that, even if Mr Freeman had a certain amount of money to spare, he would be disinclined to make any maintenance order. In those circumstances he would have to weigh up the obligation of other parties to pay mainteance for Mrs Freeman's children. Then he would have had to consider 'the general justice of the case'. Mr Freeman was being asked to pay for some fifteen years (since these are young children) as a result of what turned out to be a passing liaison, albeit one in which the couple were legally married. The registrar said that he was not going to make any order on this application.

The Freeman case provides a graphic illustation of the futility of litigation for couples operating at or near the state's Income Support safety-net. The solicitor for Mrs Freeman defended her application on the basis of the husband's responsibility, both morally and in law. But, whilst it is true that cost-effectiveness cannot be the sole criterion in determining access to Legal Aid, one is surely entitled to apply this yardstick in the case of Mrs Freeman, who cannot benefit from her own litigation.

It is possible to argue that Mr Freeman's obligation to these children ought to be sustained, albeit at some public cost, because men ought to pay for their children. However, even that argument founders in the face of state policy (the cohabitation rule, applied to Income Support claimants) which requires Mr Freeman to devote his resources to any *new* partner and children he may acquire.

One is forced to conclude that the Freeman exercise benefited no one but the lawyers. There appears to be no effective mechanism for determining whether a maintenance application is worth pursuing, or worth paying for. This is despite the fact that, in principle, the Legal Aid Scheme only supports litigation which it is reasonable to pursue.

Conclusion

Public debate concerning income maintenance upon divorce reflects two incompatible concerns. On the one hand, there is a wish to maximize the resources available to divorced families through the development of state benefits which are above subsistence level, and which are not too sharply offset against earnings or spousal maintenance. This concern would lead us to develop the relationship btween public and private funding in order to offer freer choice and, taken as a whole, more money to divorced families. Against this, there is concern (as noted, for example, by Maddens and van Houtte in Chapter 9 and Ingleby and Funder in Chapters 4 and 6) about the heavy social burden which flows from a commitment to provide subsistence income to these same families. So one can view the relationship between public and private funding in at least four ways:

1. in terms of its coherence and rationality—as in avoiding poverty traps and the associated disincentives to employment or spousal maintenance;
2. in terms of the proportion of public resources which should be devoted to the divorcing population, compared with the continuing married;
3. in terms of the appropriate division of resources (supplemented by public funds) between men, women, and children on divorce; and
4. in terms of the speed and efficiency of the mechanisms whereby private obligations are assessed and private money collected—since these are bound, in their turn, to influence the demand for public resources.

These questions can only be addressed against a backdrop of the earnings distribution, demands upon income, availability of public resources, and pattern of home-ownership to be found in any given country. For example, in the United Kingdom, no policy geared purely to divorce can overcome the inequalities and anomalies arising from the 'gift' of home-ownership. The capital value of homes has in recent years inflated at a rate far in excess of the increase in wages. This, coupled with an ideology which decreed that children should remain in the matrimonial home, can result in the man losing a large slice of unearned capital. On the other hand, as we noted above, he leaves relatively unencumbered and is granted a rough-and-ready compensation in not being required to meet the true cost of maintaining his children. It could also be argued that it is non-home-owners (whether married or divorced) who lose out. In addition the position of women who are left in a house which they partially own, trapped on Income Support, and with a large mortgage debt, is not an enviable one.

Partly because of this disparity between house prices and wages, and partly because the system of assessment and enforcement through the courts is inefficient and laborious, we observe that private maintenance is not being treated seriously as a contribution to post-divorce family income. Whatever the limitations of private maintenance as a mechanism for lifting families out of poverty, there is little doubt that some men could pay more than they do at the moment. On the basis of our own research, and utilizing the experience of researchers in other countries (Ingleby, Maddens and van Houtte, Voegeli and Willenbacher, Harrison and Garfinkel—all in this volume), it would seem that an effective system of private maintenance requires there to be a single mechanism to bear the main burden of allocating both public and private resources. It is difficult to envisage the court as a means of achieving this objective, so it is tempting to identify with the Finer Committee's preference for an administrative system—a proposal which never attracted any properly articulated and publicly formulated governmental response. Equally, it is conceded that not all administrative procedures work as they are intended to do; and that the question of the proper relationship between administrative decision-making and judicial review is a controversial and difficult one. Thus, one might have reservations about the creation of another major bureaucracy, as, for example, the Child Support Agency with responsibility for assessment, collection, and enforcement described by Harrison (Chapter 11). For many former communist countries, given their experience of administrative decision-making, this may well appear the worst solution. But our present system of lawyer negotiation and judicial discretion can appear equally hard to defend. In particular, there seems little justification for permitting judicial decision-making (or, indeed, private negotiation) effectively to determine the allocation of public resources. These resources have to be shared amongst the population as a whole; in other words, they have to be rationed. This task is performed either by the local authority or by central government. Why impose an additional judicial tier just because the family in question has experienced divorce?

This dual decision-making (administrative and judicial) in respect of the one issue is even more questionable when the private litigation is itself financed by public funds—these being rationed through yet another complex administrative process. In that case we have publicly funded private litigation determining the allocation of public resources. As a result, it can take years to arrive at a final outcome, even in simple cases. Then, having achieved a court order, the need for *enforcement* or *variation* (the latter being inevitable, given inflation, job changes, and new responsibilities or relationships) requires the whole cumbersome machinery to be brought into operation once again.

Finally, in the context of the inter-relationship between public and private provision, we would make the following points:

1. Whether the forum be primarily judicial or primarily administrative, there would seem to be a strong case for developing well-publicized formulas as the basis for such decision-making.
2. Enforcement procedures need to be improved; and there could well be scope for a further extension of administrative process in this context. The case for regarding wage-withholding as the primary method of enforcement seems now to be conceded.
4. There is a strong case for introducing a tapering disregard of both own earnings and private maintenance in an attempt to ensure that, even where dependence on public resources cannot be avoided, any maintenance paid will still be of some net benefit to the ex-wife and children.

As well as considering the mechanism whereby the parties' financial obligation is determined, our ongoing research enables us to reflect on the present levels of public financial support for the divorcing population, and to consider the consequences of different policies. There are essentially two questions: first, is there a case for treating single parents more generously than intact families? and, secondly, would a better solution be to create a more generous system of Child Benefit, thereby granting greater freedom of manœuvre to *all* parents, whether divorced or not?

Proposals for a more generous benefit system tied to divorce have always foundered on the argument that the state cannot pay people to separate. The underlying comparison is always with the continuing married, many of whom are likewise dependent upon Income Support. This was one reason why the Finer Committee's proposal for a Guaranteed Maintenance Allowance (GMA) was never implemented. The GMA would have lifted the income of one-parent families substantially above subsistence level. It would also have tapered more gradually against earnings, thus defeating the operation of the poverty trap. Finer's aim was to place lone parents in a position where they could choose between taking paid employment and staying at home to take care of the children. The subsequent introduction of a one-parent allowance was, in comparison with GMA proposal, a half-measure.

Several UK commentators have observed that the state's minimum subsistence payments were never intended to be a long-term source of income for women and children (see, e.g., Smart 1984). In many instances these women's child-care responsibilities leave them ill placed to escape the poverty trap. The key to understanding the reluctance—at least in the United Kingdom—to improve the lot of divorced parents dependent on Income Support may lie in Eekelaar's and Maclean's observation that 'western countries have been tenacious in retaining the ideology that a child should look first to its parents for the retention of its living standards, even after the collapse of the family unit' (Eekelaar and Maclean 1986: 109).

In reality, as Eekelaar and Maclean describe, private maintenance payments are comparatively insignificant as a source of income for lone parents. In England, such payments comprised no more than 10 per cent of the total income of these families (Bastard, Cardia Voneche, and Maclean 1989). Furthermore, it has been the deliberate policy of many

Western countries to attenuate the obligations of a former bread-winner towards the family from which he is separated. As previously noted, he is in effect required to devote his resources to any *new* dependents. Eekelaar and Maclean (1986: 109) argue that this development should be recognized as heightening the significance of the state for the first family. In the United Kingdom the fiction is maintained that the state is merely a *reserve* source of income, whereas all the research evidence confirms that it is the primary source for most custodial parents and their children. But as things stand, state provision for children of divorced families forms part of state policy towards the poor (Eekelaar and Maclean 1986: 113). This is unlike the position in New Zealand, where state support for lone-parent families is set at a level roughly half-way between that of subsistence and average earnings, or that pertaining in Belgium, where the subsistence income for lone-parent families is set to rise, through successive stages, to a point where it is equivalent to the minimum income of families of cohabiting spouses (Maddens and van Houtte, Chapter 9).

As to our second question—would it be preferable to introduce more generous universal child-support payments?—the trend throughout the 1980s in the United Kingdom is firmly in the opposite direction. The real value of Child Benefit (£7.25 per week per child at the time of writing) has decreased sharply. Far from placing the parental obligation for children on the community at large, it is more than ever the case that the child takes his standard of living from the income of his parents (Eekelaar and Maclean 1986: 108). This is despite the fact that, as Land (1984) has observed, the inadequacy of the wages system as a means of meeting family needs is well documented. The case for Child Benefit (or 'Family Allowance') was first identified by Eleanor Rathbone (1924). According to Land, Rathbone's analysis gains added credence in an era of large-scale family breakdown, because most single parents are women. Women, who undertake most of the child-care, do not earn as much as men. Accordingly, the strategy of treating women as individuals like men can only be partially successful in meeting the needs of mother-headed families. There would seem to be force in Land's comment that individualism is a creed which fails to recognize the needs of those (mainly women) who care for others beside themselves.

It is impossible to rectify this situation through a benefit system geared to the recipient's unemployment. That is to treat a custodial mother like an independent man. Child Benefit at least has the advantage of being triggered by the presence of children, rather than by some stigmatized condition such as unemployment, sickness, or divorce. It is designed to meet a long-term need, rather than a temporary crisis. However, state support of *any* kind is not viewed with scepticism; and those who assert the integrity of 'the Family' as a primary objective of social policy sometimes seem to have in mind a different kind of family from that with which this chapter has principally been concerned. And it is true to say that a Child Benefit scheme which actually met the basic needs of a child would be expensive, because it would mean increasing the present level four-fold. But that, ultimately, may be the only way to avoid discriminating against the children of divorced parents.

References

Bastard, B., Cardia Voneche, L., and Maclean, M. (1989), 'Women's Resources after Divorce: Britain and France', in J. Brannen and L. Hantrais (eds.), *Cross-National Studies of Household Resources after Divorce* (Aston).

Cretney, S. M. (1984), *Principles of Family Law* (4th edn., London).

Davis, G., Macleod, M., and Murch, M. (1983), 'Divorce: Who Supports the Family?', *Family Law*, 13: 213–17.

Deech, R. (1984), 'Matrimonial Property and Divorce: A Century of Progress?', in M. D. A. Freeman (ed.), *State, Law and the Family* (London).

Eekelaar, J., and Maclean, M. (1986), *Maintenance after Divorce* (Oxford).

Ermisch, J. (1989), 'Divorce: Economic Antecedents and Aftermath', in H. Joshi (ed.), *The Changing Population of Britain* (Oxford).

Hall, P., Land, H., Parker, R., and Webb, A. (1975), *Change, Choice and Conflict in Social Policy* (London).

Harrison, M., McDonald, P., and Weston, R. (1987), 'Payments of Child Maintenance in Australia: The Current Position, Research Findings and Reform Proposals', *International Journal of Law and the Family*, 1/1: 92–132.

HMSO (1974), *Report of the Committee on One-Parent Families* (Finer Committee), Cmnd. 5629 (London).

JOSHI, H. (1989), 'The Changing Form of Women's Economic Dependency', in H. Joshi (ed.), *The Changing Population of Britain* (Oxford).

KAHN-FREUND, O. (1978), *Selected Writings* (London).

LAND, H. (1984), 'Changing Women's Claims to Maintenance', in M. D. A. Freeman (ed.), *State, Law, and the Family* (London).

MCGREGOR, O. R. (1981), *Social History and Law Reform*, The Thirty-First Hamlyn Lecture (London).

MURPHY, M. J. (1989), 'Housing the People: From Shortage to Surplus?', in H. Joshi (ed.), *The Changing Population of Britain* (Oxford).

RATHBONE, E. (1924), *The Disinherited Family* (London).

SMART, C. (1984), 'Marriage, Divorce and Women's Economic Dependency: A Discussion of the Politics of Private Maintenance', in M. D. A. Freeman (ed.), *State, Law, and the Family* (London).

Social Trends, 18 (1988) (HMSO, London).

THORNTON, R. (1989), 'Homelessness through Relationship Breakdown: The Local Authorities' Response', *Journal of Social Welfare Law*, 2: 67–84.

PART SIX

Features of Divorce Management

18. Background Facts from Country Reports

Mavis Maclean

DATA from Eastern Europe, the United Kingdom, Scandinavia, Germany, Belgium, Australia, Japan, and South Africa confirm William J. Goode's analysis of rising divorce rates accompanying industrialization and the consequent separation of family roles from economic roles (see Chapter 2). The information summarized in Table 18.1, which forms an appendix to this chapter, serves as a backdrop to the chapters that follow. It shows a surprising degree of similarity among these countries. In the first column we see periods of rapid increase in the divorce rate in the 1960s and 1970s, coinciding with women's increased participation in the labour market. The second column summarizes the legal rules used for deciding when divorce is to be granted, on what grounds, and with what conditions, in each country. In particular, it is concerned with whether divorce is fault-based or based on irretrievable breakdown of marriage, and how this is measured; whether divorce is available on the request of one party only, and how far the children's interests are safeguarded; how far the outcome is predictable, and how far discretion is accepted in the interest of increasing equitable decision-making. The third column describes the arrangements for defining and dividing property, with particular reference to the family home, and to 'new property' such as pension rights and career assets, and for calculating the 'debts' of the marriage, particularly whether the opportunity costs of child-rearing are taken into account. It is interesting to see how some jurisdictions look only to the past to 'settle up', while some look to future entitlements.

Income support for wives and children is described in the fourth column. Here we summarize both the level of support and the procedures for enforcement. The fifth column is closely related to the private income-support aspect, covering the impact of divorce on the public purse, that is, how far provision for the economic fall-out from divorce is collectively shared. The final column notes current debates and policy trends in each country.

The countries for which information is presented are not ordered by their legal system—common law or civil code—nor by geographical area, nor by the kind of settlements made at divorce emphasizing property or maintenance. They are ordered instead in response to the question raised by William J. Goode in Chapter 2, that is, how far the collectivity of the family remains the individual's best investment? Now that it cannot be relied upon to last long enough to pay out, how do we produce a society that works? If marriage brings dependency for the wife by both interrupting her career and creating children who need care during their minority, how will these dependency needs be met if the marriage ends, and the key producer in the unit leaves and supports newly chosen dependents elsewhere? Are the costs of child-rearing to be borne by the biological parents, or by the mother alone, or shared by larger collectivities, whether extended family or state? We therefore look at countries ranged along a continuum from those emphasizing collective responsibility to those promoting individual responsibility for individual dependency. Firstly, Hungary and Poland where the systems were established under socialism, then the traditional welfare states Sweden and the United Kingdom, through traditional Belgium, efficient Germany, to pragmatic Australia, via the special problems of South Africa, and the private tradition of family life in Japan. Surprisingly we note a convergence—despite the great differences in tradition, legal rules, and levels of economic well-being—towards child-centred divorce. The socialist countries which began the post-war period with easy access to divorce, full female employment, full child-care, and housing shortages, are moving towards control of divorce and measures to strengthen family life and increase fertility rates. A key concern is the falling birth-rate and the increasing proportion of elderly in the population. In Hungary new procedures are being introduced, making divorce by consent more complex. State financial support for children is generous, and the child has the right to stay in the family home. In Poland the state can withhold divorce in the interests of the children, or the state, even when both parties seek it—and the role of the family and church is even more strongly emphasized. There seems to be a move from public to private values, with state support for children through generous nurturance leave for women for three years after child-bearing and guaranteed state support for children in one parent families.

In the traditional welfare states of Sweden and the United Kingdom the state assumes greater responsibility for the children of divorce, with generous income support in Sweden and with housing assurance in the United Kingdom. In Sweden state support for the child in a lone-parent family is so generous that such a child may be better off than the child with two parents in a low-income family, and there is discussion of reducing this disparity. In the United Kingdom the assumption that, if a man remarries he will support his second family, leaving the first family on state welfare, has only been seriously questioned towards the end of the 1980s. The lone mother still has the choice of whether to work or live on benefit while her children are under 16. On divorce the court is charged to seek 'the best interests of the child', which tends to allow the child (and the child's caretaker, who is usually the mother) to retain possession of the family home. In Sweden also the family home cannot be sold without the permission of both parties. But in both these countries there is discussion of reducing the level of state support. In the United Kingdom parental responsibility and access to employment are being encouraged, with the dual aim of reducing public expenditure and meeting a growing labour shortage, while in Sweden there is growing concern over the disappearance of the housewife—almost all young Swedish women are in paid work—and the importance of allowing women a choice between staying at home with children and entering the labour market.

The FRG stood alone as the only country to have a national system for sharing pension entitlements at divorce and, as such, it was one of the few countries that had taken a real step towards alleviating the major loss of future income that women, especially older women, experience at divorce. The children were also entitled to support in their own right as a primary obligation of the payer. Child support had to be paid, even if this caused problems for the non-custodial parent and an obligation equal to that towards a second family. The implications for the structure of income support of the political developments of 1990 are not yet clear. There is growing concern over mothers of children under 3 years being in employment. Belgium has a complex legal system, using fault and no-fault grounds for divorce, and community- and separate-property regimes—but it also shows a growing concern for mother-headed households, and is developing an advance maintenance payment scheme for child support to cope with non-compliance.

In South Africa the main source of support after divorce for the Black majority comes, not from the state, but from the extended family network. In Japan the emphasis also lies on private family support, but the courts have wide discretion to protect the wife—even granting emotional damages. But wives are nevertheless in economic difficulty. The high value of privacy, and the need to maintain self-esteem, are associated with low levels of litigation.

Australia and the United States (see Chapter 10) are at the far end of the continuum, with their emphasis on individualism and the responsibility of the father to provide support. This is a new development, even though the rhetoric and ideology are long-standing. But it was not until research documenting the fact that fathers were ignoring child-support orders while their children (and former wives) were plunged into poverty and near poverty—and being supported on welfare by taxpayers' dollars—that public policies were adopted to enforce fathers' obligation to support more rigorously.

Both countries have taken a strong principled stand that parents must be financially responsible for their children, and that this is not a matter of private choice, but a matter for public regulation. Thus the private obligation remains, as neither has chosen to increase public welfare support, and remains central in both countries, but the government is assuming a larger role in enforcing that private obligation by setting guidelines for uniform levels of support, and supervising enforcement and collection. In Australia the government is taking an even more active role by allocating a fixed proportion of the non-custodial parent's income as child support and collecting this money through the tax system.

Notwithstanding these new measures in both countries, the

level of child support still remains very low. It is certainly below the economic cost of child-rearing. Nor does it promote equity between the living standards of first and second families. In addition, there are still high rates of non-payment and partial payment of support orders, but hopefully this will improve as the new measures are more firmly established.

In the United States (see Chapter 14) there is also a growing concern about displaced 'home-makers', older women who cannot re-enter the labour market after long marriages and a lifetime of child-rearing, and who are totally dependent on their former husbands or the state for support. This has stimulated renewed interest in alimony or wife support, now termed reimbursement alimony or compensatory alimony, and an attempt to equalize the standard of living of the ex-spouses after divorce.

While there is a divergence among countries with respect to alimony, there is a convergence with respect to child support. The strong support for shared responsibility for child-rearing—axiomatic in socialist countries but being overtaken there by a new interest in family values—is entirely new for individualistic countries, where the view is now developing that in a period of rapid change public regulation to mitigate the consequences may be necessary. Current debates are centering on the interests of the child.

Table 18.1 summarizes the information discussed above: Chapters 19–24 then present case histories of aspects of national divorce management which are of particular interest.

TABLE 18.1. *Divorce management: Background facts*

Divorce rates	Legal rules	Property division
Hungary (per 1,000 population) 1978: 2.7 1987: 2.8 Plateau reached. Fall in new marriages. Increase in over-50s, and in numbers of children affected by divorce. Average age 30–4 at divorce.	Civil code. Clear rules. 1952: divorce by consent (no-fault) or on one party's request by court decision; 1974: Divorce at request of either party on grounds of irretrievable breakdown; 1986: pre-divorce-suit hearing now compulsory, and, if consent grounds used (the majority), all matters must be agreed, in order to make divorce less easy.	Community property on marriage unless parties contract out. Minor child has the right to stay in the family home. The court can divide the family home, as housing is scarce. 'New property' not mentioned.
Poland (per 1,000 population) 1946: 0.3 1960: 0.5 1970: 1.1 1980: 1.1 1987: 1.3 Increased proportion of cases include minor children (1960: 49%; 1985: 67%).	Civil code. Family code with wide court discretion. Divorce on grounds of irretrievable breakdown, but court can decide not to grant divorce even if both partners seek it. 1983: 65% of divorces granted without attributing fault, 26% fault of man, 37% fault of wife, 6% fault of both. Fault affects maintenance.	Common property and separate property exist in marriage. Common property is shared. Rights to use the common housing are allocated by court. 'New property' not mentioned.
United Kingdom (per 1,000 marriages) 1961: 2.1 1971: 6.0 1981: 11.9 1986: 11.9 The rapid increase of the 1960s and 1970s is tapering off; a plateau has been reached. 70% petitioners women. Fall in new marriages. Increase in over 50s and in numbers of children affected: and in redivorce. Average age 30–34 at divorce.	Common-law jurisdiction. Emphasis on maintenance, rather than property; wide judicial discretion. 1973: MCA Divorce on irretrievable breakdown based on 1 of 5 facts covering separation (rare) or behaviour (most common). Interest in mediation. 90% of divorces are dealt with on paper, but courts must be satisfied with arrangements for children. Final agreements may take 2 years to reach; legal aid is available for very low income groups.	No formal community property in England and Wales. Wide discretion, with the interests of the children to come first (1984 MFPA), but clean break seen as desirable. Courts have power over all income and property, but private pensions rarely considered. A major concern is to secure the family home for the children, even by holding on trust for sale until children independent. The property is then sold and shared in an agreed proportion.

Income support	Impact on public purse	Current policy directions
Hungary		
Spousal support: rare, as almost all women work. Can be allocated on needs grounds, but must not endanger livelihood of payor. Child support: normally assessed at 15–25% average income, and must not exceed 50% of payor's income. Court can advance the support, usually at a time of transition.	Single parent receives state benefits for maternity, child-care pay, child-care allowance, family allowance plus other social benefits, earned income, and child support. Tax is paid on alimony by payer.	Aims to strengthen family ties. There is also a concern to increase the birth-rate. Divorce is being made less easy. Aim is to increase protection for the children.
Poland		
Spousal support: the innocent party can always ask for support. If at fault, spouse can only ask for support if in poverty. Child support is the duty of parents and is assessed by the court depending on needs and resources. 60% of payments awarded are received. 1974 Alimony Fund guarantees payment to those who do not receive.	Most women are employed, have right to 3 years' nurturance leave, and return to same job. Alimony fund receives contribution from parents, state, and voluntary donations, and pays out to all custodial parents below a minimum living standard.	Note the role of the church in supporting family life in Poland at a time of severe economic difficulty.
United Kingdom		
Wife support: very rare except where there are children. Child support: agreed, without formal guidelines, in majority of cases, but amounts are low (£15 per week per child) and paid in full in less than half of cases. No effective enforcement programme. No advance maintenance scheme (although recommended by Finer Report 1977). Plans for administrative assessment and enforcement of child support announced, Child Support Act, 1991.	Heavy. Acceptance until 1990 that remarried man keeps present family, state supports first family. Over 50% custodial mothers are on welfare. As mothers of small children work part time, it is difficult to make the move from welfare to employment. Private maintenance is taken into account when assessing welfare, so does not affect household income level for the majority. Tax relief on child support abolished 1988.	Increased government interest in setting levels, and in enforcement of, child support and in removing barriers to employment for custodial mothers. Interest in mediation and family courts. There are proposals to simplify procedures, and to strengthen parent–child relationship, whatever the marital status of parents. Proposals to remove all fault statements from divorce procedure announced November 1990.

Divorce rates	Legal rules	Property division
Sweden (per 1,000 marriages) 1956: 5.0 1966: 5.47 1974: 14.99 1980: 11.16 1987: 11.06 Reaching a plateau, but perhaps affected by fall in marriage rates and increase in cohabitation (49% children born to cohabitating couples in 1987).	Civil code. Emphasis on property division, by rules. No-fault since 1920. Now a 6-month waiting period if one spouse does not consent or there are children. Joint custody automatic unless opt out. Matters usually dealt with on paper. Dispute rare. If a property dispute arises, court will appoint a property division executer (lawyer). Mediation available.	All property brought to the marriage is marital property and will be shared at divorce, unless the parties contracted out before or during marriage. A firm rule, but court can adjust if outcome unfair (e.g. a short marriage to which one party brought in a large property). Family dwelling cannot be sold without the other partner's consent.
FRG (per 1,000 marriages) 1905: 1.0 1940: 3.0 1950: 6.8 1961: 3.6 1970: 5.1 1980: 6.2 ⅓ of the present cohort expected to divorce. 70% divorcing couples childless. Divorce rate still increasing. 70% petitioners women.	Civil code. Divorce is by consent, with 1 year's separation (70%); or contested, either with 3 years' separation or hardship claimed, or with 1 year's separation (21%). There are no limits to private ordering. 70% use legal aid.	Property is held separately until death or divorce, then compensation is made at 50% of the difference in value of the separate properties. The home, if in joint names, will be split. May be sold to pay the monetary compensation. Career assets excluded. Pensions *ex officio* included in procedure when petition filed. The difference in value is split.
Belgium (per 1,000 marriages) 1910: 0.1 1920: 0.2 1940: 0.5 1950: 0.7 1970: 0.8 1980: 2.2 1986: 3.2 Rate still increasing, but slowing down. More longer marriages ending. 59% childless. Middle socio-economic groups, working women, and age group 24–5 have highest rates. Fall in number of marriages.	Civil code incorporating *dual system* divorce, by consent (now 40%) and with fault. 1956: divorce by consent made easier, with requirements of age over 23, married 2 years and 3 court appearances. 1974: new ground of de facto 5-year separation without consent. Guilt affects alimony *and* custody. Process may take 6 months to 2 years.	Divorce by consent: the parties decide. Divorce by fault: court will decide whether the marriage was contracted under the statutory property settlement. If married under separate property regimen, then each keeps the estate they owned before marriage.

Income support	Impact on public purse	Current policy directions
Sweden		
Spousal support: none, except for a transitional period (1978 Marriage Code). Child support: the economic needs and resources of parents are assessed; each can deduct a reserved amount, and the cost of child is then apportioned. State guarantees payment. Since 1964 state also pays index-linked payment, which has led to a financial advantage for one-parent families over low-income two-parent families.	The maintenance advance costs Kr. 2 billion p.a. State retrains some wives, and pays a disability pension to those over 60.	Discussion about reviewing the one parent-payment. Discussion of pension-splitting. Growing concern that Swedish women have lost the choice between work at home and in labour market, and wish to strengthen family life.
FRG		
Spousal support: none except special cases (e.g. child-care). Usually small but accompanied by pension-splitting. Child support: claimed by child as individual. Lineal support is due at any cost to payor. Fixed levels customary, depending on wage, following the reforms for ex-nuptial children. Enforcement procedures are good (90% pay) and, since 1979 Advance Payment Scheme, usually used in transition periods. 50% agreed privately, 50% by court.	Welfare is cumbersome. 14% lone divorced mothers live on welfare; 15% live on maintenance only.	There is disapproval of women with small children (0–3) working. 40% women work, 17% part time, and earnings are low.
Belgium		
Wife support: up to ⅓ spouses's income to innocent and indigent wife. Received in ⅓ fault cases, av. FB 8,000 per month (50% fault cases wife works and 78% of consent cases). Child support: agreed in 80% of cases, average FB 3,400 per month. Not all receive. Can prosecute for non-payment.	40% all mothers draw welfare compared with 23% of the total population of the same age.	Concern growing for lone mothers. Bill recently introduced to pay advances on child support if child is dependent, payor has failed for 3 months, and household is below the minimum income (FB 8,400 per month). Public Welfare Centre will reclaim the agreed payment, and keep the balance.

Divorce rates	Legal rules	Property division
Japan (per 1,000 population) 1940: 0.7 1987: 1.30 1988: 1.26 1985: 68% divorces include children, and are increasing; rate for older couples also increasing. 1984: 72% custody to mother, 22% father, no provision for joint custody.	Civil code. No-fault since 1947. Dual system: by consent (90%); by court decree (1%); by mediation in family court (9%). Wide discretion of court used, to protect wife.	Property is separate, but court can treat as joint. Private ordering can bypass court. Court has wide *discretion*; allocates according to *contribution* made. Domestic work is considered as a contribution. No consideration of previous or career assets. Court gives 25% assets to a housewife, 50% assets to a working wife. Wife can also sue for *emotional damages*, e.g. £6,000 for adultery, £5,000 for desertion.
South Africa 3 populations: White 18–50% marriages; Coloured Asian 14% Black 68%—no hard data, ⅓ marriages are not recognized, but very high rate of family breakdown.	Civil code. No fault since Divorce Act 1976. One party swears breakdown and unopposed in 90% cases. Court must be satisfied with arrangements for children. Litigation very expensive and rare. Black Divorce Court cheaper, but delays longer.	Multiple systems. Until 1984 choice between Antenuptial Contract (Whites only) and keeping own contributions. Majority married in Community with control of the property to the husband. This was abolished in 1984 Mat. Property Act offering accrual system i.e. sharing 50 : 50 assets gained in marriage. Also customary law. Pensions and career assets not considered.
Australia (per 1,000 married women) 1915: 1.0 1940: 2.0 1950: 4.0 1960: 3.0 1975: 5.5 1976: 19.0; 41% no dependent children. 1982: 14.0; 14% of divorces were redivorce. Most common profile: man 38, woman 35, two children.	Common law. Wide discretion plus new rules. 1975 Family Act: does not use term 'divorce' but marital status is terminated by dissolution on irretrievable breakdown after 12 months at request of 1 party. Counselling available to all. Always used if a child issue is contested; pre-trial hearing mandatory in financial disputes.	Property definition very broad, but a pension is a contingent interest only and excluded so far. Unwaged contributions would lead to a 50% interest in home, or 60–70% in interests of children. Career assets not included.

Income support	Impact on public purse	Current policy directions
Japan Wife support: there is no provision in 1947 Act, but court can exercise discretion in favour of wife, considering her future earning power. Child support: both parents have duty to support. Lone fathers have problems.	Some provision for lone mothers, but excludes fathers.	Concern re lone fathers. Ex-wives in difficulty despite court powers to help, as ex-husbands lack resources.
South Africa Wife support: only in high-income families. Child support: duty of both parents, to be shared pro rata in relation to income. Application can be made to Supreme Court, or to maintenance officer at Magistrates Court, which is cheaper and simpler. Amounts and compliance are low, 85% Blacks and 30% Whites default.	Blacks rely on family assistance. There is a state maintenance grant for children whose absent parent cannot pay, but this is unlikely to go to a woman of working age.	Separate policies for the different racial groups. There has been considerable change recently, and family courts and pension-splitting are discussed. A Mediation Act is in preparation.
Australia Wife support: rare and depends on need and ability to pay. But court seeks clean break. Rehabilitation maintenance used. Child support: a *primary* duty (1987) and priority over all other commitments except maintaining self and other children, with which it is equal. *Not* affected by child's other entitlements. Compliance now high, and the average amount ($20 per week before the new formulabased scheme) is now $80 per week.	Entitlement to social security is not taken into account in setting levels of private support. But welfare may be witheld if mother has not attempted enforcement. Mothers of children under 16 may choose welfare or work. 41% lone mothers work. Sole parents receive Supporting Parents Benefit developed from widowed mothers pension plus help with rent, tax relief, cost of utlities. 83% sole parents receive welfare: for 63% it is the main source of income; 56% are in lowest income group.	Plan to amend entitlement to share superannuation. June 88 Child Support Collection Agency was established in Taxation Department, to collect existing child support orders. From Jan. 1989 collects at levels set by formula, e.g. 18% of absent parent's income for first child. Child benefit is now means-tested. Need to taper earnings/benefit cut-offs and more child-care. Rising house prices are a problem. House is often given in lieu of pension-splitting.

19. Interlocal Conflict of Laws in Federal States in Matters Relating to the Family

Petar Šarčević

This chapter provides an overview of conflict of laws in family matters in federal states, showing that only in the United States has there been a move towards uniformity. Diversity remains a strong element in other jurisdictions. Federalism is generally regarded as a 'mode of political organization that unites separate states or other politics within an overarching political system in such a way as to allow each to maintain its own political integrity' (*Encyclopaedia Britannica* 1985). Of the numerous differences among the various political systems which call themselves federal, this chapter is basically interested in only one: are family matters governed by federal legislation or by the laws of the individual states, republics, or provinces? In federal states in which the federal parliament or other federal law-making body has exclusive jurisdicition over matters relating to the family, interlocal choice-by-law problems do not arise. On the other hand, if this legislative power is vested in the law districts, family matters are governed by more than one set of substantive rules and, consequently, interlocal-conflict problems occur in cases in which two or more law districts are involved. The same is true in federal states where the jurisdiction over such matters is shared by the state and its law districts.

Interlocal-conflict problems can also be found in states temporarily governed by a composite legal system. This was the case, for example, in France from 1918 to 1924, and in Italy from 1919 to 1928. Interlocal conflict of laws may also be present in partitioned states (Kegel 1987; Vitta 1985).

In some countries conflict of laws occurs in private law (particularly in family law) as a result of differences in the beliefs of ethnic, religious, or racial groups. Such conflicts, which are referred to as interpersonal conflict of laws, may occur within a non-federal country or between the law districts of a federal state (Lipstein and Szasy 1985). Here, however, it is not the territorial divisions which are decisive, but rather the fact that the parties belong to different races, or tribes, or religions. Thus the connecting factor in such cases is race, ethnicity, or religion.

Of the twenty or so federal states in the world today, this analysis is limited to Argentina, Australia, Austria, Brazil, Canada, Czechoslovakia, the FRG, India, Mexico, Switzerland, the United States, USSR, Venezuela, and Yugoslavia. The countries are divided into two groups depending on whether or not interlocal conflict of laws is present. Attention is focused on the second group of states, where interlocal-conflict problems arise in cases involving two or more law districts or one or more law districts and the federation. How are such conflicts solved by various federal states? The methods of determining the applicable law may differ significantly. As a rule, so-called choice-of-law rules are enacted, either by the federal goverment or by the law districts. Such rules contain factors which connect the relevant facts with a system of law, thus seeking to answer the underlying questions and lead to appropriate solutions (Lasok and Stone 1987).

Federal States without Interlocal Conflicts of Laws

As far as matters relating to the family are concerned, conflict of laws does not occur in federal states where family law is an integral part of civil law and a uniform civil code has been adopted for the entire country. Such federal states include for example, Argentina, Austria, Brazil, Switzerland, Venezuela, and the FRG. In the socialist countries of Eastern Europe family law is not regarded as part of civil law at the time of writing (1989), but is regulated by special codes or acts. Accordingly, there are no choice-of-law problems in family matters in socialist states where exclusive jurisdiction is allocated to the federal government. This is the case in Czechoslovakia (Ceska 1986), where matters relating to the family are governed by the federal Family Law Code of 1963 as revised.

Federal States with Interlocal Conflicts of Laws

Australia

In accordance with Article 51 of the Australian Constitution Act of 1909, the greater part of family law falls within the exclusive jurisdiction of the Commonwealth Parliament. This includes matters relating to marriage (s. 21), divorce and matrimonial causes, parental rights, and custody and guardianship of infants (s. 22) (Lane 1979: 121). On the other hand, matters such as adoption are governed by the laws of the respective states and territories (Finlay, Bradbrook, and Bailey-Harris 1986), thus raising the question of the applicable law in cases involving two or more states or territories. Such conflicts are solved by regarding the laws of the states and territories within Australia as foreign law. For example, in *Chaf and Hay Acquisition Committee* v. *J. A. Hemphill and Sons Pty Ltd* (1947) the judge noted that, for the purpose of conflicts of laws, 'South Australia is a foreign country in the Courts of New South Wales' (Commonwealth Law Reports Australia: 396). From a theoretical point of view, Nygh (1976: 6) thus concludes that judicial opinion has steadfastly denied the existence of a law of intra-Australian conflicts.

Canada

Although most family law in Canada is within provincial jurisdiction, the power to make laws relating to marriage and divorce is allocated to the Federal Parliament (s. 91(26), Constitution Act of 1867). According to Hogg, the intention was to assure nation-wide recognition of these institutions:

> If marriage and divorce were provincial responsibilities, and if markedly different rules developed among the provinces, there would be no assurance that a marriage or divorce performed or obtained in one province would be recognised by the courts of another province. (Hogg 1985: 553)

None the less, the scope of federal power has been left largely undetermined. In fact, the only federal law ever to come before the courts was one which declared that 'every marriage performed in accordance with the laws of the place where it was performed was to be recognised as a valid marriage everywhere in Canada' (Hogg 1985: 535). This is due to the

Constitution Act of 1867 (s. 92 (12)), which confers on the provincial legislatures the power to make laws relating to the 'solemnization of marriage in the province'. Despite the fact that federal authority has to be read side by side with that of the province, the courts have tended to construe provincial power liberally. As a result, most of the laws concerning marriage have been enacted by the provinces (Harriss 1987: 15; Payne 1986: 7).

In view of the extent of provincial power in such matters, interlocal conflicts of laws are bound to occur. For the purpose of conflict of laws, each of the ten provinces and two territories in Canada is a legal unit possessing its own provincial or territorial system of laws. In addition, there is a federal legal system for the country as a whole under the jurisdiction of the Federal Parliament. Since the provinces are regarded as foreign jurisdictions in relation to one another, provincial and territorial conflict rules are applied not only to interlocal conflicts, but also to international conflicts of laws, that is, in matters within the competence of the provinces and territories.

India

In India matters relating to the family are governed by the personal law of each religious or quasi-religious community. For example, the majority community, the Hindus, has its own personal or family law, as does the major minority community, the Muslims, and other minorities such as the Christians, Parsi, and Jews. This means that, regardless of a person's residence, his or her personal matters are subject to the rules and regulations of a particular religious community. As mentioned above, conflict-of-law problems arising in such circumstances belong to the special group of so-called interpersonal conflicts of law. As a rule, intercommunal and inter-religious marriages are not possible in India, and therefore Diwan (1988: 244–9) rules out the possibility of direct interpersonal conflicts of law. On the other hand, such conflicts may arise indirectly in situations where the husband or wife converts to the religion of his or her spouse. Based on the scarce case law available, Diwan proposes the following rule:

1. if both parties change their religion, then they will be governed by the new personal law;

2. if one of the spouses alone changes religion, then no matrimonial relief can be granted to the convert-spouse on the basis of his or her new personal law.

Furthermore, interpersonal conflict of laws may arise in situations where one party to the dispute pleads that the applicable law should be the law of a particular sect, either because 'the custom of the community differs from the personal law normally applicable or because the community in question is governed by a law, equally as authoritative as the personal law'.

Finally, it should be noted that any two persons belonging to any community or nationality may choose to marry under the Special Marriage Act. These are usually parties which belong to different communities and do not wish to convert or parties which simply prefer to have a civil marriage. Such marriages are subject not only to the marriage law laid down in the Act but also to other laws, such as the Succession Act.

Mexico

Mexico is a federal state consisting of twenty-nine states, a Federal District, and three territories. The Federal District and the territories are subject to the federal administration. In Mexico matters relating to the family fall under Article 124 of the Federal Constitution, which provides that the 'powers not expressly granted by this Constitution to federal officials are understood to be reserved to the States'. Since family law is not codified at the federal level, this means that interlocal conflict of laws is inevitable. For this purpose, each of the law districts may enact its own conflict rules within the limits laid down in the Constitution. According to Article 121, the interlocal-conflict rules are to be based first and foremost on the territorial principle.

> Full faith and credit shall be given in each State of the Federation to the public acts, registries, and judicial proceedings of all the others. The Congress of the Union, through general laws, shall prescribe the manner of proving such acts, registries, and proceedings, and their effect, by subjecting them to the following principles:
>
> I. The laws of a State shall have effect only within its own territory and consequently are not binding outside of that State;

II. Real and personal property shall be subject to the laws of the place in which they are located . . . (Prinz von Sachsen 1987)

Article 121 also provides that its principles are to be supplemented in detail by appropriate state laws.

USSR

In accordance with Article 14 of the Soviet Federal Constitution, the basic principles of family law and the general principles of its institutions are laid down in the Fundamentals of Legislation of the USSR and the Union Republics on Marriage and the Family enacted on 1 October 1968, as subsequently revised. The family laws enacted at the level of the Republics take into account the specific national and other local characteristics of the respective Republics in accordance with the principles of their Constitutions. As provided by the Fundamentals, these laws regulate the conditions under which a husband or wife is relieved of the responsibility to support his or her spouse (Art. 13), the consequences of the annulment of marriage (Art. 15), adoption (Art. 24), and other matters (Matveev 1985: 35).

Although the family laws of the Republics closely adhere to the principles laid down in the Fundamentals, enough diversity occurs in republican laws to make interlocal-conflict problems inevitable. Such problems are to be solved in accordance with the rules provided in Article 8 of the Fundamentals:

Marriage, relationships between spouses, relationship between parents and children, adoption, establishment of paternity, alimony, guardianship, custody, divorce, and registration of vital statistics shall be regulated by the legislation of the Republic whose organs registered or determined the relationship, or where the court action originated.

Validity of marriage, validity of adoption, validity of custody and guardianship, and validity of acts of registration shall be governed by legislation of the Republic where the marriage, adoption or custody and guardianship was entered into, or where the particular occurrence was registered.

These rules apply only to interlocal conflict of laws; special rules of private international law are provided for international cases. Recent political developments may have implications for these relationships.

United States

In the United States the same choice-of-law rules come into play in both interstate and international situations. In accordance with the Tenth Amendment to the United States Federal Constitution, choice-of-law rules are primarily state law unless subject to some important federal constitutional and statutory constraints (Scoles and Hay 1982). The Tenth Amendment reads as follows: 'The powers not delegated to the United States by the Constitution, nor prohibited by it to the States, are reserved to the States respectively, or to the people.' Although family law was long held to be under the exclusive jurisdiction of the states, this has evidently changed as a result of the rapidly growing body of US Supreme Court decisions which subject state family laws to federal constitutional provisions. These provisions do not speak expressly of the family nor of subjects such as marriage, divorce, illegitimacy, birth-control, abortion, adoption, neglect, dependency, or termination of parental rights (Krause 1986); they deal instead with fundamental rights.

Such changes have brought about a movement from diversity to uniformity, which has been further enhanced by the adoption of a uniform model law relating to child abduction and by Congressional attempts to create a national system to set and enforce child support. According to Stein (1986: 191), another factor contributing to the trend towards uniformity is state action. In this respect, he refers to the almost complete introduction of no-fault divorce and the resulting restriction of judicial discretion with respect to divorce.

Despite increasing reductions in the once unfettered jurisdiction of the states and moves towards uniformity in family law, the diversity of state laws is still so great that the use of interlocal choice-of-law rules is necessary.

Yugoslavia

The period between the two world wars (1918–1941) can best be described as legal chaos, a chaos of conflicting legal systems, conflicting marriage laws, and conflicting church and state legislation (Eisner 1950). At that time Yugoslavia comprised six legal territories with regard to family law. In most of the country the family law then in force consisted of the marriage laws of the various religions recognized at the time. Consequently, marriage disputes were settled in these territories by the competent ecclesiastical courts, whereas the ordinary civil courts had jurisdiction over such matters as family property rights (Šarcěvić 1981).

After the Second World War family law was unified throughout the country by several federal statutes: for example, the Basic Law of Marriage of 1946. This development, however, ended in the 1970s with the enactment of Federal Constitutional Amendments Nos. XX–XLII of 1971 and the Federal Constitution of 1974, which placed legislation on such subjects as marriage and the family, guardianship, child–parent relations, tenancy in the common home, etc., under the exclusive jurisdiction of the socialist republics and autonomous provinces. The diversity in the new family legislation enacted thereafter in the six republics and two autonomous provinces led to interlocal conflict of laws, thus making it necessary to enact interlocal choice-of-law rules.

In Yugoslavia interlocal choice-of-law rules fall under federal jurisdiction. Accordingly, the interlocal choice-of-law rules for matters relating to the family are laid down in the Federal Law on the Resolution of Conflicts of Laws and Conflicts of Jurisdiction in Relations concerning Status, Family, and Succession of 1979 (Official Gazette 1979). Furthermore, Serbia, which encompasses three independent legislative territories (the territory known as 'Serbia proper', and two autonomous provinces—Kosovo and Vojvodina), is authorized by the Serbian Constitution to enact special conflict rules for cases involving two or more jurisdictions within Serbia. These special conflict rules have not yet been drafted and no such legislative action had been taken at the time of writing (1989).

Finally it should be noted that international choice-of-law rules are laid down in the Private International Law Act of 1983. These rules, however, apply only to conflicts between foreign legal territories and Yugoslavia (Šarčević 1985). Thus it can be said that there are potentially three different types of conflict rules in Yugoslavia: two at the federal level, that is, one for resolving international conflict problems and the other for internal conflicts between the republics and the provinces; and the third, the Serbian conflict rules for resolving conflicts within the Socialist Republic of Serbia (which, however, have yet to be drafted).

The trend towards diversity in Yugoslavia had led to notable differences in the republican and provincial legislation. Hopefully this diversity will not endanger a uniform approach to basic questions.

Conclusion

Federal states without uniform family laws are confronted with interlocal-conflict problems which are not resolved in the same manner. In Australia, for example, the choice-of-law rules for international conflicts are also used to resolve interlocal-conflict problems. In the United States the choice-of-law rules for solving interlocal conflicts also apply to international conflicts. The situation is similar in Canada, where the courts regard another legal territory as foreign, regardless of whether it is another Canadian province or a foreign territory. This is the case only in matters falling under provincial jurisdiction, whereas the federation has its own choice-of-law rules for matters under federal jurisdiction.

In the USSR there are separate choice-of-law rules for interlocal and international conflicts, both of which are governed by federal law. Similarly, two separate sets of federal choice-of-law rules exist for interlocal and international conflict of laws in Yugoslavia. In addition, Serbia is authorized to enact a third set of conflict rules for interlocal conflicts within that republic. In Mexico the legislation of the Federal District acts as a kind of unifying force by virtue of its authority.

Finally, India is a case *per se*, since the internal-conflict problems there are not interlocal but rather interpersonal. Although the Special Marriage Act was intended to serve as a type of unifying device, it appears that it is still rarely applied. Thus interpersonal conflicts will probably remain a matter of everyday life in that country, at least for the time being.

References

Castel, J. G. (1975), *Candian Conflict of Law* (Toronto).
Ceska, Z. (1986), *Czechoslovak Family Law* (Bratslava).

Commonwealth Law Reports (Australia) (1947) (Canberra).
DIWAN, P. (1988), *Private International Law* (New Delhi).
EISNER, B. (1950), *Porodicno pravo* [Family Law] (Zagreb).
Encyclopaedia Britannica-Micropaedia (1985) (Chicago), iv.
FINLAY, H. A., BRADBROOK, A. J., BAILEY-HARRIS, R. J. (1986), *Family Law, Cases and Commentary* (Sydney).
GROFFIER, E. (1984), 'Précis de droit international', *Privé Québeçois* (Montreal).
HARRISS, B. (1987), *Family Law* (2nd edn., Toronto).
HOGG G. (1985), *Constitutional Law of Canada* (2nd edn., Toronto).
KEGEL, G. (1987), *Internationales Privatrecht* (Munich).
KRAUSE, H. (1986), *Family Law* (St Paul, Minn.).
LANE, P. H. (1979), *The Australian Federal System* (Sydney).
LASOK, D., and STONE, P. A. (1987), *Conflict of Laws in the European Community* (Abingdon).
LIPSTEIN, K and SZASZY, I. (1985), 'Interpersonal Conflicts of Laws', *International Encyclopedia of Comparative Law* (Tubingen), iii, ch. 10.
MATVEEV, G. K. (1985), *Sovjetskoe semeijnoe pravo* [Soviet Family Law), (Moscow).
NYGH, P. E. (1976), *Conflict Laws in Australia* (Sydney).
Official Gazette of the SFR of Yugoslavia (1971), No. 19 (Belgrade).
Official Gazette of the SFR of Yugoslavia (1979), No. 9 (Belgrade).
PAYNE, J. D. (1986), *Payne's Commentaries on the Divorce Act 1985* (Ontario).
PRINZ VON SACHSEN, K. A. (1987), *Das mexikanische internationale Erbrecht und seine Bedeutung fur deutsch-mexikanische Nachlassfalle* (Munich).
ŠARČEVIĆ, P. (1981), 'Cohabitation without Formal Marriage', *American Journal of Comparative Law*, 29: 174–84.
——(1985), 'The New Yugoslav Private International Law Act', *American Journal of Comparative Law*, 33: 283–96.
SCOLES, E. F., and HAY, P. (1982), *Conflict of Laws* (St Paul, Minn.).
STEIN, E. (1986), *Summary, Uniformity and Diversity of Law in a Divided-Power System: The United States' Experience* (Chicago).
VARADY, T. (1987), 'Die Eigenarten der internne Gesetzkolliisionen in Jugoslawien', *Zeitschrift für Rechtsvergleichung* (Munich).

20. First-World Solutions for Third-World Problems

Sandra Burman

The policies discussed in this book include many examples of the most successful attempts to date to deal with social problems in the countries in which they have been applied. While none is without shortcomings, they may be seen as models which, with a little adaptation, could usefully be imported into other societies. This chapter should serve as a warning against that naïve assumption. While there is a long history of importing legislative models from other countries, the list of successful imports is much shorter. In this Chapter, I hope to highlight some of the necessary conditions for such success and to discuss some of the factors which merit consideration by potential importers when the social and economic conditions in their countries are different from those of the exporting country.

The study of what factors are of importance when selecting a law to serve as a legislative model is still in its infancy, but it is clear that some types of law can be transplanted with much greater advantage than others. Commercial law tends to transplant relatively easily, for example; family law far less so. The other crucial element is the similarity of important factors between the exporting and importing countries—but deciding what the important factors are is far less obvious. To discover them, a study in two stages is required: a detailed examination of what mechanisms cause the policy under discussion to be successful in its country of origin; and then an examination of how freely such mechanisms could, and are likely to, operate in the society of the potential importer. Unfortunately, such

The research on which this paper was based was sponsored by the International Federation of University Women; the British Academy; Lady Margaret Hall, Oxford; the Nuffield Foundation; the Anglo-American and De Beer's Chairman's Fund; the Social Science Research Council; and the Human Sciences Research Council, which last also made possible attendance at the conference with gave rise to this book. I am indebted to Mr John Eekelaar and Dr Kenneth Hughes for helpful criticisms of an earlier draft of the paper.

research tends to be expensive—a luxury for wealthy countries—which frequently rules out the second stage being undertaken by the country interested in using the legislation as a model. Where the first stage of the study is done, it is usually in the country of origin and tends to take many facts as universally applicable, whereas they may not in fact apply in the society of the potential importer.

It is in this context that an examination of South African experience, especially in the field of family law, is enlightening, partly because of (rather than despite) the strange social situation to which South Africa's apartheid policy has given rise. The area has a longer history of contact with European legal systems and the money economy than the rest of sub-Saharan Africa and, as a result of its pattern of economic development, a longer history of industrialization, urbanization, and family disintegration. South Africa has imported a large number of current family-law reforms modelled on Anglo-American and European examples. These include a liberal system of no-fault divorce and an adaptation of the underlying civil-law property system inspired by Dutch law, so as to include an optional accrual system and such modern adaptations as the splitting of pensions. Yet, its apartheid policy has kept various groups and their diverse social patterns more separated and distinct than would otherwise have been the case in a rapidly developing economy. A small minority of the population has the income, social patterns, and reference group of north-west Europe; while the African majority's patterns of urbanization and family formation, though distorted by apartheid legislation, reveal many similarities to those observable in other parts of Africa.

The result, when coupled with the extremely unequal distribution of wealth within the society, is a situation in which the same imported legal policies can be observed in action against a wide range of different social and economic structures. This result may well foreshadow patterns to come in many other parts of Africa. On the one hand, some of these policies are at least moderately successful for the section of the society which most closely approximates the economic situation and life-style of the exporting country. On the other hand, a lot of the South African family-law legislation exposes the pitfalls inherent in importing Anglo-American or European family-law models into a very different society, even when that society has the essential prerequisite of a social security system, and one more extensive than is usual in Africa. To illustrate the point, this chapter briefly examines some of the consequences of one example of South African legislation inspired by the sort of foreign solution discussed elsewhere in this book. The pattern of unforeseen consequences from the imported model should be a cautionary lesson for many other countries—far beyond Africa's borders.

Making Imported Divorce Legislation Work: Necessary Conditions

South African divorce legislation, and the European models which inspired it, aim to achieve a just division of the assets of the couple, while guaranteeing the best possible economic and emotional protection for the children of the marriage. Such provisions also try, where possible, to protect the economically weaker partner of the marriage from want as a result of the breakdown of the marriage, especially where that partner was not the cause of the breakdown. However, for the legislation to achieve these aims, European experience has shown various socio-economic underpinnings to be essential.

In the first place, as can be seen from all the other examples in this book, in the countries where the policies originated financial assistance from the state in both cash and kind is necessary. Two households cannot live as cheaply as one, and only where the custodial parent—usually the woman—has sufficient income to maintain her child in her new household, or where the non-custodial parent—usually the man—can not only afford to contribute adequately towards his children's upkeep, but actually does so, can a state grant system for child support be dispensed with. The same applies to support for the wife: support is essential where she is without property or the ability to earn adequately for herself.

Even in the wealthy countries discussed in this volume the majority of custodial parents rely on state assistance after divorce. Moreover, where a spouse is without adequate means to pay for essential legal services to obtain the divorce, state legal assistance is necessary if the complex system is to work correctly, involving, as it frequently does, complicated property arrangements and actuarial calculations in order to index maintenance payments to future living costs. Adequate housing must be available if the marital household is to be able to split into two and, where the marital home is not owned, state housing stock and/or state assistance with rent is required. State assistance with child-care, either in the form of cheap state crèches or financial assistance with fees, may also be necessary. All this requires a state welfare system with enough resources to meet the demands of the poorer parts of its population and a bureaucracy and social workers with a level of education, efficiency, and integrity to run the system properly.

Even in the wealthiest of countries this places a great financial burden on the state. If it is to be relieved of paying all or part of the cost of wives and children of men who are well able to pay themselves, then an efficient system is required to ensure compliance with court orders for child support and spousal support. However, as Chapters 7 and 12 in this book show, only in the FRG and Sweden has this been achieved, as a result of excellent records being compiled on the population, thereby making it extremely difficult for defaulters to 'vanish' and enabling the system to swing into action automatically as soon as default occurs. (For this, a fast and reliable postal system is also extremely helpful in keeping costs low). Most important, however, is the fact that the combination of an efficient enforcement system and very generous state provision at all stages of a person's life makes it more sensible to pay maintenance and retain one's benefits, than to vanish and forfeit all the benefits available to citizens.

The Reality of Importing Divorce Legislation: A South African Example

The example discussed below is that of the provision made for the support of wife and children on divorce. Data are drawn from two studies reported in Burman 1987 and Burman and Beyer 1988. The only court with jurisdiction in divorce cases is the Supreme Court. However, when both parties are classified as Black,[1] they may use the Black Divorce Court.

[1] Under the system of 'race' classification set up by the Population Registration Act 30 of 1950, there are 22 categories, which are generally collected under the broad

This was introduced as a local variant of the imported court model, in order to provide cheaper and less formal divorces for the largest section of the population. It is meant to apply the same substantive law on divorce as the Supreme Court but to relax the procedural requirements, thereby reducing both its cost and strangeness for the Court's clients. However, as a result of economic stringency, it has various other disadvantages, including longer delays and the fact that some or all divisions of the Court will not hear maintenance claims, though it will allow maintenance settlements to be included in settlement papers put before it. (The Black Divorce Court is divided into three regional courts and information on current practice was available from research only on the Southern Divorce Court (see Burman 1983).) Most divorces, especially in the Supreme Court (some 90 per cent), are unopposed, agreement on custody and property arrangements having been reached out of court. Where lawyers are involved—in virtually all Supreme Court cases and in some two-thirds of Black Divorce Court cases—the parties have their settlement recorded (and usually negotiated) by lawyers, and it is generally rubber-stamped by the court. Fighting in court is prohibitively expensive. Maintenance arrangements are usually included in Supreme Court agreements and, very occasionally, in Black Divorce Court agreements, but for these a lawyer to draw up the necessary consent paper is required.

Where maintenance arrangements are not made on divorce, parties may take their cases on child maintenance, but not spousal maintenance, either to the Supreme Court which is expensive, or to a magistrate's court. The exclusion of wives' maintenance claims once the divorce is over, combined with the refusal of the Black Divorce Court to hear maintenance claims, excludes a wife unable to obtain a lawyer from getting

headings of 'White', 'Coloured', and 'Black', with 'Asian' as a subcategory of 'Coloured'. The terminology is colonial in origin but currently has uniquely South African governmental overtones. Broadly, 'Whites' are those supposedly of European descent, 'Blacks' of African descent, 'Asians' of Asian descent (largely from the Indian subcontinent and some from China but excluding those considered of Malay descent), and 'Coloured' embraces all other groups, including the (largely Muslim) descendants of Indonesians and Indians brought to South Africa by the original Dutch colonists and known as 'Malays'. Since the categories dictate administrative and legal arrangements for maintenance and the terms are used in all official documents dealing with it, the need for clarity has necessitated the use of the same terminology.

maintenance for herself. Since maintenance for an ex-wife is available only after the man has paid for his own keep and that of his children, it tends to be a luxury beyond the reach of the vast majority of the population anyway, but it is instructive to see how in this instance economics interact with legal principles to exclude many of those eligible wives from claiming maintenance.

While it is possible to sue for divorce in the Supreme Court without being represented by a lawyer, judges discourage it on the grounds that the complexities of the law make it highly desirable that the Court's clients benefit from the expertise of the legal profession in matters as important as divorce settlements. On the other hand, since the aim of the Black Divorce Court is to keep costs low and procedure less formal, litigants in undefended divorces need not have legal representation and the presiding officers therefore have an added responsibility to examine pleadings adequately beforehand. The Southern Divorce Court insists that litigants in defended divorces be represented. To give these officers the extra time required, each must either have fewer cases, which necessitates that more officers be employed, or their time spent in court must be reduced. As economic stringency precludes the former course, the latter has been adopted by excluding a time-consuming element which can be heard in a cheaper court. It is felt that if a couple have the type of income which warrants a claim for support for the wife, they can employ lawyers, who could draw up the necessary consent papers.

This, however, ignores the realities of such situations. As a result of common patriarchal attitudes, family size, and gender inequalities in pay, women frequently have far less income than men, if they have any. A husband may be well able to pay his ex-wife support, but she may not be able to afford the necessary lawyer.

Nor does legal aid necessarily provide the answer, since, although it exists, economic exigencies make for rationing. Apart from the fact that it may have been temporarily discontinued for divorce cases, due to lack of funds in the legal-aid account, the woman may fail to fulfil one or more of the strict conditions for award of legal aid. The Director of the Legal Aid Board periodically exercises his discretion to refuse all funding for divorce except in rare cases where special representations are made to him. This occurred, for example, between November 1985 and April 1986, and again in 1987. Legal aid *for divorce* has been further restricted by the imposition of a ceiling above which the client is personally responsible. For example, all applicants for legal aid for divorce must be interviewed by a social worker attached to the welfare department covering his or her respective population group. The social worker's task is to assess the applicant's qualification for legal aid, based on whether or not the marriage has irretrievably broken down. If in the social worker's opinion there is a reasonable prospect of the marital relationship being restored, he or she is obliged to recommend that legal aid be refused. The applicant may apply again if, after a reasonable time, reconciliation has not been effected. But the process can also involve such a long delay that the woman may not feel able to wait for it to run its course.

The legal-aid process is fraught with other delays. There may be a considerable wait for the initial interview with a social worker, since social-work departments are frequently understaffed, especially for some sections of the population; and, even after the interview, a social worker is unable to recommend legal aid until he or she has obtained some response from the other party, even if this is merely a refusal to discuss the matter. This can make for a further long delay.

The shortage of housing for those classified as Black is particularly acute in the cities—considerable overcrowding and waiting lists of over ten years for state housing are normal. In some areas the combination of bad relations attendant on a pending divorce, lack of alternative accommodation to which one of the couple could move, and the strongly patriarchal attitudes inherent in customary law, which categorizes moderate chastisement of a wife as a husband's right, tend to make for extremely stressful situations. Social workers on the whole exhibit a sympathetic attitude, and recommend for legal aid any wife who can prove assault by her husband, provided she has not expressed any doubt to the social worker about leaving her husband. But the woman may be forced by her interim living conditions or other considerations to abandon her application and, therefore, support from her husband. Many of these factors also apply to women in other population groups awaiting legal aid to defend a Supreme Court divorce.

Child support cannot be escaped by fathers in the same way: each parent has an obligation to support his or her children, the extent of support being pro rata to income. The amount to be paid by the non-custodial parent may be reached in negotiations between lawyers or with the maintenance officer at a magistates' court, or be ordered by a magistrate after a court hearing where agreement could not be reached. The non-compliance figures do not appear to bear out the widespread belief that, where the parent has agreed to the amount, he is more likely to comply with the order. A correlation might be found between consent and compliance if the timing, forum, and other circumstances of the consent could be taken into consideration. Research has, however, made it clear that some groups in the population accept the concept of paying for their children more readily than others, whatever their subsequent performance. This has relevance for the length and, therefore, expense of divorce and maintenance proceedings. The reluctance of the lowest-paid group to pay is supplemented by considerations partially deriving from a customary-law background. In customary law, obligatory bridewealth payments by the man's family to the woman's brought the wife's offspring into the husband's family. On divorce, the children remained with the latter or, if too young to be parted from their mother, would be sent to the father's family as soon as they were old enough. For their maintenance in the intervening period, a very low maintenance charge would be paid, since it was argued that the child would have been largely suckled by the mother during the period of its absence. Should the dissolution of the marriage have been due to the wife's misbehaviour, the husband's family could reclaim its bridewealth payment, less the part offset against the offspring of the marriage, who remained with the husband's family. Today bridewealth payment is still virtually universal practice in South Africa among the Black population, irrespective of whether the marriage is by civil or customary law and irrespective of the level of education or wealth of the parties. The amount is steadily increasing, being highest for educated women and reaching very substantial amounts. As it is now increasingly unusual for a man to claim back the bridewealth on divorce, irrespective of the circumstances of the divorce unless it occurred very early in the marriage, there tends to be a strong feeling that the man has emerged from his civil-law marriage considerably poorer and with nothing to show for it, since the court tends to award custody of the children to the wife. The proportion of fathers awarded custody of their children is, however, considerably higher in the Black population (see Burman and Fuchs 1986). Some of the same considerations appear to influence the Muslim section of the population, although only nominal bridewealth is paid. However, religious precepts dictate that the children shall remain with the father's family and this tends to influence attitudes to payment where the mother obtains custody.

In addition to the above factors, the lowest-paid sections of the population have the largest families and by far the highest illegitimacy rates, resulting in the poorest people having the highest maintenance obligations. Although it has recently become illegal for Blacks to acquire a civil-law wife in addition to a customary-law wife, the legislation (Act 3 of 1988) was not retroactive and the practice was common among temporary migrants to the cities until 1988. It resulted in many men having maintenance obligation to even more families than serial monogamy produces. It is, therefore, hardly surprising that the default rate for those classifed as Black and Coloured is over 85 per cent, while it is considerably lower for the top income group in the country, who are those classified as White.

The effectiveness of enforcement is obviously intimately related to the rate of default, since poor enforcement fails to provide either correction of the rate or deterrence. The differential ability of men from different groups to 'vanish', and their willingness to do so or go to jail, have a strong correlation with the default rate of different groups. Officially every adult in the country must have identity papers and have his or her particulars entered in the data bank in Pretoria. In practice, it is difficult enough to achieve this with a co-operative population, and becomes increasingly so when a large section of the population is illiterate or semi-literate and dispersed, without adequate transport, over large areas away from data-collection offices. Where, in addition, many of the population are suspicious of bureacracy and fear that such data is more likely to produce taxation and other undesirable effects than benefits, fully reliable data would be virtually impossible to obtain, even with a better staffed and more computer-literate bureaucracy than exists in South Africa. Added to this is a highly mobile population of unskilled labour, partly as a result of 'influx-control' legislation having ensured continuing strong rural links even among the ostensibly urbanized. In addition, the South African government's independent homeland's policy, which treats four areas of South Africa as independent foreign countries, makes for considerable legal complications if a man retreats to one of them. The equivalent available to men in other groups—flights to a foreign country, usually outside Africa—is far more expensive and difficult. Thus, in numerous respects, a man in a well-paid job or profession has much more to lose and is far more conspicuous and traceable if he tries to disappear from one at the other end of South Africa's economic scale.

Where a man does default, the staffing numbers, together with the educational level and training of the maintenance office staff available, have resulted in the retention of a system which lumbers into action only if the woman activates it over several visits and only when the police can find the time to serve the summons. For the illiterate or semi-literate woman, and those on daily pay, the system is particularly daunting. If the man is found, he cannot be made to pay if he is unemployed and, given the high rate of unemployment among the unskilled, is unlikely to be jailed for failing to get a job if he is in that category. There is, however, a flourishing informal trading economy, income from which cannot be proved but on which he may well subsist, sometimes in considerable style.

The result is that the vast majority of women, particularly at the lower end of the economic scale, are unlikely to receive support from their ex-husbands either for themselves or for their children. In countries where a tight family system still exists on which the women can rely, or where she can earn sufficient for family needs, there are alternatives, but South Africa's family system has disintegrated to a great extent. The same process is underway throughout Africa. Moreover, women's earnings, more markedly than in developed economies, tend to be considerably below men's, and particularly in unskilled categories. Other alternatives are therefore required.

The solution adopted in many of the developed economies discussed in this book is to institute a generous state system of assistance. Whether this is possible for less developed economies involves, as indicated above, such factors as levels of education, data collection and control, and taxation compliance, as well as national income. However, the South African experience is instructive.

South Africa is one of the wealthiest countries in Africa and a middle-ranking country in the world's table of national wealth. But it currently has an extremely inequitable distribution of wealth among groups within the country. This is reflected in the unequal distribution of benefits available through the welfare system, although the level of the benefits is slowly being raised for those classified as Black and Coloured, and equalization for all groups within the next few years is the goal. However, the range of benefits is small and the level low, even for the most privileged groups. Moreover, it is very possible that only the low level of uptake, especially in the most numerous low-income groups, due to stringent regulation and the type of attitudes to bureaucracy described above, enables the whole system to continue without collapsing for lack of funds. While a more democratic government would presumably abolish the expensive duplication of services resulting from the policy of separate development, and might reduce military expenditure and allocate more funds to the welfare system, the economy is currently squeezed and is likely to be considerably more so before there is a democratic majority government.

It is, therefore, totally unrealistic to expect that under such a regime benefits will approximate those currently available to Whites. They may well be considerably lower even than those now available to people classified as Black, especially if conditions are liberalized to enable more people to qualify for assistance. Some other solution to the problem of providing for remnant families must, therefore, be found.

If the models supplied by the developed economies will not work, it may be that countries too poor to follow their lead should start to rethink their family assistance from the point of view of their own strengths as well as of their own needs. Since not even the most developed economies have been able to enforce the system of child support by fathers after divorce, and since there seems very little chance of South Africa following the successful models of the FRG and Sweden, perhaps the inevitable should be accepted and the system as it stands abolished. The salaries and other funds thus freed could be devoted to alternative schemes. While people will object to allowing men 'to have their fun without paying for it', there is very little evidence that any but the wealthiest are paying for it under the present system anyway. And, while support by non-custodial parents continues to be regarded as the basic source of child support, the tendency is for a state short of funds to rely on it to pay for children even when it is patently not doing so.

Models of alternative systems for Europe and America all work predominantly on cash payment of benefits to individuals, sometimes in tandem with taxation systems to recoup money from liable parents. South Africa could revamp its taxation system to ensure payment by this means from fathers able to pay maintenance for their children but who fail to do so, and it would help to meet objections to taxpayers paying for the children of men who can afford to pay themselves. However, in a country with such low wages and so high an unemployment level among the group most affected, it could be only a subsidiary source of state funds for benefits, even if the problems of tax enforcement mentioned above were overcome.

If there is not enough money for an adequate system of cash payments to individuals, perhaps benefits should rather be concentrated on services where economies of scale could be used and the still-existing strengths of the societies built upon. In South Africa, even though the family is much weakened as a unit, opposition to the existing government has, if anything, strengthened community spirit and organization. It may be possible to utilize this strength. Child-care, for example, is currently performed in poorer households by individuals in the family, usually elderly relatives, who are often unpaid, and sometimes unable to control the children. Payments to crèches and child-care centres run by the community and staffed by its members—probably largely those same elderly—might be both cheaper than child-support grants and productive of better child-care. In some situations additional funding might also be obtained by selling places in such crèches to local industrialists for their workers. Subsidized schemes for school feeding from central kitchens, where they have existed, have until now been run by charities in the townships but are beginning to be taken over by communities in some areas, staffed in rotation by members of the community, who are paid. Subsidized and assisted across the country, they might similarly give better value for money than child-care allowances. What is required, above all else, is that countries discard the attitude that what works in Europe and the United States, is in the forefront of social planning and should be copied as soon as possible. Such schemes may provide ideas, but they are in many respects unsuitable as models for the very different countries that make up the majority of the nations of the world.

References

Burman, S. (1983), 'Roman Dutch: Family Law for Africans', *Acta juridice*, 132: 171–89.

——(1987), 'Marriage Break up in South Africa', *International Journal of Law and the Family*, 1/2: 206–47.

——and Beyers, S. (1988), 'When family support fails', *South African Journal of Human Rights*, 4: 194–203, 334–54.

——and Fuchs, R. (1986), 'When families split: Custody on Divorce in South Africa', in S. Burman and R. Reynolds (eds.), *The Contexts of Childhood in South Africa* (Johannesburg).

21. Custodial Fathers in Japan

Satoshi Minamikata

A SHARP increase in divorce cases following radical changes in family life over the last thirty years has led to growing numbers of lone-parent families in Japan. Although such families have been provided with some assistance under several Acts, they still face financial difficulties and social disadvantages in daily life after divorce as a result of the lack of sufficient legal provisions and social prejudice against them. In particular, father–child families easily get into difficulties, as many of the legal provisions are designed primarily for mother–child families. In addition, social prejudice against them is much stronger than against mother–child families. Indeed, it was not until 1981 that the Tokyo Metropolitan Government replaced the term 'mother-child families' with a more general term—'lone-parent families'—in its official reports, indicating that little consideration has previously been paid to father–child families (Tokyo Metropolitan Government Public Welfare Bureau 1986).

This chapter presents statistics concerning lone-parent families, particularly father–child families, and then discusses the various difficulties and problems facing them. Finally existing legal systems dealing with such families and assistance provided for them are described.

Divorce and Custodial Fathers

The number of divorces in 1988 declined slightly to 154,000 from 159,000 in 1987, and the divorce rate per 1,000 population during the same period fell from 1.30 to 1.26 (Asahi newspaper 1989). This decline, however, does not seem to imply that marriages are becoming more stable, as the divorce rate per 100 married couples continues to rise (Yuzawa 1987). (There is no evidence indicating that this rate has begun to decline.)

When a couple with children divorce, they are required to decide who will have custody of their children under the

Japanese Civil Code. 'Joint custody' is not available, though, in a few cases, one parent obtains custody while the other gets 'care and control' of the children.

Since the mid 1960s more mothers have begun to obtain custody, and now over 70 per cent of mothers get custody in divorce cases involving children under 20 years old. Moreover, mothers often maintain 'care and control', even if fathers have custody. As a result, the number of mother–child families is growing steadily.

One study indicates that there were approximately 890,000 lone-parent families, including over 718,000 mother–child families and 167,000 father–child families throughout Japan in 1985 (Ministry of Welfare 1985). Another national survey points out that the rates of father–child families and mother–child families per 100 households including children under 18 years old were 0.8 per cent and 4.7 per cent respectively in 1985 (Council of Population Problems 1988). Approximately 60 per cent of all lone-parent families were in that position as the result of 'divorce or separation', while 40 per cent had lost a parent through death (Yuzawa 1987).

When a father has to live without the mother's help after divorce, he is unlikely to expect direct assistance from relatives, particularly parents. More than 80 per cent of all father–child families in the Tokyo area live as a nuclear family, and only 21 per cent of them consist of three generations (Welfare Office 1987). It seems that the number of father–child families will continue to rise gradually. What difficulties and problems do father–child families face in daily life?

Custodial Fathers and their Difficulties

A father–child family faces a number of problems and difficulties after divorce: financial problems, taking care of children, social relationships, and emotional problems.

Financial Problems

The main financial problem after divorce is to maintain sufficient income. It is generally believed that father–child families are better able to maintain their income after divorce than mother–child families. In a Tokyo survey, fathers replied that only 17.1 per cent of them were concerned about financial issues after divorce, but 72.6 per cent of mothers referred to their economic uncertainty (Tokyo Metropolitan Government Welfare Bureau). According to a survey conducted by the Ministry of Welfare published in 1984, the average annual income of lone-father families was 2.9 million yen in 1982, while that of lone-mother familes was 1.8 million yen. However, in the same year two-parent families earned 4.4 million yen on average. The per-capita income in lone-father families was also lower (0.9 million yen) than for two-parent families (1.3 million yen) in 1982 (Ministry of Welfare 1984: 4, 12). In addition, it is reported that father–child families after divorce earned about 10 per cent less than father–child families after the mothers' death (Welfare Office 1987).

These statistics suggest that father–child families enjoy more financial stability than mother–child families after divorce, but that they do face serious financial difficulties when they are compared with two-parent families. In addition, while the financial situation of father–child families appears to be better than those of mother–child families in the short term, in the long term this is not so.

Child-care

The earning capacity of fathers begins to fall gradually after divorce for two reasons; first, fathers have to spend additional time at home taking care of their children, and, secondly, they need time for doing domestic chores. In other words, during marriage fathers maintain their income capacity partly at the expense of the mothers' labour. After divorce, fathers cannot escape from looking after their families every day. They have to cook breakfast, wake up their children, and take them to nursery or school; they have to leave their workplaces immediately after closing time to pick up their children, and then they have to prepare a meal for their family when they return home. If their children get ill, they have to be absent from the office without advance notice, which may cause difficulty with their colleagues. Furthermore, it is not uncommon for fathers to hire child-minders to pick up their children from nursery, if they find they are unable to get there in time. Many nurseries close between 5 and 6 p.m., and it would be nearly a miracle for fathers to finish their work and rush to collect their children on time. This may trigger off financial difficulty by adding extra expenditure for the fathers.

One indication of the stress these fathers experience is their anxiety about their health. In Tokyo, for instance, 11.6 per cent of fathers of father–child families go to hospital regularly, while only 7.2 per cent of fathers of two–parent families do (Tokyo Metropolitan Government Public Welfare Bureau 1986). This kind of life is likely to prevent fathers from doing over-time or going on business trips due to housework and health problems, so they fail to obtain extra income and often lose opportunities for promotion. Consequently, the fathers are obliged to change their occupation in order to make work compatible with family life.

In a survey, 30 per cent of respondents replied that they had had to change their jobs some time after divorce (Hirano *et al.* 1987). According to another study, 47.6 per cent of fathers from lone-parent families said that they often had difficulties in focusing their attention on work, and 25.8 per cent of them had had to give up their former jobs (Tokyo Metropolitan Government Public Welfare Bureau 1986).

If fathers work from 9 a.m. to 5 p.m. and can obtain sufficient income without doing extra work, they will have few problems if they become a one-parent family. However, such cases are exceptional under the current labour conditions and social circumstances in Japan. One lone father said:

> Both fathers and mothers from single families have financial difficulties. In some respects, I think mothers have better conditions because they can spend time with their children in the evening if they choose part-time work. But it is very difficult for a man to give up his full-time job and to find a part-time one when he gets divorced. Moreover, there are no welfare services for fathers. So, I am obliged to leave my children without proper attention . . .
>
> I know that mothers as part-time workers can earn only about 100,000 yen per month. However, they spend only seven or eight hours in the office. In addition, lone-mothers are entitled to obtain a child-support benefit—some 30,000 yen. Then, their income amounts to approximately 130,000 yen per month . . .
>
> On the other hand, it is not unusual for fathers to start working at eight in the morning and to finish their work at seven or eight in the evening. Under such circumstances, fathers earn about 200,000 yen monthly. But to be able to earn this maintaining income, fathers have to hire babysitters or leave their children at a private nursery

called a 'baby hotel' quite often. If these extra expenses for fathers are taken into consideration, the fathers finally obtain about as much money as mothers do. (Kasuga 1989)

In several studies, single fathers say that their most difficult tasks are the domestic chores. In the Koseisho survey of 1983, 54 per cent of fathers had difficulty with housework and 16.3 per cent of them in managing family finance (Yuzawa 1987). The 1984 Tokyo study, for instance, indicates that 63.3 per cent of fathers had difficulty with housework compared with only 29.1 per cent of mothers (Tokyo Metropolitan Government Public Welfare Bureau 1986).

Social Relationships

As Japanese society is based on the principle of male dominance, most people, particularly men, find it difficult to accept the appropriateness of the division of labour within families. In the case of washing up, for example, 0.4 per cent of all husbands participate compared with 93.8 per cent of all wives.

Under such circumstances, it is unrealistic to expect men to learn and develop domestic skills. In addition, it has been pointed out that fathers aged 30 to 39 spend only 11 minutes per day looking after their children, although working mothers of the same age spend more than 3.5 hours a day (Council of Population Problems 1988). As a result, fathers find serious difficulties in taking care of their children and doing housework everyday.

I could not provide appropriate meals for my children. As we could not serve nutritious meals, one of my children lost 4 kilograms in weight, the other 2 kilograms, and I lost 10 kilograms . . . I had no experience of cooking during marriage.

After divorce, I could appreciate clearly what burdensome work my ex-wife had done every day. At that time, such work did not seem remarkable to me. (Hosokawa, Ogasawara, and Kita 1981).

It is not easy for typical Japanese fathers to survive with their children after divorce under the circumstances described above. Traditional attitudes towards gender roles and prejudice against lone fathers are widespread. For instance, when they ask local authorities for help in order to continue to live with their children, it is not unusual for lone fathers to be advised by the authorities to abandon the idea of bringing up children by themselves. Instead, they are persuaded to send their children out to board. The authorities explain that it is better for children to be taken care of by female staff than by fathers.

It is often said that prejudice against lone fathers prevents them from obtaining help. In many local authorities home-help services are provided for father–child families and such services are in great demand. Fathers, however, are very cautious or sometimes reluctant to ask for those services given by female-home helpers because they do not want to give cause for gossip among their neighbours. Even voluntary workers working for the welfare department of local authorities sometimes say, 'I am concerned about what happens at the house of a father–child family when visiting alone . . . we must consider what to do if something wrong happens to a female helper at a lone father's house' (Kasuga 1989).

Emotional Problems

It is often pointed out that lone fathers are likely to have emotional problems caused by social prejudice and a lack of appropriate help. Society still holds the traditional view that, since man is the stronger sex, a divorced man is weak, simply because he is divorced and a failure as an individual. Consequently, some fathers tend to be depressed and to lose self-confidence in daily life, which cannot improve their family relationships.

Even if lone fathers ask for emotional help, they find that in current Japanese society very few agencies can offer appropriate help. Most fathers do not have any friends in the local community in whom they can confide, because they spend all day at the office and so have little time to make good friends among the neighbours. And, although there are public and private agencies providing advice or counselling, these may not be accessible for the lone fathers or may be too expensive.

In one survey only 36 per cent of lone fathers responded that they had some individuals to talk to (Welfare Office 1987). In addition, 20.9 per cent of lone fathers said that they had no communication with relatives during the three months before the survey, compared with 14.9 per cent of lone mothers (Tokyo Metropolitan Government Public Welfare Bureau 1978).

Under such circumstances, fathers of lone-parent families are likely to be isolated from relatives, friends, and the community, and such isolation may produce more emotional problems for them.

These studies make it clear that lone fathers experience a particular kind of isolation. As they leave home rather early in the morning and return in the evening, they seldom have opportunities to talk with their neighbours directly. Consequently, they find that it is difficult to obtain relevant information about useful services provided by the community. The 1978 Tokyo survey indicates that 61.6 per cent of fathers only exchange greetings with neighbours, 20.6 per cent of them talk, 11.0 per cent of them visit each other, and 6.6 per cent of them have no contact with neighbours (Kasuga 1989). Also fathers do not have extra time for visiting their children's school and participating in its events, and so often fail to understand their children's progress at school.

Legal Assistance for Custodial Fathers

While several legal remedies, welfare support, and local authority services for mother–child families have been implemented in a series of statutes and rules relating to social welfare for over forty years, these measures are rarely available for father–child families in the Japanese legal system.

For mother–child families whose annual income is below a certain amount in Tokyo, for instance, mothers are entitled to claim 'child-support benefit', which is paid monthly at between 34,000 yen and 23,000 yen per child under 18 years. In addition to this payment, some mothers also have a right to 'child-caring allowance', of 8,500 yen per child. In addition, mothers can have 2 million yen on loan from the Tokyo Local Government if they plan to start a small business, and also a loan of between 9,000 yen and 35,000 yen per month in order to pay children's school fees (Tokyo Metropolitan Government Public Welfare Board 1987).

On the other hand, lone fathers can receive only the 'child-caring allowance', and are ineligible for the other public financial support. With respect to accommodation, mothers can apply for rooms in the 'Boshiryo' (mother–child dormitory) managed by local authorities under the Child Welfare Act. Lone fathers, however, have no legal right equivalent to the mother's concerning accommodation. Tokyo Local Goverment has now opened one dormitory for father–child families for a population of 10 million.

Lone fathers are insisting that they should be treated equally with lone mothers in many aspects of daily life. Further services provided in the public sector include an advisory service for one-parent families, and home help. There are a variety of criteria for receiving home-help services, depending on the local authority. In Tokyo, for instance, twelve visits from a home-helper per month are available for a father–child family including only children under 8 years old for two years after divorce. A home-helper works between 7 a.m. and 7 p.m., looking after children, preparing meals, cleaning rooms, and washing clothes. Fathers whose annual income is over 4.2 million yen are required to make payments for such services according to the tariff.

The Future for Custodial Fathers

When one considers the legal system and social attitudes towards father–child families, it could be said that lone fathers are deprived of reasonable help, not only from the financial point of view but also from the human viewpoint. It was not until the early 1980s that people began to notice that the serious plight of father–child families almost equalled that of mother–child families.

However, as society is changing rapidly, we can now see a new development for lone-parent families. The lone fathers themselves have started to organize self-help groups in order to improve their situation, exchanging general information on family matters and providing reciprocal assistance within their groups.

Although it is difficult to predict what changes will happen to father–child families in the near future, it is possible that they will be able to obtain more help from society and gradually become free from prejudice against them.

References

Asahi Newspaper (Asahishimbun) (1989) (23 June) (Tokyo).

Council of Population Problems (1988) (Ministry of Welfare Policy Section, and Ministry of Welfare Institute of Population Studies), *The Population of Japan: Families in Japan* (Jinkomondaishingikai, Koseisho-Daijinkanbo-Seisakuka, and Koseisho-Jinkomondaikenkyusho, *Nihon no Kinko-Nihon no kazoku*) (Tokyo).

HIRANO, T., OKA, T., MACHINO, H., and AKASAKA, Y. (1987), *Father-only Families (Fushikatei)* (Kyoto).

HOSOKAWA, K., OGASAWARA, N., AND KITA, Y. (1981), *The apron that disappeared* (*Kietaepuron*) (Tokyo).

KASUGA, K. (1989), *Living on Welfare* (*Fushikatei wo Ikuru*) (Tokyo).

Mainichi Newspaper (Mainichishimbun) (1989) (26 May).

Ministry of Welfare (1984) (Children and Family Bureau), *Summary of National Survey of Mother-Headed Families* (Koseisho Jidokateikyoku, *Zenoku Boshisetai to Chosakekkano Gaiyo*) (Tokyo).

Tokyo Metropolitan Government Public Welfare Bureau (1978), *Report on a Survey of Lone-Parent Families* (Tokyo-to Minseikyoku, *Boshi-Fushisetai Seikatsujittaichousa Hokokusho* (Tokyo).

——(1986) (Committee on Research into Problems of Lone-Parent Families), *Welfare Policies for Lone-Parent Families* (Tokyo-to Tanshinkazokumondaikentoiinkai, Tanshinkatei no Mondainikansuru Fukushiseasakuno arikata) (Tokyo).

——(1987) (Children's Division), *Leaflet on Lone-Parent Families* (Tokyo-to Fukushikyoku jidobu Boshifukushika, *Tanshinkatei no Shiori*) (Tokyo).

Welfare Office (1987), *Report on Survey of Lone-Parent Families in Higashikurume* (Higashikurumeshi-Fukushijimusho, *Higashikurumeshi Hitorioya (boshi-fushi) katei Jittaichousa Hokokusho*) (Tokyo).

YUZAWA, Y. (1987), *Exposé of Family Problems in Contemporary Japan (Zusetsu Gendainihon no Kazokumondai*) (Tokyo).

22. Attitudes to Divorce and Maintenance in Poland

Malgorzata Fuszara and Jacek Kurczewski

IN POLAND the ending of marriage is not seen as a matter to be dealt with purely in accordance with the wishes of the individuals concerned. Society as a whole has a role in the proceedings, involving a complex set of duties and obligations to family, church, and state.

The law provides for divorce based on the irretrievable breakdown of marriage. No items of behaviour are listed as comprising evidence of breakdown; it is up to the court to decide. The family courts in Poland are relatively informal, many of the judges are women, and the court takes an active part in investigating family behaviour. For example, in cases of juvenile delinquency, the court takes evidence from teachers and schoolfriends and makes a 'treatment plan' involving the co-operation of school and family. Similarly, in divorce, the court does not simply 'rubber-stamp' an arrangement requested by the individual parties. Instead it investigates, takes evidence from other parties, uses social reports, refers to a specialist for consultation, and seeks to promote reconciliation. In each case a reconciliation session is obligatory.

The state has the final say on whether or not a divorce is to be granted. There is provision in the code that divorce is impermissible if it would infringe on the interests of the minor children of the marriage, or violate the principles of community life in other ways. The interests of the children may, therefore, make divorce impossible, even if the marriage has irretrievably broken down. It is also possible for divorce to be prevented if the petitioning spouse is the only guilty party, and the innocent spouse does not want a divorce. It is important to remember that a spouse may, as a Catholic, have religious reasons for rejecting divorce and regarding marriage as a sacrament, even if living together in the marriage is not a satisfactory way of life.

In Poland, attitudes towards the family, the state, and the

church are complex, and have been undergoing rapid change during the 1980s. During the post-war period, when the majority of the population were not in sympathy with the government, the family took on extra significance as almost the only group to which the individual was encouraged to show allegiance in the interests of social cohesion. At the same time, the Catholic Church in Poland also strongly emphasized the importance of marriage and the family. There was a marked degree of external support for the family—with the result that family breakdown, though increasing, tends to be defined more often in Poland than elsewhere as the result of some individual pathology such as alcoholism or violence. Marriage breakdown often results from domestic violence associated with drunkeness—but this is seldom publicly discussed as a major cause of divorce. The emphasis in public discussion is on no-fault divorce and ways of easing the process.

Things are changing rapidly in Poland, however, and the divorce rate, though low, is increasing. In 1960 the rate was 0.6 per 1,000 population. It doubled by 1970, remained stable during the 1970s, but by 1987 had reached 1.3 per 1,000 population. In a survey of 926 randomly selected men and women throughout Poland interviewed in the late 1980s, slightly over 3 per cent were currently divorced, 3 per cent remarried, 6 per cent widowed, 71% married for the first time, and 16 per cent single and never married (Fuszara 1988 and 1989). In this survey Fuszara studied current attitudes about the circumstances in which divorce should be granted or withheld, and how financial responsibilities should be shared afterwards. The study used vignettes to explore the views of Polish men and women concerning the circumstances in which divorce should be granted by the state, and how financial responsibilities should be allocated for wife support and child support after divorce and remarriage.

The first example described a couple with children, with the husband working and the wife running the home. The man seeks divorce and wishes to remarry. The wife accepts this. The respondents were asked whether the husband should support the wife at home, as she had not sought the divorce and was not at fault. Thirty-seven per cent took this view. A slightly larger group, 47 per cent of the total, agreed that the husband should support his wife but to a lesser extent, as it was reasonable that she should now go to work. However, a substantial minority, 14 per cent, said that divorce should not be granted at all, even though both partners sought it.

The second vignette described a married man with children who is having a relationship with another woman who is pregnant with his child. His wife does not want a divorce. In this case 30 per cent of the respondents said that the court should not pronounce a divorce decree, and the first family should continue, even if only in name. But 62 per cent declared that a divorce should be granted to facilitate the creation of the new family.

In both cases men with higher incomes (and who were party members) were more likely to favour the granting of divorce, the establishment of a second family, and the requirement for the former wife to go to work. These are the attitudes which resemble more closely developments in Western Europe—and perhaps also indicate a breaking away from the constraints of family and church.

In another example respondents were asked about support for a child claimed by a mother when the father disputes paternity. There are witnesses to the fact of the intimate relationship between the couple, but scientific tests cannot positively determine the paternity. In this case 31 per cent of the sample said that the woman should support the child, and 59 per cent said that the court should decide that the man is the father on the basis of evidence about the relationship and that he should support the child. Again men were more likely to support the individualistic model requiring the woman to support the child by herself.

The degree of state or community involvement in the decision-making process—with the court seeking evidence about relationships and making plans for intervention—is far greater in Eastern Europe than elsewhere.

The Polish data support William J. Goode's thesis (see Chapter 2) that increased wealth is associated with looser family ties, in that it is the higher-income men who seek acceptance of individual responsibility by the wife for herself, and for a child whose paternity is uncertain. The impact of housing shortages and inflation align with religious and patriotic feelings in supporting the traditional family. Divorce remains a luxury item.

References

Fuszara, M. (1988), 'The Judges Room', paper presented at IPSIR University of Warsaw Conference (Nieborow).

——(1989), '*Divorce and the Related Demands Concerning Property*', mimeo (WPRIPS, University of Warsaw).

23. Gender Differences in Custody Bargaining in the United States

Lenore J. Weitzman

This chapter analyses qualitative data from interviews with 228 divorced men and women and 169 matrimonial attorneys in California in 1978. (For a description of the research design, see Weitzman 1985.) It examines the ways in which men and women approach custody and support, and explores the extent to which custody is used as a ploy in financial negotiations.

In the United States the standards for child-custody awards have changed substantially in the past hundred years. The father's absolute right to custody of his legitimate children under common law shifted, by the late nineteenth century, to 'the tender-years doctrine'—a rebuttable presumption that the custody of a young child should go to the mother. Under this standard, which became known as the maternal presumption, courts were likely to grant custody to the mother automatically, unless there was substantial evidence of her unfitness. In most states this maternal presumption prevailed, at least for children of tender years, into the early 1970s.

In the late 1970s the maternal presumption waned as a new standard emerged in response to Goldstein's, Freud's, and Solnit's (1973) influential book, which urged the courts to place the child's needs first by maintaining the child's bond with the 'psychological parent'. Now custody was to be awarded in 'the best interest of the child'. Since it was not always clear just how the courts were to serve the child's best interest, these new laws typically included a list of factors for the court to consider (Kay 1990: 16).

The research reported in this chapter was conducted when the 'best-interest' standard was in its heyday in California. Since the best-interest standard is vague and subjective, and since the outcome of any specific case is uncertain, both feminists and child-advocates were concerned that the law would encourage litigation (and the threat of litigation) and allow men to use custody as a ploy in negotiations.

The aim of this chapter is to explore the accuracy of these concerns by examining, in more detail, how the major participants in the legal process think and talk about custody decisions and negotiations. All of the quotations cited below are drawn from my California research.

California Law and Custody Threats

As noted above, when California replaced the maternal-presumption with the best-interest standard in 1973, the first concern was that the vagueness and uncertainty of the new rule would permit men to use custody threats to extract better financial settlements. As one California attorney in our sample frankly acknowledged, this tactic was common: he had a standard 'blackmail letter' that he used for such purposes:

> I could write the blackmail letter by heart (although I haven't written one in a long time), but this is how it goes: Dear Mrs. Jones's lawyer, I received the proposal you offered on behalf of your client, and my client is willing to agree to everything. Although we would prefer to have custody of the children, he realizes it is probably not in the best interest of the children to contest custody. However, my client is not interested in paying alimony, and if your client is willing to waive alimony, we would be willing to accept the proposal which you suggest; if not, then all the issues will have to be litigated.'

Although most of the attorneys interviewed said they usually dismissed such threats as 'hot air' and 'posturing', the divorced women we interviewed were likely to take them seriously. These threats had a chilling effect on the financial claims of mothers who were afraid of losing custody, or were frightened by the prospect of a long-drawn-out court battle.

In theory and in the formal law, custody and support are two separate issues. But in practice they are often negotiated together and involve implicit or explicit trade-offs. In the California research only 13 per cent of the husbands requested custody on the divorce petition. But a significant minority of divorced women (33 per cent) reported that their husbands had threatened to ask for custody as a ploy in negotiations.

Many of these threats appear to be motivated by financial interests; by threatening to ask for custody men have a lever for getting their wives' agreement to less support or property.

In some cases the linkage between the two issues was explicit, as in these reports of outright threats:

> He said he wasn't going to give me any money [for support] and if I gave him any legal trouble he'd take the kids away from me.
>
> He said—straight and clear—if you don't agree to $200 a month in child support, I'll go for custody and you won't get a cent . . .

Most men were more subtle, but for many women even the hint of a custody contest was enough to stifle their determination to assert their claims to the property they were entitled to:

> One day he told me Steve [a recently divorced friend] told him to take the kids instead of turning all that money over to me. I knew he didn't want them, but it didn't matter . . . He had me—I wouldn't take any risks—I wanted to get that agreement signed.

The one phrase that was repeated over and over again was '*it's only money*'. When faced with a choice between less child support (or less alimony, or less property) and the possible loss of their children, the women said there was no choice: the support was 'only money' and insignificant in the context of a potential loss of incalculable value—the loss of their children.

Different Perspectives

Underlying these comments about support and custody negotiations are more fundamental differences in the ways that husbands and wives approach these issues.

Willingness to Consider Negotiating about Children

The first difference is a willingness to consider negotiating about children in discussions of property and support. Men are more likely to see custody as part of a total package of divorce issues that are, to some extent, 'all up for grabs'. Women, by contrast, draw a line when it comes to custody. They are more likely to consider custody on an altogether different level—it is something they simply cannot negotiate about because it is too important—it is worth any price. Since women attach such great importance to their children, they are not only willing to sacrifice financial benefits for custody; they are also willing to lose a great deal just to avoid even the *risk* of losing their children. As one woman said:

It was like a game for him . . . like trading property in Monopoly . . . but it was life and death to me . . . losing the children would be like losing my life . . . I couldn't stand back and 'negotiate' as my lawyer suggested. I couldn't let them go—no matter what.

Attorney Nancy Polikoff (1983: 195) observes that this attitude is common, and it invariably results in a disadvantageous financial settlement for women. As she states it, 'the reality is that most women faced with a contested custody hearing are unlikely to turn down a proposed settlement which removes that threat, no matter how low the child support or how disproportionate the property settlement . . . All women can be intimidated by the threat of losing their children.'

New York attorneys Henry Foster and Doris Freed (1984) call this pattern of negotiating 'custody blackmail', which they describe as follows: a husband proposes a small child-support or property settlement and threatens to take the children away if his wife does not agree to it. Because the threat of losing custody is more terrifying than the threat of losing money, she is likely to agree to his proposal. Moreover, as with other forms of blackmail, the threat may continue to hang over her: he may threaten to take her back to court to challenge her custody if she finds a new male companion, or if she works, or if he remarries. And at each point she is likely to 'pay him off'.

The detrimental combination of vague standards, differential investments in children, uncertain outcomes, and the threat of custody blackmail influenced a landmark decision of the West Virginia Supreme Court. As the Chief Judge of that court, Richard Neely stated,

Uncertainty of outcome is very destructive of the position of the primary caretaker parent because he or she will be willing to sacrifice everything else in order to avoid the terrible prospect of losing the child in the unpredictable process of litigation . . . Moreover, it is likely that the primary caretaker . . . will be unable to sustain the expense of litigation. (*Garska* v. *McCoy*, 278 SE 2d, 357, W. VA. 1981: 361)

These concerns led the West Virginia Court to institute a primary caretaker presumption in custody cases

to prevent the issue of custody from being used in an abusive way as a coercive weapon to affect the level of support payments and the outcome of other issues underlying divorce proceedings. When a custody fight emanates from this reprehensible motive, children inevitably become pawns to be sacrificed . . . (*Garska* v. *McCoy*, 1981: 361)

As Professor Agell (see Chapter 3) and other legal scholars have noted (see, e.g., Glendon 1982), clear-cut legal rules, such as primary-caretaker presumptions, discourage custody threats and the financial coercion associated with them.

It's Only Money: Economics v. Social Relationships

A second difference is apparent in the way mothers and fathers approach divorce negotiations: women are more likely to focus on the interpersonal aspects of a decision while men are more likely to focus on its economic aspects. Thus when women think about child support, they are likely to focus on how the financial transaction will affect their relationship with their former husband (and, in some cases, his family). Men, in contrast, are more likely to see child support as a purely economic matter or as a purely legal matter; they think about how much it will cost, what a judge is likely to order, and how much money they will have left.

The men we interviewed were likely to discuss economic decisions as clear-cut issues of dollars and cents. They spoke of the 'going rate', the cost, the law, and their rights:

My lawyer said that was the going rate for child support so that's what I agreed to pay.

Her lawyer was trying to get me to let them stay in the house but the law says I'm entitled to my equity . . . Why should I give her my half of the house?

As these comments suggest, for men—and it is the male perspective that the law reflects—the economic issues stand alone.

For woman, in contrast, these economic issues are embedded in social relationships, and the relationship is the primary concern:

I wanted to stay on good terms with him, so I didn't want to hassle him about the money . . . It was more important to have him as my friend and to part amicably.

I didn't want him (and his parents) to think I only cared about money. They were always talking about women who took advantage of men and just took them for a ride and I didn't want to be seen as that kind of woman . . . They lived nearby and I depended on them . . . They are my children's grandparents . . . I wanted them to respect me.

Each of these women saw 'giving in' on monetary issues as a way of maintaining her relationship with her former husband, or with his family, or between him and his children.

Other women were willing to give in on monetary issues as a means to a very different goal—*to extricate themselves from their former husbands.*

I wanted him to leave me alone. I didn't want any connection to him (including receiving his checks).

I figured it wasn't worth getting support and having to put up with his control over me . . . When we were first separated, before the divorce, he wanted an accounting of every penny—how much I spent for food, why didn't I buy hamburger meat on sale at Safeway, why didn't I buy them new shoes instead of more jeans . . . He drove me crazy . . . it wasn't worth $125 a month to have to put up with him.

The thread that links what may at first appear to be contradictory goals—one focused on maintaining a relationship, the other focused on ending a relationship—is that *the focus is on the relationship* rather than on the economic issues. Since women seem to care more about the relationship, and appear to emphasize social–emotional needs over financial needs, they are predisposed to giving up support and property in exchange for good will, control of their own lives, control of their children, and the avoidance of conflict. When these women talked about financial issues, they talked about how the money would affect their independence or dependence on their former husbands, whether it would allow them to break or maintain their relationship with him and/or his family, whether it would reduce their ex-husbands' good will and respect, and, finally, how it would affect their own feelings and actions (such as whether it would make them feel less guilty about leaving him, or more able to stand up to him and insist on what they thought best for the children). As for financial considerations, over and over again these women said, '*It's only money.*'

Willingness to Compromise

A third underlying difference in the way men and women approach these issues is their willingness to compromise. Women were more likely to talk about compromise and to say that they could understand their husbands' perspective.

I understood how he felt about money and I didn't want him to think I was taking advantage of him . . . I wanted to ask for something he would consider reasonable.

I know how upset he'd get if I pressed him . . . he's very emotional and temperamental and if he gets angry he just won't budge . . . I didn't want to get him angry by pushing him for more support [than he offered].

Men were likely to aim at 'getting the best deal' and to treat the settlement as a financial negotiation they wanted to win:

My attorney told me what was in the ball park . . . and what she was entitled to . . . so we offered about half of that for starters.

I wanted to protect my business and not get stuck with a big support order hanging over me for the next ten years . . . but it was no big deal. I knew she'd agree if we held out long enough . . . and she did.

It often seemed as if *both partners were focused on the husband* and what he wanted or offered: while he worried about his chequebook, she worried about how he was feeling, how he would react, and how she might find a solution that would please, or at least satisfy, him. Because of their greater tendency to empathize, then, women may well agree to solutions that compromise their own interests.

Avoidance of Conflict

A closely related dimension is a different tolerance for conflict. The men were more likely to ask for what they wanted in a forthright and forceful manner and to fight for it. The women, by contrast, shied away from negotiation and confrontation. When a woman says, 'It wasn't worth the fight,' she is also saying that she does not like to fight (and also, perhaps, that she does not know how to fight for herself).

Feelings of Entitlement

Finally, men and women commonly express different conceptions of their own entitlement to money and property.

Women, especially those who have been housewives and mothers throughout the marriage, are likely to devalue their entitlement to support, even if it is child support, and their right to share the assets of the marriage.

Community-property laws notwithstanding, many divorcing women still see the money their husbands have earned as 'his money', and do not feel entitled to it (especially if she is the one who initiated the divorce). In this way, women discount their own contributions to the marriage, including the value of the services they provided to help their husbands earn money.

It is easy, of course, to find the roots of these differing perspectives in sex-role socialization, that is, in the differing behavioural expectations that society imposes on males and females. What Carol Gilligan (1983) calls 'women's different voice' is reflected in women's orientation towards people, in their need to please others and gain approval, and in their preoccupation with interpersonal considerations. Men, on the other hand, are likely to be socialized to assert their independence and self-interest, and to have their claims valued and rewarded in our society.

It may appear at first glance that this analysis 'blames the victim'. That is, if women get inadequate support awards, it is only because they agree to accept these awards. But women do not make these agreements in a social vacuum. Both social norms and the legal process itself set the parameters for their expectations and structure their negotiations.

The Dynamics of the Legal Process: Risk Aversion, Bargaining Leverage, Economic Vulnerability, and Lack of Information

How does the legal system allow—and even foster—inadequate settlements for divorced women, despite the fact that at least half of the attorneys in divorce actions are paid to represent the interests of women? Surely part of the answer lies in the legal profession itself, still heavily dominated by men, and in the ways that the profession represents, or fails to represent, divorcing women. Because women typically have fewer financial resources than their husbands and, therefore, less financial clout, they often have greater difficulty obtaining effective legal representation. In addition, the legal process rewards those who are willing to accept a certain level of risk to gain their ends, and women in general show greater '*risk aversion*' than do men. Thus, women are more likely to accept a low award that is 'a sure thing' rather than chance a greater loss in court. Instead of counteracting these power differentials between men and women, attorneys who represent wives tend to play into them by allowing their clients to make 'their own' agreements.

In fact, one may look at a woman's agreement to a low-support award as a realistic economic calculus. The costs of bargaining may in reality be greater than the pay-offs she can expect. For example, if a divorcing woman's husband is aggressive and persistent, she can expect to pay dearly in terms of time and energy (and money) for any extra dollar she might obtain. Thus she may realistically calculate that she cannot bear what economists call the transaction costs of fighting him. These costs include the direct costs of litigation (such as filing fees, court costs, the cost of taking depositions, hiring expert witnesses, and, most important, attorney's fees), as well as in the indirect costs—the loss of time, the costs of not being able to use property and money while the issues are being resolved, and the emotional costs of negotiating, litigating, and living with uncertainty.

Consider the difficulties faced by women whose husbands refused to pay alimony (Weitzman 1985: 160–2). These women were often advised to 'cut their losses' by avoiding the high cost of litigation (and negotiation). Here, too, the party who cannot afford to bear the transaction costs of litigation is at a great disadvantage. Lawyers who specialize in divorce call it 'the starve out technique'— the 'illicit bargaining leverage' used by the more affluent or bread-winning spouse to extract agreement to his financial terms. As New York attorneys Henry Foster and Doris Freed (1984: 6) describe it:

> The 'starve out' technique is particularly effective where joint bank accounts have been closed, the husband's credit cut off from the wife, bills are coming in, and the wife has little or no personal income or assets. A variation of the technique may also occur where arrearages pile up and the obligee is forced into repeated court appearances in order to collect some or all that is past due.

If a woman has not been employed during marriage, and if she has no income of her own, she may be especially vulnerable. Her financial situation may be so precarious that she is willing to agree to a ridiculously low award just to have some money on which to live.

A final factor that may contribute to a party's willingness to accept a low support offer is lack of information. In most divorce cases neither party has a great deal of knowledge about what he or she might gain by going to court. A court battle might result in more litigation (and higher attorneys' fees) and little else. Thus, fighting for one's position might not pay off and most would-be contestants do not have the experience to predict whether it will. What they do know is how their spouse is likely to react to a contest—and how they can best deal with that reaction. If a divorcing woman believes her husband will insist on his position and fight to the finish, then this perception alone will shape the 'real market' in her case. If, in addition, her former husband has more money and power, can hire better lawyers, is better able to endure high transaction costs, and can better accept risk, it may well be a 'rational' decision for her to agree to what he offers.

Conclusion and Policy Implications

Obviously not all women give priority to their children, and not all men adopt the legal–economic framework observed above. But these different voices were more likely to be typical than atypical in the United States in the 1970s and 1980s. And, as long as they remain typical, discretionary custody rules will disadvantage women in negotiations about custody and money.

These gender differences in negotiations remind us, once again, of the difference between 'the law on the books' and 'the law in practice'. While the law on the books may be gender neutral, here, as elsewhere, those with greater power and financial resources will have an advantage in the negotiations that occur 'in the shadow of the law'. The reality of how the law works in practice is always shaped by this larger cultural and economic context.

These portraits have several policy implications. First, it is evident that if sociologists and lawyers are really to understand how the law works in practice, they must look behind what appears to be 'a private agreement' and be cognizant of the fact that some of these private agreements may be coerced by power differentials that may work against the explicit aim of the law. Women, and more vulnerable parties in general, are more likely to be disadvantaged in 'private agreements'.* Thus, whenever the law leaves decisions and arrangements to the parties, we must realize that the *de facto* result is to empower the powerful and disadvantage the vulnerable.

But it would be a mistake to see these women as powerless people. They are expressing a different value system and fighting for what they consider important—the well-being of their children and the primacy of relationships—in a system that rewards other values. What is distressing is that the legal system does not reward their values and therefore, to my mind, does not really act in the best interest of the child. The challenge for the law is to fashion rules and procedures that recognize this reality.

Secondly, as has been noted throughout this volume, laws that are vague and allow judical discretion foster uncertainty and encourage litigation. Not only do such laws further empower the partner with social and economic advantages, but, when they deal with decisions like custody, where (in the words of Judge Richard Neely) the mother is 'willing to sacrifice everything else in order to avoid the terrible prospect of losing the child', they allow the legal process to be used as a coercive weapon that thwarts the best interest of the child. The detrimental effects of 'custody blackmail' and 'the starve-out technique' discussed above point to the need for clear standards, such as the 'primary caretaker presumption' instituted by the West Virginia Supreme Court.

* This may also suggest that mediation of family law disputes may result in further disadvantages for women and children.

References

Clark, H. (1988), *The Law of Domestic Relations in the United States* (St Paul, Minn.).

Foster, H. H., jun., and Freed, D. J. (1984), 'Law and the Family: Politics of Divorce Process—Bargaining Leverage, Unfair Edge', *New York Law Journal*, 192/7: 6, 11 July.

GILLIGAN, C. (1983), *In a Different Voice* (Cambridge, Mass.).

GLENDON, M. A. (1982), 'Property Rights upon Dissolution of Marriages and Informal Unions', in N. E. Eastham and B. Krivy (eds.), *The Cambridge Lectures 1981* (London).

GOLDSTEIN, J., FREUD, A., and SOLNIT, A. J. (1973), *Beyond the Best Interests of the Child* (New York).

KAY, H. H. (1990), 'Beyond No-Fault: New Directions in Divorce Reform', in S. D. Sugerman and H. H. Kay (eds.), *Divorce Reform at the Crossroads* (New Haven, Conn.).

POLIKOFF, N. (1983), 'Gender and Child-Custody Determinations: Exploding the Myths', in I. Diamond (ed.), *Families, Politics and Public Policies: A Feminist Dialogue on Women and the State* (New York).

WEITZMAN, L. J. (1985), *The Divorce Revolution: The Unexpected Social and Economic Consequences for Women and Children in America* (New York).

24. Attitudes to Finance after Divorce in France

Benoît Bastard and Laura Cardia Voneche

After divorce it is clear that mother–headed families face economic problems (OECD 1990). In addition, some women report greater satisfaction and less stress after divorce, despite having reduced incomes (Weitzman 1985). For this chapter, therefore, we studied not only levels of income from various sources, but also the strategies which women develop for tackling their new economic situation. Fifty women were interviewed who had taken charge of one or more children at divorce or separation. They were chosen to include representatives of all income groups, families living in different urban environments in France (in the capital, in a large city in the west of France, and a small town in the south-east), and subgroups of different socio-economic status. The interview covered family history, the present economic situation, and the family's approach to economic problems. The analysis revealed different orientations to economic functioning, related not only to the standard of living, but also to such factors as the mother's personality and the dynamics of family interaction before and after the separation. The following analysis describes four family types and the different strategies they adopted: (1) low-income families in which the wife found difficulty in entering the labour market and relied on public welfare support at the time of the study, (2) better-off families, (3) the poorest families, and (4) the middle-income group.

The Low-Income Families

For these nine families, social security payments were the main source of income, but different coping strategies had been developed. Living on approximately 4,000 F. per month, expecting little from the father, and with little hope of the mother finding a reasonable job, these families all received housing benefits. Four women were on the Zeller Plan, a form of workfare established in 1986. They received aid in return for their part-time work in public institutions. Where the woman was unemployed, 90–100 per cent of income came from the public-transfer payments, and where the woman was employed, the proportion was 46 per cent. This group of families also made heavy use of medical and social services. The women had little educational qualifications and no continuing work experience, and had jobs such as shop assistant or kitchen aid. These women felt that finding a good job was impossible as they needed to combine work with care for their children.

Of the nine, three had no financial agreement with the father, as they had cohabited and had not been legally married. In three cases of divorce where there was an agreement for support payments, payments were never made. In any case, the amounts were low, for example 430 F. per month. The men making the payments were also in financial difficulties (see also Maclean and Eekelaar 1983). In three families, payments of 500 F. per month were received, and these included the only two of the nine families where the father saw the children regularly. Father support provided only 7 per cent of income for this group as a whole.

Problems were felt particularly by those who had lived, before separation, in a two-income household. In one case, income had been 12,900 F. per month, and after separation fell to 5,200 F. from the woman's wage, plus 1,500 F. of housing allowance. Then, the wife became unemployed and was left with total resources of 5,500 F. The families had to cut down on their food and heating, and income was often diverted to pay off debts. Some felt their situation was better than before the separation, even though income was lower, because they felt in control of the money. Their coping strategies were as follows: maximizing available resources, claiming all available rights and benefits, focusing on self-development, and living from day to day.

The women who tried to maximize available resources looked for work, not aid, and considered the Zeller Workfare Plan positively as a means to find employment. They were willing to approach relatives for financial help and child support. Some gave and received mutual help in co-operation with other women in the same position. They gained considerable satisfaction from coping well.

The low-income women who adopted a claiming strategy felt that they had the right to obtain assistance from public funds. One said, 'They help third-world children, why not mine?' 'We have a right to compensation for the father's failure to look after us.' These women were well informed of their rights and were always calculating the best approach.

One of the nine women sought *work for its own sake*, for her own *self-development* and fulfilment, as well as economic gain. But the transition from aid to salary is difficult. One woman said, 'Even today I'm afraid of losing certain forms of help, especially the housing allowance, and losing all I earn at work. It is disappointing to realize that you have almost the same standard of living if you work as if you have welfare aid.'

Three of the low-income women did not develop a clear strategy, but just lived from day to day. For example, one woman, with an income of 3,500 F. per month, plus 500 F. housing aid, worked four hours a day on the Zeller Plan, but considered it as exploitation: 'My morale is zero.' A second woman had a better per-capita income, but was saddled with debts from the marriage, particularly heavy rent arrears. She aimed only to survive. All three felt their lives were 'out of control'. They had been in 'close' marriages, where everything had been held in common. They had no experience of independence on which to build their life after separation.

The Better-off Families

In these seventeen families, the wife was well qualified and had a secure job in a field such as health, education, or culture. The father took some responsibility for the children and there were no calls on the public purse. The family of origin and friends also gave emotional and financial support.

The average household income was 11,330 F. per month, 6,420 per capita. These families were not rich but were comfortably off. They had experienced a loss in income at divorce, but had moved into relative, rather than absolute poverty.

These wives had generally worked during the marriage and described this as a source of satisfaction and personal development. Some had increased their work activity in anticipation of the separation. Some returned to study to gain qualifications. This helped to provide psychological as well as economic satisfaction: 'Work for them was a liberation.'

These professional women were able to organize their time to enable them to care for their children as well. Earnings ranged from 5,500 F. for a doctor working part time to 15,500 F. for a doctor working full time and on average made up 70 per cent of the families' total resources.

As to maintenance after divorce, thirteen out of the seventeen received some support, the average payment being 1,700 F. per child per month. The money was paid in full and regularly and without legal intervention. The fathers did not interfere in the way money was spent. In six cases the fathers also provided gifts and holidays and took care of the children. One family even spent birthdays and holidays all together. Of the five cases where the father did not contribute, in two, the women shared the care of the children, and, in two, the father had no resources.

Support from family and friends was also important for these families, but difficult to measure. In two families, a monthly allowance was made. But more often financial help was available at times of crisis or for specific purposes, such as buying a car. In wealthier families this kind of continuing support is quite unrelated to the marital status of the adult child, and was accepted rather than requested. One woman said, 'If I need a new coat, I don't ask my mother, but if she offers to buy me one, I accept gratefully.'

Friends tended to help in kind, rather than cash, by offering shelter and child-care at separation, sharing holidays and offering moral support, especially those who were in a similar position.

For some women, divorce led to loss of both income and access to the material gains made during the marriage. For seven of the better-off women, marriage had been a continuation of, even an improvement on, the privileged position they enjoyed with their families of origin. As a result, divorce was accompanied by considerable loss. A 'good marriage' led to problems on divorce. These wives of architects or doctors had not needed to work during marriage. Before separation, they had nannies and housekeepers, but on divorce their resources were halved. One woman had a quarter of the income which she had enjoyed during marriage, and had also lost social status, club memberships, and friendships. So the poverty, although only relative, was keenly felt. But some advantages acquired during the marriage sometimes remained, such as the matrimonial home. 'I am a poor wealthy women or a wealthy beggar.' Some preferred to live modestly: 'A certain marginality and a certain loss of status.' They received child support, on average 2,200 F. per month per child.

Some had experienced a marriage of equals—for example, a doctor with a doctor—and divorce made little difference. Everything was shared equally during and after marriage. The fathers could, without difficulty, transfer an amount which formed 20 per cent of the one-parent family income. Some shared child-rearing. One wife said, 'I have less than before, but I have enough.' Average income was 6, 432 F. per capita monthly. One woman said, 'I have lost out, but I think he lives less well as he organizes less well.' Having contributed to household resources during marriage was a protection against problems on divorce.

For two women the divorce brought a higher standard of living because it restored the economic and social status the women had given up on marriage. For example, a university graduate had married an immigrant worker without a residence permit and there had been quarrels with him about whether they should return to his native country. Another had married a man who had become mentally unstable and alcoholic after a traffic accident. These women had kept their jobs and their husbands had earned so little during the marriage that after separation the woman's per-capita income went up and, in addition, the uncertainty factor was removed. Both men lived in poor circumstances after the divorce.

Although there were complex marital histories among the group, it is still possible to identify the strategies which were formed as a result of these 'life paths' and which contributed to their development. These women formed plans, carried them out, enjoyed their work, and had a strong conception of personal autonomy.

The better-off women who had been richer in marriage and poorer on divorce, tended to use the two strategies already mentioned: making claims and maximizing all resources. The women using the claims strategy made demands principally against their ex-husbands rather than the public purse. One wife justified this on the grounds that her husband had left the family to live with another woman and so she had a right to receive compensation for abandonment, and to 'make him pay'. This could be accomplished in this case, as the father had plenty of money and a strong desire to remain close to his daughter.

Other better-off women in this group adopted the opposite strategy: maximizing all resources. One woman, who had taken a teaching job during the marriage while her children were small, now struggled to manage a more satisfying and interesting job in her own field while coping with the children alone. 'Self-reliance' for her meant hard work and a strict domestic routine, but also satisfaction.

Two additional strategies were observed among the better-off women. Six families were *co-operating*. This strategy coincided with a clean financial break between spouses and equal sharing of the financial aspects of child-rearing. In a sense it prolonged the marriage, through co-ordinating the separate lives of two co-parents in continuing co-parenting. One case involved two doctors with similar earnings. After separation, each lived in the home alternately with their two children. Later the house was sold, but they still shared custody. 'We are joint parents.' The five others in this group all had no serious financial disgreements during marriage and were able to co-operate afterwards.

And, lastly, two of the better-off women formulated a strategy of recovery. Since they had married badly, this was achieved by returning to work, renewing close contact with kin, and making new friends; one said, 'If I work, I stay on my feet;' 'I cope by looking outwards.'

The career success of these women from the higher-income marriages was both the cause and effect of their better situation afterwards. Their experiences after divorce make it very clear that 'capital' for a woman is training and a career. This analysis confirmed that the ability to find a well-qualified job is the best, perhaps the only, effective protection against poverty after divorce.

The Poorest Families

These eleven families had severe problems, including chronic unemployment, ill health, alcoholism, violence, and child abuse. Separation resulted in not only a fall in income, but also a serious threat to the very survival of the family as a unit. These families had a long history of contact with social services, and had been at risk of having the children taken into care. These were often large families with children by different fathers, the mothers having had a very early first pregnancy and consequently a complex family history.

The absence of the father for these families could be a solution, rather than a problem. For seven families, the fathers had been unemployed for a long time and had no financial or caretaking responsibilities within the home. None of these fathers paid any wife or child support after divorce. Two men returned to their native country and were never heard from again. One woman said, 'He has never given any sign of life.' For these women a career was only a dream. Some worked, but at low-paid unskilled jobs and usually only for short periods. Since it was impossible to find a reasonable job without qualifications, a better job was no more than a point to aim at, which helped in coping with the situation.

The only resource these families could draw on were those provided by the welfare state: public-transfer payments, charitable gifts, clothes, and food. This situation was usually a continuation of what had happened during the marriage.

The women found the state benefits difficult to understand. Amounts paid varied without warning (e.g. at one time one mother received 3,600 F., the next time 1,300), and some benefits were available only temporarily. It took time and energy to collect the benefits due. Earned income, even modest wages for work, led to a reduction in payments and also limited access to medical aid and school meals. Remarriage was rare, especially for those with a large family: 'With six children it is difficult to find anyone to take us on.'

These families saw themselves as condemned to live in poverty without escape, living only from day to day. Nevertheless, the separation was often seen by these women as liberation, a chance to save the family. 'Me, poor? Now I am rich. I have a dining-room, I eat beefsteak.' 'My children are doing well at school, they have nice clothes, they eat well. I am more independent.'

In spite of their difficulties, these women had plans for working and keeping their families together to show that they were good mothers with normal family lives. Paradoxically, living in poverty was not the main issue for the very poor—the first question was the survival of the family.

The Middle-Income Group

For this group a key factor was the failure of traditional conjugal roles.

During marriage, this middle-income group of thirteen families had behaved in traditional ways with the men earning money and the women caring for children. However, it was impossible to maintain this division of labour after divorce. So the women had gone to work—five in offices, seven in service industries, and one in a textile factory. Their earnings were less than among the higher-income wives (who averaged 8,548 F.) but still reasonable (6,339 F. per month). These women had 5,055 F. per capita monthly (cf. 6,420 F. for the better-off families; 2,990 F. for the low-income group). Seventy-four per cent of their household income derived from their earnings. The secondary source of income for them, however, was not the non-custodial parent, but the state—'allocation familiales' and 'aide au logement' (i.e. the benefits targeted not just at one-parent families only but at all families in need).

The dominant strategy for eight out of the thirteen was maximization of all resources available through finding work and taking care of the children, even though this involved complex domestic routines and lower income. This group, having been 'professional mothers' by choice, were particularly sensitive about risks to their children's interests. One woman, talking about worklife and home, said, 'I have tried to reconcile the two, but it is so difficult, so hard.' These women had particular difficulties as they were low on the occupational ladder and could not secure flexibility in their hours of work. Morevoer, child-care was expensive.

Some of these women found great satisfaction in coping through their own efforts. They descibed having put their own wishes in abeyance during the marriage and being constrained, as individuals, in many ways. Since divorce they had recovered and redeveloped these interests. 'After 12 years of marriage, I hardly existed in myself; now a great bond is broken.' These women were not satisfied with traditional marriage and were redefining family roles and seeking personal autonomy and work satisfaction.

Amongst this group there were no feelings of victimization, or need for compensation. Perhaps this was because some women had rejected their conventional marriages and did not feel dependent on the former partner, or the state. Others sought escape from a *mésalliance*, a marriage involving peculiarly difficult circumstances due to their ex-husband's incapacity.

Summary and Conclusion

The study reported briefly here identifies a typology of five key financial strategies adopted by women after divorce.

1. *Maximizing all available resources*: this strategy for the lone parent is centred around self-reliance and self-development—in practice, finding a way of putting together a package of resources over which she has control.
2. *Claiming rights and benefits*: the lone mother who adopts this approach sees herself as a victim of the separation, let down by the father of her children. She seeks, in whatever way she can, to make someone pay for the cost of the marriage breakdown. She approaches public assistance organizations, and her ex-husband if he has sufficient resources.
3. *Recovery*: in this case the wife seeks to return to the situation she enjoyed before marriage, by recovering from the inability of her cx-husband to provide for the family.
4. *Survival*: in this case the woman does not have a clear strategy but lives from day to day and aims only at survival.
5. *Co-operation*: this final strategy is perhaps the most 'modern'. Both parents, now ex-partners, continue to work together to provide for the upbringing and education of their children

These contrasting approaches were found in different social groups according to the availability of access to certain kinds of resources but not always related to the household's standard of living. The maximizing strategy was found in all social groups, but predominantly among the better-off women rather than the middle-income women; the final strategy, co-operation, was found almost exclusively among the better-off families. The poorest families were mainly concerned with survival. They did not see poverty as their main problem. However, in trying to improve their economic situation, they relied on strategies such as claiming social benefits or maximizing their resources.

This classification of the families studied is exploratory only, but it is hoped that this conceptual framework will be helpful in approaching policy development for dealing with the problems arising from family breakdown.

References

MACLEAN, M. and EEKELAAR, J. (1983), *Children and Divorce: Economic Factors* (Oxford).

ORGANIZATION FOR ECONOMIC CO-OPERATION AND DEVELOPMENT (OECD) (1990), *Lone Parents: The Economic Challenge* (Paris).

WEITZMAN, L. J. (1985), *The Divorce Revolution: The Unexpected Social and Economic Consequences for Women and Children in America* (New York).

25. The Way Ahead: A Policy Agenda

Mavis Maclean and Lenore J. Weitzman

COMING from a wide range of national backgrounds and academic disciplines, the participants at the Bellagio meeting revealed—despite differences in terminologies and methods—an extraordinary level of agreement about the nature of the economic consequences of divorce, and the direction in which they would proceed to navigate a way out of the present troubled waters. This chapter presents the attempts of the group to look ahead, and make choices of the directions to follow.

The societies represented are both rich and poor, prospering and declining in economic terms; socialist and capitalist in political terms; collectivist and individualist in social policy terms. Within this diversity lies a multitude of perspectives and goals for the family, the law, and society. The family was viewed variously as a constraint on individual development; as a defence against powerful administrations; as a guardian of moral values; or simply as the most efficient child-rearing device to hand. Family law also was characterized in different ways: as designed for the minority of conflicts which could not be resolved by administrative rules; as the effective professional decision-making body for dealing with family matters; or as the only independent source of the kind of discretion necessary for achieving equitable rather than merely predictable outcomes. The state was seen as the source or organizer of secure financial support for dependent members, as neutral arbiter, or as the source of arbitrary and unpredictable power.

Divorce—as a clearly visible sign of change in family organization—was widely perceived as a kind of consumer good, representing one of the many choices which become increasingly available to the individual as prosperity increases. Of itself it may or may not be perceived as problematic, depending on whether marriage is seen as an individual contract, a religious sacrament, or a social institution. If any view other than that of an individual contract is taken—a view which is difficult to maintain after children are born—

then divorce, even if commonly followed by remarriage, involves a degree of disruption and economic stress. This stress was held by the participants to have a disproportionate impact now on the women and children involved. Rather than simply recording this stress, the group addressed ways in which the costs of divorce might be reassigned. The editors report here the views formulated by the participants to the best of our ability. We do not accept that these costs should lie where they now fall. With increased understanding of the economic processes involved, we hold that it should be possible to improve strategies for dealing with the current detrimental outcomes of divorce.

Specialization of function within the family still, despite high levels of employment for women, leads to persisting wage differences and high costs in human capital to women who marry. These costs are concealed while the family is intact but are revealed on the breakdown of marriage. In the past the economic problems of divorced women, particularly women with custody of children, have tended to be regarded as somehow due to the divorce, and have been dealt with by devising legal rules to allocate resources fairly at divorce. These rules have been applied at a time of dispute and distress, and become associated with all the conflicts associated with marriage breakdown. Thinking back a little, and accepting that these economic inequalities are an integral part of marriage, might help devise clearer guidelines for all those marrying, and separate out financial allocation of resources from the divorce dispute. This allocation would not only include the private resources of the couple, but would also pay attention to the public resources associated with earning capacity, that is, public and private pension rights, and social security benefits. In this context wife support or alimony could be renamed compensation for the costs of marriage revealed at divorce and would stand quite separately from the process of sharing financial responsibility for the children of the marriage.

Concerning child support, we increasingly turned towards collectivist universal support, regarding children as a vital communal resource to be valued and cherished by society as a whole. With falling birth-rates in Western Europe and an ageing population, a heavy burden of support will fall on the next generation. If a society accepts mass divorce and fails for whatever reasons to secure adequate private support from individual parents for children, then society as a whole must accept responsibility for the support of the children affected, both during a period of crisis and in the long term.

We now turn from these general perspectives to more specific recommendations. We begin with the legal rules for divorce concerning the resolution of disputes, property division, and income support for women and children. Then we examine society's response, and the interplay between the two.

Legal Rules for Divorce

With respect to grounds for divorce, the participants believe that the law should contain only one single ground for divorce and that the desire of either spouse to terminate the marriage should be respected. There is also unanimous agreement on the desirability of having some period of reconsideration—the length to be discussed—between an application for divorce and the issuance of a divorce decree. It should not be necessary to claim that the spouses live apart during the transitional period. This acceptance of unilateral divorce was held to be unavoidable, in that it represents what most often happens in marriage breakdown (see Vaughan 1986).

Dispute Resolution on Divorce

The dilemma over whether to seek judicial discretion within statutory guidelines in the interests of justice, or to seek instead increased statutory regulation in the interests of predictablity, was more difficult to resolve, and there were marked national differences. For example, in Japan the judge is regarded as the appropriate professional person to make decisions—and there is no difficulty in accepting his discretion. In the FRG, on the other hand, the judiciary rationalized their own discretion, when the Court of Appeal set out its own guidelines. In Denmark administrative application of rules is regarded as quicker and cheaper—whereas in Poland administrative justice is seen as arbitrary and judicial discrimination is limited by statute.

Overall, we expressed a wish for increased forseeability of

decisions to reduce individual feelings of unfairness, bearing in mind that judges do not have the necessary information to look into complex social problems and should not be expected to do more than judge equal cases equally. Statutes will always involve an element of discretion—but this discretion should be applied within clear statutory guidelines. The level of discretion should vary; for example, it may need to be greater in custody matters. On economic matters the rules should be clear, and outcomes predictable.

How far should private ordering extend, and how extensive should public rules or public supervision be? The lawyers at the meeting argued for the necessity to reach agreement over custody and finance before divorce could be finalized, though strong reservations were expressed about the decree being used as a bargaining counter by the stronger partner. Not all matters should be left to private ordering. Public supervision is essential to safeguard the interests of children and women. Agreements affecting public policy, for example concerning pensions, must be under public control. Property and income settlements must have rules. Other matters may be settled privately, with public monitoring of the interests of weaker parties. Child support should always be paid in advance and through a public authority, and, if parties make a different agreement, it must be at least as good as the state minimal provision.

Property Division

We propose that at the time of marriage all couples should register any property they wish to keep as separate. In our ideal marital-property regime all other property, with the exception of gifts and inheritances, would be considered jointly owned marital property. All property and assets acquired during marriage would be under joint ownership and joint control. While gifts and inheritances remain separate property, the increase in the real value of separate property becomes marital property. To minimize the time and expense spent on discovery, the parties would be required to file a financial declaration when they file for divorce—including their employment position, assets, pensions, insurance policies, and even lottery winnings.

In general we endorse the equal division of marital

property, but this does not require that each item will be equally divided. We also endorse specific rules for the family home, career assets, and pension entitlements.

The Family Home The basic principle, if there are any children, is that the home should follow the children. This may mean that the home could be held in joint ownership after divorce, with use and possession awarded to the custodial parent. When the children leave home, the house may be sold and the proceeds shared. Entitlement to remain in and occupy rented accommodation should also follow the children. The principle of the home following the children suggests that, if custodial arrangements change, arrangements for the home may follow. There was some concern expressed that an outright award of the family home might encourage custody litigation, especially in the United States where there is already concern about the use of insincere custody litigation for economic gain. It is, therefore, important that the home be reserved for the children's custodian—and not be used as a reward for the parent who 'wins' an initial custody suit.

Career Assets We endorse the principle of sharing the gains that either spouse acquires during marriage, including (but not limited to) the acquisition of pensions and other employee benefits (such as social security and medical insurance), professional education, and enhanced earning capacity. Our ideal would be a national data bank, in which each couple's yearly acquisitions (of, let us say, social security credits) would be deposited, with half of the yearly total credited to each spouse. This is in line with the principle articulated above, of equalizing benefits during the marriage, rather than retrospectively at divorce. To produce a figure for yearly compensation, a formula is proposed based on the national earning capacity of each spouse. This formula multiplies the years of marriage by half the difference between any net appreciation of the husband's earning capacity and the net depreciation of wife's annual earning capacity. Brief childless marriages would be excluded, and the formula might need to use an upper limit in the case of very long marriages. This is the most effective strategy we could devise to take into account the negative impact of marriage on a woman's earning capacity and the enhancement of the husband's earning capacity.

Pension Entitlements State and private pension entitlements should be calculated at the end of every year for everyone, and for married couples should be divided equally between spouses. To calculate the value of pension entitlement at the time of divorce, the years of marriage should be divided by the years of working life. Recipients could then receive pension entitlement at retirement, or be allowed to cash in the pension; this way marriage is treated as a career, with built-in pension rights not to be lost on divorce, as often happens at present.

Income Support

The objectives for child-support policy were found to be threefold: first, and above all, to produce economic security for children, both as an aim morally desirable in its own right and also as an investment recognizing the need to nurture and maintain the next generation, in view of low birth-rates in the developed countries and an ageing population worldwide; secondly, to promote good parenting; and, thirdly; to reconcile good parenting with economic independence, involving some participation in paid employment by both parents. Child support paid invisibly during marriage and visibly after divorce could best be viewed as an insurance system to which both parents contribute and on which the custodial parent will draw—though the mechanisms for administering this to ensure prompt and regular payment may be taken into public hands.

The role of the state is to contribute on a flat-rate non-contributory universal basis to all children, to provide retraining for mothers, and to organize or provide child-care to enable parents to work within a framework of labour law which allows both parents to reconcile the demands of home and work. For example, such a law should guarantee the availability of parental leave at birth, and time to care for sick children. If a lone parent of young children wishes to work part time, his or her wages should be topped up by social security—but it is not appropriate for the state to fund the role of full-time parent on a long-term basis. Social assistance should be available in cases of special need, for example, during sickness, unemployment, or retraining, or during a crisis period following divorce or bereavement. There can be no question of 'clean-break' settlements applicable to children, except where large sums of capital are available for endowment to yield an income for the child's support. The aim is to maximize the economic independence of both parents and their integration into society through work. But state support, through income support, tax incentives, and regulation of conditions of employment, is necessary in order to reconcile this aim with the overriding objectives of providing economic stability and good parenting for all children, including those with divorced parents.

The question of spousal support, often held to be more open to the clean-break solution than child support, is in our view not quite so easily resolved. As a long-term goal we fully accept the desirability of ending the financial dependence of one ex-spouse upon another. However, at the present time, the economic resources of most families are not sufficient to provide both spouses with enough capital to achieve this goal at the time of the divorce. This often leaves alimony as the only means of achieving equity and parity between spouses.

Divorce is not an economically acceptable choice unless there is compensation for lost human capital. The ex-wife must be compensated for what she has forgone. This may be possible through property adjustment. For example, in Australia a notion of rough equivalence seems to be developing, equating the value of the family home usually awarded to the wife with the value of pension entitlements kept by the husband. He, with his earning power intact, can fund a second house purchase. She, with the capital accrued in the home, can fund re-entry or training for increased effectiveness in the labour market. But if sufficient property is not available, then compensation may need to be made through periodic payments. This may look like alimony, but it is not a simple transfer payment perpetuating the dependence within marriage—it is compensation for the losses resulting from the withdrawal of expectation of support and shared parenting at the end of a marriage. This is different from marriage and child-bearing. The part of that loss resulting purely from gender should be shared by all, not only divorcing men.

Society's Response to the Cost of Divorce

As we stated in the introduction, we are not concerned in this volume with divorce as the ending of individual pair-relationships but with divorce as the ending of marriage as an institution within society, thereby leading to a chain reaction affecting parents, partners, children, employers, and the taxpayer. Society has a choice. The response may be to promote the well-being of family groups within society or it may be to maximize individual freedom of choice. Do we then accept collective responsibility for the welfare of individuals—particularly dependent children—directly, or do we rely on the family to do the job of nurturing children?

At a time when society as a whole accepts widespread changes in family structure through divorce and remarriage—and is apparently unable to enforce private obligations to support children by non-custodial parents—it seems that, unless we forgo the aim of providing equal opportunities for children, society as a whole (whether characterized as the state or 'the taxpayer') needs to accept at least some of the responsibility for the financial support of children and for organizing child-care. A universal non-means-tested child benefit for all children represents a public manifestation of the value that society places on children, and works alongside, not instead of, family obligation. In addition, during the crisis period of divorce, families may need additional financial and social aid from the larger society.

We conclude by returning to some of the basic issues raised throughout this volume: the need to renegotiate the private social contract within the family, with the aim of balancing the needs of individuals against the needs of the family group. Such a process would seek to reduce dependency and hence the possiblity of exploitation by freeing women from their economic dependence on men—through equal wages and public child-care—and also to free men from their domestic dependence on women, by reducing the length and rigidity of working hours.

Finally, we end by reiterating a point made throughout this chapter and throughout this book—we need to renew the public social contract between state and families by encouraging the state to underpin the family, taking a share with the family in accepting responsibility for the next generation.

References

Vaughan, D. (1986), *Uncoupling* (London).

Index